FROM UNDERDOGS TO TIGERS

From Underdogs to Tigers: The Rise and Growth of the Software Industry in Brazil, China, India, Ireland, and Israel

ASHISH ARORA AND ALFONSO GAMBARDELLA

OXFORD
UNIVERSITY PRESS

OXFORD
UNIVERSITY PRESS

Great Clarendon Street, Oxford OX2 6DP

Oxford University Press is a department of the University of Oxford.
It furthers the University's objective of excellence in research, scholarship,
and education by publishing worldwide in

Oxford New York

Auckland Cape Town Dar es Salaam Hong Kong Karachi
Kuala Lumpur Madrid Melbourne Mexico City Nairobi
New Delhi Taipei Toronto Shanghai

With offices in

Argentina Austria Brazil Chile Czech Republic France Greece
Guatemala Hungary Italy Japan South Korea Poland Portugal
Singapore Switzerland Thailand Turkey Ukraine Vietnam

Oxford is a registered trade mark of Oxford University Press
in the UK and in certain other countries

Published in the United States
by Oxford University Press Inc., New York

© Oxford University Press, 2005

British Library Cataloguing in Publication Data
(Data available)

Library of Congress Cataloging in Publication Data

From underdogs to tigers : the rise and growth of the software industry in Brazil,
China, India, Ireland, and Israel / Ashish Arora and Alfonso Gambardella.
    p. cm.
Includes bibliographical references and index.
ISBN 0–19–927560–2 (alk. paper)
  1. Computer software industry.   2. Globalization.   I. Arora, Ashish.   II. Gambardella,
Alfonso, 1961–
    HD9696.63.A2F76 2005
    338.4'7005—dc22   2004026997

ISBN 0–19–927560–2

1 3 5 7 9 10 8 6 4 2

Typeset by Newgen Imaging Systems (P) Ltd., Chennai, India
Printed in Great Britain
on acid-free paper by
Biddles Ltd., King's Lynn, Norfolk

CONTENTS

LIST OF FIGURES

LIST OF TABLES

NOTES ON THE EDITORS

Ashish Arora has a PhD in Economics from Stanford University and is Professor of Economics and Public Policy at Carnegie Mellon University, Pittsburgh. Arora is also codirector of the Software Industry Center at Carnegie Mellon University. His research focuses on the economics of technological change, the management of technology, intellectual property rights, and technology licensing. In addition to publishing pioneering studies of the Indian software industry, he has published extensively on the economics of patents, technology licensing, the growth and development of biotechnology and the chemical industry, and software quality and security. His recent book, *Markets for Technology: Economics of Innovation and Corporate Strategy*, coauthored with Alfonso Gambardella and Andrea Fosfuri, was published by MIT Press. He has also coedited (with Ralph Landau and Nathan Rosenberg) *Chemicals and Long Term Economic Growth*, published in 1998 by John Wiley & Sons.

Alfonso Gambardella obtained his PhD from the Department of Economics, Stanford University, in 1991. He is Professor of Economics and Management at the Università Commerciale 'L. Bocconi', Milan, Italy. His main research interests are in the economics of technological change, applied industrial organization, and strategic management. He has published in leading international journals in these fields, and participated in several international research projects, including projects sponsored by the European Commission and the Sloan Foundation. He published *Science and Innovation* with Cambridge University Press in 1995 and *Markets for Technology* (coauthored with Ashish Arora, Carnegie Mellon University, and Andrea Fosfuri, Universitat Carlos III, Madrid) with MIT Press in 2001. He has also coedited *The Organization of Innovation Activities in Europe* (with Franco Malerba, Bocconi University, Milan) and *Beyond Silicon Valley: Building High-Tech Clusters* (with Timothy Bresnahan, Stanford University), which came out in 1999 and 2003 respectively from Cambridge University Press.

LIST OF CONTRIBUTORS

Ashish Arora, Carnegie Mellon University

Suma S. Athreye, Open University, London

Antonio J. Junqueira Botelho, Instituto Gênesis, PUC, Rio de Janeiro

Dan Breznitz, Industrial Performance Center—MIT

Alfonso Gambardella, Carnegie Mellon University

Marco Giarratana, Universitat Carlos III, Madrid

Devesh Kapur, Harvard University

Steven Klepper, Carnegie Mellon University

John McHale, Queen's University

Alessandro Pagano, University of Ubino, Italy

Anita Sands, Carnegie Mellon University

Giancarlo Stefanuto, University of Campinas, Brazil

Salvatore Torrisi, University of Camerino, Italy

Ted Tschang, Singapore Management University

Francisco Veloso, Carnegie Mellon University and Universidade Católica Portuguesa

Lan Xue, Tsing Hua University

1
Introduction

ASHISH ARORA AND ALFONSO GAMBARDELLA

The raison d'etre of this book is simple. During the 1990s several emerging economies developed sizable software industries. By 2001, there were several countries with software revenues between $7 and $10 billion, including Brazil, China, South Korea, and India, Israel, and Ireland. The latter three, dubbed the 3Is in this book, standout for their rapid growth and high share of exports. India's software revenues, for example, grew at over 30 percent per annum over the last decade, and the industry went from being practically nonexistent in the 1980s to accounting for 3 percent of India's GDP, a fifth of its exports, and employing about 230,000 Indians by 2003. Similarly, both Israel and Ireland have established themselves as major software exporters.

Brazil and China also recorded double digit growth rates in software revenues over the past decade, but were largely pulled along by domestic demand rather than by exports. Nonetheless, the size of their respective markets implies that their software industries are large, even by international standards. Moreover, if Brazil and China do succeed in becoming exporters in the future, as they are attempting to do, their impact on the international industry will be significant, particularly since they would have demonstrated an alternative path to international competitiveness in the software industry, different from that of the 3Is, especially India and Ireland.

Since software is commonly viewed as a high-tech industry, it is intriguing that such spectacular growth has occurred in countries where one would not typically expect high-tech activities to flourish. This raises several questions. What accounts for the spectacular growth of software in these emerging economies? What is common and what is different between the successful exporters, the 3Is, and Brazil and China, which appear to be taking a different path. Does the apparent success of the 3Is in becoming internationally competitive in a high-tech sector suggest new possibilities for other developing countries? Are there lessons to be learnt by other emerging economies from their experience? These are the questions we address in this study.

The book is organized as follows. The five country chapters describe the rise and growth of the software industry in the countries in question. They also provide interpretations of the patterns, forces, and causes underlying the development of the industry. These five chapters are complemented by three others that deal with important horizontal themes that recur in the country chapters. The first draws upon recent research on the origins and evolution of four US industries—automobiles, tires, TVs, and lasers, to understand the origins of the software industry in the five emerging economies. Our goal is to identify some of the fundamental forces underlying the growth of new industries, and thereby to highlight some of the forces central to the dynamics of capitalism. The history of the four US industries highlights the importance of organizational competencies in firm formation and firm performance. Though there are important differences between industrial evolution in a pioneering nation such as the United States and that in late-comer nations, and between software and industries such as automobiles, the sources of organizational competencies remain important for understanding the growth and evolution of the software industry in the five emerging economies.

External sources of organizational and technological competencies have been important in the growth of software industry in the five countries studied in the book, and especially in the 3Is. However, the 3Is differ in how important multinational corporations have been and in what role they have played. Thus, the second of the three chapters dealing with horizontal themes looks at the impact of multinational corporations in the 3Is, the various channels through which multinational corporations have influenced the growth of the software industry, and the differences in importance of these channels across the 3Is. The chapter provides a very useful complement to the individual country descriptions by providing cross-country comparisons using a variety of data sources, including data on patenting and on firm linkages.

The third horizontal chapter focuses on the international migration of human capital from and to the 3Is. All three have sizeable diasporas, and in the 1990s population flows from and to have been relevant factors in the development of their respective software industries. The chapter provides quantitative evidence on extent and nature of the population flows and assesses how these flows have affected the 3Is, and especially the role of the expatriate nationals in the growth of the software industry in the 3Is.

In the concluding chapter, the editors organize and re-examine the material provided in the preceding chapters with a view to developing a framework for addressing some of the broader questions they raise.

The growth of the software industry doubtless owes much to the tremendous growth in IT demand in the 1990s. However, this book has tried to understand why a selected group of *underdog* countries alone appear to have been able to leverage this window of opportunity to grow their software industry. Thus, one element of the framework is to distinguish between factors responsible for the *initial* growth of the software industry in our 'underdog' regions from the forces that sustained this growth even as plausible sources of initial advantage (such as cheap and abundant human capital) diminish in importance over time.

This brings into question whether comparative advantage is by itself sufficient for understanding how underdog economies could become software tigers. Though undoubtedly the 3Is have a comparative advantage in software, so do Brazil and China, and as do plausibly many other countries. Comparative advantage cannot by itself explain why these countries and not others have developed an internationally competitive software industry, nor can it explain by itself why growth has continued even as the initial advantages diminish. For understanding the factors that sustain growth, we look to firm level capabilities, both organizational and technological. Firm capabilities are related to country level endowments of human capital and technological capability but also depend upon distinctive country specific institutions and of course, on chance. This interplay between the macro and the micro foundations of success, between comparative advantage and firm capabilities, is how we see the growth of the software industry in emerging economies.

The book is the outcome of a two-year research project on the software industry in five emerging economies—India, Ireland, Israel, Brazil, and China. The authors of the country chapters hail from the countries in question, though several now work abroad, putting them in an excellent position to assess the industry both from the standpoint of their respective countries of origin and from a global perspective. All the country studies are based on original interviews and material obtained from field work. Over the two-year period, the group met in three workshops to discuss and revise the individual chapters. These meetings were extremely useful in developing and disseminating ideas, in improving the overall structure of the book and of the individual contributions, and in helping to generate the intellectual stimulus necessary to sustain an endeavor such as this. The book is thus the outcome of a tightly controlled editorial process, involving several revisions of the various chapters. The project was carried out under the aegis of the Software Industry Center (SWIC), Carnegie Mellon University, Pittsburgh, and sponsored by the Alfred P. Sloan Foundation and the Commonwealth of Pennsylvania. The Sloan Foundation deserves special thanks for laying the foundation for this project by supporting an initial study of the Indian software industry in 1997–98 at Carnegie Mellon University. We also gratefully acknowledge support from the following corporate sponsors: IBM, TCS, PWC, i-Flex, Marconi, and InformationWeek.

Many colleagues have been generous with their time and expertise. We are grateful to Rafiq Dossani, Manuel Trajtenberg, David Mowery, and Giovanni Dosi for providing very helpful comments and suggestions on individual chapters at the two workshops in Pisa and Pittsburgh. We are indebted to Rafel Lucea and Jay Horwitz who displayed initiative in data collection and analysis well beyond what one can expect from research assistants. We are also very grateful to Diasmer Bloe and Marica Passarelli for their energy and enthusiasm in helping us put this book together for publication.

PART I

COUNTRY CHAPTERS

2

The Indian Software Industry

SUMA S. ATHREYE

1 Introduction

In the last fifteen years, India has emerged as a major exporter of software services in the international economy. This feat has been accomplished through the extraordinary growth of the Indian software industry: between 1995 and 2000, software sales grew at a compound rate of over 50 percent. Despite fears that the market for Indian software would collapse in the midst of a recession in the United States, software growth continues, albeit at a slower pace, and the industry has diversified into other geographical and related markets.

The industry is emerging as a major contributor of export earnings in India: the proportion of software exports to merchandise exports grew from insignificant amounts in 1990 to 18 percent in 2002–03. The sector's contribution to India's overall invisible receipts is more remarkable and accounted for about 59 percent of receipts in 2002–03. Despite this impressive export performance, the software sector's share in overall GDP and employment is small—contributing less than 3 percent of India's GDP and employing 500,000 people in 2002–03. The domestic market for IT, although growing, is minor and the industry has no links with other domestic sectors. This is supported by the fact that exports account for a high share in total software revenue. Nonetheless, the Indian software industry accounted for over 28 percent of India's GDP growth between 2000 and 2002.[1] So, although the size of software services in India in terms of GDP and employment is small, it is one of the fastest growing sectors of the economy. In the last two years the more phenomenal growth has come from the IT-enabled service sector, which grew at a rate of 70 percent in 2001–02 and employed an estimated 106,000 persons at the end of March 2002.[2]

Software is more than just another industry—it is a central intermediate good in the new digital economy. Its role is analogous to that played by the capital goods sector in an economy based on mechanized technologies. Like capital goods, software is characterized by a large number of specialized (service) suppliers. Put differently, the number of firms that produce software or employ

The author gratefully acknowledges all those whose comments helped shape this chapter, notably Ashish Arora, Anthony D'Costa, Rafiq Dossani, Alfonso Gambardella and participants at the two globalization meetings. The usual disclaimer applies.

software developers is larger than the number of firms usually labeled as software firms, for example, Microsoft or Oracle. Thus, 'packaged software' is only a fraction of the total software industry. Indeed large banks, insurance companies, finance companies, and virtually every organization of any size ends up producing, maintaining, and enhancing a considerable amount of software. Much of this software is specialized, consisting of standard 'platforms' such as an SAP ERP system or an Oracle accounting system tailored to users' needs. Over two-thirds of all the software development effort is spent in maintaining and enhancing the existing software code, rather than in producing new software.[3]

Despite the steady increase in the supply of software technology and tools, much of these activities still require suitably trained people, the demand for whom exceeded supply in the developed world as the information technology revolution took hold in the 1990s. However, a substantial portion of these activities could be outsourced from the user organization. This type of demand formed the basis of the initial growth of the Indian software industry.

At first glance, this seems ironic since India has some of the lowest figures for IT penetration. Yet, the needs of such software production seem particularly suited to the resource endowments of the Indian economy, which has an abundance of labor and a relative scarcity of capital and physical infrastructure. Software services are intensive in the use of skilled labor and require relatively little capital.[4] Firms can begin as a single software development team or temporary employment agencies, requiring a minimal space to set up a handful of PCs and a telephone. The production of software does not depend heavily on physical infrastructure such as roads and ports. However, a steady supply of electrical power is critical, as is ready access to PCs, workstations, and communications infrastructure—airports, phones, faxes, and increasingly, the Internet.

This paradox of India's success in a technology service industry when the economy itself is technologically backward excites debate even as it raises hopes of similar success in other developing economies. The primary question is: What accounts for India's success and what has been its broader impact? This chapter will approach this question by looking in detail at the evolution of the software industry in India. The chapter is organized as follows: Section 2 will review the existing explanations for the growth of Indian software and explain why they are incomplete, and Sections 3 and 4 outline the main trends in Indian software growth. Section 3 identifies four phases of growth, based primarily on the changing policy and economic environment facing domestic software producers. It also highlights the evolving business model of software outsourcing adopted by Indian firms in response to the opportunities and constraints of each phase. Section 4 details the development of suitable managerial and organizational capabilities by Indian firms in lieu of changing constraints in the labor market. Section 5 concludes.

2   Salient Facts and Existing Explanations

2.1   The Growth of Indian Software

Figure 2.1 plots the growth of software revenues between 1984 and 2004.[5] Several important features of India's software growth are discernible. First, export sales were crucial to the rise in industry revenues. In 2000, more than two-thirds of the software industry's sales were due to exports. This percentage is still climbing, with exports accounting for 72 percent of industry sales in 2000–01. Second, the figure shows the sharp growth of the industry in the mid-1990s and the slow-down after 2000. Third, Indian software was earning export revenues even in 1984. Though these revenues were insignificant compared to those accrued in the mid-1990s, they did exist, suggesting that an industry was in place more than a decade before the export boom took place.

The predominance of exports marks the Indian software industry as an export-led industry, and as such is different from its counterparts in countries like China and Brazil. When compared with the equivalent exporters like Israel and Ireland, Indian software growth also manifests differences.

Unlike the Israeli industry, the Indian software industry was built around customized software services rather than products. As previously stated, the

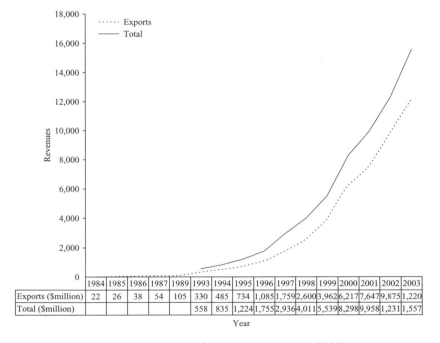

	1984	1985	1986	1987	1989	1993	1994	1995	1996	1997	1998	1999	2000	2001	2002	2003
Exports ($million)	22	26	38	54	105	330	485	734	1,085	1,759	2,600	3,962	6,217	7,647	9,875	1,220
Total ($million)						558	835	1,224	1,755	2,936	4,011	5,539	8,298	9,958	1,231	1,557

Year

FIGURE 2.1. Indian Software Revenues (1984–2003)

TABLE 2.1. India's Manpower
and Revenues/Man-year

Year	Rev/employee ($)
1993	6,200.00
1994	7,076.27
1995	8,742.86
1996	10,968.75
1997	14,833.33
1998	15,600.00
1999	34,606.90
2000	35,129.55

Note: Figures for 1999 and 2000 are computed by adding revenues and employment of
all firms in the NASSCOM register.

Source: Author's computations based on
NASSCOM, various years.

customized software services market is a large volume market. Many types of
services, such as those involved in the maintenance of data/legacy systems, are
low value. The Indian software industry has predominantly specialized in relatively low-value activities. To some extent this low-value content of the software
services industry is also reflected in Table 2.1, which shows that the revenues per
employee for Indian software is much lower than similar figures for Ireland and
Israel. There are signs of change visible in Table 2.1, which shows that revenues
per employee have risen over time. The industry is evolving and a small proportion
of firms have advanced into providing higher value services in the form of larger
and more complex projects.

Unlike the Irish industry, Indian software growth was led by domestic rather
than foreign firms. India's software exports are largely the products of Indian firms.
A number of multinational subsidiaries, foreign (US) firms set up by expatriate
Indians, subsidiaries of Indian business houses, and entrepreneurial firms, often
set up by IT professionals were attracted to the profit opportunities presented by
the software industry in India. Indeed one can observe all of these types among the
leading firms in Table 2.2. Of the top twenty exporters in 2000–01, only five firms
were foreign subsidiaries. If we look at more recent figures (that exclude firms not
incorporated in India) we can also see the diverse origins of the domestic firms—
spin-offs serial entrepreneurs, joint ventures, business house subsidiaries, and
MNE subsidiaries are all represented. In particular, Indian software has attracted
a large amount of entrepreneurial talent from IT professionals.

It is significant that among the leaders, entrepreneurial firms (often set up by
IT professionals) were almost as prominent as business house firms. Table 2.3—
based on a classification of firms by the industry association directory (henceforth
NASSCOM) according to entrant type—shows this clearly.[6] The share of industry
revenue and employment by type of entrant in 2000–01 shows that revenues

TABLE 2.2. Top Twenty Exporters and the Origins of the Firms
(Ranked by Annual Revenue)

Name of firm	Year established	Origin/type of firm
2000–01		
Tata Consultancy Services	1968	Business house subsidiary
Wipro Technologies	1980	Business house
Infosys Technologies Limited	1981	Entrepreneurial (IT professionals)
HCL Technologies Limited	1991	Entrepreneurial (IT professionals)
Satyam Computer Services Limited	1987	Business house
IBM India Limited	1987	Multinational subsidiary
Cognizant Technology Solutions	1994	US firm with Indian back office
NIIT Limited	1981	Entrepreneurial (IT professionals)
Silverline Technologies Limited	1992	US firm with Indian back office
Pentasoft Technologies	1995	Business house subsidiary
Pentamedia Graphics	1976	Business house subsidiary
Patni Computer Systems	1978	Entrepreneurial (IT professionals)
Mahindra British Telecom Limited	1988	Joint venture
HCL Perot Systems	1996	Joint venture
DSQ Software Limited	1992	Business house subsidiary
Mascon Global Limited	1995	US firm with Indian back office
Mascot Systems Limited	1993	US firm with Indian back office
Tata Infotech Limited	1977	Business house subsidiary
I-flex Solutions Limited	1989	Spin-off from MNE subsidiary
Mphasis BFL limited	1992	Joint venture
2003–04		
Tata Consultancy Services	1968	Business house subsidiary
Infosys Technologies Limited	1981	Spin-off (Patni Computer Systems)
Wipro Technologies	1980	Business house
Satyam Computer Services Limited	1987	Business house
HCL Technologies Limited	1976	Entrepreneurial (IT professionals)
Patni Computer Systems	1978	Entrepreneurial (IT professionals)
I-flex Solutions Limited	1989	Spin-off from MNC (Citibank)
Mahindra British Telecom Limited	1988	Joint venture with British Telecom
Polaris Software	1993	Entrepreneurial (IT professionals)
Digital Globalsoft Ltd.	1988	MNC (now part of HP)
NIIT Limited	1981	Spin-off (HCL)
Perot Systems TSI (HCL Perot Systems)	1996	Joint venture with Perot Systems
IGate Global Solutions (Mascot Systems Limited)	1993	US firm with Indian back office
Birlasoft Ltd.	1995	Business house subsidiary
Mphasis BFL limited	1992	Joint venture (Citibank spin-off & BH)
Mastek Ltd.	1982	Entrepreneurial (IT professionals)
Hexaware Technologies Ltd.	1992	Entrepreneurial firm
Larsen & Tubro Infotech Ltd.	1996	Business house subsidiary
Tata Infotech Limited	1977	Business house subsidiary
Hughes Software Systems	1991	Multinational subsidiary

TABLE 2.3. Entry Dates and Composition of Firms, 2000–01

Type of entrant	Year established						Number of firms	Share in revenues	Share in employment
	Pre-1980	1981–84	1985–91	1992–99	2000–01				
Business house firms	10	2	10	60	5		112	26.24	26.89
Multinational enterprises	1	3	24	80	20		128	11.29	16.28
US–Indian	0	0	10	38	10		58	7.87	7.87
Entrepreneurial firms	1	1	4	13	3		22	1.44	0.85
Entrepreneurs with prior IT experience	11	8	46	129	35		229	36.99	34.10
Others	7	2	5	26	3		44	8.08	7.97
All firms							657		

Notes: 1. For classification of type of entrant, see Appendix to the chapter. 'Others' includes Joint ventures and PSU. Many firms did not report year of establishment.
2. Shares of employment and revenue do not add up to 100 because of missing data on year of establishment. Total number includes firms with missing data on year of establishment.
3. Ten Multinational subsidiaries were established in 1991, and twenty-five were established following the second wave of liberalization of foreign investment rules in 1995–96.

Source: Author's computations based on NASSCOM [1].

TABLE 2.4. Looking Back: Instability of Market Shares Over Time of the
Top Ten Firms in 2000–01

Firm	1994–95	1995–96	1996–97	1999–2000	2000–01
TCS	13.44	12.28	11.43	8.35	8.32
Wipro	5.01	5.64	4.44	4.41	5.21
Infosys	2.13	2.23	2.28	3.62	4.91
HCL	7.63		4.68	2.60	3.38
Satyam	1.31	1.20	2.54	2.78	3.36
IBM India	n.a.	n.a.	n.a.	1.22	2.20
Cognizant	n.a.	n.a.	0.75	1.70	1.87
NIIT	1.99		3.37	3.07	1.81
Silverline	2.10	2.05	1.23	1.80	1.73
Pentasoft/Pentafour	2.26	2.69	2.72	3.27	3.22
CR5	0.336	0.256	0.266	0.222	0.252
CR10	0.449	0.342	0.373	0.316	0.345

Notes: 1. Market shares are firm sales as percentage share of total industry sales revenue for that year.
2. Pentafour Technologies was split into two firms, Pentasoft and Pentamedia. For comparability the sales revenues of the two firms have been added up in the later years.
3. The CR 5 and CR 10 ratios are computed as the proportion of industry sales with the five and ten largest (by sales) firms.
Source: Computed from NASSCOM [1] registers, various years.

are evenly shared between foreign firms (including those owned by US-based expatriates) and entrepreneurial firms, followed by business house subsidiaries. Thus, about two-thirds of industry revenues accrued to domestic firms.

There are other features unique to the Indian case. The software industry in India retains a largely competitive structure, with the top five firms accounting for roughly a quarter of all industry revenues. The top five and top ten firms (reported in the last two rows as CR5 and CR10) have always accounted for a minor proportion of industry (see Table 2.4). The market shares of 2000's top ten firms over the period 1994–2001 show signs of Schumpeterian creative destruction with new entrants (such as Cognizant and IBM India) becoming top ten revenue earners.

Contrary to popular perception, the industry is not clustered in Bangalore but dispersed over the south and west of the country. The number of firms in each region and their share of revenue and employment indicate this. However, foreign investment in software is concentrated in Bangalore (see Table 2.5).

2.2 Explanations for Indian Software Industry Growth

The phenomenal success and growth of the Indian software industry is quite extraordinary when one considers that India is a very poor country with poor infrastructural investment (generally and in IT) and an illiteracy rate over 33 percent. So how did the software industry happen? Different explanations have been proposed, and in this chapter we shall add to the list of such explanations. Before proceeding to do so, however, we look at the existing explanations and their limitations.

TABLE 2.5. Entry Dates and the Regional Location of Firms, 2001

Location	Pre-1980	1981–84	1985–91	1992–99	2000–01	Number of firms	Share in revenues	Share in employment
Bangalore	3	3	19	50	15	126	23.7	24.52
Mumbai/Pune	9	11	32	63	8	149	32.47	30.12
(Pune)	(1)	(0)	(8)	(17)	(2)	(35)	(2.24)	(3.97)
Chennai	3	5	9	34	6	67	13.20	15.29
Delhi: of which	5	4	25	63	17	156	23.49	15.48
(Noida)		(1)	(6)	(18)	(4)	(34)	(18.26)	(5.75)
(Gurgaon)			(1)	(9)	(2)	(25)	(1.16)	(1.80)
Hyderabad/Secundrabad		1	6	29	8	63	5.22	9.07
Calcutta			9	8	4	26	0.66	0.48

Notes: 1. The first five columns are computed from NASSCOM [1] after excluding government departments, liaison offices and firms with missing data on years of establishment (N = 449). Firms that provided IT-enabled services were also excluded.
2. The last three columns have a larger number of firms (N = 658) as they include firms which have missing data on year of establishment. As a consequence employment and revenue shares add to less than 100.

TABLE 2.6. International Differences in the Salaries Paid to Software Professionals
(US$ Per Annum): 1995–99

	USA	UK	Ireland	India
1995				
Project leader	54,000	39,000	43,000	23,000
Systems designer	55,000	34,000	31,000	11,000
Development programmer	41,000	29,000	21,000	8,000
Quality assurance specialist	50,000	33,000	29,000	14,000
1999				
Project leader	65,600	47,400	52,300	33,700
	(21.5)	(21.5)	(21.6)	(46.5)
Systems designer	66,900	41,300	37,700	16,100
	(21.6)	(21.4)	(21.6)	(46.4)
Development programmer	49,800	35,300	25,600	11,700
	(21.4)	(21.7)	(21.9)	(46.3)
Quality assurance specialist	60,800	40,100	35,300	20,500
	(21.6)	(21.5)	(21.7)	(46.4)

Note: Figures in parentheses indicate percentage change in salaries on 1995.

Source: www.man.ac.uk/idpm/ for 1995 data, World Employment Report, 2001 for 1999 data.

The earliest explanation, advanced by Heeks [3], is that the Indian software industry's success has been due to the wage advantage enjoyed by software programmers, as they are the key to understanding Indian exports. Cast in the terminology of trade theory, Heeks's argument suggests that India had an absolute advantage over the rest of the world in terms of software wage costs and this explains the large software exports from India. During the early stages of software growth, wage differentials were crucial in explaining the profitability of firms engaged in this business.

However, the export boom through 1995–2000 cannot be explained by absolute advantage alone. Table 2.6 compares international software salaries between two points, 1995 and 1999. Even though salaries in India remained lower than those in the United States, United Kingdom, and Ireland in 1999, Indian software salaries rose and its growth rates were more than double of those observed in the other countries. If wages were the only advantage, based on this evidence the export boom of the mid-1990s should simply not have happened. Absolute advantage would have diminished once relative scarcity increased, eroding profitability and reducing Indian exports of software in favor of the exports of other cheaper wage nations. This dissonance arises because the wage advantage explanation ignores that software exports are driven not only by absolute (cost) advantages but also by comparative advantage. The two can coexist, but comparative advantage is the crucial factor determining Indian software exports.

To see this, consider that wage costs in India (relative to the rest of the world) are low also for a range of manufacturing and agricultural products. Why have these wage differentials not translated into good export performance? One explanation

TABLE 2.7. Comparative Advantage in Software Production Across
Selected Countries, 1995

Country	All manufacturing	Software	Comparative advantage
($ '000)	Value added per employee (1)	Revenue per employee (2)	Index (1)/(2)
Israel	38.30	100.00	2.61
Ireland	117.10	142.24	1.22
India	4.10	8.93	2.18
France	77.143	161.32	2.09
Finland	76.16	83.46	1.10
USA	98.20	126.02	1.28

Notes: (a) Data in column (1) is taken from the UN Industrial Statistics, 1998 and 1999 published by UNCTAD. Exchange rates used to convert local currencies into $ are average exchange rates (line rf) from the International Financial Statistics published by the International Monetary Fund.
(b) Data in column (2) are derived from the following national and international sources: Data on India are from NASSCOM (www.nasscom.org), Israel from Israeli Association of Software Houses (www.iash.org.il), Ireland from National Software Directorate (www.nsd.ie), Ireland, and for France, Finland, and USA from The Software Sector: A Statistical Profile for Selected OECD Countries, OECD (www.oecd.org/ dsti/sti/it/infosoc/index.htm).
(c) Figures for Israel are obtained by dividing Israeli software revenues by estimated employment. Figures for Ireland are obtained by excluding multinationals from the calculation, and therefore, may underestimate revenue per employee in software in Ireland.
Source: Adapted from Arora and Athreye [4, table 4].

is that productivity in these industries is not as high in India as in other parts of the world. Yet, software productivity levels are lower in India compared with other parts of the world (notably Ireland and Israel as remarked earlier). Therefore a more accurate explanation is that software is far more productive relative to manufacturing sectors in India compared with other countries. Table 2.7 compares the relative productivity of labor in software and manufacturing for several countries based on crude productivity figures. Software productivity is measured as revenues per employee, while we measure manufacturing productivity as value-added per employee.[7] Admittedly the indices of productivity are crude, but this is one way to get an estimate of relative productivity that is consistent across a range of countries.

Indian firms producing software are more productive per unit of labor employed than their counterparts in manufacturing. When we compare the ratio of labor productivity in software to that in manufacturing and the differences in this ratio across countries, we see that India has the second highest ratio. For instance, productivity in software is more than twice that in manufacturing in India, as compared to 1.3 times in the United States.

There is also some indication that this ratio of relative productivities has been growing in recent years. Arora et al. [5] noted the rapid growth of revenue per employee figures (shown in Table 2.1), an index of the increases in the productivity of Indian software firms since the late 1980s. This has led to the continued entry of domestic firms—especially established business houses—into software from other sectors. This microeconomic counterpart of the changing allocation of resources in the domestic economy demonstrates the increased profitability of the software sector compared to less lucrative sectors in manufacturing. Absolute costs are still important—the absolute levels of wage cost and labor productivity do influence profitability of software production for export from India—but are not the sole determining factors. Table 2.7 also hints that comparative advantage is necessary but perhaps not sufficient. For example, France has a favorable relative productivity in software but is not a major software exporter. This could be because of the predominance of English as the language for communicating software needs (often cited as a reason for the success of the 3Is), or the absence of firm capabilities needed to translate favorable conditions into software exports.

A second explanation, advanced by Ghemawat and Patibandla [6], is that software represents the success of 'liberalization' after government investment in human capital formation during the previous two decades of import substitution. As we saw from Figure 2.1, the most phenomenal rise in software industry revenues came after the mid-1990s. This sharp increase in revenues could be attributed to the success of liberalization policies, since the boom happened soon after the reversal of these policies in 1991. However, such a conclusion would be erroneous because, as we showed in Figure 2.1, by 1988 the industry was already an important foreign exchange earner and the firms that would emerge as industry leaders were already well established. If one is reasoning the success of the industry in the 1990s, the explanation must hinge on changes that took place in the 1980s.

There is some truth in the liberalization argument, though one needs to be careful about the use of the term 'liberalization'. Indian industry in the 1960s and 1970s was shackled by an industrial policy beset by a number of problems. Chief among these were excessive regulation and constraints on domestic entry into sectors, high levels of tariff protection, and restrictions against the entry of new foreign competition. In common parlance, liberalization refers to the reversal of all three, which happened in 1991. However, being a service industry, software fell outside the purview of industrial capacity licensing and the domestic market was small and virtually nonexistent for the industry to gain from protective tariffs. For software, liberalization related only to the reversal of tariffs on inputs and the removal of restrictions against foreign competition.

Table 2.8 lists the important policy changes that affected the Indian software industry. Notice that tariffs to protect hardware imports continued through the 1980s, except for 100 percent export oriented units, which could import hardware at world prices. The Foreign Exchange Regulation Act (FERA) that required foreign companies to dilute equity holdings to 51 percent also governed foreign investment in this sector. This governed foreign investment in other sectors of the economy as well and famously caused the exit of IBM and Coca-Cola in the late 1970s. Though it is claimed that, in granting Texas Instruments the right to invest

TABLE 2.8. Policy Changes Affecting the Software Sector: 1972–99

Year and policy	What the policy did
Software Export Scheme, 1972	Permitted the imports of hardware for purposes of hardware development on the condition that the price of hardware was recouped through foreign exchange earnings within 5 years.
Liberalization of policies related to software industry, 1976	Hardware import duties reduced from 100% to 40%
	Faster clearance of software export applications
	Software could take advantage of export incentives including location in Export Processing Zones
	Nonresident Indians were allowed to import software for purposes of export. Export obligation was 100% of all output produced.
Software Export Policy, 1981	Import duties on hardware raised to encourage use of indigenous computers
	Firms allowed to import hardware to write software for both domestic and export purposes
	Software exporters could also import 'loaned' computers.
New Computer Policy, 1984	Import procedures simplified
	Import duties on hardware reduced from 100% to 60% for software developers
	Access to foreign exchange was made easier for software firms
	Income tax exemption on net export earnings lowered from 100% to 50%
	Software exports were sought to be promoted through satellite based communication links with overseas computers, and the national computer network Indonet was made available for exports from public sector and small firms.
Software Policy, 1986	Software growth seen for the first time as independent of hardware growth in the domestic economy
	Imports of hardware liberalized and duties on them abolished for exporters of software
	Export obligations for hardware importers, however, increased: export obligations ranged from 250% to 150% of foreign exchange used, to be repaid to the government in four (rather than five) years. A penalty fine was also imposed on nonfulfilment of the export obligation
	Imported software attracted a 60% duty on its value
	Special export obligations governed the use of dedicated satellite links.

TABLE 2.8. (*Continued*)

Year and policy	What the policy did
Software Technology Parks of India, 1988	Established under the Department of Electronics of the Government of India, the STPs were autonomous bodies to encourage and support small software exporters, by giving 100% export-oriented firms a tax-free status for five years within the first eight years of operation. In addition, they were provided with office space and computer equipment, access to high-speed satellite links and an uninterrupted supply of electricity. STPs also provided services such as import certification, software valuation, project approvals, market analysis, marketing support and training and 'single window clearance' for projects. STPs are connected by an integrated network, so subscribers can lease a point to point digital channel, and have access to the Internet with their own TCP/IP number, which would give them e-mail, remote log in, and file-transfer services as well as access to the World Wide Web
	Export obligations applied to firms in the STPs using telecom infrastructure.
New Economic Policy, 1991	Devaluation and partial convertibility of the rupee
	Abolition of foreign exchange for travel tax
	Reduction in telecommunication charges for satellite links
	Export obligations on STPs removed
	Reduction of hardware import duties.
Import duties on imported software, 1992–95	Reduced to 20% on applications software and 65% on systems software in 1994
	Reduced to 10% on both in 1995.
Income-tax exemptions, 1993–99	Software exports were exempt from income tax and this tax-free status was confirmed every year till 1995 after which it became open-ended. There is talk of ending this status in 2001.

in Bangalore in 1984, the Indian government broke twenty-five different rules, this was very much the exception rather than the rule.[8]

Furthermore, through the 1980s software policy seemed to be in a strange bind. While it was recognized early that Indian software had the capacity to become a major foreign exchange earner, the government saw the development of software as inextricably tied up with planning for self-sufficiency in hardware manufacture until 1984.[9] This paradox led to policies, which shackled software through restrictions on the import of equipment and high tariffs, even as the government targeted software as a potential export sector. Planners and technology policy makers who saw India's potential in software were frustrated by the government's excessive preoccupation with indigenous hardware development [8]. Indeed, one could turn the liberalization argument on its head and say that software exports were in fact the creation of a regulated policy regime, which needed foreign exchange badly and recognized an opportunity to earn it in software exports.

Furthermore, the software industry was more influenced by post 'liberalization' policy. Similar to Israel, Indian software was a beneficiary of innovative policies designed by the government. Chief among these was the Software Technology Park of India (STPI) initiative to overcome infrastructural constraints with regard to telecom access and distribution. The launching of the STPI initiative brought telecom links within reach of the majority of small software exporters. This was followed by a universal slashing of the costs of establishing those links. As a result, Internet access costs decreased dramatically in the mid-1990s.

As for the availability of human capital, there is also no evidence to suggest that the Indian government had been developing human capital particularly for equipping the software industry. India's achievements in tertiary education in the mid-1980s were the result of an overinvestment in education in preparation for general manufacturing import substitution, which did not happen. That these achievements in tertiary sector enrolment were impressive and well above those of countries at a similar per capita level (such as China) and at higher per capita levels (such as Continental Europe) had been noted in a prescient paper by Sen [9]. Yet in the late 1980s engineers in India were a demoralized lot, they had undergone stringent education for employment in a manufacturing economy that was not willing to pay them enough.

In terms of explaining the evolution of the industry, it is also difficult to see how liberalization could account for some of the other features of software growth during this period: the sort of increase in productivity observed for Indian software in Table 2.7, the increases in expenditures on training by firms, the variety of services that the Indian software industry now provides, and other aspects of industrial evolution such as the gradual polarization of the industry into the top five firms and the rest.

3 Evolution of the Indian Software Industry: Phases of Growth

Characterizing any growth process by phases is an arbitrary imposition since growth is an ever-unfolding process, with each stage building upon the previous in several and often complex ways. Therefore, 'periodization' usually reflects what the writer wants to highlight—in our case the story of software growth in terms of the growth of individual firms' capabilities in response to changing opportunities offered by the external economic environment. Changes in the external environment came from two directions. There were policy-induced changes as the Indian economy moved from regulation, to de-regulation, liberalization, and postliberalization. There were also important changes in the world demand for software as computerization spread and as business administrative processes became increasingly automated in the Western world. Thus it is useful to think in terms of the following four periods in the growth of the industry:

Pre-1984: The major thrust of government policy was achieving self-reliance in hardware capability and the major event for fledgling software firms was the dramatic exit of IBM in protest against the draconian FERA rules.

1985–91: The worldwide crash in hardware prices and de-regulation of import licensing policy in India coincided with an acceleration of demand for software programmers worldwide as large multinational firms moved from mainframe to client-server systems. From 1986, software policy was de-linked and made independent of policy for the development of the indigenous hardware sector.

1992–99: There was large-scale financial liberalization by the Indian government, large-scale entry by multinational firms, a peaking of worldwide demand for software, and the phenomenal growth of the Internet. In the policy arena, Indian software saw innovative attempts to develop the telecommunications infrastructure and to broaden low-cost access to the Internet via the STPI scheme.

2000–present: There was slowdown in the demand for software but an expansion in the demand for outsourcing more generally, forcing some consolidation in the industry.

The changing constraints and opportunities in each phase of growth, whether induced by policy or changes in external demand, had many implications for the direction of evolution of the software industry. These changing nature of constraints and opportunities favored some categories of entrants and types of business models over others. This, in turn, affected the evolution of the industry. Competition by heterogeneous entrants affected the building of firm capabilities and profitability principally through two routes: the selection of business models in the product space and the building of organizational capabilities. We discuss each in turn, paying attention first to the selection of business models.

3.1 Early Entry: Pre-1984

By 1972, there was a dawning realization of the importance of software as a foreign exchange earner. The Electronics Commission and the Department of Electronics (DOE) were set the task of energizing these exports. Computer hardware imports would be allowed (subject to export obligations) to those who developed software for export. Export performance remained poor though parties claiming to have developed software for export imported several computers. This appears to have had an indelible influence on a decade of policy that followed, which saw allowing hardware imports for software exports as a major loophole, which needed to be fixed, in the interests of indigenous hardware development.

Analysis of poor performance of exports by the head of DOE singled out the inability of Indian software to break into markets as the main factor constraining software exports. Tedious procedures governing foreign exchange and inevitable delays in obtaining permissions for imports also prevented early software firms from maintaining pace with changing markets.[10] In addition, small firms with few contacts were discriminated against by export obligations on imports.

The single most dramatic event of this period, however, was the departure of IBM in protest against the FERA rules, which required it to dilute its equity holding to 40 percent in 1977. The departure created an import substituting opportunity for domestic manufacturers of computers, and a demand for programmers that could write the proprietary software to run computers produced by domestic hardware firms. The exit of IBM also provided an opportunity for sales of (micro) computers by other foreign hardware manufacturers. Foreign companies such as Burroughs depended upon software programmers in India to write software conversion programs which could be used by non-Burroughs (mostly IBM) clients in order to switch to Burroughs computer systems.[11] The public sector company Computer Maintenance Corporation (CMC) was also established in 1976 to service IBM computers when the company's decision to exit in protest against the FERA laws became known. Ex-IBM employees started up small entrepreneurial computer companies. Domestic attempts at building nuclear and space capabilities located in the public sector were also an early source of demand for programming skills.

Despite a small installed base of computers domestically, software programming in India started early, and supported a large variety of software platforms and a range of projects that varied in their complexity. This variety proved to be an important asset for the industry when demand for software skills grew in the subsequent decade. There was a gradual build-up of programming skills and knowledge of software languages—those meant for legacy systems as well as knowledge of newly emerging software platforms and languages, such as UNIX. The Indian government in its few computerization projects because of its nonproprietary nature particularly favored UNIX.

The dependence of software on hardware components during this period constrained potential entrants to the Indian software industry. As India was still trying to build a domestic hardware industry through import substitution, duties on hardware components were high and importers had to endure a complex set of rules and regulations in order to obtain imports of hardware components. Hardware was a more profitable business than software at this stage, but it had severe barriers to entry. The rules and regulations imposed by the government on the hardware sector are described in Brunner [11]: while FERA regulations kept foreign competition out, MRTP regulations prevented large business houses from entering the lucrative hardware manufacturing until 1985. Software was, however, an open field and free of the compulsions of licensing. Both the public sector and some big business houses, such as the House of Tata, entered this business.

Early companies (such as TCS, Patni, CMC, Datamatics) were established in this period. Tata Consultancy Services (TCS) was a subsidiary of the business house of Tatas. CMC, as we noted earlier, was a public sector company. Datamatics and Patni were Indian companies promoted by expatriate Indians. Although diverse in origin, all companies had strong links with foreign hardware manufacturers. Examples include TCS with Burroughs, Datamatics with Wang, and Patni Computer Systems with Data General.[12] This feature of the early Indian firms echoed an attribute typical of the software industry worldwide, when software was mostly provided with hardware. The important difference in the Indian case was the predominance of non-IBM computers and non-IBM software.

The software projects executed abroad by Indian companies in this early period often took the form of data conversion projects executed on-site for foreign firms. It was often easier to 'hire out' the services of an engineer rather than try to do the work in India. In this way the software skills of Indian programmers could be leveraged for maximum benefit and neither the supplier nor the buyer had to accumulate the higher costs due to India's protectionist policies. Furthermore, the client was assured constant monitoring—an important guarantee in the early 1980s when the reputation of Indian exports was one of poor quality and unreliability in delivery. Indian firms provided the labor for client projects. The established names of the early firms (e.g. Tatas) also helped them to draw the best engineering talent in the country. Thus, the on-site model for software service delivery—where the software-exporting firm provided the personnel to execute the project while the client firm provided the specifications and the needed capital equipment—emerged and became the popular business model for software firms. It was pioneered by Tata Consultancy Services.

The basic infrastructure required for software production, viz. stable electricity and good communication, were available only in some regions. The Bombay–Pune region was particularly favored for its stable electricity and the first export-processing zone began there. Bangalore, which had several space and electronics research labs, was another favored location. Delhi was also a favored location, possibly due to its proximity to the central government. Business houses and private limited firms with professional entrepreneurs dominated entry in this period (see Table 2.3). These firms located around a few cities, viz. Bangalore, Mumbai/Pune, and New Delhi (see Table 2.5).

The big achievement of Indian firms operating in this period was that they developed the ability to compose a team of talented software programmers to deliver highly bespoke (technical) services on a variety of software systems to large foreign firms. Their relative specialization was porting data from one platform to another and maintaining legacy systems on old mainframe platforms.

In spite of this early success, the early 1980s saw renewed policy attempts to make software development conform to the needs of hardware self-sufficiency and grow at the pace of the hardware industry. Thus the Software Policy of 1981 stated:

[T]he revised policy and practices place emphasis on the generation and export of software using the existing computing capacity in the country, rather than on the import of computers, let alone the import of a particular type of computer, for such software generation.

The Computer policy in 1984 reiterated the export obligations and import tariffs required of the industry. It was not till 1986 that policy allowed software to grow independently of domestic hardware.

3.2   New Entry and Experimentation: 1985–91

The spread of computerization in the United States and in Europe received a major boost with the advent of personal and networked computers in the mid- and late 1980s. Networked computing was a particularly important development as it allowed large amounts of data to be stored on several small computers that could talk to each other. It was a more flexible (and less capital intensive) method for storing data than the earlier mainframe computers. At the same time, networked computing accommodated both small and large users of data. Thus, the shift to networked computing in the West opened up a huge new source of demand for software services.

These developments created a huge demand for software services in addition to the maintenance of legacy mainframe systems, the speciality of several Indian firms. There was demand for customized software that would allow firms to migrate from mainframe to networked systems and install and maintain enterprise resource systems. Many of the tasks were routine enough to be outsourced but required knowledge of diverse software languages and protocols that were expensive to acquire for firms wishing to computerize their operations.

However, for many such firms local outsourcing was less competitive in this period than outsourcing to Indian firms. Indian firms, by now, had considerable experience working with the migration of data across different systems. Also, the increased credibility of Indian software professionals in the Western world created a positive externality that helped new entrants during this period. More importantly, it was in this period that foreign firms first realized the large cost advantage of employing Indian programmers.[13] There are no systematic data on the movement of software salaries overtime, but the following anecdote is illustrative. A salary survey undertaken by the magazine *Dataquest* and published in 1989 revealed that the salary earned by a computer professional was around Rs. 8,000 a month ($5,486 per annum), well below salaries in other industries. Posts in the Middle East offered salaries of Rs. 14,000 per month ($9,600 per annum with benefits and without taxes). In the same period Microsoft was prepared to offer $40,000 plus re-location expenses and a green card to Indian software engineers.[14] The higher rewards to training in software became readily apparent to Indian engineers, many of who migrated to the United States.

The Software policy of 1986 broke away from earlier policies by allowing software to grow independently of domestic hardware. Hardware imports were de-licensed and made duty free for exporters, though they continued to be subject to export obligations. Concurrently, hardware prices in the world economy fell dramatically and importing hardware necessary for software production was much cheaper. This meant that set-up costs for a software firm were lower than in the previous period. Software still faced numerous problems on account of high import duties on imported software code and foreign exchange obligations (payable to the Indian government) on the exports of software. The latter often favored larger over smaller software exporters. The Government also experimented with preferential procurement of domestic software and put a duty on all imported software.

Despite all these policy measures, some of which greatly dampened profitability from software activities, the rate of entry into the sector increased modestly. As Table 2.3 reveals, both entrepreneurs and business house subsidiaries increased their share in entry during this period. Some entrepreneurial firms that had been set up by IT professionals in the early 1980s, for example, Infosys and NIIT, matured. Indian firms that had entered as hardware firms seized the opportunity to leverage their technical resources out of hardware and manufacturing into the more profitable software production. For example, WIPRO Technologies (a wholly owned subsidiary of a vegetable oil conglomerate) and Hindustan Computers Ltd. (an entrepreneurial firm promoted by an expatriate Indian), initially established as hardware firms, entered the software business later in this period. Other business houses, for example, Satyam, Ramco, and Pentafour, saw the opportunity to move from low profitability sectors (e.g. manufacturing) into software production in the late 1980s. Established business houses also set up joint ventures with multinational firms.

The lack of proximity to end users (mainly foreign firms) and the primitive state of the communications infrastructure still posed a major problem and limited the growth of export sales. These problems were resolved in a variety of ways. Regional pockets that were well endowed with the relevant infrastructure were given tax breaks and other incentives to attract investment in software and facilitate exports. These areas were called Science Technology Parks (STPs) and became popular from 1988. The promise of adequate infrastructure in STPs was never fully realized and soon private sector firms were allowed to set up communications facilities and invest in power generation.

Though infrastructure constraints imposed large fixed costs on outsourced software projects, there were offsetting factors. Very important was the time difference between India and its most important trade partner in software, the United States. The 12-hour lead enjoyed by Indian firms allowed them to economize on set-up costs by investing in dedicated satellite links that would allow Indian firms to utilize hardware facilities lying idle in the United States. At the same time overall productivity increased as the time difference effectively extended the US working day. Combined with the cost advantage in software salaries, this conferred enormous cost advantages to locating in India. Some multinational firms quickly recognized this and located their global computerization operations in India. Thus Texas Instruments and COSL located operations in India, despite the considerable restrictions on foreign investment that still existed in this period.

On the demand side, some things had changed in the domestic market. The advent of microcomputers and personal computers, coupled with the fall in hardware prices, facilitated the spread of computing to small users in the domestic market. The installed base of computers between 1983 and 1987 in India was estimated to have grown from 3,500 systems to 26,560 systems.[15] Possibly this gave rise to expectations of creating a mass market in Indian software package products, though duties of 60 percent on imported software may also have played its part in creating a profitable domestic market opportunity. The Indian market saw the entry of the first domestic market-focused product firms such as Sonata and Mastek. Mastek was also the first to experiment with a product model based on the use of tools. Infosys and Wipro also developed products aimed at the domestic market in this period. Entrepreneurial entry in the 1980s was thus diverse both in terms of product spaces occupied by new entrants and business practices.

Domestic demand had increased but was not sufficient to sustain software product businesses that targeted the domestic market. Thus, product firms like Wipro, Sonata, and Mastek soon reverted to the on-site services model. Firms also realized that though they had the technical ability to write product software, they lacked the business acumen and marketing ability needed to make it sell. Furthermore, the per unit profits on service exports were far more stable than those on domestic products or services. The on-site services model emerged as the dominant business model by the end of this period. The main reasons for its dominance lay in its ability to overcome problems caused by poor communications infrastructure in this sector and to avoid the large financial risks that committing upfront costs to product development involved.

3.3 Imitative Entry and Financial Liberalization: 1992–99

The year 1991 witnessed many changes in the Indian economy. Most important among these changes were the sharp depreciation of the rupee and the liberalization of financial flows. The depreciation of the rupee kept wage costs in dollar terms down even as software salaries began to rise in the domestic economy. Using quarterly data, Sen [9] shows that between 1990 and 1993 almost half of the export growth was accounted for by the rupee's devaluation (see Table 2.9).

The liberalization of financial flows from 1992 meant that foreign capital could move in relatively easily. This was particularly opportune for the Indian software industry. The changes wrought by networked computing in the late 1980s affected large multinational firms the most. Many had a real need to connect and computerize all their global operations, and the client-server architecture offered a basis for doing so. The experience of COSL and TI had demonstrated that

TABLE 2.9. Decomposing the Annual Growth of
Indian Software Exports, 1987–93

Period	Total growth (%)	Real growth (%)	Exchange rate (%)
1987–93	46	28	18
1987–90	41	29	12
1990–93	52	28	24

Source: Sen [9] as cited in Parthasarathy [10].

an Indian subsidiary of an MNC could operate as a low-cost outsourcing center for global software needs. Through the 1990s, when foreign investment norms were liberalized, a steady stream of multinational subsidiaries, often managed by Indian software professionals, followed. Therefore, software was first developed at the Indian subsidiary and then installed on-site by teams of Indian software professionals.

Another hybrid type of entrant in this period was the foreign subsidiary established via expatriate (usually the United States) links between the foreign market and local entrepreneurship. Such companies usually had a front office in the United States responsible for marketing the technical services of an Indian based and managed team. Early and successful examples of this type of entrant are companies like Silverline, IMRI, Mastech, and CBSI.

Multinational entry into the sector was interesting in that their operations demonstrated the possibility of what was to become a new kind of business model for software services: the offshore model. Domestic firms like TCS and later Infosys had already demonstrated the profitability of the on-site model. But as MNC subsidiaries explored for greater cost saving by only implementing software on the site of computerization, they demonstrated elements of what a successful offshore model would involve.[16] The benefits of this model were quickly realized and adopted by leading domestic firms, though they were entrusted with autonomy by foreign customers only for fairly small, specific, and noncritical tasks. The dramatically decreasing cost of telecommunications access and its vast outreach due to the STPI scheme also meant that offshore operations came within the reach of smaller firms as well. Desai [13] argues that offshore operations became popular as many firms switched to web-based delivery made possible by the STPI scheme.

Domestic firms faced competition from imitative entry by other Indian firms and a flood of US–Indian firms, which benefited greatly from the opening up of the financial market and liberalization of foreign capital. The strengths that different types of entrants brought to the basic outsourcing model were, however, different. MNCs relied upon their own internal markets and grew with stable revenues. Business houses competed with reputation and diverse client base. These selling points affected revenues and firms that were able to attract larger, diverse, and more reputable clients were assured a more rapid growth.

Even though the heterogeneity of entrants (and their abilities) increased, the industry as a whole seemed to be converging on some basic economic underpinnings in their business model. Products and a focus on the domestic market were out and software services based on exports were in. The dominant value proposition and capability was the ability to deliver a working team of software professionals to any part of the world to do any software engineering job.[17] The experimentation that happened in this period was focused around increasing value in software service offerings: developing the offshore business model and fixed price projects. These were more sophisticated variants of the service model rather than a radical departure from it. However, the firms were competing against each other in the same product space. This is confirmed by the Arora et al. [5] survey of Indian firms. They found that the main competition to Indian firms came from other Indian firms or US firms.

Therefore, leading firms also devised strategies to differentiate themselves from the pack. This was as much a strategy for avoiding direct competition as it was for increasing the value of the service provided. The first strategy of differentiation was acquiring certification and becoming involved in commencing certification norms for service production, such as those proposed by the CMU-CMM. This signaled a commitment to providing accountable, reliable, and error proof services. By the end of 1998, more than half of software firms receiving four and five in SEI-CMM rankings were Indian. Many had also acquired ISO-9000 certification. It is a moot point, of course, whether these rankings were indicative of better software ability or no more than a signaling device in an increasingly competitive market. For example, Arora et al. [14] found no evidence that having ISO certification improved productivity per employee for Indian software firms. Unlike ISO certification, CMM rankings are fewer and more selective. They are also used by MNC subsidiaries with little need to signal in their largely captive markets (see Table 2.10). This suggests that certification has some value in indicating organizational efficiency as it relates to software service delivery.

Firms also paid attention to acquiring domain expertise, often through collaborations in the so-called development centers. Even if the actual distribution of contracts does not show this, the intentions of the leading companies in the annual reports and declarations to their shareholders suggest that there was a picking of domains: TCS and Infosys concentrated on financial and insurance domains, Pentafour concentrated on creating digital assets in animation, Satyam sought to concentrate on software for automated systems in transport manufacturing, and Wipro in telecom and R&D services.

Lastly, many firms went public, sometimes listing in the United States. Financial liberalization greatly facilitated this. Infosys became the first Indian firm to list on NASDAQ, and other firms soon followed suit. Listing on overseas markets added an important element of visibility and credibility in the technical services business. Ironically, the firms who listed on these stock exchanges had very little

TABLE 2.10. Incidence of Certification Among Various Types of Entrants in 1999–2000

Entrant type	Business house subsidiaries	Multinational enterprises	US–Indian	Entrepreneurial firms	Entrepreneurial (professional IT)
Relative incidence of certification	1.18	1.54	1.53	1.00	0.64

Notes: (1) Firms that had any type of certification, ISO or SEI-CMM were counted.
(2) Relative incidence is computed as: proportion of firms in each category that had certification/ average proportion of firms in the industry that had certification. A relative incidence greater than 1 indicates that sub-group had an average certification that was higher than the industry average, which was 0.274.

need for external finance.[18] Their successful listing also drew venture capital financed funding into India and encouraged entrepreneurial start-ups by providing exit routes to entrepreneurs. Inorganic growth through acquisition of other firms was flagged as a possible strategy, though very few acquisitions were actually made in this period.[19]

By the end of this period of unfettered demand, the Indian software industry had built both a general capability (for outsourced service delivery) and some firm-specific capabilities (in particular domains and software process management). Evidence of such differentiation is provided in Table 2.11, which reports some characteristics of firms in the median and third quartile. The larger scale and higher capital intensity of the third quartile firms is noteworthy.

Experimentation with business models was much less radical than in previous periods since it basically involved developing more profitable variants of the

TABLE 2.11. Characteristics of Firms in the Median and Third Quartile

	1994–95 N = 105	1996–97 N = 225	1999–2000 N = 237	2000–01 N = 457
Median firm				
Size of authorized capital (Rs. million)	7.8	12.5	35.00	42.50
Sales revenue (Rs. million)	28	38.36	49	53.15
Export revenue (Rs. million)	20	25	27.3	39.45
Total employment	85	115	100	101
Employment of software professionals	66	90	67	70
% software professionals in total employed	77.6	78.26	67	69.30
Revenue per employee (Rs. million)	0.33	0.33	0.49	0.52
Third quartile firm				
Size of authorized capital (Rs. million)	37.89	48	110	110
Sales revenue (Rs. million)	143	130	225.25	270.28
Export revenue (Rs. million)	115	90.6	147	172.60
Total employment	230	315	235	288
Employment of software professionals	192	218	174	200
% software professionals in total employed	83.5	69.2	74.04	69.44
Revenue per employee (Rs. million)	0.62	0.41	0.95	0.93

Notes: (1) N = number of firms with no missing data on any variable.
(2) The quartile data have been calculated using the Tukey's Hinges method.

Source: Author's computations based on NASSCOM registers.

outsourced service model: application to different domains and progressing from
on-site to offshore project execution. There were two outliers to this general rule:
the successful development of a banking product by COSL (Flex-cube) and the
less successful development of an ERP product (Marshall) by Ramco. The larger
profit margins of the product business still seduced, and both these products were
targeted at smaller, overseas customers. Most existing firms, however, were either
unprepared to take the financial risk or thought they needed more domain knowledge to anticipate market needs. It was difficult to forget the lessons learned in the
previous period and the lack of a domestic market was perceived to be a handicap.[20]

3.4   Consolidation and Slowdown: 2000 Onwards

This period brought a lot of changes for the industry. The slowdown in demand
came on the heels of the dot com crash and the recession in the United States, the
industry's largest market. Many firms had anticipated an eventual slowdown and
they made attempts to enter other markets, such as the European, Japanese, and
African markets. The long awaited bill allowing private investment in telecommunications was passed and costs of connecting to the Internet fell sharply, affecting
businesses that used the Internet.

The most dramatic development in 2001 and 2002 was the growing size of
outsourcing projects secured by the leading domestic firms. Recent NASSCOM
estimates suggest that top Indian companies have been routinely securing multi-
year offshore contracts valued at about $75 million or 300 man-hours, much
higher than the $10–15 million contracts of prior years (although those were
dispersed over many more firms).[21] Table 2.12 lists some of the deals reported in
the national press and the values and number of years involved. This list is not
exhaustive but demonstrates the large size of single outsourcing projects, the longer
time commitments, the large offshore nature of operations, and the fixed-price
nature of the contracts.

To put these figures in perspective, it is useful to contrast them to the dimensions
of a typical export project reported by Arora et al. [5] based on interviews conducted
in 1997 when billing by Indian firms was typically in terms of time and materials
costs:

The typical export project is to the US, small (10 manyears) worth about $1million and
involves maintenance, porting an existing application from a legacy platform to a client
server platform or Y2K work. Between 33% and 66% of the work is executed offshore
(in India).

Table 2.12 thus testifies to the growing process capability of the leading Indian
software firms. Many of the deals reported have been preceded or followed by
some acquisition activity. HCL acquired a Belfast call center prior to its deal with
BT, as part of the Ericsson deal Wipro took over employment in Ericsson's R&D
centers, and in the TCS deal with GE the latter took over development centers
created by TCS.

TABLE 2.12. Large Contracts Bagged by Indian Software Firms Reported in National Newspapers (2001–03)

Month/Year	Indian firm	Contracting client firm	Contract type	Value (period)
August 2003	L&T Infotech	Motorola	Unknown	$70–90 million (3–5 years)
August 2003	Satyam	Certain Teed (USA)	Outsourcing contract to implement end-to-end supply chain solution. Fixed cost	$15 million (9 months)
June 2003	HCL	Airbus	Embedded software	—
April 2003	HCL	British Telecom Group (UK)	Outsourcing contract for business telemarketing, billing, and conferencing work	$160 million (5 years)
April 2003	Progeon (subsidiary of Infosys)	BT group (UK)	Second service provider for BPO services	— (5 years)
March 2003	Patni Computer Systems	Guardian Life Insurance Co. (US)	70% offshore contract for gap analysis and implementation of IT systems in the market place	$35 million (7 years)
March 2003	Ramco–Boeing	Aloha Airlines (US)	Technical services with main marketing by Boeing (50% of revenues for each)	—
November 2002	TCS & Wipro	Lehmann Bros.	IT outsourcing	$50–70 million annually
October 2002	Wipro	Ericsson	'Total' R&D outsourcing with Wipro taking over the Ericsson R&D centres in India	—
July 2002	Wipro	Transco (UK) (formed as a result of merger between Lattice group and National grid)	Application, maintenance support and integration services around SAP tools	$20 million
January 2002	TCS	GE medical systems	'Take or pay' model, whereby GE is committed to making a fixed payment irrespective of work done by TCS	$100–120 million (2 years)
July 2001	Wipro	Lattice Group (US)	Outsourcing	$70 million (3 years)

Source: Author's compilation based on newspaper clippings from the following national newspapers: *Business Line, Business Standard,* and *Economic Time.*

Even as the leading offshore firms were growing in size, a new segment of the software market opened up in the form of small niche companies. These were often focused in new areas such as DSP (digital signal processing) software, embedded software, and system on chip (SOC). Further, firms in these areas are increasingly turning to a product-based model using some kind of Intellectual Property. A notable example of this is Sasken, previously Silicon Automation Systems—an embedded telecom solutions company that writes software across the telecom value chain. Other examples include: Impulse Software which has a software product that enables appliances to talk on the blue tooth standard, Tejas Networks which manufactures optical switches for telecom carriers, Xybridge (started by two ex-Nortel employees and is a second generation spin-off) which manufactures a 'soft' switch that can be deployed on networks that carry both voice and data traffic, and Ishoni Networks which builds chips for home gateway boxes that will enable home networks to be both secure and capable of connecting many small devices.

There are some curious features of these newer firms. They are product companies and, though they are physically based in India, they also operate out of Silicon Valley, using global networks for initial customers and financing. Their products are grounded in what they perceive as emerging future needs as the global adoption of digital technologies proceeds. They also bet on particular standards while competing with similar companies. Some of these firms are spin-offs or set up by groups of academics, though we are still far from assessing the proportion of each.

The top five companies are aware of these developments and almost all of them have set up corporate venture funds, possibly to scope the potential of these activities. They have also realized that in order to succeed, many of these products require manufacturing capability on a large scale, which India lacks. Therefore, a new dimension to the industry has been the exploration of possibilities for locating and manufacturing in China by some of the leading firms (TCS, Wipro, and Infosys). Again, this evidences a competence and confidence in managing global operations by a few leading software firms and a preparedness to risk large investments to corner a new niche should one become visible.

The explorations of other domains for application of the offshore model had already begun in 1998, often by new firms. These included the provision of e-services, web hosting, data transcription, e-CRM services etc. These attempts received an unexpected impetus from the recession, which heightened foreign firms' sensitivity to cost pressures. The most surprising and dramatic growth in the recent period has thus come from the growth of IT-enabled services such as:

1. Customer interaction services—with adequate telecom infrastructure where customer related support in areas such as marketing, selling, information dispensing, and technical troubleshooting is provided round the clock. Includes voice calls and e-mail management.
2. Back office data processing—for large banks, in finance and HR activities, where raw data and paper documents are sent to remote locations for entry.

TABLE 2.13. ITES-BPO Revenues by Service Lines

Type	2001–02 employment	(US$ mil) revenues	2002–03 employment	(US$ mil) revenues	2003–04 (est) employment	(US$ mil) revenues
Customer care	30,000	400	65,000	810	95,000	1,200
Finance	15,000	300	24,000	510	40,000	820
HR	1,500	30	2,100	45	3,500	70
Payment services	7,000	110	11,000	210	21,000	430
Administration	14,000	185	25,000	310	40,000	540
Content development	39,000	450	44,000	465	46,000	520
Total	106,500	1,475	171,100	2,350	245,500	3,580

Source: Estimates reported on NASSCOM web site (www.nasscom.org/images/itesbpo-p66.gif).

3. Medical transcription, including billing, ensuring compliance with standards, and health care outsourcing.
4. Content development—for web sites, GIS, engineering services for plant design, and also animation content.
5. Other services such as remote consultancy on market research, remote education, and remote data search.

Most of these segments recorded remarkable growth during the downturn (see Table 2.13). Growth of back office operations and customer interaction services have been particularly rapid. Both new and old firms have been involved in this process. The most famous old firm example is the call center Progen, which was incubated in Infosys, and recently spun-off. The existence of older players in many of these activities suggests a commonality of business and organizational capabilities involved in these new IT service areas.

4 Tight Labor Markets and the Pressure on Organizational Capability

The outsourced business model required a certain organizational capability in human resource management and in software process management to ensure reliability of the service product. Indeed the business model would not have been successful without this parallel process management capability. The interesting question is what forced Indian firms to develop such capabilities? This is not a trivial question and it is not a question that can be answered with reference to the complementarities between the business model and the specific capability alone. While these qualities were desirable from the point of view of the higher productivity they would impart to the outsourced model, the huge mass of unemployed engineers in India did not encourage firms to invest in such capability. It would have been far easier if they could have employed one cheap programmer after another rather than invest in incentives and organizational capability development. In the other success stories of Indian exports, gems and jewelry and leather exports, this is what Indian firms have done to keep their exports competitive. However, software firms departed from this norm. To understand why they did so, we need to look closely at the labor market for software firms and understand how it changed over the same time periods.

As Arora et al. [5] argue, the initial growth of the Indian software industry was undoubtedly due to the fortunate circumstance of an excess supply of engineers and scientific labor. As the cost–quality advantage of Indian programmers was realized there was fierce competition for the scarce resource—Indian software programmers—both by foreign competitors who persuaded their governments to relax immigration laws and increase visa quotas for Indian programmers and later by MNC subsidiaries that came to set up firms in India. The stock of engineers rapidly depleted and by the mid-1990s there were signs of a growing tightness in the labor market. A state of 'educational emergency' was declared by the government in 1998–99 in response to the growing scarcity of engineers as demand for them mushroomed. The three new Indian Institutes of Information Technology were set up and private training institutions boomed. In interviews, firms confessed to pooling labor to alleviate temporary scarcities. Thus, if firm A had a shortage of a particular type of skill (say a Java programmer) and knew firm B had employees who could do the job, firm A would 'rent' the employee from firm B rather than leave the job incomplete. This was unlikely to happen in offshore jobs but was quite frequent for on-site jobs.

Wages in the software industry grew at over 30 percent per annum in the mid-1990s and attrition rates were high. Despite this, Arora et al. [5] report that when asked in 1998–99 to list the top three problems they faced, more than half of all firms (out of a sample of over 100 firms), irrespective of age, size, or market orientation (either export or import), selected manpower shortage and employee attrition as the most serious problems affecting them.

The vulnerability to employee attrition and upward pressure on wages created two different sorts of problems for the domestic firms in the software sector. Rising wages (see Table 2.6) decreased a company's profitability and put pressure on firms to restore profitability by increasing productivity in other ways: more efficient practices, the use of non-engineering labor whose quality was raised by firm-specific training, and the use of software tools. Attrition created different kinds of threats and problems—the loss of employee-specific knowledge and the possibility that the organization's knowledge was lost to a competitor. When attrition is at senior levels then it is also likely that a firm loses some of its customer base to the competitor. Interviews with US-based clients of Indian software firms reported by Arora et al. [5] indicated that many of them saw employee attrition as an important problem. Several clients commented on the delays due to entire project teams leaving in the midst of a project in response to a more lucrative offer. Such delays were particularly troubling for smaller clients and for product focused clients with a need to shorten product development cycles. In both cases attrition threatened to open up the credibility gap which earlier firms had strived to close.

Firms responded in some measure by adopting procedural norms that would make their software development immune to such attrition. One of these was to rely heavily on documentation and another was to start using proprietary tools wherever possible. New organizational structures evolved in order to keep a mix of new and old employees as an informal deputizing system. Skill gaps were identified and firms developed training programs that would help retain skill set. In time, firms were also able to use these procedures to institute better process control.

The growing scale and offshore component of projects facilitated a careful splitting of tasks. Thus, in many offshore projects, process control allowed something like a 'Babbage effect' in the growing specialization of the industry in outsourced services.[22] The best quality programmer could be used for suitable tasks while less able/experienced programmers could be assigned the lower-level tasks, each paid according to their productivity. This separation of tasks allowed huge increases in productivity—recent NASSCOM estimates suggest that offshore billing rates on an average are one-third the billing rate of similar on-site projects.

The offshore model adopted in the mid-1990s also addressed some of the problems created by the relative scarcity of talented software particularly well. On-site projects in contrast needed to be manned by people who could do the most complex tasks as well as the least complex ones. Since the size of the team had to be kept relatively small, these workers also had to do the lower-level work. Put differently the offshore model allowed Indian firms to realize more fully the productivity benefits of large-scale specialization. But in order to realize these benefits firms had to learn how to split up the tasks involved and also exercise judgment on how to recombine the results.

Employee attrition and wage increases also prompted software firms to explicitly introduce human capital management strategies comparable to those adopted by their international rivals competing for the same labor. These included:

(1) an increasing role for private investment by software firms in software education and training for their employees;
(2) organizational practices designed to retain the interest and loyalty of employees such as Employee Stock Options (ESOPs) and attention toward charting a management career path for technical personnel in firms— perhaps the first signs of a technocracy;
(3) organizational innovations designed to diffuse and recombine employee-specific knowledge in a variety of different ways, most notably through flat hierarchies, team working, and the use of embodied forms of software knowledge such as tools or where possible through the use of licenses and intellectual property.

The adoption of ESOPs and the charting of career paths in management for technically qualified professionals have had at least one unintended outcome. Technically qualified persons now view entrepreneurship quite differently. It is a logical extension of the managerial tasks they hope to perform as their careers grow, with an added element of risk that promises large rewards. It has also been an important mechanism by which organizational and managerial lessons learnt in software have been leveraged in other similar service areas.

Though there is little systematic evidence on the origins of software firms, anecdotal evidence suggests that ex-employees of HCL and Wipro have also been particularly active entrepreneurs. TechSpan, NIIT, Pertech Computers, Global Infotech, InfoTech Enterprises, STG, and Infogain were all set up by ex-HCL employees. Similarly, product-based ventures such as Jamcracker, Microland, e4e Ventures, Tarang Software, iLantus, Jumpstart, Qsupport, and Mindtree Consulting have been set up by ex-Wipro employees. The leading software firms are sensitive to these concerns suggesting that such spin-off activity may pose threats for the existing firms. Satyam has sought to avoid such attrition by investing in corporate venturing. Plans announced by TCS indicate that they too will start a venture capital fund to encourage employees with innovative ideas. All this is also reflected in Table 2.3 where entrants that have had prior experience in IT are the largest single category of entrant type.

5   Summary and Implications

This chapter has painted a picture of the evolution of the Indian software industry. The chapter detailed how the different variants of the outsourced service model developed in response to changing opportunities available to Indian software firms. These models still leverage their unique cost advantage in software programming vis-à-vis the rest of the world. The chapter then argued that the development of new business models was allied to an evolving capability in software process control and large-scale labor management.

The specific capabilities successful firms developed were in process control, team management, and profitable implementation of good organizational and human resource practices. This happened in response to the pressures from competition in the labor market—just as new business models developed in response to competitive pressures in the product market. However, it is the winning combination of particular organizational capabilities and new business models that differentiate Indian software firms from other software providers in the global marketplace, allowing them to hold a fifth of the global market for custom software.

What about the implications for industrial development more generally? It is often argued that the excessive export dependence of Indian software has made it a less useful source of growth for the domestic economy. Productivity improvements in software do not transmit to the other sectors of the Indian economy since domestic demand is still small. However, there are other ways by which productivity improvements can 'infect' other sectors of the economy and contribute to overall industrial development and growth. Consider the innovation of the manufactory in the case of cotton textiles, the principles of mechanical engineering design in the case of machine tools and the mastery of manufacturing design in the case of the four dragons. In all these cases, leading firms of the industry developed organizational capabilities that were also generic and applicable to other industrial areas. These capabilities were later leveraged for greater productivity in other industrial sectors and general economic growth.

The Indian software services industry also shows these characteristics. The outsourced business services model can, in principle, be applied to a range of business processes: payroll management, data transcription, call services, technical support, R&D services, to name just a few. If the organizational and managerial capabilities learnt in the process of software service outsourcing can be successfully applied to different sectors, the Indian economy may enjoy a great externality due to the development of the software boom, even if domestic demand for domestically produced software is limited.

Appendix on Data Sources

Figure 2.1 is based on two sources of data. Data for 1984–89 are as quoted in [12], while data for 1993–2001 are based on NASSCOM reports.

Tables 2.2, 2.3, and 2.5, 2.10, and 2.11 of the text are based on computations from the NASSCOM registers. The data source is described and the computations are explained in this section.

The National Association of Software and Service Companies was established in the late 1980s as the Industry Association and its membership has grown steadily since. NASSCOM brings out yearly registers, which contains information about its member companies. The data reported are not the company's balance sheet data but are based on a questionnaire required of their members by NASSCOM. The register gives details about the sales revenues (export and domestic), certification, employment, and the years of establishment of various firms. These data are signed by the auditors of each company and as such represent the most reliable data with broad coverage for the industry as a whole. Table 2.2 is based on direct extrapolations of this data.

We also added to the NASSCOM register in two ways: first, we visited the web sites of firms to classify them as software product or service producers or ITES service providers. The latter type of firm has grown in number since 1999. A number of software firms also diversified into ITES: if they are still reporting some software work we have retained these firms for our analysis. However, we excluded firms that were ITES only in our computations of Tables 2.3, 2.5, 2.10, and 2.11.

Second, we added a classification of entrant type by visiting the web sites of different firms in the 2001 register. The following different types of entrants (reported in Table 2.A1) were identified and are used in Tables 2.3 and 2.5.

TABLE 2.A1. Types of Entrant Firms

Entrant type	Description
Missing	If the origin of the firm could not be determined
Professional entrepreneur	If a firm was started by professionals with prior experience in IT or IT management
Entrepreneur	If a firm was started by an existing individual entrepreneur in fields other than IT
Multinational enterprises	If a firm was started as a multinational subsidiary
US–Indian	If a firm was started by people of Indian origin and incorporated in the United States
Public sector enterprises	If a firm was started as a public sector unit/enterprise
Business house subsidiaries	If a firm was started as an arm of an existing business house
Joint ventures	If a firm was started as a joint venture

Notes

1. GDP grew by $14,288 million between 2000 and 2002, while NASSCOM reports the software revenues in this period grew by $4,016 million.
2. By 2003, employment in Indian software industry is about 230,000; software professionals employed in user organizations are about 260,000, and employed in IT-software enabled services (e.g. call centers) are about 160,000. Data are from www.nasscom.org/artdisplay.asp?Art_id=1608.
3. See ref. [2].
4. Software products on the other hand are known to be capital intensive.
5. The data for Figure 2.1 are collated from different sources in order to have as long a series as possible. These sources are detailed in the Appendix. Figures for 2003–04 are estimated figures based on NASSCOM revenue projections.
6. The classification employed is detailed in the Appendix.
7. Manufacturing uses more bought inputs (raw materials) in production than does software and using value-added adjusts for this.
8. See Lateef [7] for this claim.
9. This premise was given up only in 1986.
10. Based on the account in Subramanian [8].
11. These details are based on the author's interview with one of the software firms established in the pre-1980 period.
12. Other examples include TUL with Unisys, Hinditron with DEC.
13. Interview with one of the early multinationals to set up a subsidiary, November 1999.
14. Dataquest figures are as cited in Subramanian [8]. The conversion rate used is Rs. 17.5 = $1, which was the exchange rate in 1990.
15. Estimates from Lakha [12].
16. Satyam was probably the first firm to try the full offshore model in 1991.

17. A CEO of a large software company set up as a joint venture claimed this in an interview with the author.
18. See Palepu and Khanna [14] for a discussion of this point in the context of Infosys.
19. The scoping of M&A as a successful strategy, however, also suggests some prevalence of economies of scale in the business of outsourced software services, though the sources of such economies are not well understood in the literature.
20. These comments summarize the conclusions of a panel discussion (August 2000) in IIM, Ahmedabad titled 'Services not Products?'
21. NASSCOM vice president Sunil Mehta as reported in 'Indian software sector sees recovery', The Washington Times, 15 October 2002.
22. Babbage added a fourth source of increase in productivity within a firm due to the division of labor. This was that specialization of tasks within the firm allowed the firm to employ fully and pay each type of worker according to their ability. Thus, an engineer could be employed only for engineering tasks and a transcriber could be employed only for transcribing tasks and they would be paid differently.

References

1. NASSCOM. *Indian IT Software and Services Directory*, various volumes.
2. Raymond, Eric (1999). *Cathedral and the Bazaar: Musings on Linux and Open Source by an Accidental Revolutionary*. Cambridge, MA: O'Reilly Press.
3. Heeks, R. (1996). *India's Software Industry: State Policy, Liberalization and Industrial Development*. New Delhi: Sage Publications.
4. Arora, A. and Athreye, S. (2002). The software industry and India's economic development. *Information Economics and Policy*, 14(2), 253–273.
5. Arora, A., Arunachalam, V.S., Asundi, J., and Fernandes, R. (2001). The Indian software services industry. *Research Policy*, 30(8), 1267–1287.
6. Ghemawat, P. and Patibandla, M. (2000). India's exports since reforms: three analytic industry studies. In J.D. Sachs, A. Varshney, and N. Bajpai (eds.), *India in the Era of Economic Reforms*. New Delhi: Oxford University Press.
7. Lateef, A. (1997). Linking up with the global economy: a case study of the Bangalore software industry, New Industrial Organization Programme, discussion Paper/96/1997. International Institute for Labour Studies, ILO, Genova, ASBN 92-9014-599-4.
8. Subramanian, C.R. (1992). *India and the Computer: A Study of Planned Development*. New Delhi: Oxford University Press.
9. Sen, Pronab (1994). Software exports from India: a systemic analysis. *Electronics Information and Planning*, 22(2), 55–63.
10. Parthasarathy, Balaji (2000). Globalization and Agglomeration in Newly Industrializing Countries: The State and the Information Technology Industry in Bangalore, India. Doctoral dissertation, University of California at Berkeley.
11. Brunner, H.P. (1995). *Closing the Technology Gap*. New Delhi: Sage Publications.
12. Lakha, S. (1994). The new international division of labour and the Indian software industry. *Modern Asian Studies*, 28(2), 381–408.

Suma S. Athreye

13. Desai, M. (2003). India and China: an essay in comparative political economy. *Paper for Imf Conference on India/China, Delhi, November* 2003.
14. Palepu, K. and Khanna, T. (2001). Product and Labor Market Globalization and Convergence of Corporate Governance Evidence from Infosys and the Indian Software Industry. Harvard Business School Working Paper No. 02-040.

3

The Irish Software Industry

ANITA SANDS

1 Background

1.1 Introduction

In Ireland the inevitable never happens and the unexpected constantly occurs.
Sir John Pentland Mahaffy (1839–1919)

The Irish software industry constitutes the first example of a successful high-tech indigenous industry in Ireland. In this respect, and insofar as the Irish software industry has prospered by drawing on an abundant supply of skilled human capital and is highly export oriented, there are clear similarities with India and Israel. On the other hand, unlike their Indian counterparts, the leading indigenous Irish software firms are not mere service providers. Instead, they offer solutions, based on sophisticated software products. In this respect, the Irish industry is more like the Israeli software industry. Breznitz's chapter on the Israeli software industry (Chapter 4), however, clearly shows it to be founded on a broader industrial base and to be technologically more advanced than the Irish software industry. Moreover, as Giarratana, Pagano, and Torrisi (Chapter 8) also point out in their chapter, differently from Israel, multinational corporations have played a very important role in the birth of the Irish industry, and even today, continue to account for over half the employment and the majority of the revenues. However, the 1990s did see the emergence of a burgeoning indigenous sector, populated by a rapidly growing number of start-ups, several of which have gone on to become market leaders in their respective areas.

By the end of 2003, the Irish software industry is estimated to have consisted of 900 firms, employing a total of 24,000 persons with revenues of US$18 billion and exports of US$17.3 billion.[1] According to the OECD, the United States and Ireland accounted for almost two-thirds of OECD exports of software goods in 1998 with Ireland being the largest exporter in the world (Information Technology Outlook, 2000, p. 28).[2] Despite employing only about 1.5 percent of the Irish workforce, revenues from the software sector accounted for approximately 13 percent of Irish GNP and 14 percent of total Irish exports in 2002.[3] Though the significance, both quantitative and qualitative, of the software industry to Ireland is undeniable, these statistics exaggerate it, in large measure because the revenue and export figures for multinationals reflect accounting decisions, not economic realities. Despite this, there is no denying that the Irish software industry is a success story.

1.2   The Emergence of the Irish Celtic Tiger Economy

The development of the Irish software industry is inextricably linked to the remarkable transformation of the Irish economy over the past fifteen years. The laggard Irish economy of the past, characterized by double-digit unemployment, crippling national debt, and staggering levels of emigration has been transformed, catapulting Ireland onto the international stage. When Ireland joined the European Union (EU) in 1973, *The Economist* magazine labeled it 'the poorest of the rich' because national income was a mere 64 percent of the EU average. By the end of the 1980s, Ireland's national debt was running at 125 percent of GNP and rising. Budget deficits in the order of 12 percent of GDP were the norm and Ireland was using all its income tax revenues just to service the national debt. As a result, unemployment soared, reaching 17 percent by 1986, and emigration became a way of life, with 44,000 people departing Irish shores in 1989 alone [1].

Fifteen years later, Ireland's economic profile is very different. Economic growth in Ireland throughout the 1990s was more than double the European average reaching a staggering 11 percent in the year 1999.[4] Unemployment fell to 4.3 percent in 2000 and the national debt was only 37.4 percent[5] of GNP by 2001. *The Economist* magazine heralded Ireland as 'Europe's Shining Light' because national income had reached 118 percent of the European average in 2001, and GDP per capita is now the second highest in the EU. In a remarkable historical turnaround, Ireland has also experienced net inward migration every year since 1996, including a reverse diaspora phenomenon, which as Kapur and McHale discuss in their chapter, was a critical component of Ireland's success in software (Chapter 9).

Key to this turnaround, and also to the rise of the Irish software industry, was the implementation of a highly successful policy of foreign direct investment, which has resulted in Ireland becoming home to over 1,050 foreign companies, 46 percent of US origin. Prompted by severe economic decline and record levels of emigration in the 1950s, Ireland instituted a policy of 'industrialization by invitation', which was spearheaded by the IDA—the Industrial Development Authority—whose remit it was to lure foreign companies to Ireland through a series of tax-based and financial incentives. The job of the IDA was made significantly easier when Ireland joined the European Community in 1973. This immediately opened up a market of over US$300 million, making it an attractive, English-speaking location for foreign firms seeking to access the European common market. In the period from 1972 to 1984, the share of total Irish exports accounted for by the UK market dropped from 61 to 34 percent while exports to other EC countries increased from 17 percent in 1972 to 34 percent in 1984 [2, p. 14].

The origins of the IT industry in Ireland can be traced back to this time when the IDA made the decision to selectively target companies in potentially high-growth, high-tech sectors. This strategy resulted in a wave of foreign investment in the 1970s in electronics and computer hardware with Digital Equipment Corporation becoming the first company to establish a mini-computer manufacturing operation in Ireland in 1971 [3]. Others soon followed including Amdahl (1978), Apple (1980), and Wang (1980). Criticisms of the IDA's policy emerged in the early 1980s, when it became apparent that these operations were little more than sub-assembly plants with few linkages to the domestic economy. The Irish government responded by shifting financial incentives away from fixed asset support, focusing resources on internationally traded manufacturing and service industries. Another milestone in Irish policy in the early 1980s was the introduction of a 10 percent corporate tax on manufacturing and selected services, which was guaranteed for twenty years, only to be replaced by a uniform corporate tax rate of 12.5 percent in 2003.

Following these two decisions, foreign investment inflows into internationally traded services started to increase and the software industry was born.[6] These investments, alongside a similar influx of multinational companies in pharmaceuticals, hardware, medical devices, financial services, and call centers transformed the Irish economic landscape. Employment in the Irish software industry grew by 125 percent between 1993 and 1997, outpacing that of other sectors, making it the fourth largest source of employment and one of the fastest growing sectors of the Irish economy.[7] Throughout the 1990s, employment in the software industry increased at an average annual rate of over 20 percent, an impressive figure when compared with an overall annual growth rate in employment of 6.4 percent [5, p. 5].

2 The Software Industry in Ireland

2.1 Growth and Performance

The Irish industry evolved from humble beginnings comprising just 365 firms at the beginning of the 1990s, employing fewer than 8,000 persons. Over the next decade the industry expanded rapidly with impressive growth in the number of companies, employment, and sales, and even faster growth rates in exports (see Table 3.1). Between 1991 and 2001, total employment grew by 304 percent from 7,798 to 31,500. As the number of software MNCs located in Ireland continued to increase throughout the 1990s, so too did the number of indigenous start-ups and by 2000 there were 760 indigenous software companies in Ireland along with 140 foreign firms, compared to 291 Irish firms and 74 foreign firms in 1991.

Although the majority of firms are indigenously owned and employment has traditionally been equally divided between the domestic and foreign sectors, revenues and exports have always been dominated by the MNCs. Total industry revenues grew by an impressive 577 percent in the 1990s increasing from

TABLE 3.1. Overview Statistics for the Indigenous and Overseas Sectors of the Irish Software Industry (1991–2003)

Year	No. of companies			Employment			Revenue (US$M)			Exports (US$M)		
	Irish	Overseas	Total	Irish	Overseas	Total	Irish	Overseas	Total	Irish	Overseas	Total
1991	291	74	365	3,801	3,992	7,793	231	2,428	2,660	94	2,379	2,473
1993	336	81	417	4,495	4,448	8,943	363	2,698	3,061	178	2,652	2,830
1995	390	93	483	5,773	6,011	11,784	593	4,012	4,605	347	3,971	4,320
1997	561	108	669	9,200	9,000	18,200	787	6,089	6,875	551	6,027	6,578
1999	690	132	822	11,100	13,791	24,891	1,546	7,680	9,226	958	6,931	7,889
2001				15,000	16,500	31,500	1,825	14,001	15,826	1,486	13,271	14,831
2003	760	140	900	10,710	13,200	23,930	1,652	16,469	18,021	1,333	16,046	17,379
Growth 91–95 (%)	34	26	32	52	51	51	157	65	73	268	67	75
Growth 95–01 (%)				160	174	167	208	249	244	328	234	243
Growth 02–03 (%)				−15	−14	−14	−11	10	7	−16	13	11

Source: National Software Directorate, downloaded from www.nsd.ie in June 2004. Industry Revenues and Exports converted from Euros to US$ at rate of €1.00 = $1.21.

a modest $2.66 billion in 1991 to over $18 billion by 2002, with MNCs continuously accounting for almost 90 percent of the total. Growth in exports was even more rapid, rising from $2.47 billion in 1991 to over $17 billion in 2001 (a 603 percent increase), again dominated by the MNCs who account for over 90 percent of this total. The indigenous sector accounts for 760 (84 percent) of the 900 companies and employs just under half the industry's workforce, yet it accounts for only 9 percent of the industry's revenues and 8 percent of its overall exports.

Revenue per employee, which is found to differ by almost an order of magnitude between the indigenous and multinational sectors, offers further insight into the nature of the dichotomy that exists within the Irish software industry. Using gross industry statistics (total revenues/total employees) revenue per employee on the part of foreign firms is found to have ranged from $608,000 in 1991 to over $1.2 million by 2003. Our survey of fifty-five indigenous companies (71 percent of which had fewer than twenty-five employees) found average revenue per employee to be $78,400.[8] This is consistent with NSD findings in 1998, which cited average revenue per employee to be in the order of $80,000 for small firms (<25) and ranging from $142,000 to $180,000 for firms with over 100 employees. Though these figures might be a rough approximation, it does not detract from the extent to which total industry figures are inflated by the activities of the MNCs. If one assumes, for example, that the value added per employee in the MNCs is also in the order of $160,000 this would imply that the software industry in Ireland had revenues of approximately $3.8 billion in 2003—a factor of six lower than the reported figures.

This obvious disparity in productivity for both sectors explains why one should remain cautious while citing overall industry figures for Ireland as it is highly unlikely that the MNCs are truly so much more productive than their indigenous counterparts. Rather these figures are undoubtedly inflated by transfer price fixing activities on the part of overseas companies in Ireland, which 'arises mostly because the output of overseas subsidiaries in Ireland consists of final products, and much of the value embedded in those products is actually generated, not by the subsidiaries and employees in Ireland, but upstream in the value chain by the R&D and management activities of the parent companies located in other countries' [6, p. 17].

The MNCs use Ireland as an export platform for the European market, while taking advantage of the favorable tax environment. Given the limited size of the domestic market, however, exports are equally important to the success of indigenous companies, who have certainly improved in this regard. Indigenous exports as a percentage of indigenous revenues increased from 41 to over 80 percent during 1991–2001 whilst the proportion of total industry exports attributable to indigenous firms also doubled from 4 percent ($94 million) in 1991 to 8 percent ($1.33 billion) in 2003.

Although the Irish software industry underwent rapid expansion throughout the 1990s, the industry has contracted for the past two consecutive years in the wake of the recent downturn in the global ICT industry. It appears, however, that the indigenous industry has suffered to a much greater extent than the overseas sector. In the year 2001–02, employment in the indigenous sector fell by −16 percent from 15,000 to 12,600 and by a further −15 percent to 10,700 in 2003. There were also job losses in the MNC sector, although to a lesser extent. Employment in the overseas sector decreased from 16,500 to 15,300 in 2001–02, a drop of −7 percent, and by a further −14 percent to 13,200 in 2003. Somewhat surprisingly though, overall industry revenues and exports have continued to grow. Both revenues and exports for the industry as a whole grew by 6 percent in 2001–02 and there was a further 7 percent increase in revenues and an 11 percent increase in exports in 2003. Significant losses on the part of the indigenous sector (which in 2003 saw its revenues fall by −11 percent and its exports by −16 percent) have been offset by continued strong performance in the foreign sector, which despite cutting jobs, has seen an increase in revenues of 10 percent and exports of 13 percent in 2002–03.

2.2   Evolution of the Industry—Firm Origins in the Irish Software Industry

Although some of the older firms began operations in the 1970s, and the majority of software overseas investment took place in the mid-1980s, it was not until the 1990s that the indigenous sector gained critical mass. As O'Riain notes, there are two branches of the industry: an overseas sector, dominated by US multinational companies engaged primarily in software logistics, localization, and development, and an indigenous sector populated by small and medium-sized Irish-owned firms, engaged in software development activities, many of whom are 'gaining growing recognition in international markets' [7, p. 185].

2.2.1   Evolution of the Overseas Sector. The success of the IDA in attracting both Microsoft and Lotus Development (now part of IBM) to Dublin in 1985 had a catalytic effect on the development of the Irish software industry. Both companies produce off-the-shelf products for mass markets and their Irish operations were initially responsible for the manufacturing and distribution of these products, including tasks such as duplicating disks, printing manuals, and assembling shrink-wrapped packages. As time progressed, both companies added localization work (i.e. the translation of already developed software products into the languages and formats suitable for different European and Middle Eastern markets) to their Irish operations [7,8]. These two were soon joined by others and by 1992, fifteen of the world's top forty software companies had bases in Ireland [9].

Today 140 of the 1,050 foreign companies located in Ireland are in the software sector and can generally be divided into three main categories: companies focusing on the manufacturing, distribution, and localization of mass market software; companies providing systems integration and software services; and firms with dedicated software development centers [4]. The leading foreign firms in each of these three categories are shown in Table 3.2 and the main activities pursued by

TABLE 3.2. Leading Software Multinational Corporations Located in Ireland

Company	Year located in Ireland	Nationality	Estimated employment
Manufacturing, Logistics, Localization, Porting, Testing			
Microsoft	1985	US	1,700
Oracle	1987	US	1,067
Novell	1993	US	80
Corel	1993	Canada	150
Informix	1992	US	100
Lotus (now IBM)	1985	US	570
Symantec	1991	US	450
Sun Microsystems	1993	US	220
Bowne Global Services	1991	US	75
Software Supporting Sub-contractors (translation, turnkey services, disk duplication, localization)			
Berlitz Globalnet	1985	Japan	440
BG Turnkey Services LTD	1984	US (originally Irish)	200
Bowne Global Solutions	1991	US	500
Client Logic Co	1990	US	350
Modus Media International	1984	US	900
Zomax Ireland		US	600
Systems Integration, Sales and Consulting, Bespoke Development			
Amdahl DMR Ireland	1978	US	160
IBM	1983	US	4,000
EDS (Ireland) Ltd	1989	US	400
Accenture	1987	US	400
Banta Global Turnkey Ltd	1984	US	250
Sonopress Ireland Ltd	1994	Germany	350
Bull Cara Group	1965	France	300
Cambridge Technology Partners	1995	US	70
Software Development Centers			
Ericsson	1979	Sweden	1,185 (150 sw)
Alcatel	1982	France	85
Siemens	1983	Germany	950
Lucent Technologies	1985	US	800 (140 sw)
Motorola	1981	US	550
Silicon Software Systems (S3)	1986	Netherlands	220
Compaq (now HP)	1976	US	500
Logica Ltd (tookover Aldiscon)	1988	UK	450
Marconi	1990	UK	
ADC	1994	Canada	200
Cognotec	1994	UK	180

Note: Employment figures should only be considered as estimates, as figures may have changed since data was submitted and in some cases figures pertain to total company employment in Ireland and in others only to employment in software development.

Source: O'Riain [7], Crone [8], and author's own web-based research.

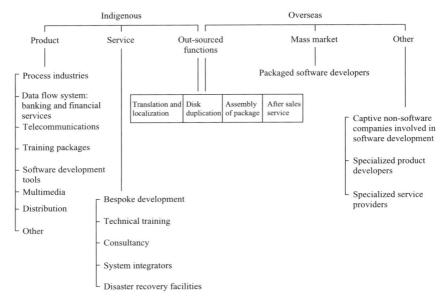

FIGURE 3.1. Principal Activities of Software Firms in Ireland
Source: Taken from O'Malley and O'Gorman [6].

both foreign and indigenous firms in the Irish software industry, is demonstrated in Figure 3.1.

According to O'Riain [7], some MNCs kept the localization and translation activities 'in-house', attracting bilingual graduates from all over Europe to Dublin. Most others outsourced the actual translation (either to independent contractors in the country of destination or to translation bureaus in Dublin) and focused on the associated programming tasks and managing relations with translators. Arora et al. state that 'the majority of foreign-owned firms in Ireland, such as Microsoft, Claris, and Symantec, concentrate their local operations on low-value-added, low-skill activities such as porting of legacy products on new platforms, disk duplication, assembling/packaging and localization' [5, p. 13], and add that companies such as Oracle, Corel, and Novell outsource most of their work and specialize themselves in project management and administrative or sales back-office activities (including multilingual customer support).

Although these kinds of activities may employ both language graduates (involved in translation) and graduate software engineers (who conduct the associated programming tasks), the manufacturing and distribution component, however, typically employs few graduates and involves lower-skilled process tasks.[9]

The evolution of activities among the MNC sector from mere manufacturing and distribution to localization did, however, present an opportunity for outsourcing and subcontracting to domestic suppliers and stimulated the development of a local base of specialized supporting vendors including localization/translation bureaus, printers, disk manufacturers, and logistics specialists. However, there was limited outsourcing to software firms and many of these suppliers remained highly dependent on their MNC clients.

During the mid-1990s an increasing number of overseas companies added software development to their portfolio of Irish activities. These dedicated software development operations undertake work of varying degrees of sophistication but typically employ a much higher percentage of computer science graduates and software engineers than the firms engaged primarily in just localization activities [8]. Some of these development centers are arms of major computer services or IT consulting MNCs (e.g. EDS, IBM, and Accenture) and are involved in specialized or customized software development for internal or external clients. There are also a number of non-software companies—including several telecoms MNCs such as Motorola and Ericsson—who undertake the development of embedded software and software applications for ICT hardware devices (e.g. mobile phones) in Ireland. Recent announcements in the industry seem to suggest that software development activities are becoming more prevalent among the Irish arms of many foreign subsidiaries, including several outside the software industry.[10]

2.2.2 Evolution of the Indigenous Sector. As the overseas software sector emerged and evolved in Ireland from the mid-1980s, it was accompanied by a parallel process which saw increasing numbers of indigenous firms entering the market. Although MNCs were critical to changing Ireland's economic and industrial landscape, they had a limited effect in terms of stimulating the development of a national system of innovation and directly spawning the growth of Irish-owned software companies. A number of factors prompted the emergence of the indigenous Irish software industry, among them the rapid growth in international demand for information technology, the low barriers to entry associated with software, the specialized pool of labor and skills accumulated in the domestic economy, and the return migration of people who had worked abroad or who had gained valuable experience working for MNCs in Ireland. However, by the end of the 1980s, the domestic software industry was still dominated by very small firms providing services and consultancy to businesses which were beginning to adopt IT systems [7,10].

Over time Ireland, unlike India, did not follow the trajectory of providing international software services, but rather developed a range of firms which sell software products in international niche markets in systems software and enterprise applications. The products provided by the indigenous industry tend to be quite technical and virtually all the companies have avoided direct competition with dominant US firms in consumer packaged software markets [7]. The routes by which Irish software companies began to emerge in the late 1980s and early 1990s, can be summarized as [7,8]:

Services to Products. Several Irish software companies started out by providing 'bespoke' or custom services to businesses, expanding this into consultancy kits and then products, which many then succeeded in exporting. O'Riain [7] notes that several of these firms relied significantly on IT development projects from MNCs located in Ireland and questions whether there would have otherwise been sufficient domestic demand for such companies in the absence of foreign-owned MNCs.

Many firms which began by developing software applications for particular clients in niche markets managed to expand internationally, but more often than not, remained in the same vertical sector. A prominent example of such are companies in the banking and finance industries including notable successes such as Kindle Banking and Fineos. Kindle Banking was formed in 1978 having received an important contract from the Ansbacher Bank in Dublin to develop a software product for the ICL platform (ICL was a leading British computer company now part of Fujitsu), which they leveraged to land a series of such contracts, eventually converting its products to other platforms as well. The Kindle story highlights the importance of multinational corporations and their associated technologies (in this case access to the ICL platform) in the early history of the industry in providing an initial source of demand and facilitating access to international markets [5].

Government Contracts and MNC Spin-offs. Other Irish software companies came into existence either as a result of government initiatives or contracts (including spin-offs from state-owned entities) or when firms in other industries, such as telecommunications or computer hardware, spun off their software divisions. One such example is Datalex, founded in 1985 when the software development team in Aer Lingus' (the state-owned national airline) IT department spun off and began developing business application software and services for the global travel industry. Another example is Amdex Systems, established in 1989 when the founder was working on a contract for a state company, which he then leveraged to secure a number of projects in the travel industry, eventually developing a generic reservation system suitable for all travel and tourism businesses.

The overhaul of the telecommunications system by the Irish government in the 1980s also opened up further opportunities for aspiring software companies. One of the industry's former leaders, Baltimore Technologies (e-security solutions) was founded in 1982 by a university lecturer and, in 1984, hired Dr. Jim Mountjoy as its managing director, who had previously worked for the Department of Posts and Telegraphs and for the National Board of Science and Technology. Mountjoy then went on to found Euristix, a specialized telecommunications software company in 1990 following a dispute within Baltimore [4, p. 155]. Aldiscon (since acquired by Logica, UK), another well-known indigenous company, which creates software applications for telecommunications, was founded in 1988 by the owner of the company which had the main contract for laying telephone cables for the new telecommunications system in the 1980s.

Although some began by undertaking specialized contract work for a MNC or government customers in Ireland, others came about as a direct result of spin outs from MNCs including Airtel ATN (from Vertel, a US telecommunications company), and Allfinanz (from Siemens). Irish companies also benefited from the presence of MNCs who served as former employers or first customers.

One such example is Transware PLC, formerly DLG Software Services, which is a specialist e-learning localization company. Formed in 1996 by David Ayres (who previously worked as a Project Manager at Lotus Development from 1990 to 1994), the accessibility and opportunity brought about by the presence of MNCs in Ireland along with the personal contacts proved critical. Ayres himself considers Transware's 'sophisticated MNCs or large Irish MNCs customers (such as Baltimore, Symantec, Corel, Lotus, Oracle) to have been a very important source of local competitive advantage'.[11]

Another legacy of the MNC sector in Ireland arose, ironically, from one of its most significant disasters. Digital Equipment Corporation established its manufacturing operation in 1971 and employed 1,800 persons in the 1980s. When Digital closed its Irish operations in 1993 the laid-off employees launched several new entrepreneurial ventures including companies such as Parthus-Ceva and Sybernet.

Parthus-Ceva (formerly SSL and then Parthus) was established in 1993 by a core team from Digital Equipment Corporation in Galway on the west coast of Ireland. Prior to the DEC closure, the team had been engaged in developing IP solutions for the semi-conductor industry. Although it focused initially on hardware, the company expanded to become one of the leading indigenous companies in the Irish software/hardware sector and currently employs over 250 people in eleven locations throughout the world. Following its merger with an Israeli company, Parthus-Ceva is now headquartered in San Jose, CA.

Other companies sprung from government-led initiatives in education and training, which has subsequently spawned the emergence of an indigenous subsector specializing in computer-based training and e-learning. Initial entrants into this niche included companies such as CBT (now Smartforce/Skillsoft) and Courseware Interactive in the 1980s. The most successful of these companies, Smartforce (now Skillsoft), was established in 1986 by Pat McDonagh backed by an initiative by the Irish Government to develop and encourage computer-based training. The company has now gone on to provide enterprise e-learning solutions to over 2,500 major corporate customers. Riverdeep, another of Ireland's most successful companies, is a Smartforce spin-out and was also founded by McDonagh, in 1996. Riverdeep designs interactive, multimedia software, mostly in the area of mathematics and science for secondary school pupils serving primarily the US market.

Academic Spin-outs. Several of Ireland's most successful indigenous companies have their origins in the university environment. University spin-offs are among the most technically oriented and rapidly growing firms, operating in areas such as development tools, system software, computer-based training tools, and telecommunications. This is undoubtedly a legacy of Ireland's significant and ongoing investment in higher education and the accumulation of national expertise in the area of computer science and software engineering.[12]

Ireland's most successful indigenous software company, IONA Technologies can trace its roots to the EU Esprit grants for distributed computing research in the Computer Science Department of Trinity College, Dublin. Founded in 1991, by the head of the distributed systems group, Dr. Chris Horn, IONA provides customers with standards-based enterprise middleware solutions, making diverse software components work together in a reliable manner. IONA was originally incorporated as a Trinity College campus company in 1991 but owing to a lack of capital the company survived on domestic consulting, services, and training contracts for the first two years to bootstrap its investment while it developed its first software product. IONA attributes its success to two main things; first, its leading edge innovative technology, and second to its decision to focus on exporting to the US market as soon as it had a developed product.

Trinity College has spun out a number of other successful companies as well. Trintech (financial software company, specializing in card payment and electronic commerce solutions) was founded in 1986 on the basis of a student project in the Engineering Department and Havok (which uses real time physics software for digital entertainment and web-based applications), spun out of the Physics Department in 1999. Other Trinity College spin-offs include EUnet (founded in 1991 as Ireland's first provider of Internet solutions to the corporate market, later acquired by ESAT Telecom Group) Wilde Technologies and Aurium. Other campuses have had their fair share of success with companies such as Piercom (business critical software systems) emerging from the University of Limerick in 1994, Scientific Systems from Dublin City University in 1998, and WBT Systems in 1995 from University College, Dublin. Another highly successful university spin-out is ChangingWorlds, winner of the technical innovation award at the Irish Software Association's annual awards ceremony in 2000. ChangingWorlds develops advanced personalization technologies and is one of a growing number of successful Irish companies focusing on the digital mobile/wireless markets. The company was founded in 1999 by Barry Smyth and Paul Cotter to commercialize technology developed as part of a research program at the Smart Media Institute at University College, Dublin.

Entrepreneurial Start-ups and Spin-outs from Latter Stage Indigenous Companies.
The mid-1990s saw an upsurge in entrepreneurial start-ups many of whom are product oriented from the outset, focused on international markets, have obtained VC funding, and have the fortune to avail the managerial expertise of seasoned software industry veterans. A significant proportion of these later entrants are formed by individuals or groups with previous experience and technical expertise acquired from working for established indigenous firms. Our survey found that 40 percent of new firms were founded by people who previously worked together, in many instances for indigenous companies (see Table 3.5). As the industry evolved successful firms such as Baltimore Technologies, Smartforce (Skillsoft), and IONA acted as 'role models' in the industry creating a 'follow-the-leader effect'. Unsurprisingly, IONA has become the single most significant parent of new indigenous companies, with almost twenty spin-outs to its credit. Although many of these (e.g. Prediction, Rococo, and Cape Clear) entered the software market, there are

a number of them that diversified into unrelated areas such as sales, services, and even recycling.

When one examines the sources of competitive advantage among newer companies, it is found to be somewhat correlated to three factors:

(1) spinning out from, or being founded by people who previously worked for a leading indigenous Irish software company;
(2) spinning out from academia;
(3) entering areas which are internationally recognized as specializations within the Irish software industry.

One only has to look at companies such as Macalla software and Netrisk which were established by people who previously worked for Quay Financial Software (before it was acquired by CSK Software). Cape Clear was founded by three former IONA employees including senior executive David Clark in 1999 and were later joined by IONA cofounders Colin Newman and Anrai O'Toole. Rococo Software was founded by Sean O'Sullivan, who ran the global professional services arm of IONA, whereas the four founders of the Wolfe Group (the first IONA spin-off in 1998) all worked internally on IONA's own IT system and spotted a niche for other companies to outsource this function. Another successful Irish company, Prediction Dynamics, hired a former 'IONAian', Paul Donnelly as its CEO in 2000. Other recent successes such as WBT Systems and ChangingWorlds have continued to spin out of Irish academic institutions.

When one examines the new companies which have been successful in securing one or more rounds of venture capital backing, one immediately sees the companies from academia (such as ChangingWorlds) or those with links (either via founders or board members) to recognized industry leaders such as Openet Telecom (founded by Barry Murphy, former head of the National Software Directorate), Sepro (Jim Mountjoy and Chris Horn serve as non-executive directors), Prediction Dynamics (ex-Iona employee as CEO), or Headway Software, Duolog and Corvil Networks, which also have Jim Mountjoy (former MD of Baltimore and founder of Euristix) as a board member. Finally, other successes are entering well-recognized areas of technical and market competency including CR2, Eontec, CardBASE, Orbiscom, and Phoenix in the financial/e-payment sector and Network365, NewSymphony Technologies, Itsmobile, and OpenMind Networks in the mobile/mobile payment/wireless sector.

2.3 Characteristics of the Indigenous Irish Software Industry

The indigenous Irish software industry obviously differs greatly from the MNC sector. Until 1990, indigenous firms were largely reliant on the provision of software services (mainly bespoke software development), but the mid-1990s, saw a major switch taking place from services to products, and from servicing the local market to exporting. Details on the leading indigenous software companies are given in Table 3.3.

TABLE 3.3. Leading (Top Thirty) Indigenous Irish Software Companies

	Company name	Year founded	Specialization	Employment (2002)	Exports as a % of revenues (2002)
1	Conduit Software (Ireland)	1996	Call center service and solutions provider	592	41
2	Smartforce (Skillsoft)	1983	Enterprise e-learning solutions	375	97
3	FINEOS Corporation	1993	Banking and insurance software	203	91
4	Iona Technologies Ltd	1991	Middleware e-business infrastructure and enterprise portals	183	3
5	Proscon Solutions	1978	TurnKey integrated solutions for the process industry	156	19
6	Eontec Ltd	1994	Component-based solutions for banks and financial services organizations	154	81
7	Trintech Manufacturing Ltd	1987	Transaction management and payment infrastructure solutions for finance industry	149	
8	Esat Business (now owned by BT plc)		Telecom services provider	120	
9	VISION Consulting	1984	IT consultancy company	108	
10	Baltimore Technologies	1976	e-security products, application, and cryptographic devices	92	
11	Connect Business Solutions Ltd	1998	Globalization and software testing solutions, tailored to meet the requirements of corporations involved in global commerce	88	42
12	SDL Technology	1992	Translation services and technology solutions	84	72

TABLE 3.3. (*Continued*)

	Company name	Year founded	Specialization	Employment (2002)	Exports as a % of revenues (2002)
13	VistaTEC Ltd		Software localization services	82	
14	Accuris Ltd	1997	Software solutions to the global telecommunications market	81	97
15	Datalex Communications Ltd	1985	Technology solutions for global airline and travel industry	78	
16	Interactive Services Ltd	1993	Custom learning solutions and training	75	
17	AMT-Sybex (Software) Ltd	1990	Consultancy and systems integrator entirely focused on the utility, transport, and energy retail industries	74	77
18	Precision Software Ltd	1984	Specialized export and import solutions (shipping, logistics, freight, transport etc.) for a range of industries	73	91
19	CR2	1997	Channel banking and card payment solutions	71	98
20	ESBI Computing Ltd	1989	IT Solutions	65	19
21	Network365 (now Valista)	1999	Electronic and mobile payments software	63	97
22	QUMAS Limited	1994	Enterprise compliance management solutions to Pharm, lifescience, and healthcare corporations	63	92
23	Cape Clear Software Limited	1999	Web services software products to enable easy creation and integration of software applications	60	

TABLE 3.3. (*Continued*)

Company name	Year founded	Specialization	Employment (2002)	Exports as a % of revenues (2002)
24 PMI Software Ltd	1986	Package and custom software	60	19
25 Systems Solutions Ltd	1987	Solutions for the pharmacy sector	60	25
26 I.T. Alliance Ltd	1997	Outsourcing, software testing, and project management services	59	
27 Softco Ltd		Document and process management solutions	58	
28 CardBASE Technologies	1993	Smart card solutions for secure e-commerce	56	100
29 Am-Beo	2000	Rating and revenue settlement solutions to the communications industry	52	100
30 Orbiscom Ireland Ltd	1998	Online payment technology	47	100

Note: Employment figures should only be considered as estimates, as figures may have changed since data was submitted and in some cases figures pertain to total company employment in Ireland and in others to total global employment.

Source: Crone [8] and data given to author by NSD in 2003.

Indigenous software companies are generally small. In 1992, 65 percent of Irish firms employed fewer than ten people and only 5 percent had more than fifty employees. By 2002, 45 percent of companies employed less than ten people, 71 percent employed less than twenty-five, and 13 percent employed fifty or more.[13] These figures indicate that the indigenous sector remains highly fragmented with a significant bias towards small firms. Both the NSD data and our survey of fifty-five companies found average employment in indigenous companies to be twenty-eight, but median employment to be only thirteen. A dichotomy also exists in terms of the distribution of indigenous employment, revenues, and exports (Table 3.4). In 1998, the 316 small companies (<10), constituted 50 percent of all indigenous companies, yet accounted for only 15 percent of employment, 11 percent of revenues, and 6 percent of indigenous exports. On the opposite side of the scale, the thirty-four big companies (>50), which accounted for only 1.6 percent of all indigenous companies, were responsible for 43 percent of indigenous employment, 56 percent of revenues and 68 percent

TABLE 3.4. Size Analysis of Indigenous Software Companies (1998)

Company size (by employment)	No. of firms	% of firms	% of total indigenous employment (9,255)	% of total indigenous revenues ($1.1B)	% of total indigenous exports ($685M)	Exports as % of revenues	Revenue per employee ($)
0–10	316	50	16	11	6	36	187,324
11–24	112	18	19	14	9	40	121,339
25–40	58	9	22	19	17	55	102,959
50–100	24	4	20	20	20	63	86,055
100+	10	2	23	36	48	81	81,445
Unknown	110	17					
Total	630	100	100	100	100		

Source: Given to author by NSD in 2002 [10].

of indigenous exports. Our survey also found most companies to be young, 53 percent of which were less than five years old, and 75 percent of them had reached profitability, taking an average of just over two years to do so.

The most notable distinction to be made within the indigenous sector is between firms involved primarily in the production of products as opposed to the provision of services. Arora et al. [5, see table 7], suggest that from their analysis of 500 companies in the NSD database, 44 percent of indigenous firms are involved in the development of software products or 'service intensive products' that require a variety of related services (such as installation, training, systems integration, and support). In his 1997 survey of firms, O'Riain [4] found that firms are split relatively evenly between a focus on product development (41 percent obtaining over 50 percent of their revenues from products) and providing services (37 percent of firms obtaining over 50 percent of their revenues from services). Over time, the share of indigenous firms earning larger proportions of their revenues from products rather than services has grown. Our results found that in 2000–01, 11 percent of companies earned 100 percent of their revenues from products, with 31 percent earning over 80 percent and 64 percent earning over 50 percent of their total revenues from products. This compares to 14 percent who earn 100 percent of their revenues from services and 34 percent who earn 50 percent or more of their revenues from services.[14]

As indigenous companies increasingly move toward product provision, they do so in niche (or vertical) markets. O'Malley and O'Gorman [6, p. 29] state that 'indigenous producers of software products and services to a lesser extent, usually follow a strategy of specialization in market niches'. The reasons for this are twofold. First, this specialization implies firms can succeed without having to be very large, an important consideration given the limited size of the domestic market. Second, there can be relatively lower barriers associated with entering vertical markets, which often sees firms starting out by providing a custom-based product for a single customer and using this success to secure other customers in the same niche (often in Ireland or the United Kingdom), while at the same time developing their application into a generic product suitable for export.

To date, many Irish companies have successfully pursued this strategy with more than ten floating on public stock markets: Smartforce (now Skillsoft), IONA Technologies, Baltimore Technologies, Trintech, Riverdeep, Pathus, Datalex, Horizon Technology Group, Conduit, and Alphyra (formerly ITG Group). Led by these early successes, Irish companies have gone on to develop notable technical specializations concentrating on enterprise application integration (including middleware) and wireless technologies (both applications and infrastructure) while developing strong niches in areas such as CRM and e-learning, focusing on key industries such as banking/finance and telecommunications.

A number of firms are now providing solutions targeting the financial sector, in both front and back-office administration systems, having built up specified capabilities in customer relationship management (CRM), workflow management, electronic payments, mobile telephony, security, and document processing. These firms serve a variety of customers in the retail, corporate or Internet banking sectors, card processing companies, insurance, and stock broking houses. As well as vendors of specialist financial solutions, builders of 'infrastructural' software (e.g. IONA) have found a ready market for their products. In recent years, a growing number of companies have started to focus on the telecommunications, primarily the mobile/wireless applications market including newcomers such as ChangingWorlds, Cyantel, OpenMind Networks, and Itsmobile. Niche specializations that have emerged in the indigenous sector are [8]:

- Financial services applications/solutions (Fineos, Eontec, CR2, Norkom)
- E-security/secure payment solutions (Baltimore, Eurologic, Trintech, cardBASE, Orbiscom)
- E-learning/computer-based training (Skillsoft, Riverdeep, WBT Systems)
- Open systems-based middleware (IONA technologies, Cape Clear, Macalla)
- Telecommunications (mobile) software developers (Euristix (now Marconi), Network365, Xiam, Amphion, MobileAware, Propylon, WEST Global)
- Hardware/Software designers (Parthus-Ceva, Massana)

As noted, Irish firms are increasingly export oriented. In 1991, an estimated 63 percent of all indigenous firms were engaged in some form of export activity, a number which had grown to over 80 percent by 1997, with approximately 44 percent of these earning at least half their revenues from exports [8, p. 61]. Not surprisingly indigenous exports are dominated by the larger firms and export activity is more prevalent among product-oriented companies. O'Riain [4] found that 45 percent of all exporting Irish firms earned over half their revenues from product sales and 25 percent earned over 80 percent from products. He also found that the mean percentage of revenues from product sales was 46 percent among exporting firms and only 30 percent among non-exporting firms. The vast majority of indigenous companies (some 70 percent) now have offices overseas.

Despite their export orientation, domestic demand continues to play a catalytic role. Our survey (of mostly small Irish software firms) found that for 80 percent of the companies, their customers in the first year of operation were in Ireland. Of these, 47 percent were MNCs (about 60 percent of which were foreign), 29 percent were indigenous Irish companies (not software), 13 percent were Government agencies and 11 percent were other indigenous software companies. The dependence on customers at home does decrease with time with the proportion of Irish customers falling to approximately 63 percent within 3–5 years of formation.

Indigenous firms have also had to contend with their fair share of challenges. In our case studies, entrepreneurs continually cited lack of capital as the singularly most significant challenge they faced in starting up. During the industry's early years, VC funding was not available, and it was only following the establishment of a government VC fund in 1996 that private investors started to appear. Our survey found that 94 percent of companies were self-financed either in whole or in part and over a third (34 percent) of them were 100 percent self-financed. This had significant ramifications for the industry as companies were forced to undertake consulting and service contracts to bootstrap their growth. As one entrepreneur put it 'the biggest challenge we faced was capital. We are 100 percent self-financed and got no loans, grants or investments from anyone, so over the first few years things were a bit lean at times.' As a result, many Irish firms had limited growth profiles and the majority grew organically. This has changed in latter years once VC became available. Younger companies, many of whom have successfully secured venture financing, tend to have a more dynamic profile, focusing on product development from the outset and aggressively targeting export markets.[15] The indigenous industry has also matured to the point where successful serial entrepreneurs can be identified.[16] Another factor now influencing the decision of potential investors is the expertise and track record of the people behind these new start-ups, many of whom benefit from the expertise of industry veterans.[17]

3   Why Ireland? Why Software?

Identifying and analyzing the factors behind Ireland's success, not just in software, but in terms of general economic development leads one to the conclusion that it was a case of 'fortune favoring the well prepared'. Although Ireland did not initially set out to directly develop an indigenous software industry, it did design and implement a national strategy to promote industrial development in high-tech industries, albeit initially focused on the attraction and development of foreign-owned industry. As O'Riain correctly states, 'the indigenous software industry has its roots in the unintended consequences of state policy aimed at attracting foreign investment' [4, p. 188]. The factors driving this success can be categorized into two main areas—domestic input factors, which include a good public policy and investments in education; and external factors including an increase in international demand, the role of multinational corporations, returning diaspora, and the acceleration of globalization and European integration.

3.1   Domestic Input Factors

3.1.1   National Vision, Public Policy, and Creating a Pro-Business Environment. Beginning in the 1950s, Ireland adopted a relatively standardized foreign direct investment, export-led growth model, the success of which is inarguable.[18] National policies designed to encourage overseas investment also created an environment conducive to the growth of indigenous firms. This is especially true of the investments in human and physical infrastructure including the overhaul of the Irish telecommunications system undertaken by the Irish government in the 1980s. In the year 1980, Ireland's telecommunications system was among the worst in western Europe. The IDA became an important lobbying force, making clear to government the linkages between creating new jobs and upgrading a primitive telecommunications system. Because of this the government committed to investing £1,000 million to transform the semi-state body Telecom Eireann. By 1987, digital switching was available throughout the country and Ireland had established itself as a recognized leader among European telecommunications entities offering favorable international business rates as opposed to domestic/residential rates [1, p. 544; 4, p. 108].

The jewel in the crown of Ireland's pro-business initiatives was naturally the introduction, in 1981, of the 10 percent and then 12.5 percent corporate tax rate, which when compared with corporate tax rates of 39.5 percent in the United States, 40 percent in Germany, 30 percent in the United Kingdom, approximately 34 percent in Belgium, France, and the Netherlands explains why Ireland had little difficulty in competing for international investment.[19]

3.1.2   Investing in Education and Human Capital.   The restructuring of Ireland's educational policy formed the cornerstone of the country's success resulting in an education system that was specifically designed to meet the needs of industry, providing an ample supply of highly skilled graduates from educational institutions that demonstrated a flexibility rivaled by few. The accumulation and building up of the national stock of human capital in Ireland began well before the international skill shortage became a serious bottleneck and was undoubtedly assisted by a skewed demographic profile. In 1999, 47 percent of Ireland's population was aged twenty-nine and under, ten percentage points more than the EU 15 giving the Irish government an abundant supply of 'raw material' with which to work.[20]

Ireland's first priority in addressing its educational requirements was to significantly increase funding for all levels of education, particularly at the tertiary level. The share of public expenditure on education in GNP doubled in the 1960s, from 3 percent in 1960/61 to 6.3 percent in 1973/74 [5, p. 15] and in 1997, expenditure on all levels of education as a percentage of GDP (5.5 percent) was comparable to the European average.[21]

Of particular significance was the decision to spend a larger proportion of structural funds received from the EU on human capital as opposed to physical infrastructure. Ireland as a designated Objective 1 region (meaning that it was relatively economically deprived and eligible for considerable assistance) received ECU 4.5 billion from European Structural Funds between 1989 and 1993 and a further ECU 5.6 billion for 1994–98 [2, p. 41]. The National Development Plan covering the first period of Structural Funds (1989–93) prioritized human resource development which with funding of over $3 billion comprised the largest single category of expenditure. During the second funding period (1994–99), Ireland allocated 44 percent of its structural funds to human resources and 20 percent to physical infrastructure. This differs greatly from other Objective 1 regions such as Greece which distributed 25 percent of its funds to human capital and 46 percent to infrastructure, or Spain, which allocated 28 percent to human capital and 40 percent to infrastructure [2, p. 31]. The priority given to training and human capital development sets Ireland aside in this regard and undoubtedly contributed to its subsequent success.

3.1.3   Restructuring the Education System to Meet the Needs of the Industry. Alongside the large investments in higher education, Ireland also significantly restructured the system of higher educational institutions in the 1970s in anticipation of the labor demands of new international investment. In doing so, the government created more institutional diversity by establishing three new kinds of institutions in addition to the traditional universities. Vocational Education Committees (VECs) were established to run vocational secondary schools oriented towards technical and apprenticeship education for teenagers destined to directly enter the labor market. At the tertiary level, a network of thirteen Regional Technical Colleges and two National Institutes of Higher Education (NIHEs) were instituted, both explicitly designed to 'refocus the educational system towards the labor market needs of the economy' [4, p. 110]. Over time the Dublin colleges in this network were integrated to form the Dublin Institute of Technology and the RTCs were recently re-designated as Institutes of Technology (IoTs). The two National Institutes of Higher Education (which had been built on the Boston MIT model) have since gained full university charters becoming the University of Limerick and Dublin City University.

More importantly, however, these three institutions—VECs, RTCs, NIHEs— were much more directly controlled by the state than the existing schools and universities, which had traditionally been buffered from state intervention by the religious orders and others. In creating these new institutions therefore, the state simultaneously increased its ability to influence the education system and its outputs, particularly the supply of technical labor. The state was more than willing to leverage its new found capacity to influence the labor supply and did so with remarkable effectiveness. As O'Riain puts it, 'the state effectively pushed the population away from the historically popular professions, using its unusual capacity to shape labor supply to disproportionately expand the number of vacancies in engineering, computer science and other technical fields throughout the 1980s and 1990s' [4, p. 206]. For example, the expansion of engineering and computer science education undertaken in the late 1970s was accomplished through increased state funding earmarked specifically for those disciplines—including £1.725 million extra in funding put aside in 1979 [4, p. 111]. Currently, there are over twenty-five degree programs in Irish third-level educational institutions in computer science/software engineering. There are also eleven additional courses (e.g. computation linguistics) where computing or software engineering is the major subject and a further ten that have up to 50 percent computing content.

Enrolments in higher education have increased significantly in the past four decades undoubtedly assisted by the government's decision to abolish university fees in the 1990s. The total number of full-time students (all years) in higher education (universities, institutes of technology, colleges of education, and others) increased from 21,143 to 116,548, an increase of 404 percent between the years 1968 and 1998 [12, table 2, p. 20]. The growth was much greater in enrolments in the Institutes of Technology reflecting the success of introducing institutional diversity.[22] The emphasis placed on software-related disciplines also bore fruit. From 1980 to 1998, enrolments in technology disciplines consistently accounted for about 25 percent of total new entrants into the higher education sector.[23]

This outcome of increased enrolments is obviously increased graduation rates. Here, Ireland's success is worthy of considerable note. Latest figures from the OECD now show that Ireland ranks third highest among OECD countries in the share of its population aged 25–64 with tertiary level education. In 2001, 35.6 percent of the Irish-working population had a tertiary education, a figure surpassed only by the United States (41.6 percent) and Canada (37.3 percent) and well above the OECD average of 26.4 percent and the EU average of 22.2 percent. Again, what sets Ireland aside, however, is the disproportionate representation of graduates in technology related disciplines. OECD figures also show that in the year 2000, 30 percent of all new degrees awarded were in science and engineering, compared to an OECD average of only 21 percent. European figures which track the number of tertiary graduates in science and technology per 1,000 of the population aged 20–29 show that in the ten years from 1993 to 2002, Ireland has consistently ranked number 1, with the proportion of S&T graduates being double that of the EU average.[24]

Ireland's educational investments paid dividends in the 1990s with many software MNCs citing the availability of a highly educated, technical workforce as a primary driver behind their location decision [5, table 12]. The indigenous sector has also been a huge beneficiary of the education system both in terms of the entrepreneurs themselves and the broader make up of the indigenous software workforce. Our survey of fifty-eight Irish software entrepreneurs found them to be highly educated with 90 percent having at least a Bachelor's degree and 46 percent with at least a Master's level qualification. Generally, these were in technical areas. Of the thirty-nine founders with Bachelor's degrees 38 percent of them were in computer science or software engineering, 27 percent in other forms of engineering, and a further 24 percent in mathematics or science.[25] Of the founders with certificate/diploma qualifications 22 percent were in management/business studies and not surprisingly 72 percent were in technical fields such as computer science, computer applications, engineering etc. indicating the success of the RTCs and IoTs in generating people with the right skills for the high-tech industry.[26]

3.2 External Factors

In addition to domestic inputs on the part of the Irish government, there is little doubt that the Irish software industry emerged as the result of a large number of external factors, including the increased demand for software products and services throughout the late 1980s and the early 1990s and the increasing pace of globalization and European integration, particularly following the introduction of the single market in 1992. Ireland was fortuitous to be one of only two English-speaking members of the Union and the only one to partake in European Monetary Union. Ireland's historically close relationship with the United States, which stems largely from the continuous outward migration patterns post-famine of 1847, has had a marked impact on the propensity of US firms to look favorably to Ireland as an investment location.

3.2.1 Impact of Foreign Investment and Multinational Corporations. The efforts of the Irish state to create the right infrastructure and to provide incentives for a knowledge-based industry bore fruit, as we saw in Section 2, in the large number of MNCs which located software operations in Ireland through the 1980s and 1990s. The central tenant of industrial policy in Ireland since those times was the creation of jobs, a strategy that has undoubtedly been highly successful.[27] Although the entrance of software MNCs to Ireland did not have the desired effect of producing large numbers of direct spin-outs, they did have a number of significant indirect benefits, serving as a source of demand to several early indigenous companies but more importantly acting as a training ground for aspiring Irish entrepreneurs. Knowledge spillovers did occur between the foreign and indigenous sectors facilitated primarily by the mobility of labor. O'Malley and O'Gorman [6] found in their survey that most of the indigenous entrepreneurs they interviewed had been working in Irish indigenous firms immediately prior to starting their companies, about half of these being indigenous software firms. About one-third of the founding entrepreneurs had been working in MNCs immediately prior to start-up, and not just confined to companies in the IT sector, but more broadly in the IT activities of a range of other sectors. Whereas only a minority of the founding entrepreneurs worked in foreign MNCs immediately before starting their own firms, a majority, of about two-thirds of them, had gained experience working in a foreign-owned MNC in Ireland at some stage in their careers. About half of

TABLE 3.5. Work Experience of Irish Software Entrepreneurs

	Number of companies ($n = 38$)	Number of founders ($n = 58$)	% of companies ($n = 38$)	% of founders ($n = 58$)
MNC	25	32	66	55
Abroad	29	33	76	57
Indigenous software company	16	23	42	40
Studied abroad	8	10	21	17
Academia	2	4	5	7
Other	7	13	18	22

Source: Carnegie Mellon University Survey 2001–02.

them had also worked abroad in software or a related sector prior to starting their own company, and about half had at some time worked in a sector which now constitutes a major customer for their company.

These results are consistent with the findings from our survey conducted in 2001–02 (see Table 3.5). Our sample set which included information on fifty-eight founders from thirty-eight different companies found that 66 percent of the companies were established by founders who had worked for a MNC at one stage in their career. Our results found that 75 percent of the (thirty-eight) indigenous Irish software companies were founded by people who had previously worked abroad, a figure that translates to just over half (57 percent) of the fifty-eight founders. Not surprisingly 75 percent of those who did work abroad did so for a multinational corporation. We also found that approximately 40 percent of the companies and founders who had experience working for an indigenous Irish software company and approximately 17 percent of the founders had studied abroad. These results appear to suggest that Irish software entrepreneurs are more likely to be employed in an indigenous Irish company (probably software) rather than a MNC directly prior to start up, notwithstanding the fact that the vast majority have had MNC experience, either at home or abroad, at some point in their careers.

Overseas companies also served as an important early source of demand to indigenous companies. Among the indigenous software firms interviewed by O'Malley and O'Gorman [6, p. 25], one-third of them had half or more of their sales in Ireland going to subsidiaries of overseas MNCs in a variety of different sectors such as pharmaceuticals, telecommunications equipment, computer hardware, software, financial services, and other manufacturing sectors. At the other extreme, they found that more than one-third of the companies sell little or nothing to overseas MNCs in Ireland. Our survey, which covered mostly smaller Irish firms, found that a third of the companies had MNCs as customers in the first year of operations. According to O'Malley and O'Gorman [6, p. 25], a quarter of Irish companies explicitly stated that overseas MNCs in Ireland were important initial customers in the early years of their business.

MNCs also served a role as exemplars of international standards. It has been said that because overseas MNCs in Ireland had 'relatively sophisticated and demanding standards, their influence as purchasers of software from Irish firms would have tended to push their suppliers to achieve relatively high standards in their products and services, and hence to develop a competitive advantage' [6, p. 25]. Overall, it appears that employment in a MNC helped Irish entrepreneurs to 'understand what world class meant and what's expected at the level' and also leads us to the conclusion that this, coupled with demand from overseas MNCs as customers, had a significant influence in strengthening the capabilities of many indigenous software firms. Linkages and interactions between domestic software companies and foreign MNCs in Ireland also helped to adequately prepare them for the standards required abroad in addition to 'directly helping to provide access to export markets through referrals by overseas MNC customers in Ireland to foreign affiliate companies or others abroad' [6, p. 26].

Finally, Irish entrepreneurs we interviewed were overwhelmingly of the opinion that MNCs significantly raised Ireland's international profile and reputation. As one founder put it MNCs were 'useful in putting Ireland on the map. Before this, people would not have thought of Ireland as having a software industry. That's been a very good thing.' That said the MNCs also had some negative influences. As one interviewee put it they 'pushed up the wages we must pay and have taken the cream of the engineers from the indigenous companies, who are generally poorly funded in comparison'.[28]

3.2.2 Diaspora/International Linkages. Ireland's young population, a growing number of immigrants, and an increase in the number of women rejoining the workforce, meant that Ireland did not suffer significant skill shortages throughout the 1990s on the same scale as in other international software industries. The most interesting element of inward migration into Ireland in the course of the 1990s was the fact that it was largely accounted for by returning Irish emigrants. In 1994, 55 percent of immigrants into Ireland were returning Irish emigrants.[29] In fact, O'Riain makes the argument that 'the 1980s set in motion a new type of migration circuit between Ireland and the rest of the global economy—the substantial migration of professionals, the formation of emigrant communities, and the significant and increasing return migration among professionals' [4, p. 251].

The decision to expand technical education, while beneficial in the long run, appeared to have led to a 'brain drain' of dramatic proportions in the 1980s. In 1988, 20 percent of all graduates had gained employment overseas within a year of graduating, a figure that had fallen to 5.6 percent by 2002.[30] Emigration was even more prolific among science and engineering graduates. According to O'Riain, in the mid-1980s, almost half the graduates in electronic engineering and over a quarter in computer science had left Ireland within a year of graduating.[31] By the 1990s, this trend had slowed down with 55 percent of computer science graduates gaining employment at home compared with 13.5 percent overseas in 1992. By 1996, the proportion gaining employment in Ireland had grown to over 82 percent although the last few years have seen a fall in the number gaining employment at home (74.3 percent in 2000) and a slight increase in those finding work overseas (from 9.8 percent in 1996 to 11.6 percent in 2000). This persistent (albeit decreased) trend towards emigration among computing and engineering professionals is attributable in part to the over-education of these graduates, which led them to 'emigrate rather than work on relatively mundane tasks in production oriented MNC subsidiaries' [4, p. 257]. Over-education also prompted some Irish graduates to start their own enterprises. As one of our interviewees put it 'we got started in 1989 owing to dissatisfaction working for the State and/or large companies which were the primary sources of employment at the time. There was just a lack of other interesting opportunities.'

Once abroad, many of these professional emigrants formed strong networks among themselves and with their counterparts back at home, a fact that undoubtedly facilitated their return when the economy picked up in the 1990s. Even since the 1980s, the rate of return migration has been increasing rapidly, taking off in the mid-1990s, when the benefits of the growth became clear and employment opportunities became available at home. The 1996 census found that 10.8 percent of the Irish population in residence at that time had lived outside Ireland for at least a year. The 2002 census, however, found this figure to have risen to 16.5 percent, with 42 percent of these people returning between 1996 and 2002, indicating a significant increase in recent return migration (Chapter 9). Between 1981 and 1990, an average of 10,300 people returned to Ireland per annum. From 1991 to 1996, this had more than doubled to 26,800 per annum and in the year from 1995 to 1996, it had doubled again to 40,500 [4, p. 264]. Net migration also increased significantly in the decade between 1989 and 1999. In 1989, 70,600 emigrated, 26,700 immigrated, resulting in net outward migration of $-43,900$. By 1999, only 29,000 emigrated, 47,500 immigrated leaving Ireland with net inward migration of 18,500.[32]

Although these trends refer to the entire population, it is likely that return migrants were disproportionately professionals.[33] As Kapur and McHale (Chapter 9) point out in their chapter, although the 1980s saw significant levels of emigration among Irish graduates, most immigrants into Ireland in the 1990s were returning Irish emigrants and moreover, most had university degrees. Of the 47,500 people who immigrated to Ireland in 1999, 26,000 were returning Irish nationals and 21,500 were non-Irish nationals. Labor force survey data from the mid-1990s confirm that the returning Irish were relatively highly educated with 58 percent of returning Irish emigrants—that is, those born in Ireland but not resident in Ireland twelve months previously—having a third-level degree (see Chapter 9). They also point out that a wage premium existed for these returnees and was highest for those in the computer sector. The return of Ireland's computer science and technical graduates, many of whom went on to found software companies upon return, undoubtedly enhanced the competitive advantage of these companies as the entrepreneurs brought with them valuable international experience and extensive connections to overseas markets.

4   Conclusion

As discussed, the Irish software industry is a tale of two industries each with its own background and profile. The development of the multinational sector—the outcome of a successful FDI policy by the Irish government—had a catalytic effect on the Irish economy and contributed, indirectly, to the emergence of the indigenous sector. Although Irish companies are generally small and until recently relatively poorly funded, their increasing orientation toward products as opposed to services, and their focus on niche markets, particularly buoyant sectors such as financial services and telecommunications has been a source of success although many of them remain highly vulnerable to downturns in the market.

The Irish government did not set out with the express intention of developing an indigenous software industry, but they were highly successful in luring software MNCs and in generating the right input factors, notably overhauling the telecommunications system, creating a favorable business (tax) environment, and investing heavily in the national stock of human capital, particularly in science and technology disciplines. Ireland's membership of the EU and strong historical connections to the United States, facilitated by significant patterns of international migration (including a returning Irish diaspora in recent years), also contributed to its software success.

Looking ahead, for Ireland to retain its competitive advantage, not just in software, it must reduce its over reliance on MNCs and focus on moving up the value added chain. This need is reflected in recent government initiatives such as the €600 million investment in Science Foundation Ireland, which is designed to increase the national R&D capacity, along with efforts by state agencies to embed overseas companies in Ireland in the face of growing competition, particularly from eastern Europe. The focus will now be on the indigenous sector, the success of which depends not necessarily on generating new start-ups, but rather on encouraging growth among established firms, something which remains inextricably linked to the availability of financing and the ability to successfully compete in export markets. Speaking at the launch of another major review of industrial policy in July 2004, Ireland's Minister for Enterprise, Trade and Employment said that 'in the future we will have to put a greater emphasis on creating our own Michael Dell or Bill Gates rather than importing them'. Should Ireland succeed in doing so, it shall have little difficulty in retaining its reputation as Europe's 'Silicon Isle'.

Appendix: Research Methodology

Original data reported in this chapter results from a survey of indigenous Irish software companies conducted by the author in 2001–02. Using a database listing of over 500 Irish software companies, from the National Software Directorate in 1999, and having conducted a pilot survey among five firms, we solicited fifty-five responses, constituting a response rate of approximately 10 percent. There was a significant bias towards small firms among respondents (75 percent of which employed fewer than twenty-five people at the time of the survey in 2002).

In the survey, firms were asked to provide information on company formation and activities, revenues, customer base, educational and professional background of the founder(s), and profile of the company workforce. A copy of the survey instrument and other details about the respondents are available from the author upon request. We also conducted twenty-five case study interviews, fifteen of which were with company founders and the other ten with representatives from Enterprise Ireland (National Software Directorate), IDA Ireland, Irish Software Association, County Enterprise Boards, Department of Trade, Enterprise and Employment, Venture Capital firms, and several of the Institutes of Technology.

Notes

1. Statistics taken from National Software Directorate (www.nsd.ie/htm/ssii/ stat.htm) in June 2004 and converted from Euros to US$ at rate of €1.00 = $1.21.
2. The downturn in the global ICT industry in recent years has taken its toll on the Irish software industry, which having grown at an annual rate of up to 20% throughout most of the 1990s, has contracted for the second year in a row, with employment falling by 11% in 2002 (to 27,900) and by a further 14% in 2003 (to 23,930), down from a peak employment of 31,500 in 2001.
3. Irish labor force estimated at 1.88 million in 2002. Software Revenues (2002) €113,869 million/GNP (2002) €103,429 million = 13.4%. Software Exports (2002) $12,997/Total Exports €93,626 = 13.8%. Source National Software Directorate (www.nsd.ie) and Central Statistics Office (www.cso.ie).
4. Real GDP Growth Rate (1994–2000) averaged at 9.4% in Ireland compared with 2.6% for the EU (fifteen countries).
5. Statistics from Irish Department of Finance (June 2004) www.budget.gov.ie/2003/table9.asp.
6. Household names such as IBM (1983), Microsoft (1985), Lotus (1985), Oracle (1987), Claris (1988), Symantec (1991), Corel (1993), in software were joined by other providers such as Ericsson (1979), Motorola (1981), Siemens (1983), and EDS (1989).
7. Employment in software was approximately 19,000 in 1997, compared to leading manufacturing sectors such as Metals and Engineering (93,000), Food (40,300), and Chemicals and Pharmaceuticals (20,100) which experienced growth rates 1993–97 of 35%, 15%, and 30%, respectively relative to 125% in Software [4, table 2.10, p. 79].
8. The Appendix provides more details on the Carnegie Mellon survey and case studies.
9. Coe [9] described the typical workforce profile of one such operation in Ireland suggesting that approximately 40% of staff are employed in manufacturing and distribution jobs, 30% in localization, and 30% in other support tasks (accounts, administration, customer services, marketing, purchasing, software support).
10. In June 2004, Intel Ireland announced that they were to add a software R&D facility—'IT Innovation Centre'—to their current €4.5 billion investment. Likewise IBM

Corporation announced a €22 million investment to significantly develop its Irish R&D software facility—the IBM Dublin Software Laboratory—which grew from the original Lotus Development organization.

11. Interview with David Ayres by Arora et al. [5].
12. A number of schemes were put in place to encourage academics to commercialize their research. One such initiative was the EU (ESPRIT) funded program in distributed computing which came to full fruition as emphasis on network computing and the Internet increased in the 1990s.
13. Based on analysis of data for the years 1992 and 2002 on 249 indigenous companies given to the author by the National Software Directorate.
14. In our survey, we categorized 'product' revenues as those from software development, licensing, and custom products and 'services' as being bespoke software, consultancy, and other services.
15. In the first half of 2004, almost $1 billion was invested in 27 Irish technology companies including $12 million in mobile software first Network 365 with Corvil Networks, ChangingWorlds, and Aepona also raising rounds of more than $12 million in the past two years. *Source*: Ion Equity (www.ionequity.com).
16. Serial entrepreneurs include Pat McDonagh (CBT-Smartforce-Riverdeep) and Jay Murray and Gilbert Little who provided the entrepreneurship and funding for the Aldiscon-Apiion-Aepona series of companies.
17. One such example is Dr. Jim Mountjoy, former managing director of Baltimore Technologies and founder of Euristix who serves as a non-executive director of Duolog Technologies, Corvil Networks, and Headway Software as well as chairman of Tsunami Photonics.
18. Ireland wins a disproportionate share of FDI given that it represents less than 1% of the EU population including 41% of all software projects and 12% of all FDI into the EU in ICT [11, p. 5].
19. Why Ireland? Statistics on corporate tax rates and hourly labor costs downloaded from IDA Ireland website, www.ida.ie.
20. Data from FAS: Ireland's Training and Employment Agency. *Source*: The Age Structure of Ireland's Population and Labour Force. Labour Market Update 2/00—2000 (www.fas.ie).
21. Expenditure on all levels of education as a percentage of GDP still lags countries such as Sweden (8.5%), France (6.4%), and Germany (5.9%). *Source*: OECD Education at a Glance, 2003.
22. In 1968–69, 78% of enrolments of full-time students in higher education were in the universities, compared to 6.3% at the Institutes of Technologies, and the rest being to Colleges of Education etc. By 1989–99 this distribution was 54% universities and 37.3% Institutes of Technology (IoT) representing an increase of 251% in the university sector and 2900% in the IoT sector during the period 1968–98 [12, p. 19].
23. In 1998, for example, technology had 26% of new entrants compared to 21% in commerce, 12% in science, and 5% in medical sciences [12, p. 30].
24. Data on tertiary graduates in science and technology per 1,000 of population aged 20–29 years taken from Eurostat in June 2003 (http://europa.eu.int/comm/eurostat/), Science and Technology Statistics.
25. Interestingly only 10% of company founders had studied business studies or commerce, although 35% of the Masters degrees obtained were MBAs.

26. O'Malley and O'Gorman [6, p. 19] found that in about four-fifths of the companies, 70% or more of the staff were third-level graduates, while in two-fifths of them, at least 90% of staff were graduates.
27. Employment in IDA supported (i.e. foreign) companies in Ireland grew from 73,000 in 1990 to 141,000 in 2000 (an increase of 92%) but dropped by almost 10% to 129,000, by 2003. The largest growth in new jobs between 1999 and 2003 was in the ICT sector followed closely by international and financial services sector, both of which employ over 40,000.
28. Comments made by Irish entrepreneurs in case study interviews done undertaken by the author in 2000–01, available upon request.
29. Data taken from ICMS: http://migration.ucc.ie/irishmigrationinthe1990scharts.htm, June 2004.
30. Higher Education Authority—First Destinations Surveys: www.hea.ie.
31. In 1987/1988, 25% of male computer science graduates and 45% of male electrical and electronic graduates emigrated within a year of graduation (compared to 26% of all graduates) [4, p. 256].
32. Data from the ICMS taken from http://migration.ucc.ie/irishmigrationinthe1990scharts.htm, June 2004.
33. Labor force surveys indicated that 28.4% of those who returned to Ireland between 1983 and 1988 were in the professional or technical occupations, by far the largest occupational category among return migrants [4, p. 265].

References

1. Burnham, J.B. (2003). Why Ireland boomed. *The Independent Review*, VII(4), 537–556, ISSN 1086-1653.
2. Higgins, T. (1999). *The Relationship Between Science, Technology and Broad Industrial Policy, Ireland*. Dublin: CIRCA Group.
3. Tallon, P.P. and Kraemer, K.L. (1999). *The Impact of Technology on Ireland's Economic Growth and Development: Lessons for Developing Countries*. IEEE Published in the Proceedings of the Hawaii International Conference on System Sciences, Jan 5–8, 1999, Maui, Hawaii.
4. O'Riain, S. (1999). *Remaking the Developmental State: The Irish Software Industry in the Global Economy*. Doctoral dissertation, Department of Sociology, University of California, Berkeley.
5. Arora, A., Gambardella, A., and Torrisi, S. (2001). *In the Footsteps of Silicon Valley? Indian and Irish Software in the International Division of Labour*. (SIEPR) WP No. 00-41, Stanford University, California. Published with the same title in Timothy Bresnahan and Alfonso Gambardella (eds.), *Building High-Tech Clusters*, 2003. Cambridge: CUP.
6. O'Malley, E. and O'Gorman, C. (2001). Competitive advantage in the Irish indigenous software industry and the role of inward foreign direct investment. *European Planning Studies*, 9(3), 303–321.
7. O'Riain, S. (1997). An offshore Silicon Valley? The emerging Irish software industry. *Competition and Change*, 2, 175–212.

5

The Brazilian Software Industry

ANTONIO J. JUNQUEIRA BOTELHO,
GIANCARLO STEFANUTO, AND FRANCISCO VELOSO

1 Introduction

During the 1990s, Brazil developed a large and dynamic software industry which experienced double-digit growth rates over the decade. Its share in the Brazilian IT market increased, surpassing hardware to become (together with related services) the most important segment after 2000. Between 1991 and 2001, its share of GDP more than tripled to 1.5 percent and the Brazilian software market became the world's seventh largest, valued at $7.7 billion, and comparable in size to the Indian and Chinese markets. Despite recent economic turmoil in the country, the Brazilian software industry has continued to post growth rates above both the national industry average and the average for the global software industry. A remarkable feat given that exports were a mere $100 million in 2001, 2 percent of the total market![1]

The current industrial pattern dates from developments in the early and mid-1990s. The precursor of the current industry was an amorphous proto-software sector characterized by extensive in-house software development activities in both user firms and hardware producers and sellers [1,2]. Domestic firms occupied niches and foreign firms provided mainly system products and large applications. Following the liberalization of the Brazilian economy in the early 1990s and the economic stabilization achieved by the 1994 Real Plan, domestic demand for software grew steadily, as local business users facing increased foreign competition in their sector markets refocused on core business activities and, consequently, outsourced software development instead of developing it in-house. At the same time, after two decades of protection, hardware prices declined as imports were liberalized, further expanding the demand for software [3,4].

Authors are listed alphabetically. We would like to thank Carolina Vaghetti, Bruno Gianelli, and Nelson Hochman for excellent research assistance. We would also like to thank Alice Amsden, Ashish Arora, Alfonso Gambardella, David Mowery, Marcio Spinosa, Ted Tschang, Kival Weber, and the participants in the Carnegie Mellon Software Industry Center Globalization Workshop for comments and suggestions. Financial support from the following sources is gratefully acknowledged: the Brazilian Ministry of Science and Technology, Softex, Intel Brazil, and IBM Brazil. All errors and omissions remain our own responsibility.

The industry's dynamic growth and the shaping of its unique structure have been grounded in evolutionary path-dependent domestic market expansion. Although imports have been climbing steadily, reaching $1 billion in 2001, domestic software firms have expanded their share, particularly in critical semi-customized products and in services. Therefore, the Brazilian software industry offers a sharp contrast to those of India, Ireland, and Israel, the most widely cited success stories among developing and industrializing countries, based principally on their success in software exports. Given this disparity, one may ask whether a focus on the domestic market necessarily implies an inability to develop an internationally competitive industry, or whether, on the contrary, it represents an alternative strategy for preparing and structuring the means to enter more competitive international domains [5,6].

The overarching objective of this study is to understand the attractions and the perils of adopting an inward-looking approach to drive software growth in the context of the Brazilian software industry. It explores the ways in which a strong reliance on the local market can have a stifling effect on the development of the industry and conversely examines how some Brazilian software firms have been able to leverage the domestic market and build competitive positions and a platform for international expansion. As explained in this chapter, success has been rooted in two critical aspects. The first is the presence of lead domestic client sectors for software firms with demands close to those of major international firms. These provide opportunities for learning and competence deepening similar to those found when exporting to foreign competitive firms. The second required condition is the existence of competition and selection mechanisms, that induce successful firms to structure capabilities, while winnowing out firms that fail to learn.

The chapter is organized as follows. Section 2 reviews the emerging prescription for success in the software industry based on what are regarded as the three lead success stories, India, Ireland, and Israel. Section 3 highlights the key stages and events associated with the development of the software industry in Brazil, and positions the sector in the national industrial context. Section 4 elaborates on how the domestic market can act as a curse that stifles the development of the software industry. Turning the argument of Section 4 around, Section 5 shows how the domestic sector may also be seen as a driver of success in the industry, and seeks to specify the conditions under which this may happen. Section 6 briefly analyzes the early forays of Brazilian firms into the global software market. The last section summarizes the arguments of the chapter and distills some useful lessons relating to the development of the software industry.

2   International Players and Emerging Prescriptions for the Development of a Software Industry

During the last few years, there has been an increasing interest in the growth of the software industry in developing nations [7–12]. Much of this interest has been sparked by the export-oriented software markets of Ireland, India, and Israel.

TABLE 5.1. Software Market in Selected Countries in 2001[a]

	Sales (10⁶ USD)	Sales/GDP (%)	SW Industry Dev. Index[b]	SW Industry Dom. Dev. Index[c]	Exports (10⁶ USD)	Employees (10³)
US[d]	200,000	2.0	0.5	0.5	n.a.	1,042
Japan[e]	85,000	2.0	0.8	0.8	73	534
Germany	39,844	2.2	0.9	0.9	n.a.	300
UK	15,000	1.0	0.4	0.5	n.a.	n.a.
India	8,200	1.7	**7.8**	**1.9**	6,220	350
Brazil	*7,700*	*1.5*	*2.2*	*2.2*	*100*	*158*
Korea	7,694	1.8	1.1	**1.1**	35	n.a.
Ireland[f]	7,650	7.4	**3.4**	0.5	6,500/ 3,000[g]	25
China	7,400	0.6	**1.8**	**1.7**	400	186
Spain[e]	4,330	0.7	0.4	0.4	n.a.	20
Taiwan[e]	3,801	1.2	0.7	0.6	349	n.a.
Israel[e]	3,700	3.4	**1.8**	0.5	2,600	35
Finland	1,910	1.6	0.7	0.6	185	20
Singapore	1,660	1.9	0.7	0.5	476	n.a.
Argentina[e]	1,340	0.5	0.4	0.4	35	15
Mexico	<1,000	<0.2	0.2	0.2	n.a.	n.a.

[a] It is important to note that statistics on software are illusive. Depending on the data source, they may or may not include software-related services, as well as sales of software developed by foreign enterprises in a particular region (e.g. by the Microsoft office in Ireland). Most of the sources are not very specific about what they include. Therefore, these values should be interpreted as proxies for the industry, not as definite numbers. Authors' compilation from various sources; n.a.—not available.
[b] Software Industry Development Index. Sales divided by the size of the economy, measured by GDP, and its level of development measured through GDP/Capita.
[c] Software Industry Domestic Development Index. Same as index of column 4, but only with domestic sales of software.
[d] 2002.
[e] 2000.
[f] The fact that giants like Microsoft and Oracle use Ireland as a base for their European Union sales—because of the lowest tax rate in Western Europe—significantly distorts results. For example, eliminating Microsoft exports would change the share of software sales in GDP to 4% and the industry development index to 1.9, making the overall performance of the country in the context of international software still interesting but not quite as stellar.
[g] Second number excludes Microsoft exports.

Table 5.1 presents a set of key indicators for the software industry in a range of selected countries. As one would expect, the industry in large developed nations like the United States, Germany, and Japan, home to the top twenty largest firms in the world, is of an order of magnitude greater than other nations.[2] Nevertheless, it is also readily apparent that software has become a large industry in developing nations such as India and China, whose industries are almost double the size of the industries in countries like Finland or Spain. Yet, these absolute figures for industry revenues mask the real magnitude of the domestic market. A better measure for the relative importance of the industry might be its share of GDP. These values, presented in the third column of Table 5.1, suggest that the software industry represents between 1 and 2 percent of the economy in most countries. By such a measure, industries in the United States, Germany, and Japan remain major leaders, but figures for Israel and Ireland immediately reveal the disproportionate relevance of software to their economies.

But high-tech industries such as software typically have a smaller share of GDP in poorer countries. Thus, the fourth column of Table 5.1 presents an overall Software Industry Development index that represents industry revenues divided by country GDP to control for size and then again by GDP/Capita to control for level of economic development (then multiplied by 10^6 for normalization purposes). This index attempts to measure which countries have been able to develop software industries that are larger than might be expected given the size and level of development of their economies. The results confirm the preeminence of India, Ireland, and Israel (the 3Is) and indicate that China, Brazil, and Korea have been able to develop relatively large software sectors. But of equal interest is the calculation of the same indicator restricted to sales in the domestic market, to proxy for the relative level of development of the domestic demand. Most countries converge in index values between 0.5 and 1 while China, India, and particularly Brazil appear to belong to a category by themselves, with Korea showing a degree of similarity.

Existing work on the 3Is would suggest that the path toward a successful software industry is a large export base, preferably associated with US clients or direct investment by the United States [8]. In India, the focus has been low-value-added software services geared toward the export market, primarily the United States [7,9] (see in particular Chapter 2 by Athreye). In this process, the Indian diaspora in the United States and the knowledge of English language have played a key role in facilitating contact with American companies. Ireland pursued a similar strategy—multinationals are 'lead clients' for the local industry in low-value-added activities and a strong English-speaking diaspora aids transactions—but differed by growing through foreign investment in the country [9,13] (a detailed account of Ireland is included in Chapter 3 by Sands). Multinationals are responsible for a disproportionate share of the industry: roughly 80 percent of the sales and 85 percent of the exports [13]. Israel's industry differed by focusing on high-value-added activities and developing significant capabilities in specific areas such as real time applications, avionics, and communication systems, again mostly selling in the United States [14,15] (Chapter 4 by Breznitz). Israel has also been able to create both a successful venture capital industry and to attract investment from some of the leading US software firms.

As a result, perspectives on how to successfully develop a software industry in developing nations are increasingly tied to the common characteristics of India, Ireland, and Israel: an abundance of human capital, strong links to and a diaspora in the United States, the English language skills, the presence of multinationals, and a strong entrepreneurial culture. Presumably, the strengths of these industries were matched by a strategy of choosing products and service offerings which complemented those of leading (especially American) firms, or at least avoided direct competition with them (see [16], for a summary of these issues).

However, a policy issue arises when one tries to extend this hypothesis to countries like China or Brazil (and Korea). As seen in Table 5.1, the software markets of these countries are as large as those of the 3Is and, correcting for size and level of development, represent markets that are as or more developed than those of countries like Spain, Finland, or Mexico. One of the most striking contrasts is the difference in levels of development of the software industries of Brazil and those of Mexico and Argentina, two Latin American nations boasting higher levels of development than Brazil. Mexico, like Brazil, is a large country, with a population of slightly over 100 million (Brazil has 176 million) and nearly 1.5 times as rich as Brazil. Moreover, it is part of NAFTA bordering the large and sophisticated US software market. Yet, its performance in the software industry has been dismal [17].

Unlike India, Ireland, and Israel, very limited knowledge exists regarding the current realities of and prospects for Brazil's or China's software industries, which have developed very differently from the 3Is. Lacking familiarity with English, a key export language, these large countries rely upon a strong local demand for the production of software through their economies' commitment to Information and Communication Technologies (ICT). According to the World Bank [18], in 2001, Brazil spent 8.3 percent of its GDP on ICT, exceeding the 7.9 percent spent in the United States and more than double the magnitude of such expenditures in India (3.9 percent). China too spent more than India with its expenditures at 5.7 percent of GDP.

The need to study China and Brazil more closely is important because some of the key factors that support software industries are as present in China and Brazil as in India. First, human capital production in all countries are comparable, with India and China leading the way in absolute figures and Brazil in relative terms. In 2000, Brazil graduated close to 18,000 people in IT areas (author calculations based on [19]), China produced 41,000 (CSIA reported in Chapter 6), and India 71,000 [20]. When population size is considered, Brazil graduates 101 persons per million inhabitants, while India has a figure of 32 and China 69 per million. The recent effort in Brazil to increase the number of IT graduates has resulted in the award of approximately 87,000 bachelors and over 5,000 masters degrees in IT-related areas between 1996 and 2001. Moreover, for every 18,000 students who complete an IT-related bachelors degree each year, there are an additional 22,000 in specialized non-degree-granting training courses (with more than 1,000 hours of training), as well as 340,000 graduates from short-term (e.g. 40 hours) IT tools training programs who enter the job market every year (see [21]). Brazil and China are not lagging behind in terms of availability of venture capital either. In 1999, at the peak of the market, Brazilian firms raised $832 million worth of venture capital [22], against $620 million raised in China [23] and $500 million in India [20].

The key question that arises in the face of such an important disparity of market orientation when compared with any of the 3Is is whether a focus on the domestic market is necessarily synonymous with inferior capabilities, revealing an inability to develop an internationally competitive industry; or whether, on the contrary, it represents an alternative strategy for preparing and structuring the means to enter more competitive international domains [5,6].

3   Evolution and Current Structure of the Brazilian Software Industry

As is true of many other countries, the Brazilian software industry was born along with its hardware industry [24,25]. At the beginning of the 1970s, Brazil had a military government favoring an import substitution model of development. In 1972, it established an Informatics policy, based on a principle of market reserve, which protected Brazilian producers of minicomputers (and later microcomputers) and their peripherals from imports. The intent was to build capabilities that would make local enterprises internationally competitive, but the response of internal producers was inadequate. Government support was tepid and the government was reluctant to rein in excessive fragmentation as firms diversified into a multitude of protected areas, failing to acquire the envisioned international competitiveness. The result was higher prices than the international market, thereby retarding IT adoption in Brazil. The decade-long economic recession in the 1980s and rising political instability during the transition from dictatorship to democracy eventually lead to a shift toward greater openness in the early 1990s.

There is no consensus about the impact of market reserve. Some [26] have argued that the neo-liberal policy was an adequate response to inferior results yielded by the market reserve regime, which caused higher prices, a delay in adoption of new technologies, and general consumer dissatisfaction. Others [27] maintain that liberalization was the last example of US pressure on the Informatics Policy. But our focus here is how the market reserve policy conditioned the creation and early evolution of the Brazilian software industry. In this regard, it can be said that:

1. The focus of the early Informatics Policy was hardware development, but it created the base for the subsequent development of the Brazilian software industry by increasing the number of professionals in computer science and related disciplines.
2. Although the Brazilian Informatics Policy was not successful in establishing a truly competitive industry, it gave the IT companies a nationwide dimension, facilitated technology acquisition by local firms through foreign alliances, and generated some highly specialized niches, such as banking and telecommunications systems.
3. The Brazilian software market reached $1.1 billion, a third of the total local IT industry, in 1991 [28].[3]

Beginning in 1992, Brazil sharply reduced state intervention in the economy. The market reserve regime was replaced by a market competitiveness policy to leverage already developed capabilities and prepare local firms for global competition. The main instrument for implementing these goals was the introduction of a new Informatics Law (8248/91) in 1993. This law provided fiscal benefits to hardware companies if they manufactured their products locally and invested 5 percent of their revenues in R&D activities, 2 percent of which needed to be in partnership with research centers or universities. From 1993 to 2001, this law benefited 428 firms and generated upwards of $1 billion in R&D activities, with 63 percent spent on corporate research and 33 percent on contracts with research centers and universities. Hardware companies (especially multinationals) benefited the most with direct tax exemptions but software companies benefited indirectly, albeit on a smaller scale since approximately a quarter of total R&D funds were spent on software development.

Overall, the introduction of new technologies, the economic stability from 1994 to 1998, the fall in hardware prices, and the advent of the Internet propelled the evolution of a domestic software industry. Older software companies created before the 1990s, often as arms of hardware producers (CPM, Scopus, Itautec), changed track and improved their managerial skills in order to deal with stronger market competition. In addition, firms were created with new strategic visions and concomitant technologies.

The SOFTEX Program, created in 1992 as part of a major national project for Informatics development (the DESI project), played a role in this developmental path. The Program (initially called SOFTEX 2000[4]) has built a significant support structure, implementing a wide network of agents (twenty-two cities in twelve states), introducing entrepreneurship and business plan culture in universities, certifying entrepreneurs and promoting national and international businesses in the area of software, mainly small- and medium-sized firms (see [29] for an independent account of the success of the program).

At the beginning of the 1990s, the Brazilian software market began to grow rapidly. As seen in Figure 5.1, from 1991 to 1996 the annual revenues growth rate was of the order of 20 percent. During the second half of the decade, despite the economic turmoil that affected the country and led to an overall decline in (in US Dollar) GDP, the average annual growth rate was close to 30 percent

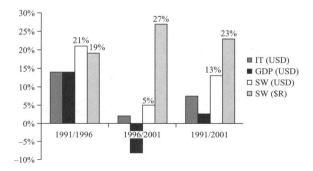

FIGURE 5.1. Average Annual Growth of IT Market in Brazil (Current Values)

Source: SEPIN (28). Growth rate for software based only on software products (excluding services); $R—Brazilian Real.

TABLE 5.2. Main Indicators for the Brazilian Software Industry[a]

(Values in $billions)	2000		2001	
	USD	%	USD	%
Hardware	7.0	40.7	7.2	40.0
Services	3.0	17.5	3.1	17.5
Software (Products and Services)	7.2	41.8	7.7	42.6
Products (Package, Custom, and Embedded)	3.2	18.6	3.6	20.0
Services (*Outsourcing*, Development, Integration, and Consultancy)	4.0	23.2	4.1	22.6
Total IT industry	17.2	100.0	18.0	100.0

[a] Brazil has the largest packaged software market and accounts for over a third of the total software market in Latin America.

Source: Authors' own elaboration from data in SEPIN/SOFTEX [30]. See Appendix for detailed explanation of the calculations.

a year, 5 percent if converted to dollar equivalent sales values. Overall, during the 1991–2001 decade the share of software in the IT market grew by two-thirds and exports increased from less than $1 million in 1990 to $100 million in 2001. Software industry sales as a percentage of GDP grew more than threefold, from less than 0.5 to 1.5 percent, while the IT market share increased from 1.7 to 2.9 percent of GDP. As seen in Table 5.2, by 2001 the software industry in Brazil had sales of $7.7 billion. Software now represents 42 percent of the total IT market in Brazil, exceeding the hardware share of the market, with sales of products and services more or less balanced.[5]

The growth of the Brazilian software market over the course of the last decade resulted in a formidable increase in the number of software development companies (program developers, data processing, and database activities) from 4,300 in 1994 to 5,400 in 2000, out of a total of 10,700 companies with potential software activities (against 7,000 in 1994). In the same period (1994–2000), the number of employees of firms with potential software activities increased from 112,000 to 167,000. Software development firms grew the most in terms of number of employees with an increase of 45 percent [30].

The slower growth in the number of employees (7 percent average annual growth in 1994–2000) as against industry revenue growth (27 percent CAGR) can in part be attributed to productivity gains. However, this may have been due to the very fast growth of packaged software revenues during this period, a possibility for which the significant rise of software imports (from $194 million in 1995 to $1,021 million in 2001) offers indirect support [31].[6]

As suggested by Table 5.3 the leading activity in the software industry in Brazil is system integration, followed by processing services, and hardware and software support.[7] These top four categories represent 57 percent of total IT

TABLE 5.3. Brazilian IT Services Market in 2002
(Share of Revenues)

Areas	Share (%)
Systems integration	17
Processing services	15
Hardware support	14
Software support	11
Outsourcing Internet services	9
Application development	8
Network consultant	7
Training	7
Network/desktop outsourcing	6
Internet consultant	4
Outsourcing application	1

Source: Executivos Financeiros Magazine (2002); excludes
a substantial part of product (packaged) software sales.

service revenues. In terms of specific markets, adequate expenses data across areas is unavailable and must be extrapolated from firm samples. A recent survey of 147 major firms in Brazil [32] about their software investment revealed that 60 percent of them were investing in customer relations management software, 57 percent in data warehousing, 53 percent in business intelligence, 41 percent in supply chain, and 39 percent in e-commerce.

Brazilian software companies are regionally concentrated as well. The southern and southeastern areas of the country had 22 and 59 percent, respectively of total companies in 2001. A similar pattern is observed in marketed volume (11 and 72 percent, respectively) and employment creation (16 and 54 percent, respectively). These regional patterns can be explained by policies of the 1970s and 1980s, which preferred the southern and (especially) the southeastern areas of the country when it came to investment in R&D. As a result, these areas, which were already the most industrialized in the country and also had better R&D infrastructure, had their role as leaders in the development of this technology in the country reinforced. The State of São Paulo stands out, because it accounts for approximately 40 percent of the total software market. The city of São Paulo is one of the largest and most sophisticated markets for software with its financial sector, telecommunications, and trade.

Today's industry is comprised mainly of micro firms (82 percent), followed by small (14 percent), medium (2 percent), and a few large companies (2 percent). A recent survey of 681 firms, showed strong and growing firm-creation activity, especially in the latter half of the last decade (Table 5.4). The table also suggests that some younger firms have grown enough to move across size categories. By 2001, although none had reached the 500 employee benchmark, thirty-six firms created during the 1990s moved to the third largest category, and fifteen to the

TABLE 5.4. History of Firm Creation in Brazil by Company Size
(Survey of 681 Firms)

Employees: Creation	≤10 Micro	10–49 Small	50–99 Medium	100–499 Large	500+ Very large
≤1980	4	4	4	20	14
1981–90	39	85	26	33	6
1991–95	84	106	23	8	0
1996–2001	118	87	13	7	0
Total	245	282	66	68	20

Source: SEPIN/Softex [30].

second. This growth trend seems to be especially prevalent among leading firms. A recent survey of fifty-five of the leading Brazilian software firms, representing 22 percent of industry revenues, showed that group sales in the period 1997–2001 grew at an average annual rate of 37 percent, while overall industry annual growth rate was 25 percent [33]. This strong pattern of both firm creation and growth is important because success in new industries is associated with both firm creation and, especially, growth [16]. However, Table 5.4 also shows that young firms (established in the 1990s) and middle-aged firms (established in the 1980s) have not yet grown large enough to be significant players in the international context. Furthermore the ten largest national companies have average sales below $100 million, whereas their equivalents internationally have sales of the order of $1 billion or more (Table 5.5). In India, the top three national firms have revenues exceeding $1 billion.

Table 5.5 also shows the importance of foreign players in the sector. Since the advent of liberalization and until the sector's worldwide slowdown in 2001, IT was one of the top three destination sectors for foreign direct investment in Brazil. Attracted by the strong growth in market demand, a number of software product and service companies invested in software development units, especially in more recent years. This strong inflow of foreign firms has brought new technologies and familiarity with current software tools to Brazil, erasing the backwardness of the earlier autarkic period.

Top software firms in Brazil have a particular set of origins. The recent report, mentioned above [33] that surveyed a sample of leading companies in the country showed that a majority were outgrowths of existing firms (see Table 5.6). Some were established as true spin-offs, in the sense that the 'mother' company started and had a stake in the new firm (e.g. Trópico resulted from the commercialization of a technology developed by CPqD, and Itautec became a separate office automation arm of ITAÚ bank). However, the majority are separate companies created by employees of the 'mother' firm who spotted a particular opportunity and decided to create a new firm, often without any direct support and sometimes even in competition with the 'mother' firm (IBM and Siemens are among the most prolific 'nests' for these fledgling entrepreneurs). The large number of spin-offs from existing firms contrasts with the low number of university spin-offs, indicating

TABLE 5.5. Largest Software Firms in Brazil in 2001

Company	Millions of USD	Origin
'Pure' nongovernment software firms		
Microsoft	362	US
Computer Associates	260	US
Oracle Brazil	182	US
SAP Brazil	124	GER
Consist	77	US
Microsiga	*72*	*BR*
CPqD	*64*	*BR*
Datasul	*41*	*BR*
Novell	25	US
RM Sistemas	23	US
JD Edwards	21	US
Symantec	21	US
PeopleSoft	19	US
Sybase	17	US
Eversystems	*15*	*BR*
Digitro	*14*	*BR*
Logocenter	*14*	*BR*
Adobe Systems	12	US
Baan	12	UK
Network Associates	10	US
Consulting/software services firms		
EDS	240	US
Accenture	194	US
DBA	*62*	*BR*
CTIS Informatica	*57*	*BR*
Proceda	*52*	*BR*

Sources: Exane Informatica (2002). *Exane Info 2002.* Agosto, 2002—
(software); Gazeta Mercantil (2002). Balanço Anval 2001. Informática e
Tecnologia da Informação—(consulting).

that most entrepreneurs had some firm experience before deciding to create their
own companies.

Another important characteristic of the industry is the prevalence of government software firms among the major players. These government firms originated
before the 1980s. The largest of all, SERPRO, employs close to 9,000 people and
had revenues totaling $372 million in 2001. The figures presented in Table 5.6
also highlight the fact that several multinationals have a long and established presence in the country, dating from the market reserve period, while recent entrants
are trying to capitalize on the growth and liberalization of the domestic market.
Finally, as in most other nations with vibrant software sectors, there are a large
number of start-ups. These start-ups are diverse, ranging from software factories
to e-commerce, component development, and management software firms.

TABLE 5.6. Dates of Firm Creation for Sample of Leading Companies

Creation date	Firm origin					
	Govt.	Multinational	Firm spin-off	University spin-off	Start-up	Total
Before 1980	5	4	4	1	4	18
1980–89	0	1	12	0	6	19
1990–95	0	0	6	0	2	8
1996–2002	0	2	5	0	3	10
Total global	5	7	27	1	15	55

Source: Botelho et al. [33].

TABLE 5.7. Comparing Software with the Overall Brazilian Industry

	Software	Total industry
Sales growth (CAGR %—1995–2000 current values)	24%	2%
Growth in number of workers (CAGR %)	7% (1994–2000)	−1% (1994–99)
VA/employee (10^3 R$—1999)	97	26/60 (Hi Tech[a])

[a] High Tech is an average of nine sectors that range from pharmaceuticals, to electronics and aircraft.

Source: Own calculations and data from the IBQP-PR and IBGE for Industry, accessed at www.ibqppr.org.br; SEPIN [28] and Botelho et al. [33] for software.

Table 5.7 presents a comparison of key competitiveness statistics for Brazilian industry overall and the software sector in particular. The differences are quite significant on every level. The software sector is growing at a much faster pace than industry in general in terms of sales and job creation.[8] The software industry also has a higher value-added per worker, both in comparison to overall industry figures as well as to those for the high-tech subgroup.

Although policy makers have begun to recognize the importance of the software industry in Brazil, current supportive policy instruments are still quite narrow, confined for the most part to a few timid financial incentives.[9] Recent policy emphasis has been placed on the development of export consortia and open source software. For example, in Congress, the House of Representatives has chosen not to renew its MS Office software licenses. In Brazil's southernmost state, Rio Grande do Sul, free software has advanced further, mostly in schools and small municipalities, and continues to expand to include even the municipality of Porto Alegre, the state capital.

Another recent development is the creation of an institution to organize and coordinate venture capital in Brazil. In 2000, the Brazilian Association for Venture capital (ABCR) was established with government agencies such as FINEP[10] playing an important role in its creation. Between 2000 and 2002,

183 firms received roughly \$2.8 billion in venture capital [34]. Although firms with computer-related activities, communications, and media represent 46 percent of total recipients, only twenty-three firms valued at \$30 million are in 'pure' software and services. Thus, software firms are either using other financing mechanisms or are being included under other computer related categories (e.g. all Internet firms are placed in a separate category).

The brief history of the Brazilian software industry provided above portrays a relatively young but sizable sector with a substantial growth pattern. However, it is also inward oriented, regionally fragmented, and composed mostly of small players. These contrasts require us to probe further into the nature of local companies, their capabilities, and their interactions with the market.

4   The Curse of the Domestic Market

One could expect the large and fast growing market in the 1990s to have led to a healthy mix of mostly local or regional custom development service firms, together with national general purpose (packaged) software, as well as firms specialized in vertical (industry) segments and horizontal niches (e.g. components). The reality is different: smaller unfocused regional players, with thin competence sets and limited ambitions still dominate important parts of the sector. Only recently has this pattern begun to change, with the emergence of more specialized firms on the national level, especially in some subsectors, a development explored in the next section.

In the decades preceding the 1990s, IT users, private and public sector alike, perceived software development as an essentially auxiliary activity performed in-house by IT-user organizations and hardware producers. That is, software production activity did not have either a corporate or an industrial identity and was mostly an afterthought, a marginal activity within firms. Moreover, with market reserve pushing cost considerations to a back seat and amidst a generally soft labor market for human capital in the sector, the drive for an organizational culture oriented towards the acquisition of efficiency-driven and business model sensitive managerial capabilities was virtually absent. As a result, the emergence of a market-based software industry had to await economic liberalization.

The slow decline in high costs of hardware (as a result of hardware import liberalization in 1992) and the low cost of software personnel made IT end-user firms increasingly reliant on software to meet the competitive challenge of foreign competitors entering the Brazilian market after 1990. As the software industry came into being, the emerging firms, many of them spin-offs of former hardware producers or large software users, inherited organizational and cultural legacies of disorganized production and inattention to cost. Vertical integration, bundling of hardware with software, and full in-house software development, with a few notable exceptions, hindered the development of collaborative strategies among firms, and the development of subcontracting networks were the norm. Conversely, the end-user organizations were unsophisticated in their use of software, with a few early exceptions in the banking and telecom sector and later in the federal government, which, however, continued to rely on in-house capabilities.

This lack of sophistication among user and developer firms was a key feature of an expanding domestic market also characterized by strong regional fragmentation. In addition, there was a rapid and massive increase in software imports in the 1990s. The result was an environment that encouraged customization of products to individual customers and growth through diversification in regional markets instead of specializing in general purpose products for the national market. Thus, numerous small regional firms lacking strategic focus appeared and have succeeded to date.

The counter-specialization bias was further reinforced by the persistence of large captive in-house software markets in sectors such as banking and government. In 1999, the banking sector's in-house expenditures on software development were almost 50 percent higher than its expenditures on external purchases.[11] From 1995 to 2002, government IT expenditures rose 214 percent from R$808 million to R$2.5 billion (about $800 million). Concurrently, government expenditures on external software acquisition and licensing grew only 13 percent and 133 percent, respectively, jointly accounting for a mere 1.3 percent of total IT expenditures. However, total government expenditures (internal, i.e. paid to state-owned developers, and external) on professional technical services in the area grew a substantial 305 percent in the same space of time, reaching 24 percent of total national IT expenditures versus 18 percent in 1995 [35].

Two additional factors aggravated the negative effect of these captive markets on software specialization. First, since large state-owned software firms were mostly self-contained, their unique process capabilities and expertise has seldom been transferred to external firms competing in the local and international market. Second, as most large organizations were no longer confined to purchasing IT services from domestic sources, they quickly moved to adopt international software solutions as a means to catch up with international competitors entering the local market.

Finally, features of both human and financial capital markets also affected the growth of specialized software firms. Existing social and labor regulations dramatically increased the cost of direct employment, discouraging service-oriented software firms from investing in organizational and managerial capabilities.[12] With the high-end tier of the market closed to them because most large users favored in-house sources or established suppliers (mostly multinationals), budding domestic software firms competed mostly through lower costs, implying high levels of labor outsourcing and high turnover. This, coupled with financial constraints such as high interest rates and onerous collateral requirements, made it difficult to invest in technology or organizational capabilities.

The market trap generated by the set of conditions described above was neither correctly understood nor dealt with early enough through appropriate policy measures. The government's focus was on eliminating a mounting balance of payment deficit and exercising the fiscal restraint required by its stabilization macroeconomic policy. Therefore, policy efforts took on an 'export at any cost' character and were unmindful of any potential leverage that a strong and large domestic software market could have for long run export success. In addition, the relatively small size, newness, and geographic dispersion of the emerging Brazilian software industry meant that it did not possess the political clout relative to other industrial sectors to obtain differentiated financing for exports.[13] This lack of appreciation for the potential importance of the domestic market as a driver of competitive domestic firm growth was evident in the limited nature of national policies directed at the software industry in the 1990s. The few policy instruments that did exist (i.e. Softex and Prosoft) were governed by a nationalistic bias towards development of software products, ignoring the potential of service-oriented firms and initiatives. The problem was that products were often developed (and financed) as 'toy products' for pet regional clients , without a clear perception of whether or not a real market potential existed, and with no serious marketing effort nationally or internationally. In addition, the informal nature of a large segment of Brazilian economic activity coupled with the size and fragmented structure of the domestic market for software led to the growth of piracy, particularly in the packaged software product segment geared towards small business. Weak distribution channels and geographic dispersion make it hard to enforce anti-piracy policies. The PC market is dominated by gray market producers that usually bundle pirated software and aggravate the problem. Therefore, the results are particularly damaging to domestic software product development firms.

The ultimate impact of this curse of the domestic market is found in the immature and distorted industrial structure of the domestic software industry and the weakness of its attendant institutions. First, there is a dearth of large lead firms capable of serving as exemplars. For instance, in the segment of 'ERP—Enterprise Resource Planning' for small- and medium-size firms, there are three small- to middle-size firms that are prominent (Datasul and Microsiga are the two largest players), each offering somewhat similar solutions in their individual regional markets. Although they have experienced reasonable growth, they are still small by international standards, which puts them at a disadvantage when competing with foreign firms. Second, cooperation efforts such as strategic alliances, joint marketing agreements, and product development partnerships, are key in the context of software and Internet product development [36] but, until recently, few Brazilian firms have been involved in such efforts [33]. Third, the industry lacks a unified voice and is torn between different regions, expectations of SMEs versus large firms, and product versus software services-oriented firms. Although there are two different industry associations, neither is seen as truly representative of the sector, a stark contrast to NASSCOM in India.

5   The Promise of the Domestic Market

Developed nations such as the United States or Germany often nurture industrial capabilities by leveraging their strong, sophisticated, and large domestic markets, but it is unclear whether developing countries can do the same. This section will argue that two complementary conditions must be met for such a possibility to materialize, overcoming some of the difficulties highlighted in the previous section. First, software firms must have a set of lead client sectors whose demands are close to those of leading international users, providing learning opportunities. Second, there must be competition and selection mechanisms that force firms to structure capabilities and weed out firms that fail to measure up. In addition, one needs a strong entrepreneurial culture that promotes risk taking and experimentation.

5.1   Leveraging Leading Sectors

While Brazil is a developing country in most respects, several sectors of the domestic economy are particularly well developed, even by international standards. One such area is banking. The financial turmoil experienced by Brazil, its large and complex market, as well as its aggressive policies for stabilizing currency and capital markets have generated high-performing institutions. This was true before liberalization [37,38] but their strength has been confirmed over the course of the liberalization process initiated in 1994. A recent study, using as indicators leverage rate, equity, profitability, net margin, revenue of operating assets, and cost to revenue ratio, showed that, unlike many other developing nations, foreign entrants in Brazil neither exhibited better operational indicators upon entry nor better evolution after entry in comparison to domestic players, except in terms of revenues from operating assets [39].

Another area where local industry is extremely sophisticated is telecommunications. From the late 1970s to the early 1990s, Brazil had a strong policy supporting the establishment of an indigenous telecommunications industry. As a result, and very much at the expense of the final consumer, significant technological capabilities in telecommunications have been created, including a relatively developed cluster around the city of Campinas involving CPqD, the R&D center for Telebrás (the former government telecom monopoly), universities, other research institutions, equipment suppliers, and operating companies [27]. Initially, most players were locally owned firms. Since the deregulation in the early 1990s, foreign firms have bought most of them. Moreover, through the informatics law, these companies faced strong fiscal incentives for R&D, which has guaranteed a continuing investment in their technological capabilities in Brazil.

Foreign direct investment (FDI) in both financial and telecom sectors has been significant. In 2000 and 2001, they represented 52 and 30 percent of total FDI, respectively, a preeminent position they have occupied since the mid-1990s. The financial and telecom sectors are sophisticated clients and strong developers of

TABLE 5.8. Knowledge Intensity of Firms Developing
Software for Leading Sectors Versus Average

	Telecom software	Banking software	Average
R&D/software sales (%)	17	47	13
R&D/total sales (%)	11	5	6
R&D expenses/HR in R&D	32,238	182,178	52,092
R&D expenses/HR	16,599	1,043	8,742
R&D HR/HR (%)	60	32	41
HR with graduate level/HR (2) (%)	15	5	11
Share of direct software revenues (%)	38	45	71

Source: Botelho et al. [33]. The R&D activities should be interpreted as
involving the software development process. HR: Human Resources.

software systems, which are critical to their success. According to Banco Hoje [40],
the Brazilian banking system is the largest single investor in IT in Brazil, accounting for 30 percent of total expenditures. For most hardware telecom products,
software already represents 50 percent of product cost and its relative importance
is likely to increase over the next few years. Table 5.8 presents key indicators in
research and software development gathered from the recent study of fifty-five of
the leading Brazilian software companies [33]. Firms developing telecom software
are above average on virtually all indicators of knowledge intensity. In banking
software most indicators are also salient, although the ratio of expenses on human
resources in knowledge activities to the total is low, perhaps reflecting many other
activities in banking that are of low knowledge intensity.

The Brazilian Payment System (SPB) is a particularly good example of how
idiosyncratic local needs can spur the development of capabilities. In 1999, the
Brazilian Central Bank decided that, by 2002, Brazil should have installed an
advanced payment system in accordance with the most up-to-date Internet technology recommended by the Bank for International Settlements. With SPB, funds
clearance is immediate resulting in real time control of bank reserves, preempting
overdrafts and dramatically increasing overall system reliability and trustworthiness. This highly complex system entailed the installation of a dedicated
backbone structure and the provision of a software system to reliably and securely
link together the central bank, various clearing houses, and each individual bank
in the network. Banks spent over R$1.7 billion (over $800 million) on adapt-
ing their technological infrastructures to the requirements of SPB [32]. Microsoft
named the establishment of SPB as the biggest IT project ever in the Latin American
banking sector and assigned over 200 professionals to work on it with their local
partners [32].

While several of the 170 banks in the Brazilian system used their internal resources to develop solutions, a significant number hired outside firms, creating an immense market opportunity for local and foreign software firms alike. Fees from system development and maintenance are a source of significant and sustained revenues. Moreover, products and services developed in the context of SPB can serve as foundations for subsequent products and services. Several dozen Brazilian and international software firms and consortia bid for the development of software products for the SPB. Ultimately, the majority of the contracts went to Brazilian firms and several leading foreign banks in Brazil, including Bank-Boston, UBS Warburg, JP Morgan, and Bank of America, among others, opted for purely domestic solutions. Five other Brazilian software providers established partnerships with foreign suppliers such as Microsoft and Computer Associates. Only two foreign firms (besides Microsoft and IBM which provided base software technologies to most SPB projects), Getronics and Unysis, won contracts. This example clearly illustrates the level of competence domestic software firms in the banking sector have achieved [32,41].

In telecom, the first interesting pocket of competence relevant to the software industry is associated with embedded software. One of the leading examples among foreign players is Siemens. The company entered Brazil in the 1970s and is now the largest in the electronics and electrical engineering sector in the country, employing roughly 8,900 people in twelve production facilities and thirteen sales offices nationwide. Siemens' Brazilian operation also includes a Telecommunications Technology Research and Development Center with over a hundred full-time researchers and several hundred others affiliated through university grants and contracts. The research laboratory is a world competence center for four product lines, including low-end private branch exchange switches ('PBXs'), and will soon include a competence center for GSM cellular technology. The unit has global full cycle product responsibilities, including research, development, and manufacturing for these lines. Like Siemens, Ericsson has close to 500 people in its Brazilian research unit, all devoted to research and development in software. The Brazilian unit is responsible worldwide for full cycle development of software for several systems in its fixed and mobile telephony. It is also a worldwide competence center for the development of the TDMA telephony system. Others, such as Alcatel and Motorola, have a number of local and global competence centers and extensive development programs in the country.

A second pocket of competence is CPqD, the former government telecom research lab converted into a company following market liberalization. The firm is a leader in research and development in software—due to continuing government subsidies—and has consistently been responsible for several key products and spin-offs in the industry. Among its several products, perhaps the most interesting has been Trópico, the fixed commuter terminal system developed originally by CPqD and now sold by a spin-off company also called Trópico. Of the 42 million fixed network terminals currently installed in Brazil, 8.5 million are Trópico [41]. Initially, the sale of such systems was due to protectionist policies. But since the privatization of telecom in the late 1990s, the company has had to compete in the open market for contracts, battling international giants such as Siemens, Ericsson, Lucent, and Nortel. In 2001, Cisco acquired a minor share in the spin-off firm, attesting the value of the technology. The firm has been able to withstand competition, holding roughly 20 percent of local sales at present.

Start-ups are a third area of interest in telecom in particular for cell phones. Demand for cell phones has grown at a double-digit rate over the past few years, reaching thirty-three million active phones by the end of 2002 and is expected to continue to grow in the future. As a result, a number of very innovative local firms have jumped into the development of games and applications for cell phones. CESAR, a development team geared towards software games and based in Recife, was one of the five winners of the first Asia Java Mobile Challenge and had a second game place in the top twenty at the same contest. This was a 2002 global competition organized jointly by the six leading Asian cell phone operators and involved over a thousand participants from twenty-three countries around the world. As the result of these awards, the two games are now being distributed to over forty operators by iiL Corp (Information is Life) in Asia and LDC Network in Europe. Since 2000, CESAR has a partnership with Motorola, for whom they have developed more than twenty-five cell phone games. This is only one of a growing number of examples of software start-ups critical for the future of the industry. These start-ups also promote the view of Brazil as a country of entrepreneurs. According to the Global Entrepreneurship Monitor published by Babson College, Brazil has always ranked among the top five and often led the list of most entrepreneurial countries in the world.

It is not only the private sector that has played an important role in the development of the software industry. Public administration can also be considered a lead sector and an anchor for the development. The Brazilian government is very large, with sophisticated needs and requirements in terms of information processing. To meet these needs, the strategy has been to create public firms that supply software and IT services across states and sometimes across the entire country. These companies have a combined employment of over 10,000 and have developed a rich pool of competencies. This effort has made Brazil one of the leading countries in this area, with important flagship projects such as electronic voting and electronic tax declarations. In the last presidential election, all the voting was done electronically with over 90 million votes in the world's largest electronic election and by 2002, 96 percent of all the people filing annual tax returns did so electronically [42].

Another area where the Brazilian government is a world leader is in the adoption of 'free' software such as Linux. At least eleven Brazilian cities have passed laws giving preference to or requiring the use of 'software livre' and a number of other municipalities, states, and the national government have considered similar legislation [43,44]. Such a strong push towards this technology is important because of its rising significance as an alternative to proprietary software. IDC estimates that around a third of the computers in Latin America will run on Linux in 2003.[14]

The discussion above illustrates how lead sectors can play a very important role in structuring software industry capabilities, helping local producers to escape the low-value-added trap discussed in Section 4. The size and sophistication of clients in areas such as banking and telecoms steer the work and provide opportunities for software firms to focus their competence and invest in general and in ever more complex products and services. As they improve, they will work in projects with greater relevance for international markets, creating a strong foundation for potential internationalization.

5.2 Structuring Competencies

Although local demand for sophisticated software products can produce technical acumen, it may not be enough to compel local firms to establish a sound business model. For this, two additional, and complementary, factors are necessary: international competition in the product and input markets and the development of capital markets.

Increased liberalization of the Brazilian market and the prospect of strong and continued economic growth attracted international software developers to invest in the local market and compete with domestic incumbents. Table 5.5, which lists the top twenty software firms currently operating in Brazil reveals the presence of familiar international names. In services, high-level systems analysis and software development, firms such as EDS and Accenture have grown at double-digit rates over recent years and have higher sales than any local private software firm, though they face strong competition from leading domestic software service providers such as DBA and CPM. Product firms have been experiencing comparable competitive pressure. A good example is the ERP segment. Through the mid-1990s, Microsiga and Datasul, two of the largest Brazilian software firms, had the market to themselves. But liberalization attracted giants such as SAP and BAAN to the business opportunity the Brazilian market presented. While these global producers have quickly taken over the large software firm market (mostly from internal development, as this segment had never been the major target of local developers), the battle now is over ERP systems tailored to cater to medium-sized companies. SAP is now aggressively pursuing this market through a version of its system. However, local ERP producers claim that they are not losing market share and have also begun exploring the Latin American and even the US market.

Liberalization acted as a competitive shock for local firms, leading them to hone and sometimes reshape their strategy and business model. Under pressure, successful local firms learned to leverage their knowledge of domestic market idiosyncrasies (e.g. the tax code), existing systems, and local corporate organizational culture. Alternatively, foreign entrants' focus on large corporations turned local firms toward the huge SME market. Given the fragmented and uninformed nature of this demand, successful local firms had to dramatically sharpen their organizational and service skills, becoming leaner and more flexible. For example, some local software service firms adopted flexible software factory development models in tandem with partnerships with other smaller vertical firms with deep market knowledge.

As important as market competition was the disciplining role of capital markets. In the early stages of the industry, virtually all firms' growth was financed through reinvested earnings. The absence of a venture capital market and financial instability (high and volatile interest rates) created a strong bias against external financing. Nevertheless, the dramatic growth of the industry allowed firms to finance their own (modest) growth. In the mid- to late 1990s, local financial stabilization and an international appetite for technology-based firms created a completely different scenario. Figure 5.2 shows the results of a recent survey of the leading firms in Brazil [33]. Of the fifty-five firms surveyed, sixteen had accessed some form of private venture capital (mostly international) and twenty had received funds from a competitive government fund to finance software firms. Moreover, the figure reveals a significant growth in access to venture capital and special funds toward product development. Together with the much needed cash, a new discipline in business, management, and technology emerged.

Firms interviewed [33] reported that the prospect of entry for external private capital provided an important impetus to the development of the firm along two major axes. First, it forced firms to define a clear business model, usually providing a sounder basis along which to structure their competence. To access external funds, firms had to prepare detailed business plans and explain how they would stay competitive in the local and international markets. This effort forced companies to seriously grapple with the issues of strategic planning, budgeting, and marketing, placing them in a coherent and integrated plan. Second, the entry of external capital, both private and public, enhanced the hitherto weak managerial

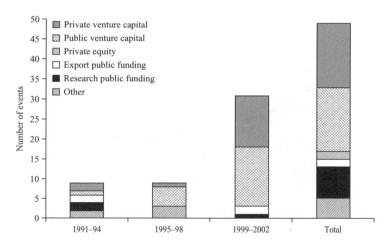

FIGURE 5.2. Growth of External Financing in a Sample of Lead Brazilian Software Firms
Source: Botelho et al. [33].

capabilities of domestic firms, either by supplying management talent to companies or forcing them to secure such competencies as a condition of being granted access to capital.[15]

6 Going Abroad

Virtually every leading local company is trying or has plans to globalize. In a recent survey mentioned before, 60 percent of them reported export activities [33]. However, many of them are still making timid inroads into foreign markets. Among the firms surveyed that reported export activity, the average share of sales devoted to the external market was only 12 percent.

Firms have been using an array of internationalization strategies. As seen in Figure 5.3, half of the firms that responded to the survey mentioned earlier use internal multinational channels as their main export route. This includes firms that are themselves multinationals operating in Brazil, as is the case with Siemens or Ericsson. It also includes branches of multinationals operating in Brazil which adopt software developed locally and then use it in their international operations. Examples of this are the sale of banking software by Software Design to Goldman Sachs in New York, or the sale of Trópico PBX devices and related software to Telefonica across Latin America. This strategy dominates because of the local strength in vertical specialized software (products and services), especially in banking and telecom, two strong areas described earlier.

In addition, there are more traditional international expansion modes. Sales through delegations and Value Added Resellers (VARs) to expand to foreign markets are being explored in areas such as ERP and niche products, which use the Latin American market as the natural route to the extension of domestic regional

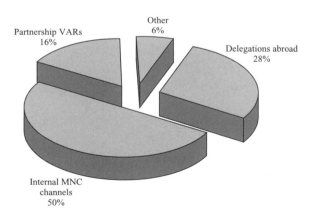

FIGURE 5.3. Export Strategies for Sample of Fifty-five Leading Software Firms
Source: Botelho et al. [33].

growth. For example, Eversystem has exported its financial management application packages to Argentina and Mexico, where it has established offices. CPqD, which already exports its telecommunication management application systems (Promus, Flexflow, Sagre, Terus, SGE e dotIP) to the United States, Italy, Bolivia, and China, recently launched an aggressive export strategy based on partnerships with Brazilian and local firms to sell its solutions in Chile, Venezuela, Colombia, Uruguay, Peru, and Argentina.

Some companies are more aggressive and have broken into the US market directly. Eversystem, one of the leading Brazilian software firms and an internationalization success story, reported more than a third of its sales (over \$32 million) out of its Miami office in 2002. Interviews with firms [33] suggest that this could become the norm soon. More recently, the earlier local experimentation with software factories has blossomed, with firms aggressively entering the international outsourcing market based on their superior knowledge of vertical markets and relatively low cost of labor. In late 2003, fifteen Brazilian firms joined efforts in creating 'NEXT—Núcleo de Exportação de Tecnologia', a unique company aiming to commercialize vertical banking products and services in the United States [45].

These emerging experiments are also seen by industry experts as representing a promising, yet still under-explored, growth path for the industry, the area of export services. A number of recent moves by international firms clearly signal that Brazil is increasingly seen as a destination for localizing development. These include recent announcements of plans by Dell and Microsoft to create or expand software development platforms involving hundreds of people. Export services also includes smaller firms—as development arms for European retailers and software factories producing for clients in the United States and Europe. Finally, Brazil is attracting the interest of leading Indian services firms such as Tata Consulting Services, which announced a joint venture with TBA, a local firm, to create a software development operation expected to grow to 3,000 professionals in five years [46]. In early 2004, it was the first software firm in Brazil to receive CMM level 5 certification.

These examples bode well for the prospects of internationalization of the Brazilian software industry over the next few years. Strong business models, mature technologies, and deep domain knowledge in key vertical areas may propel the industry to interesting levels of internationalization both in products and services, with the latter consisting of specialized vertical offshore projects. However, until exports materialize in larger numbers, this area will be one of the critical challenges for the continuing success of the industry.

7 From Laggard to Second Mover?

The evolutionary path-dependent trajectory followed by the Brazilian software industry over the past decade reveals that the curse of the domestic market can be turned into a blessing with appropriate institutions and incentives.[16] Starting in the early 1990s, a growing and increasingly open Brazilian economy spurred extraordinary development in the domestic IT and software sectors. Released from trade constraints that limited access to foreign technology during the 1980s, firms across the economy invested in IT, software in particular, and created a strong and dynamic domestic demand for the nascent software industry. However, the market incentives drove a number of software firms toward serving numerous regional clients with limited technical sophistication. Alternative strategies such as developing innovative products for the national market, growth through mergers and acquisitions, and pursuing internationalization, especially of services, were dismissed by many firms due to the high risk, high cost of capital, and lack of effective management. As a result, Brazilian companies matured more slowly compared to India and other developing countries emerging as lead players in the international software market.

Industry prospects changed when at least two conditions were established. One of these is the presence of lead domestic client sectors for software firms with demands close to those of leading international firms. These clients provide opportunities for learning and competence deepening similar to those found when exporting to foreign competitive firms. The examples of banking and telecom explored in Section 5 illustrate this dynamism. But the opportunity to learn is not always enough. The second required condition is the presence of competition and selection mechanisms, which induce successful firms to structure capabilities, while winnowing out firms that fail to learn. In Brazil, both local competition by international players as well as private and public venture capital played such disciplining role in structuring business models and shaping competence building. When the two dimensions are coupled with a third, a strong entrepreneurial culture, the result is also healthy experimentation in the product market space, a first step toward generating entrepreneurial growth firms capable of leveraging the international market. These observations are critical, not only to understand the dynamics of the industry in Brazil but also to demonstrate that there are alternative paths to those followed by India, Ireland, and Israel in the acquisition of competencies in the software industry.

In fact, one could argue that an alternative development path grounded on the domestic market is especially suitable for a country such as Brazil. On one hand, unlike India, Ireland, and Israel, the cultural and personal ties with the United States are much thinner. Moreover, while English is a widely known language in Brazil, there is not the same degree of confidence and widespread use as in the other three nations. On the other hand, the existence of large and sophisticated local demand reduces the need to rely on foreigners as leverage for competence acquisition and market growth.

This focus of the software sector on the domestic market may also have important multiplying effects for Brazil. Recent studies at the company and country levels have shown that investment in information technology is positively related to corporate and national economic performance [48–50]. This is especially important for sectors that Kraemer and Dedrick [48] refer to as 'production close to use' sectors, where IT use is very close to or overlaps with production. Therefore, while a robust software industry partially emerges as a result of a vibrant and dynamic economy, *ceteris paribus* on the level of economic development, a stronger domestic software sector may bring benefits to the rest of the economy that go beyond its value added [51].

A related potential advantage of the domestic market route, especially the one observed in Brazil, is that it naturally builds vertical industry segment specific skills in the local software supplier firms.[17] Software services can easily become a commodity, so that suppliers face intense competition and pricing pressures. Indeed as noted by D'Costa [54], many Indian software firms are developing vertical industry segment specific knowledge to move up the value chain, trying to escape from such intense competition. Brazilian firms naturally have an advantage, given that they have grown through close cooperation with users, especially in finance and telecommunications. Several Brazilian financial software firms (Eversystem, Logocenter, Disoft, Mintter) have developed 'generic' market software products out of pilot (joint product development or continuous service) projects with financial institution users, which they can leverage to service other financial institutions as well. Similarly, ERP providers to SMEs have adopted strategies to make cooperation on the part of final users mandatory. Some make use of local partners, and thus can respond more quickly to ongoing client requirements. Others make extensive use of call centers to establish this cooperative bond as well as to add required vertical market knowledge to the product.

While there are a number of factors in the domestic market that have propelled the success of the industry over the last decade, several important challenges must be met if Brazil is to fruitfully parlay its set of domestic competencies into international market success. First, it is important to note that finding the right combination of market segment and business model in the global market is difficult, for both service and product firms. In the international service and related-system integration arena, currently dominated by India, entry does not require sophisticated technological capability but rather low costs and process capability. Firms can signal such capability either through reputation or investment in process certification schemes, such as CMM. Both are difficult to manage in the Brazilian environment. Strong growth in domestic demand means that most of the attention of Brazilian software producers is still within national borders, where they have established reputations, bypassing the drive for certification. The strong devaluation of the Real and an anticipated decline in local demand will perhaps reverse this trend. In addition, attempts of some Brazilian firms to enter the US service verticals market anchored at higher entry points in the value chain (relative to India) are still timid and a successful business model has not yet been established. Product firms also face important difficulties. Successfully launching and marketing products on an international market entails large scale and deep pockets to finance the long and arduous process of market learning and client trust building. Since most Brazilian product or service firms are smaller and face strong competition from larger foreign firms, these challenges suggest the need for consolidation through mergers and acquisitions or collaborative alliances, and policies which will facilitate them.

Second, while domestic software enterprises are trying to internationalize, they face foreign competition in their local markets, putting them in a bind. Large domestic users tend to favor established foreign suppliers, whereas smaller users are often unwilling to pay a premium for the domestic firms' unique knowledge. Domestic software enterprises must therefore continuously use their local knowledge advantages to find new market segments and generate margins to finance the development of component-like products and some of the extra costs associated to internationalization. Subsidizing early users of new products and providing incentives for research centers to assist firms in turning their vertical service experience into component-like products may ameliorate the problem.

An important missing institutional link has been the state. Amsden and Chu [55] suggest that state-led networking is the strategy available to latecomers willing to acquire second mover advantage in the service sector. This requires the state to partially substitute for personal trust and market mechanisms that shape and strengthen networks in classic producer sectors, influencing firm size, structure, and degree of specialization so as to induce the creation of firms with capital and project management capabilities large enough to contest foreign competition. Larger firms that are able to aggregate some of the capabilities now dispersed over several smaller players will have the expertise and the ability to enter foreign markets and diversify into 'newer' mature service lines. Be it in Taiwan, where it plays the role of networker, or in Ireland, where it becomes a flexible developmental instrument [56,57], the state's ultimate goal should be to join forces with large capital enterprises in acting as a seamless enabler of second mover advantage, an important role the Brazilian government has not been able to play. While it is important for the future of the industry that the government engages in such role, it is critical that it does so without hindering the role of market forces as mechanisms for selecting capable firms and willing management.

To conclude, this chapter has argued that the curse of the domestic market may be neutralized by gearing development in the software industry to the local demand of strong vertical markets and establishing robust firm disciplining mechanisms, with an explicit goal of leveraging domestic experience to expand to the global marketplace. The evolution of the Brazilian software industry shows how an appropriate balance of these dimensions can lead to very strong development, while the particular evolutionary path of the local sector makes it well poised to take advantage of emerging trends in the global industry. Clearly, challenges remain, but the prospects were never brighter.

Appendix

The sources consulted and the calculations used aim to reach values that are in line with the values adopted by India and Ireland, which include software outsourcing and packaging services in the total. So, the values for 2001 are obtained as described below:

- The 2001 values were converted using the annual average exchange rate 1$ = R$2.3504.
- Hardware sales values are directly obtained from SEPIN statistics.
- For services, estimated software services sales are subtracted from total IT services sales reported by SEPIN.
- Software Products correspond to software sales data reported by SEPIN— a narrow criterion for defining software.
- Software Services. We verified that the services reported by SEPIN were mostly hardware related, making the figures difficult to compare with other international statistics. Using data from INFO Exame [58] we arrived at a conservative estimate for software services in 2001. Data for software is thus calculated as follows: Revenues for the top twenty in the Outsourcing segment amount to $1.2 billion. The segment Providers adds another $500 million. And Development and Integration add a further $1.1 billion. Consulting (top ten) accounts for $260 million. Compiling these four segments into a single Software Services category, we reach $4.06 billion. According to the same source (INFO Exame [58], the top twenty software sellers reported revenues for 2001 amount to $1.6 billion, far below the reported SEPIN value of $3.6 billion for Product revenues. The difference is probably accounted for by the more than 3,000 other SMEs that make up the bulk of the highly fragmented Brazilian software industry.
- Adding SEPIN's Products value of $3.6 billion to our estimated $4.06 billion for Software Services, we come up with a total value for the industry of $7.66 billion.
- The Software revenues for 2000 were calculated using the following methodology. First, we calculated the percentage value of Services in 2001 (Reais equivalent) over the total for IT, as reported by SEPIN (21.36%). Next, based on this share, we calculated the value of the Services segment (R$5.5 billion). Finally, we subtracted this value from the value for IT services reported by SEPIN to arrive at the value for Software Services in 2000, R$7.31 billion. These values were then converted using the annual average exchange rate 1$ = R$1.8302.

Notes

1. Brazil has the largest packaged software market and accounts for over a third of the total software market in Latin America.
2. Existing statistics for software exports by the United States are below the US$1 billion, which understates the true figure because sales by US corporations abroad are typically not included in official statistics.

3. The true figure was probably higher because no detailed accounting of software services was done, the focus having been on products.

4. When SOFTEX was created, its specific mandate was to increase the exports of Brazilian software to $1 billion in 2000. While it fell short of its quantitative objective, it did play an important role in developing an export mindset as well as in some of the early experiments. In many ways, the program was clearly ahead of firms' capability levels. Later its mandate was broadened to include overall industry promotion, including exports and entrepreneurship.

5. Except when noted, all the figures for Brasil used throughout this document are based on data of the Secretaria de Política de Informática—MCT/SEPIN and Sociedade Brasileira para o Desenvolvimento de Software—SOFTEX, especially the presentations [28,30]. See also www.mct.gov.br/sepin/.

6. IDC Brazil estimates that in 2001 the packaged software market in Brazil reached 2,087 million dollars, equaling the rest of Latin America combined. Cited in [28].

7. The figures focus on services do not account properly for sales of software products, especially those sold as stand-alone packages to end customers.

8. While software added 55,000 jobs during the 1994–99 period, industry in general, as well as all individual industry sectors at the 2 digit SIC level, lost jobs.

9. One of the most important instruments is the SOFTEX Program, already mentioned above. In 1997, Softex, in partnership with the National Banks for Social and Economic Development (BNDES), launched a pilot credit program for software firms: PROSOFT. The program, expected to end at the end of 2003, has $35 million budgeted for investment. Its funding analysis takes into account the risky nature of the software business and thus is managed as a portfolio. It provides loans of up to $2 million to software firms with gross revenues under R$100 million (approximately $30 million) and collects returns as a function of firm results. By the end of 2002, it had invested half of its budget in twenty-nine firms.

10. FINEP is the arm of the Ministry of Science and Technology whose mission is to fund research, development, and innovation projects that can contribute to the economic development of Brazil. Its broad mandate enables it to be involved in a large number of initiatives, from pure research to venture capital. It also manages sector funds, which includes the one for IT mentioned before.

11. In that year, total software expenditures reached R$874 million or about $300 million dollars [32].

12. Other relevant factors include the structural gap between academic research and industry and the historical pattern of consumption of imported technologies.

13. Mineral and agricultural products and related items account for almost two-thirds of Brazilian exports.

14. The Brazilian company Conectiva, which exports throughout Latin America, has quickly risen to the status of a major player world of open-source software. In 2001, Marcelo Tosatti, a Conectiva employee, was chosen to take over maintenance of the current 'stable' Linux kernel. This position was previously held by Alan Cox, a major figure in the Linux community and its long-time maintainer.

15. Access to subsidized government funds had a similar yet indirect impact on firm management. In 1997, BNDES and Softex created the Prosoft initiative mentioned in Section 3. Unlike traditional venture capital, this extremely competitive line of credit does not require relinquishment of equity and has therefore been very popular among companies. As with a potential venture capitalist investment, firms interested

in receiving Prosoft had to prepare a business plan demonstrating the viability of the company and merit of the project. BNDES, the Brazilian Development Bank, established an agreement with Softex to analyze the merit of the applications before granting financing, making the process extremely demanding. These two developments are transforming the industry, making firms much more aggressive, focused, and generally more competitive.

16. Conversely, Ireland has strived to reverse the curse of the export market, by stimulating the growth of a domestic software industry capable of adding greater value [13,47].

17. See Helper et al. [52] for a discussion of the importance and dynamics of such links using the example of the auto industry; see Sabel [53] for a full elaboration of the related learning-by-monitoring concept.

References

1. Botelho, Antonio J. (1987). Brazil's independent computer strategy. *Technology Review*, May/June, 37–45. Reprinted in Tom Forrester (ed.), *Information Technology in the Human Context*. Cambridge, MA: MIT Press, 1989.

2. Botelho, Antonio J. (1991). The political economy of technology transfer: the institutional basis of the Brazilian informatics industry. In D. Vajpey and R. Natajaran (eds.), *Technology Transfer and Third World Countries—Some Managerial and Policy Issues*. New Delhi, India: Rathwall Publishers, pp. 279–309.

3. Tigre, Paulo (1992). Current dilemmas and future options for informatics policy. In P. Evans, C. Frischtak, and P. Tigre (eds.) *High Technology and Third World Industrialization: Brazilian Computer Policy in Comparative Perspective*. Berkeley, CA: IAS/University of California.

4. Tigre, Paulo (1995). Liberalização e capacitação tecnológica: o caso da informática pós-reserva de mercado no Brasil. In S. Schwartzman (coordenador) *Ciência e Tecnologia no Brasil: Poítica Industrial, Mercado de Trabalho e Instituições de Apoio*. Fundação Getúlio Vargas Editora.

5. Sabel, Charles F. and Zeitlin, Jonathan (1985). Historical alternatives to mass production: politics, markets and technology in nineteenth century industrialisation. *Past and Present*, 108, 133–176.

6. Sabel, Charles F. and Zeitlin, Jonathan (eds.), (1997). *World of Possibilities: Flexibility and Mass Production in Western Industrialization*. New York: Cambridge University Press.

7. Schware, Robert (1992). Software industry entry strategies for developing countries: a walking on two legs proposition. *World Development*, 20, 143–164.

8. Heeks, R. and Nicholson, B. (2002). *Success Factors and Strategies in Developing and Transitional Economies*. Development Informatics, Working Paper Series No. 12.

9. Arora, Ashish, Gambardella, Alfonso, and Torrisi, Salvatore (2001). In the footsteps of Silicon Valley? The software industry in India and Ireland and the international division of labor. In Timothy Bresnahan and Alfonso Gambardella (eds.), *Building High-Tech Clusters*. Cambridge: Cambridge University Press.

10. Heeks, Richard (1996). *India's Software Industry*. New Delhi: Sage.

11. Correa, C. (1996). Strategies for software exports from developing countries. *World Development*, 24(1), 171–182.

12. Cochran, R. (2001). Ireland: a software success story. *IEEE Software*, March/April, 87–89.
13. Crone, Mike (2002). A Profile of the Irish Software Industry. Northern Ireland Economic Research Centre. April. Irish Software Project: Report 1 (web version): www.qub.ac.uk/nierc.
14. Khavul, Susanna (2003). The emergence and evolution of Israel's software industry. London Business School, April, mimeo.
15. Teubal, Morris, Avnimelech, Gil, and Gayego, Alon (2000). Globalization and Firm Dynamics in the Israeli Software Industry: A Case Study of Data Security. August. First report of a four-year study of Israel's high tech industry.
16. Bresnahan, Timothy, Gambardella, Alfonso, and Saxenian, Anelenne (2001). Old Economy Inputs for New Economy Outputs: Cluster Formation in the New Silicon Valleys. *Industrial and Corporate Change*, December.
17. Secretaria de Economia (2002). Programa para el desarollo de la Industria de Software, Mexico.
18. World Bank (2003). ICT at a Glance Tables. Accessed www.worldbank.org/data/.
19. Instituto Nacional de Estudos e Pesquisas Educacionais (2002). *Sinopse Estatística da Educação Superior 2001*. Brasíla: Ministéro da Educação da Brasil.
20. Nasscom (2003). Various industry statistics gathered from www.nasscom.org. Last accessed on July 2004.
21. Behrens, Alfredo and D'Ippolito, Eliane (2002). Formação em Tecnologia da Informação no Brasil, oferta de mão-de-obra. Paper presented at INTERTECH 2002, ASEE.
22. Stratus (2003). Brasil Venture News. Ano IV - No. 19 Dez 02/Jan 03. Accessed through www.stratusbr.com.
23. AVCJ (2001). *Asian Venture Capital Journal*. The 2001 Guide to Venture Capital in Asia. Annual Edition.
24. Mowery, David (ed.) (1996). *The International Computer Software Industry: A Comparative Study of Industry Evolution and Structure*. Oxford, England: Oxford University Press.
25. Campbell-Kelly, Martin (2003). *From Airline Reservations to Sonic the Hedgehog: A History of the Software Industry*. Cambridge, MA: MIT Press.
26. Tigre, P.B., Botelho, A.J., Dedrick, J., and Kraemer, K.L. (2001). Brazil meets the global challenge: I.T. Policy in a post-liberalization environment. Special issue of *The Information Society* on 'The Impacts of Economic Liberalization on IT Production and Use', 17(2), 91–104.
27. Evans, Peter (1995). *Embedded Autonomy: States and Industrial Transformation*. Princeton University Press.
28. SEPIN (2002). Brazil IT Sector. Power Point presentation, November.
29. UNDP (2003). Software Success: Brazil. In *Sharing Innovative Experiences*. Volume 1—Examples of Successful Initiatives in Science and Technology in the South, pp. 59–66. Accessed http://tcdc.undp.org/tcdcweb/experiences/scitech/cases/st2braz.htm on 09/20/03.
30. SEPIN/SOFTEX (2002). Indicadores do Setor de Software Brasileiro—Uma Parceria SEPIN & SOFTEX. Power Point presentation, August.
31. SEPIN (2003). Setor de Software—Geral Revisado. Power Point presentation.
32. Gazeta Mercantil (2001). Edition for March 20, and Gazeta Mercantil (2002), edition for March 20, and edition for April 22.

33. Botelho, Antonio J., Stefanuto, Giancarlo, Spinosa, Marcio, and Veloso, Francisco (2002). *The Software Industry in Brazil: Strengthening the Knowledge Economy.* Campinas: Softex.
34. ABCR (2003). Pesquisa ABCR/Thompson—2ª etapa, accessed on September 15 at www.venturecapital.com.br/.
35. Queiroz, L. (2002). Gastos com e-Gov somaram R$2.5 bi em 2002. IDG Now! Accessed http://idgnow.terra.com.br/idgnow/business/2003/01/0035/imprimir.html in 03/10/2003.
36. MacCormack, A. and Iansiti, M. (1997). Developing products on 'Internet time': the anatomy of a flexible development process. *Harvard Business Review.* September–October, 1997.
37. Lisfield, Robert and Montes-Negret, Fernando (1996). Brazil's Efficient Payment System: A Legacy of High Inflation. World Bank Working Paper Series No. 1680: 1–38. Washington, DC: World Bank, Financial Sector Development Department. November, 1996.
38. Botelho, Antonio J. (1998). Meeting the liberalization challenge: technological learning in the Brazilian banking automation industry. *Science, Technology and Society,* 3(1), 111–128.
39. Vasconcelos, M.R. and Fucidji, J.R. (2002). Foreign Entry and Efficiency: Evidence from the Brazilian Banking Industry. Presented at the 11th International 'Tor Vergata' Conference on Banking and Finance: Monetary Integration, Markets and Regulation. December.
40. Banco Hoje (2002). Economic section, Editorial—February.
41. Personal communication (2002). Interviews with relevant companies.
42. www.fazenda.com.br.
43. CNET (2001). Governments push open-source software. News.com August 29. Last accessed on July 2004.
44. Estadao (2002). Editions for January 6 and December 15. Accessed www.estadao.com.br.
45. TI, Revista. Software Verde-Amarelo. March 31, 2004.
46. Pressconsult (2002). Accessed www.pressconsult.com.br/textos/tba/27.htm on 06/01/03.
47. Regional Technology Strategies, Inc. (2001). Information Technology Skills Shortages and Responses in Four Countries A Report to the National Assessment of Vocational Education, U.S. Department of Education. March.
48. Kraemer, K.L. and Dedrick, J. (1999). Information Technology and Productivity: Results and Policy Implications of Cross-Country Studies (February 1). Center for Research on Information Technology and Organizations. I.T. in Business. Paper 132. http://repositories.cdlib.org/crito/business/132.
49. Mckinsey (2002). U.S. Productivity Growth, 1995–2000. Mckinsey Global Institute Report. October 2001.
50. Gordon, R. (2003). Five Puzzles in the Behavior of Productivity, Investment, and Innovation. September 10, 2003 draft of chapter for World Economic Forum, Global Competitiveness Report, 2003–2004.
51. Mokyr, Joel (1990). *The Lever of Riches: Technological Creativity and Economic Progress.* New York: Oxford University Press.
52. Helper, S., MacDuffie, J. P., and Sabel, C. (2000). Pragmatic collaborations: advancing knowledge while controlling opportunism. *Industrial and Corporate Change,* 9, 443–487.

53. Sabel, Charles F. (1993). Learning by monitoring: the institutions of economic development. In Neil Smelser and Richard Swedberg (eds.), *Handbook of Economic Sociology*. Princeton, NJ: Russell Sage and Princeton University Press.

54. D'Costa, A.P. (2003). Uneven and combined development: understanding India's software exports. *World Development*, 31(1), 211–226.

55. Amsden, Alice and Chu, Wan-wen (2003). *Beyond Late Development—Taiwan's Upgrading Policies*. Cambridge, MA: The MIT Press.

56. O'Riain, Sean (2000). The flexible developmental state: globalization, information technology and the 'Celtic Tiger'. *Politics and Society*, 28(2), 157–193.

57. O'Riain, Sean (2004). *The Politics of High Tech Growth: Developmental Network States in the Global Economy*. Cambridge University Press (due in January 2004).

58. Exame Informatica (2002). Info 200. August, 2002.

6

The Chinese Software Industry

TED TSCHANG AND LAN XUE

1 Introduction

The Chinese software industry, like the China of the past, is somewhat enigmatic. Its status is difficult to determine, in part because its strengths vary considerably, and because the industry is still in its infancy. In few other places in the world has a domestic economy provided such a powerful impetus and such ample opportunities for foreign and local software firms alike. Yet the leadership of the software industry is strongly government influenced, and its development needs to be understood within the context of powerful governmental mechanisms. The Chinese software industry thus offers a strong contrast to its Indian counterpart, in terms of the role of the state and the choice of growth paths, and also in terms of language and business organization. The two emergent software industries have fundamentally different cultures. Whereas the Indian industry is primarily export driven, its domestic products market is largely dominated by multinationals. In contrast China's domestic firms command about 33 percent of its domestic market, with official policy being to increase this to 60 percent in 10 years [1].[1]

Chinese government policies, as in the past, are very supportive of science and technology. Partly as a consequence, many software and IT firms have originated in the state- or state-supported sectors. Although China's hardware manufacturing industry is better known around the world, software has become an important part of the official strategy for new industrial development.

There is a conventional belief, shared by the government and industry watchers alike, that the Chinese industry is made up largely of small firms, with weak capabilities.[2] Rampant software piracy and high employee turnover are also believed to contribute to the smaller size and weaker capabilities of China's

Ted Tschang, Singapore Management University, Lan Xue, Tsinghua University; The authors would like to thank Professor Chen ShenBin, Professor Sun JiuLin and Dr. Cai YuLin of the Chinese Academy of Sciences for their cooperation on this project, particularly in procuring and interpreting new data, as well as Ms. Amritha Mani for her tireless research assistance. The authors are also grateful to Dr. Masaru Yoshitomi and the Asian Development Bank Institute for funding the fieldwork for the study, and Professors Ashish Arora and Alfonso Gambardella for their valuable comments. The Software Industry Center at Carnegie Mellon University provided partial financial support.

software firms. In addition, Saxenian points to government and gaunxi—the network of dense personal relationships—as factors holding back the development of the Chinese software industry [3].

However, twenty years ago one might have said the same about the Indian software industry or the Chinese hardware industry, when they were also in their infancy. Instead, the story we tell in this chapter is of an industry in transition— one that is suffering its share of growing pains, but that is by no means a lost cause.[3] To understand the current state of the industry and its prospects, we also have to examine the historical roots and growth of the Chinese software industry, in particular, the government-supported nature of these capabilities. In addition, the nature of the domestic market and the manner in which it creates opportunities are also highly relevant to understanding the state of the industry. The large size and broad, rapid economic growth of the Chinese economy and its increasing use of IT can generally benefit the industry by providing demand for software. Certain sectors hold out more promise as well, because of their larger size, or because of their unique conditions. Furthermore, the uneven nature and poorer IT capabilities of many domestic customers might provide Chinese software firms with better opportunities than multinational firms to service these customers.

In addition to using a variety of secondary data sources, we also interviewed executives and collected information from a sample of small- and medium-sized firms that were focused on product development, as well as several of the larger firms. In Section 2, we will analyze the performance and composition of the industry at the aggregate level. In Section 3, we will examine the origins of a representative sample of the larger firms and better performing small firms, and how their roots in government policy have become a factor in determining their current capability. In Section 4, we will examine the nature of the market in detail, highlighting the factors that benefit the industry, by the type of sector and product. Finally, in Section 5, we will analyze the factors influencing the industry's current growth path, particularly the short- and medium-term constraints that it faces.

2   The Structure of China's Software Industry

Foreign firms currently command a majority of the Chinese software market. However, given our interest in the domestic firms, most of our statistics relate to domestic firms, which tend to sell a broad range of software, services, and hardware.

2.1   Structure

The Chinese software industry is comprised of proportionally more software firms than India, in part because of the small size of firms in China. There were 6,282 software enterprises in 2002, which represents an increase of 110 percent over the previous year. A survey of 4,500 enterprises shows that those whose sales exceed $1.21 million comprise one-fourth of the industry, while only nineteen enterprises have sales exceeding US$120 million [4]. The largest ten Chinese firms in 2000

TABLE 6.1. Number of Firms by Software and SI Sales (in USD)

	>0.12 billion	>60.5 million	>12.1 million
2001	11	16	100
2002	19	35	192
Increase	8	19	92

Source: CSIA [4].

had average sales of US$159 million, which was not too far off from the average sales of $303 million of the largest ten Indian firms in 2002; however, the Chinese numbers may also include a lot of lower-level systems integration work.

The small size of companies is also reflected in the employee statistics, as Table 6.1 shows. According to the CSIA [4], while China has 300,000 software professionals in the industry, about half of these may be at the technician level. With about 160,000 software professionals distributed across over 6,200 software companies, the average firm size is extremely small, at about twenty-five software developers.[4]

2.1.1 Classifying Domestic Software Firms. China's software firms can be loosely classified into two groups. The first, which includes many of China's largest software firms, are systems integration (SI) firms. Systems integration involves large custom projects where the software firms provide a combination of hardware and software and services, including customized software. Of the sixty-nine largest firms with over US$1.21 billion in sales in 2000 [2], thirty-two were mainly engaged in SI, while another nineteen were engaged in a mixture of SI and product development. The second type of firm focuses primarily on product development, although for various reasons, also ended up doing SI and services.

Table 6.2 shows the largest twenty firms in the industry out of a sample (of mostly large firms) that the CSIA examined in 2000.[5] As can be seen from the table, while many of the large firms were systems integrators, they also provided a wide range of services, including product development, solutions, and other services. They also operated across a wide variety of sectors (with government work being especially important to many).

For example, Tsinghua Tongfang develops and applies an array of core technologies in various areas, and has grown 'vertically' to the point where it can provide a 'one stop' solution consisting of equipment, products, and IT solutions. It has also developed horizontally across sectors, including the e-government, e-commerce, urban, and e-learning sectors. Like other Chinese firms, it has also ventured outside of the high-tech industries, being active in the energy and environment industry, architectural engineering, and urban environmental engineering. The almost endless array of activities that the largest Chinese firms are engaged in implies that their revenues are not comparable to those of the Indian software service firms. It also points to the 'revenue chasing' nature of many Chinese software firms. The 'holding company' organizational structure of typical Chinese

TABLE 6.2. Top Twenty Software Firms by 2000 Sales

Company	Rank	Software products and services	Sectors	Size	Origin	Software capability
Founder	1	Diversified IT products and services company Software products: electronic publishing, word processing, fingerprint technology, digital media (also PC hardware and peripherals, rare earth materials) Customized industry solutions for information security, banking, network integration, e-business, multimedia call centers, digital publishing, digital broadcasting	Government, insurance, postal, banking, security	5,000; >1, 000 S/W engineers	Beijing University Founded in 1986	ISO 9001
Pu Tian	2	IT products and service provider for telecoms industry (Holding company for over fifty other companies) Fixed and mobile communications products and services: including network management, services (e.g. operation support such as billing), equipment	Telecoms	>54,000 employees	State-owned Founded in 1980	—
Legend	3	Diversified IT products and services company IT services: system and security, system operation services, IT consulting Customized applications for: finance, telecom, government application, insurance (also PC products and peripherals)	Government, insurance, telecom, finance	12,000	Scientists from the Chinese Academy of Sciences Established in 1984	—

				Employees		Certification
Dong Fang (Neusoft)	4	Application software supplier and solution provider: provides comprehensive solutions, products, technology etc. Developed application systems, public platforms, middleware products and consulting, and embedded software and system products etc. Solution provider for various industries. Other activities: training, medical imaging equipment etc.	Telecommunication, electric power, finance, social insurance, government, enterprise, taxation and service, hospitals	>5,000 employees	Academics from local university Founded in 1991	—
CS&S	5	Specializes in software product development, systems integration, information services, software outsourcing. Technology and products: operating systems, machine translation software, information security products, ERP, supply chain management (SCM), finance, e-commerce, miscellaneous business (office automation), middleware	Taxation, railway, telecom, government, medical, others (military, finance, transportation, postal-service, trading, tourism and tobacco etc.)	2,020	State-owned, set up by Planning and Development Commission Established in 1990	ISO 9001
Pansky	6	(Information for: Pansky Sci-Tech—subsidiary of Pansky Holding Int. Ltd.) Products and solutions for: banking, international clearance business information, airport information systems (IS). Airline flight operation systems, securities transaction system, taxation	Banking, securities, aviation, taxation and social security	700	Shareholders: CICC, Morgan Stanley, Singapore Government, AB (Sweden), China Bank of Construction Founded 1995	—

TABLE 6.2. (*Continued*)

Company	Rank	Software products and services	Sectors	Size	Origin	Software capability
Tsinghua Tong Fang	7	Developer of technology and solutions Develops core technologies for information systems, computer systems and broadband telecommunications Provides solutions and equipment for: e-government, e-commerce, digital city initiative, e-learning, etc.	Two main industries are information industry and energy and environment	—	Academics from Tsinghua University (with support from state leaders)	—
Yan Tai Dong Fang	8	Yan Tai Dongfang Electronics Information Industry Co. Integrates R&D, manufacturing and support for electric power automation products	Electric power	2,021 technicians	State-owned Started in 1983	ISO 9001
CVIC	9	Software development and systems integration: 40 copyrighted products including industry application software, infrastructure software, and other digital products (e.g. broadcasting, middleware, finance)	Banking, transport, government, TV stations, retail	>600[a]	Founded in 1991	—
Sichuan TOP Group	10	Application software and complete solutions for major industries Products: middleware, database application systems, embedded Linux operating systems, e-government administration information systems, ERP software, e-tax information systems, OA software etc.	Government, finance, and securities, telecommunications, transport, petroleum, hotels, medicine, construction	>6,000 [Top S/W had 788 in 2001]	Academics from the University of Electronic Science and Technology of China (UESTC) Founded in 1992	ISO 9001 SEI-CMM3

	No.	Activities	Sectors	Employees	Ownership	Certification
		Services: networking, technical support, IT management consulting SI for: software R&D, information services for supply chain management, vocational training and education in IT, operations services Other activities: computer hardware, LED display systems, digital precision technology, IT education, IT industry parks, software outsourcing services, ecology and gardening services				
UFSoft Co. Ltd.	11	Major vendor of management (including financial) and ERP software for industry management ERP Systems, consulting, solutions for various sectors (see sectors column)	e.g. e-government, manufacturing, finance, circulation service	>3,000 employees (600 in software development)	Private Founded in 1988 by ex-government employee	—
Kingdee	12	Develops enterprise applications: e.g. ERP/CRM/SCM, knowledge management, e-commerce packages, middleware software	Manufacturing, telecom, e.g. financial, transportation, energy, real estate, and government	>2,200	Private Established predecessor company in 1993	CMM-3 (Dec. 2002) ISO 9001—2000 (2001)
Tai Ji	13	—	—	—	—	—
Nanjing Luan Chuang	14	—	—	—	—	—

TABLE 6.2. (*Continued*)

Company	Rank	Software products and services	Sectors	Size	Origin	Software capability
Beida Jade Bird Group	15	Holding company including Jade Bird Sci-Tech Universal: core business is embedded software products. Also developing MEMS-based (microelectronic machinery) products, IT training, etc. Products: global positioning system (GPS) application and application specific integrated circuit (ASIC), network security, smart card, wireless fire alarm (based on own software development (CASE) system)	—	180 (91 R&D staff) (Jade Bird Sci-Tech Universal only)	Beijing University spin-off (Government supported)	—
Hua Dong	16	—	—	—	—	—
Tian Cai	17	—	—	—	—	—
Digital China	18	IT products distributor and systems integrator Major activities are: distribution of IT products, systems integration and networking products; for supply chain management, S/W and IT services, and networking solutions Systems integration: application software includes 'Smart Banking' product, 'Smart Boss' billing system, taxation management, ERP systems Design, development and sales of networking products and delivery of technical services	Telecom, finance, government, manufacturing	3,800	Spun off from Legend in 2001	—
Shanghai Ji Suan	19	—	—	—	—	—
HS Digital	20	—	—	—	—	—

[a] Author's interview.

Source: SW Firms Sales 2000, CSIA [2].

TABLE 6.3. Largest Packaged Software Vendors by
Revenue and Market Share

	Mill US	%
IBM	77.99	6.08
Microsoft	65.07	5.07
Oracle	58.28	4.55
Sybase	30.93	2.41
Informix	26.33	2.05
Computer Associates	25.74	2.01
UFSoft	23.30	1.82
Novell	21.49	1.68
Lotus	17.53	1.37
Kingdee	16.25	1.27

Source: IDC (2001). *China Software Market Overview,
2000–2005.* IDC # CN380204H, June 2001.

firms also allows firms to expand by adding independent business units that are
very different from one another.

Two other points worth noting are the number of companies that were university
or state-supported spin-offs, and the low level of software capability in the overall industry. Capability was defined by what the industry itself uses, which was
either some level of organizational capability, based on the Software Engineering
Institute's (SEI) Capability Maturity Model (from level one to five, where five
is the highest level of attainment), or achievement of the International Standards
Organization (ISO) 9000 quality standard.

2.1.2 Foreign Competition in China and the Major Software Vendors. Finally,
a number of major multinational corporations are also in China competing in
the software products market. Most foreign multinationals either sell financial or
enterprise software (e.g. SAP), middleware, and enterprise solutions (e.g. IBM),
or packaged software for desktops (e.g. Microsoft). However, since most multinationals are still exploring the Chinese market, they have not created strong local
operations dedicated to localizing and customizing their software. This provides
opportunities for domestic firms at the lower end of the market.

As shown in Table 6.3, of the ten largest packaged software vendors in China,
the largest are the multinationals, and only two are Chinese—UFSoft and Kingdee.
These two are the largest accounting vendors in China, but like many other
financial/accounting software firms, they have moved into other types of management software such as enterprise resource planning (ERP) software. Saxenian
notes that both of these companies benefit from the preferential purchasing policies
of the government [3].

2.2 The Domestic Market

As with the Brazilian software industry, the Chinese software industry relies heavily on the huge market of users and domestic producers (see Chapter 5; [5]). The

rapid and fairly diverse industrial growth of China has led to a large surge in domestic demand. As of 2000, China's software comprised 37.9 percent of the overall computer industry, but was still only 0.67 percent of the country's GDP.[6] The actual size of the software industry varies substantially depending on which statistics are used. For the aggregate statistics, we use the Chinese Software Industry Association's figures, since they have a longer time series. However, these statistics reflect an industry that is far larger than do those compiled by others such as IDC. For instance, as shown in Table 6.4, CSIA reported that China had US$3 billion as revenue from sales of software products in 2000, and $4 billion from services, while IDC reports $0.935 billion from services and $1.057 billion from packaged products. Many of the largest CSIA firms report being mainly systems integrators which suggest that there is a large systems integration component reflected in the CSIA's numbers but not in the IDC figures.

The share of products as a proportion of the industry has steadily increased, to the point where it has just exceeded that of services. The proportion of export-based output has more than doubled, reaching 11.27 percent in 2002, which is still low compared to the 76 percent reported for India in the fiscal year 2001–02 [6].

Finally, in Table 6.5, a further product-wise category breakup shows rapid growth in all three categories.[7] The rate of growth of sales of total software products has been increasing over the last few years.

2.2.1 Location of Industry. Most of the industry is concentrated in the largest cities, particularly Beijing, which has a large proportion of the firms and output,

TABLE 6.4. The Chinese Software Industry's Sales by Major Sectors (in billion USD)

Year	Software products	Services	Exports	Software total	Products as % of SW	Services as % of SW	Exports as % of SW
1999	2.202	2.886	0.254	5.342	41.22	54.02	4.76
2000	2.880	3.896	0.399	7.175	40.13	54.30	5.56
2001	3.993	4.913	0.726	9.632	41.46	51.01	7.54
2002	6.140	5.670	1.500	13.31	46.13	42.60	11.27

Source: CSIA [4].

TABLE 6.5. Growth in Sales of Types of Products for Selected Years (billion USD)

	1992	1996	1998	2000	2001	2002
System software	0.019	0.103	0.211	0.402	0.605	0.823
Supporting software	0.065	0.242	0.434	0.600	0.991	1.338
Application software	0.155	0.768	1.025	1.876	2.397	3.978
Total	0.240	1.113	1.670	2.880	3.993	6.140
Growth over preceding year (%)	330	35	23	31	38.7	53.8

Sources: CSIA [2,4].

followed by cities such as Shanghai, Shenzhen, Jinan, and Xian. Many of these cities are in the prosperous eastern part of the country, where much of the high-tech industries are located and where the bulk of foreign investments are made, but increasingly, other industrial cities such as Xian in the west and Shenyang in the northeast are gaining recognition for their strong software firms and industries. These areas are characterized by the presence of universities with strong IT programs, government support for the industry, and vibrant industrial or commercial activity. In some cases such as Neusoft (also known as Tongfang) in Shenyang, or TOP in Chengdu, a single large firm rather than a concentration of firms dominates the city. These large firms play such a significant role in the region's software activity that the mere *numbers* of firms would not be a meaningful measure of software activity.

3   Rise of the Chinese Software Industry

In addition to having a direct influence on software R&D and the formation of software firms, the government was also deeply involved in how the hardware industry grew. This has ramifications for software firms in two ways. First, some of the larger hardware firms have developed software arms, or are combining software and hardware in systems integration activities. Second, some hardware manufacturers provide business to software firms, with needs for software (to run on their products) ranging from desktop applications to embedded software.

3.1   The Origins of Software Firms

3.1.1   The Early Hardware Firms: An Exemplar for Software. The earliest and most well-known hardware companies have had their origins in a variety of sources, with the more technology intensive ones coming from the various government research institutes, universities, and 'green-field' start-ups. In the case of the hardware sector, case studies of four prototypical firms and their sources of formation were compiled by Lu [7]. The firms were:

(1) Founder, a private enterprise which commercialized university-researched technologies;
(2) Legend, a spin-off from the government-funded research institutes in the Chinese Academy of Sciences;
(3) Great Wall, a spin-off from a state run firm;
(4) The Stone Group, a green-field start-up.

These enterprises all benefited from government-supported research. Founder, which got its start developing electronic publishing systems, relied partly on research from the government-funded Project 748 at Beijing University, which was created by the State Planning Commission to deal with a perceived critical need in 1974 for a Chinese language information processing system based on

Chinese character fonts. Founder has now become dominant in the electronic publishing business and in PC manufacturing. Similarly, Legend, which started out making PC language cards and is now a full-fledged PC manufacturer, was initially established as a 'reaction by a state research institute to the changes in the state's science and technology policy' [7]. All eleven founders were from the Chinese Academy of Sciences' (CAS) Institute for Computing Technology (ICT).

Thus, through the provision of intellectual capital, training, research funding and capability, and incentives, the Chinese government has had a profound influence on firms of every provenance. It has also contributed to the hardware (and broader IT) industry by its direct involvement in state run computer companies. Some, like Great Wall, were eventually privatized as successful PC makers. Perhaps more important is the fact that a number of the early hardware firms have also moved into software, at first as offshoots of their earlier software competencies or systems integration activities (integrating hardware and software). In the case of Legend, a separate entity—Digital China—has been newly spun-off as a software group.

3.1.2 Origins of Software Firms. The preceding discussion of hardware firms is illuminating, since the Chinese government exerted an early influence on the software industries via means similar to those used in the hardware sector.

Government sponsorship of the IT industry's development is also reflected in the origins of software firms. As shown in Table 6.2, of the approximately thirty firms in the sample we interviewed, four came out of the CAS, another seven came out of the universities and three had government origins, making the proportion of our sample having state and university origins about 50 percent.[8] Equally striking is the fact that of the largest twenty firms, nine out of thirteen (for which we had data) had government or university origins, as shown in Table 6.2 (not including Digital China). Most of the others that we had data on had origins in the private sector. In the rest of this section, we examine the firms that we interviewed for obtaining more details on their origins.

3.1.3 CAS Spin-offs. Software firms that are spin-offs from research institutes such as the Chinese Academy of Science institutes or universities tend to have a stronger basis in research than would firms with origins in the commercial sector. Indeed, most CAS spin-off firms have gotten more involved in high-end software sectors and products, such as security software and operating systems. Examples of such firms from our sample include firms that appeared to match the model of hardware firms (represented by Legend) spun off from the CAS institutes. Three software firms were first gestated in, then directly spun out of CAS institutes (Red Flag, CASS, and Supermap), while at least two more—Anyware and Beijing Listen—relied heavily on CAS talent. All also had to rely on government or private capital to help them start up.

The fact that the two companies that produced operating systems—CASS and Red Flag—had CAS backgrounds indicates the importance of scientific knowledge to the production of operating systems (OSs).[9] It also indicates the importance that the government placed on the development of key technologies. CASS's original staff consisted partly of a hundred personnel trained at Beijing University as well as at various American universities. It now has five subsidiary companies making everything from operating systems to enterprise resource planning and e-commerce software. In 1999, CASS designed its own Hopen embedded operating system, and has leveraged this to great effect in the electronics manufacturing sector.

Red Flag is a small company employing about 100 people. Their experience with Unix (the foundation for Linux) goes back to 1979, when CAS Professor Zhong XiChang started his research on the subject. In 1999, Red Flag began to research Linux, an open source software substitute for Microsoft's Windows and other proprietary systems, and by 2000, the company was in operation.[10] Red Flag was co-funded by the Chinese Academy of Sciences' Software Research Institute (CASS) and Shanghai New Margin Venture Capital in June 2000, with additional venture capital from the government-linked CCID Capital.[11] Continued government support helps to sustain them, along with some commercial successes (discussed later).

3.1.4   University Spin-offs. Many of the more recent software arrivals have come out of universities. In our sample of about thirty firms, at least seven arose directly from universities, started either by students (two firms) or faculty (five firms). The firms spun off by universities (i.e. started by university students or faculty) were Grand Horizon, SLJ, TongRan (or Neusoft), ASTI, Calkai, Kingstar, and Human Technology. In addition, three firms had split off from parent companies that were formerly university-affiliated, namely, Digital China (from Legend), But One, and Tsinghua DASCOM, and some firms were setup by recent university PhDs who had decided to become entrepreneurs.

As with the CAS spin-offs, we might expect that the spin-offs from universities would typically have stronger technology or access to it than the average commercial firm. Our interviews appear to bear this out. Fudan Grand Horizon was established in 1988 by a group of professors from Fudan University located in Shanghai, one of the country's leading universities. The lead management of the firm as well as faculty and students of the university continue to have joint appointments and other close ties with it. However, like many companies of its size, Fudan Grand Horizon has also diversified into multiple product lines: network security, education and distance learning, broadband and streaming media, and touch screen technology.

3.1.5   Other Origins. Finally, other sources of software firms exist, including private entrepreneurs from other sectors who decide to fund software firms. Some firms in our sample have come into being thanks to private entrepreneurs or venture firms putting in the seed capital to start a company. At least one came about partly from a former government employee who had some connections to start with. The venture capital industry in China is such that many actors, including the government, the association/consultancies such as CSIA and CCID (which are both government connected), and even other industries such as the utilities and telecoms companies, provide 'venture' funding.

3.1.6 Role of the Government. Given that the state continues to fund most of the significant scientific activity, and that most of the best people were working in state-funded organizations, it is only natural that a significant part of the industry has had its origins in a variety of state- or state-supported institutions. As much as 30 percent of enterprises are government-owned [2]. When spin-offs from universities and research institutes (i.e. institutions with state-supported origins) are counted, one gets an even larger figure.

3.1.7 The General Role of the Government in Forming Technological Capabilities. Through its long-standing programs on high-technology fostering and incubation, China created the preconditions for some of its more important industries, including the hardware industry. However, the role of the government itself has evolved from a central planning/state-controlled one in the period 1978–85 to an innovation system focused on more advanced R&D (and not just the state sector) during 1985–91, and finally, to the market-oriented reforms of 1992 to the present [8]. Saxenian [3] notes that the reforms from 1978 to 1992 were meant to address the problems of weak R&D, poor technical skills, inefficiency, and an overly exclusive focus on defense and heavy technologies. This was done by seeking to acquire foreign technology, through foreign investment and training, by promoting university-based research, and through high-technology funding schemes. The market reforms begun in 1992 involved significant regional experimentation where government control was significantly loosened, foreign investment dramatically accelerated, and the technology sector opened up to other (non-state) forms of ownership.

In aggregate, the government has helped to significantly increase the R&D resources of the economy. The total number of 'science and technology personnel' increased from 2.29 million (including 1.32 million scientists and engineers) in 1991 to 2.91 million (including 1.60 million scientists and engineers) in 1999. Total domestic expenditures on science and technology went up from $3.68 billion in 1990 to $10.7 billion in 1995, although this expenditure as a proportion of GDP actually went down from 1.72 to 1.52 percent in the same period. The government share in total domestic science and technology expenditures went down from 45.67 to 34.13 percent, reflecting the stronger role of the private sector, and the government's transition from a controlling to a guiding role [8]. Between 1995 and 2000, the gross expenditure on R&D rose from $4.22 billion to $10.8 billion, moving expenditure as a percent of GDP from 0.6 to 1.01 percent over the same period [9]. However, these numbers overstate R&D activity. Of the R&D institutions in operation in 1995, about 51 percent did not take part in R&D activities. Of 799 institutions that were government-supported, 82,000 of the 320,000 staff were full-time R&D staff, and of these only 50,000 were actually employed on R&D tasks [8].

The pace of reform accelerated through the 1990s, and many state research institutes, including the CAS institutes, were pushed to obtain their own funding sources or risk going under. New market oriented policies like tax credits were instituted and technology-picking was abandoned. The CAS Institute of Software which performed fundamental theoretical and applied research reduced its workforce from 500 to 125 between 1999 and 2001 [3]. In fact, the total number of CAS institutes also shrank as a result of mergers and job reductions.[12] Another recent development was the development of National Engineering Research Centers, of which 100 out of a planned 200 had been established by 2000 [8].

For the more fundamental technology and scientific fields, perhaps the most significant development of the reform period was the government's funding of a broad array of basic research projects, started during the science and technology reforms of the 1980s. This was aimed at creating an impetus for developing more advanced, market-oriented technologies. These included the setting up in 1986 of the Ministry of Science and Technology's National High Technology R&D Program, commonly known as the '863' program, which had funded 5,200 projects and 230 topics by 2000 with a total of $1.21 billion of government funds (a further $1.21 billion came from enterprises and other sources) [3,9]. More recently, the research and tenure system underwent fundamental overhaul. Older researchers have been retired, and tenure for all but a small proportion of research faculty has been replaced by a system of renewable contracts. Many research institutes face simultaneous cutbacks and encouragement to seek funding from the private market and from international sources.

Another major program that also had much to do with IT was the Torch Program, which was started in 1988 in order to develop high-tech industrial zones, market high-tech products, promote international cooperation with China's high-tech industries, and train and attract talent [9]. The Torch program had surpassed the 863 program by 1999, having supported 2,742 projects with $3.51 billion in funds. It orchestrated the construction of nineteen software parks[13] around the country, requiring local authorities to submit their own policies for encouraging the growth of the local software industry, and then granting approval for the parks.

Some of the government research projects actually became the basis for Founder, Legend, and other by now leading hardware companies. More recently, the government started a number of 'Golden' projects to expand the country's e-commerce, infrastructure, and various applications in e-government areas [10]. There are now twelve of these Golden projects, which are in different stages of development. These include the Golden Bridge—China's own information superhighway; Golden Card—a nationwide financial network to jump-start the use of electronic money; Golden Customs—to let users calculate export taxes, settle foreign exchange accounts, and check export statistics; and Golden Tax—to computerize the tax-collection system.

3.1.8 Procurement Policies. Another government tool commonly used in China, including at the regional and municipal levels, is government procurement. There are by now a range of policies addressed to fostering the software sector's competitiveness. Procurement by government was about 14.2 percent of the overall software market in 2002 [11]. A considerable amount of this is for systems integration work, although the use of packaged software is increasing. The government maintains a list of key software enterprises, numbering 106 by the end of 2002, which can enjoy preferential tax treatment [4, p. 91]. In recent years, the government has used procurement policies strategically to further support specific firms deemed to be doing software in the national interest, including Red Flag's Linux, CASS's Hopen, and Beijing University's Jade Bird and its database management program (intended to rival Oracle's).

This strategy has also been effectively implemented in many cities like Shanghai and regions like Shandong. Many of the larger systems integrators like Wenda in Shanghai and Top in Chengdu have benefited directly from this policy. Recently, the government has reinforced this by putting in place a number of high-level directives targeting the software industry. The most prominent of these has been the State Council's Document Number 18, called the 'Notice of Certain Policies to Promote the Software and Integrated Circuit Industry Development' [12].[14] By putting these two industries in the limelight, the state council was effectively recognizing that they were so crucial to the development of China's other industries as to merit preferential treatment.[15] To accomplish its objectives, the central government of China will invest more than $0.48 billion during the period covered by the tenth Five Year Plan. Of this sum $0.12 billion will be used to support the development of the software industry; and the remaining $0.36 billion will be applied through the electronic information industry development fund, the '863' fund on special items, national outlays on science and technology to tackle 'key problems' etc., though not especially for software development.

3.1.9 Inefficiencies of State Intervention. Not all government policies necessarily have favorable outcomes.[16] The government continues to strategically target and support selected firms and software sectors, but in recent years, the results have been mixed at best. While government procurement in some product markets may have been more beneficial by way of getting some firms started, too much support may make them wholly dependent. Systems integrators that have relied too much on large government contracts may not be able to foster other customers, and so their growth may be limited in the future. Many provincial and municipal government systems integration contracts favor local firms, which appear to cause some of these firms to be continually dependent on these large contracts. According to one government source, the Shanghai-based firm Wenda was originally an institute staffed with CAS trained people, but still continues with its largely systems integration focus, aided by sizeable government contracts. This situation of firms having comfortable relations with government or other larger customers for 'easy project work' can cause them to be less competitive in evolving markets. Finally, a number of the newer software parks (many of which are privately invested and supported by local governments) unfortunately appear to be more focused on the real-estate development aspects of the business, or have over-invested in real estate and building infrastructure, sometimes in regions without any clear edge in software capabilities.[17]

4 The Domestic Market and the Growth of Software Technologies and Sectors

The main factors supporting the growth of the domestic software industry thus far have been government support and the domestic market. The domestic market results from the Chinese economy's spectacular growth over the last decades. Since 1978, the Chinese economy has reportedly grown an average of 9.5 percent, and is projected to be one of the world's main growth engines for the foreseeable future [13].[18] The economy itself has undergone major structural changes, going from a mainly agrarian to a largely manufacturing base, with growing service sectors. Although China's exports are considered by many countries to be a competitive threat, in 2001 nearly 80 percent of its demand was still internally generated, presenting opportunities for domestic and foreign firms alike. Nevertheless, the share of exports in total demand is continually rising. Although China's exports of $266 billion in 2001 were the sixth largest in the world in absolute terms, up to 50 percent of its exports were made by foreign enterprises, and up to half of its exports relied on imported intermediate products.

With its sustained growth and advancing economy since the 1980s, China's domestic need for information technology (IT) has increased and provided opportunities for domestic IT firms, including software firms. In general, the economy has also been undergoing a transition, from a labor intensive one to one that is based on productivity enhancements, not the least being enhancements based on IT. Business and government spending has been especially significant on infrastructure, including IT infrastructure ranging from computers to software. In addition to the large enterprises, small- and medium-sized enterprises are becoming a major source of demand for IT in China. The rise in household incomes has also led to an increase in household spending on computers and other durable goods. Installed personal computers in both households and businesses reached nearly 21.7 million in 2001, up 35 percent from the previous year [1]. Of the desktop PC sales in 2001, 39.6 percent were sold to consumers [14]. Finally, the industrial production of products requiring software as intermediate inputs (e.g. software to run the hardware) has been increasing along with the economy and its exports.

4.1 Economic Advantages for the Software Industry

The overall growth of the Chinese economy can be an advantage for the development of the software industry in different ways. As shown in Figure 6.1, three firm size and strategy effects are possible. First, the large size of the economy can provide opportunities for the emergence of sizeable software firms. Second, widespread growth across sectors allows software firms to enter into a number of them, diversifying the software sector as well as individual firms. Third, with the

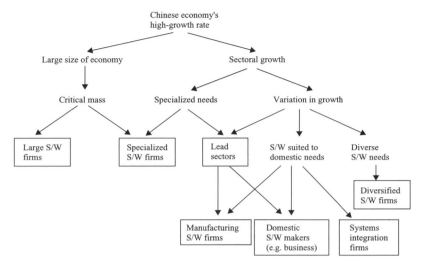

FIGURE 6.1. The Possible Impacts of the Chinese Economy's Growth on Software Firms

growth of individual sectors, software firms also have the opportunity to specialize in types of software applications specific to those sectors.

The evidence we have collected suggests that most of these effects are indeed at work in the Chinese software industry. We are seeing firms of significant size emerging, and firms emerging in a diversity of sectors. Although most of the larger firms are systems integrators, this is a consequence of large customers' needs for IT. The entry of a large number of firms has also made the market highly competitive, which may cause individual firms to either try to diversify across software sectors, or to specialize in specific areas. In our interview sample (see Appendix), some firms have chosen to specialize while others have chosen to diversify. Other reports corroborated this by showing software enterprises as focusing more on specific segments, as well as shifting themselves towards higher-value-added products [15].

4.2 Major Factors Creating Advantages for the Software Industry

Our fieldwork has illustrated at least five factors relating to the economy and its software use, and which are distinctive to China's software industry (as also partly indicated in Figure 6.1):

- Lead software-using sectors
- The need for software infrastructure and products
- Manufacturing and other opportunities for software products
- Local business needs
- Systems integration as a vehicle for software

Each of these is discussed in the sections that follow.

4.3   The Leading Software Using Sectors

The main software using sectors are shown by industry in Table 6.6. According to the table, it appears that banking/finance and communications (including telecommunications), followed by government, consumer, and manufacturing, are the largest sectors in terms of annual revenue. Domestic firms are doing particularly well in financial software. In part, the demand comes from banks which need a variety of software to effectively restructure their operations, including back office software like Enterprise Resource Management (ERM), network development, Customer Relationship Management (CRM), and data warehousing. Commercial enterprises like banks, and especially small- and medium-sized enterprises, have idiosyncratic processes and legacy systems that are difficult to change [16]. This may give Chinese software firms making industry-specific applications an edge over multinational vendors. Indeed, 60 percent of the accounting software, an area known for its highly local practices, is made by two domestic firms—UFSoft and Kingdee [12].

In terms of both size and growth rate, the telecommunications industry is one of the more important sectors, and projections show that it will continue to grow and will eventually surpass finance as one of the largest sectors. The hardware

TABLE 6.6.   IT Market by Industry Verticals (US$ M)

Industry	Software revenue in 2000	% of total software revenue	Software growth rate
Banking	144.2	13.6	21.5
Communications and Media	189.5	17.9	31.0
Construction	3.4	0.3	8.4
Discrete Mfg	70.3	6.7	22.2
Financial Markets	72.2	6.8	21.5
Health Care	20.5	1.9	130.3
Insurance	35.6	3.4	257.3
Process Mfg	3.3	0.3	23.7
Resource Industries	20.7	2.0	104.2
Retail	8	0.8	71.4
Services	5.3	0.5	8.9
Transportation and Transportation Services	37.5	3.5	17.1
Utilities	18.4	1.7	43.8
Wholesale	11.3	1.1	170.4
Education	63.9	6.0	59.1
Government	187.6	17.7	29.5
Consumer	165.4	15.6	67.2
Total	1,057.1	—	—

Source: IDC (2001). *PRC IT Spending and Industry Segmentation*. IDC # AP380126H, Aug. 2001.

component of the telecom IT growth appears to be slowing down, and is being outpaced by software applications such as billing and customer service systems, and network management [17]. The telecoms area in China is still maturing, so the lack of standardized processes in many telecom firms means that they still cannot 'absorb' packaged software to the extent that US telecom firms can. Consequently, software firms have to do more systems integration for these telecom companies.[19] Other infrastructure sectors, such as transport, will see similar growth patterns.

4.4   Software Infrastructure and Products

With the growth of the both consumer and commercial demand (across the user sectors identified previously) has come a substantial demand for software infrastructure such as operating systems, middleware and security software, and applications software. The multinationals appear to dominate some areas of the market, particularly the Windows-based environment. However, some local companies have managed to develop products in niche areas. Companies such as Kingsoft have advantages in application areas that require more intimate knowledge of the Chinese language or cultural domain. In software infrastructure areas such as middleware, private companies such as TongTech are doing well, even with the intense competition from multinationals. On the other hand, in areas like operating systems and security software, a combination of strong government support and private demand is creating opportunities for domestic software companies such as Red Flag (which makes an open source Linux-based operating system). The government is increasingly targeting strategic areas such as Linux, security, middleware, electronic government systems, and even Internet videogames for such support. The goal has been to insulate the country from the security problems inherent in using commercial (US) software, as well as to gain a share of the very large market and to ensure that China has its own 'technology base'. Some technologies such as security products and operating systems have the broadest government support and are the largest in terms of revenue.

4.5   Manufacturing: The Rise of Embedded Software and New Opportunities

With its strong growth and substantial capabilities, the manufacturing sector offers opportunities for China's software firms. There is increasing demand for embedded software in all varieties of electronic products, ranging from personal data assistants (PDAs) and mobile phones to more intelligent household appliances and automobiles. Thus, a number of Chinese firms are heavily involved in this application area. The availability of substantial engineering talent is one requirement for success, as is the availability of software engineering talent, both of which China has in abundance.

    In some sense, this is a promising area for Chinese firms, some of which have developed good technical know-how but have poorer competitive assets or market positions. Working with China's manufacturers may give them a better insight into how to fulfill requirements, much in the same way that Taiwanese contract manufacturers learnt from their best customers. CASS produces operating systems for a variety of manufactured products. CASS's Hopen OS, based on their earlier work on the Unix operating system now competes favorably with Microsoft for Chinese customers who manufacture handheld and other smaller electronic devices. In part, the Hopen OS's penetration of the market was due to the software being specifically developed for devices requiring less functionality and with lower memory requirements and cost, and being flexible enough to tailor to a variety of products.[20] They have managed to secure contracts with large Chinese companies, for example, Legend's lower-end products, and a maker of television sets. This was an opportunity typical of a market which tends to offer less advanced but lower cost products than those on offer in developed countries.

Recently, the Hopen system was further developed as the NUWA project,[21] in anticipation of the increasing market for embedded software. The NUWA project focuses on developing the NUWA-Hopen OS as a basic embedded software platform to work across a variety of information appliances. Like the TRON system in Japan, the NUWA product is a pervasive computing platform which allows intelligence to be embedded in a variety of household products, along with the ability to communicate among each other. Currently CASS is actively cooperating with chip manufacturers (including Motorola, Panasonic, National Semiconductor, and Winbond), appliance manufacturers (e.g. Legend, ChangHong, and TCL), and software developers in other fields such as mobile computing platforms, home information environments, communication computing platforms, in-car computing platforms, industry/business controlling platforms, and e-commerce. In one example of cooperation, CASS collaborated with Legend to develop the 'TianJi810', which was used in PDA products. Another application is TCL's HiD299e high-definition TV, which uses the NUWA Hopen embedded real time operating system (RTOS).

While CASS operates as a contract supplier, a few other firms are attempting vertically integrated strategies. For instance, the TOP Group (within which TOP software is a unit) has, invested 300 million yuan (US$36.3 million) in manufacturing facilities in its home city of Chengdu, with an annual production capacity of 1 million cell phones, 500,000 palm computers, and 200,000 laptop computers [18].

Another well-known vertically integrated telecoms manufacturer is Huawei. Modern advanced networking equipment such as switches can comprise 50 percent or more of embedded software. Since software is critical to their success, Huawei is making strategic investments in software, including a large development center with over 400 engineers in Bangalore. They set up shop in Bangalore as opposed to developing their software in China suggesting that in the medium term at least, Chinese software process capability, even in embedded applications, may not be as good as that of India's. Our interviews with Huawei executives in Bangalore showed that they believed that India's process capability was superior to China's, even though the Chinese were more advanced in terms of telecoms domain knowledge and had at least as much knowledge of software theory.

China's software companies are developing software for a broad range of applications, including manufactured and industrial products. For instance, the Shandong Luneng Jicheng Company (SLJ) develops software products for electrical network automation, for example, the automation of electric power dispatching. While their products currently only support the electric power industry, they will be branching out into other industries. They have only two or three domestic competitors in China at the moment, but they also compete at the high end against foreign companies like Siemens and ABB, sometimes with favorable results.

4.6   Do Local Business Practices Provide a Window of Opportunity for Software Industry Growth? The Case of Enterprise Resource Management Software

Small- and medium-sized enterprises (SME) are becoming a major source of demand for IT in China. However, in 2001 about 50 percent of SMEs still had not been computerized to any degree whatsoever, and only 4 percent had adopted IT applications [19]. In fact, most companies—large and small—are not sophisticated users of IT. This requires software firms to sell a mixture of products and services in order to help such customers. Often, these less sophisticated users will need their software applications customized, and this has benefited local software firms.[22]

A case in point is enterprise resource management software—one of the major software product areas in use across a variety of business sectors. While the ERM sector is not the biggest sector overall, it is the largest sector of the applications market.[23] The enterprise resource planning market consists of applications that deal with financial management, human resource management, distribution and inventory control, and production and operations. According to IDC, the more advanced part of this sector—ERPs—only made up 3.8 percent of China's total software market in 2000, but the ERP sector was growing at the rate of 26.9 percent in 2000. This reflected not only the gradual growth of the software customer enterprises' capability, but also the fact that enterprise software was being adopted in a broad range of software sectors. In 2000, the largest user of ERPs was the manufacturing industry, at 68.2 percent of the total ERP market, followed by the distribution, transportation, telecom, and health industries [22].

Various estimates put the number of SMEs in China between 8.6 million and 20 million, and the number of large enterprises at 15,000.[24] This provides a broad and substantial business user base. Whereas 60 percent of Fortune 500 companies have an ERP installed, only 2 percent of the top 500 Chinese firms have one, suggesting that there is considerable market potential [22]. This base of users is expected to expand the domestic (packaged) software market from

TABLE 6.7. China ERP Software Market Revenue
Breakdown by Vendor, 1999–2000

	Mill US	% share
SAP	14.52	29.74
QAD	4.40	9.01
Oracle	4.21	8.62
Fourth Shift	3.30	6.76
Symix	2.60	5.32
SSA	2.21	4.53
Beijing RIAMB	1.93	3.95
CASE	1.73	3.54
Attention	1.48	3.03
Kingdee	1.41	2.89
Others	11.04	22.61

Source: IDC [22].

US$10 billion to $100 billion in 5–8 years [2]. However, as noted earlier, many of these enterprises have difficulty absorbing software. Many enterprises and their top management, especially state-owned enterprises, do not have a good under-standing of their own business processes, let alone a good idea of what ERPs can do for them. Furthermore, their IT budgets are small and internal IT staff weak. All these make successful implementation difficult [22]. Many enterprises value service more than anything else, and require ERP vendors to have strong customer support, something Chinese vendors are more prepared to do than multi-nationals, which would rather just sell a product with minimal additional cost of localization.

Multinationals like Oracle and SAP dominate the high-end of ERP. Table 6.7 shows that of the top ten ERP makers, all but three were multinationals.[25] In 2000, whereas the top ERP supplier—SAP—was used in 290 sites; Scala, the leading supplier in terms of number of sites (but not in the top ten in terms of revenue), was used in 315 sites; and the leading domestic supplier, Beijing RIAMB, was installed in seventy sites. However, this gives Beijing RIAMB a revenue per site of $27,571, versus $76,421 for SAP and $30,730 for Oracle (which took third place in terms of number of sites).[26] This sug-gests that in the current market, the top local suppliers' capabilities for handling projects of a certain size are actually matched with the foreign suppliers' capabilities [22].

Chinese software firms compete heavily with each other at the 'lower' end of areas such as office automation and basic ERPs, but revenues are harder to build up because these clients are less sophisticated or well-off and tend to require uniquely developed projects or much handholding (i.e. consulting or customer service) which works against the software firms achieving scale economies. Many firms that we interviewed were developing or getting into the development of

ERPs, including CASS, But One, Calkai, Digital China, and ChongRan. The ease of entry into some subsectors like ERPs could be due to the technology barrier being relatively lower in these sectors, although domain knowledge is quite important. This results in heavy competition among local firms.

With the growth in use of ERP has come a gradual deepening of IT capability in some Chinese software firms, reflected in their development of more sophisticated products. For instance, in 2001, Kingdee offered a more advanced product with twenty-two application modules and ten modules with web-based capability [23]. They also allowed upgrading to supply chain management and customer relationship management modules, which gave their domestic customers an upgrade path from simpler capabilities to advanced ones. At the same time, ERPs are used in many sectors, so the heterogeneity of business practices across these sectors has caused some local ERP software firms to specialize in specific sectors. Two examples are CASS's ERP division which focuses on manufacturing concerns, and But One's ERP products which are geared to the telecoms sector.

4.7 Systems Integration and the Fulfillment of Highly Customized Needs

Systems integration has tended to dominate software development in many sectors in China, in part because of the recent maturing of the IT infrastructure. As Table 6.8 shows, a large percentage of the total IT spending in various sectors is on hardware, indicating the need for large amounts of rudimentary systems integration.

These numbers provide a powerful reason why so many software companies— product firms and systems integrators alike—are doing systems integration. In our interviews, many firms, including product firms, noted that it was difficult to survive on products alone. Even Digital China, the software arm of Legend, focused on SI in order to gain additional revenue (as related to us by one of its executives).

In 2002, a selection of the twenty largest systems integrators appeared not to be growing as fast, suggesting deeper problems. Putian's revenue growth was −2.13 percent, Neusoft's was 9.02 percent, and CS&S was about 4 percent. One possible reason for the slower growth rate is that at such sizes, these firms may be having trouble securing new large-scale work in order to sustain

TABLE 6.8. Hardware–Software Breakdown for Total IT Market

	HW (%)	SW (%)	Services (%)
1999	87.6	6.9	5.5
2000	87.6	6.6	5.8

Source: IDC (2001). *PRC IT Spending and Industry Segmentation*. IDC # AP380126H. Aug. 2001.

growth. This may also indicate a lack of standardization across customers or standardized work that limits the opportunities that software firms have for realizing economies of scale and scope. Many observers have also noted that some of the largest firms have been unable to move beyond the more rudimentary systems integration work, such as the installation of hardware and simple software applications, and into higher-value-added systems integration software work and other services. In one large state-related firm that we visited, the software work being done ranged all the way from (low-end) localization of products, to product development.[27]

5   Factors Influencing the Growth of the Software Industry

5.1   Scale and Capability of Enterprises

It would appear that while software companies in China have several factors in their favor, these also come with concerns. One problem is that even though local software firms have a lot of work requiring highly customized, domestic-oriented systems and systems integration work, it is difficult to derive scale economies in such uneven markets. A second problem that Chinese software firms face is the problem of high competition. Many local firms compete with each other at the low end. At the higher end of the market in certain sectors, there is also the increasing presence of foreign firms. Despite the seemingly large number of firms, in a number of product sectors, good software firms are few in number, and so a further weaning of the population of firms or consolidation is possible.

As shown earlier, the industry is composed of many smaller firms. The small scale of firms limits their ability to compete for larger-scale work, especially in terms of systems integration. One small firm noted that since they did not have the size to compete for such work, they were trying to expand their payroll in order to do so. Many firms also spread themselves out over a wide number of sectors—partly reflecting opportunism, partly the need to grow. This behavior can keep companies from specializing, that is, achieving the scale and depth in particular areas, which is necessary to be able to compete for larger sized (and more complex) work. The quandary facing domestic firms is that less technical sophistication is needed if firms are only satisfying the domestic need for less advanced products, but this could also jeopardize their ability to compete in markets for advanced products. A similar situation exists with regards to outsourcing. Currently, Chinese software firms are doing some outsourcing for Japanese firms, but many of the jobs are lower-level ones that do not have much scope for improving the sophistication of the firms' capabilities.

Another problem facing software firms in China is the ability to get financing. While many of the firms that we interviewed were able to get the first stages of venture financing, the traditional capital markets are not as forgiving. Since

China's banking system requires an asset mortgage or third party guarantee in order to secure loans, software enterprises without traditional assets face a unique problem. Furthermore, the capital markets offer little help to software firms. Of the 1,000 listed companies in China, only eleven are software enterprises. The accumulated financing of the listed software companies is about $0.61 billion, as opposed to $60.4 billion for the entire securities market in 2000 [18].

5.2 Human Resources: Looming Quality and Quantity Problems

Highly skilled human resources are a key to the support of IT industries, and China's large, fairly well-trained pool of human resources are an important reason why it has been able to move into most software sectors somewhat effortlessly. However, while Chinese software workers have the theoretical knowledge to handle the basic tasks and are fairly sophisticated analytically, they lack the software process skills of Indian software workers. Only about 10 percent of the IT workforce has experience with complex programming tasks, and project management ability continues to lag behind that of India's.[28]

The main measure of organizational process capability is the Software Engineering Institute's Capability Maturity Model (SEI-CMM). However, many product firms viewed CMM certification as a lower priority for producing good products, and there is only one firm at level 5 (the highest) in China—Neusoft. Of the eleven listed companies in 2001, only two had passed CMM level 2 and another two had passed CMM level 3. The companies most interested in exporting software will be the ones seeking higher CMM certification earlier. Table 6.9 shows that the total number of graduates in computer-related fields and workers in the software industry is steadily growing. Other estimates put the pool of Chinese IT professionals in the year 2001 at about 150,000, versus about 522,000 in India, based on graduates of 50,000 and 73,218 per year, respectively, and a total demand of 350,000 and 400,000, respectively [1]. Like India, China also suffers an outward

TABLE 6.9. Software Workforce

Year	Number of software professionals	Number of graduates in computers and software
1998	132,000	29,000
1999	150,000	33,000
2000	186,000	41,000
2001	250,000	62,000
2002	300,000	89,000

Source: CSIA [4], Tables 1-24, 1-26.

migration of graduates (often from leading institutions like Tsinghua University) to the United States and other countries.

Many universities do not have computer science or software engineering programs. It has also been reported that many software workers need retraining after they have entered the workforce, suggesting that the educational system is not meeting the needs of companies [18]. Recognizing that the quantity and quality of software graduates is far too low, the national and local governments are instituting larger-scale plans, such as the designation of thirty-five universities nationwide as national software engineering programs. This will contribute another 17,500 graduates a year to the industry. Cities like Shanghai and Jinan are actively developing software engineering curricula and enlarging existing institutions to feed their growing local industries. However, with the industry's comparatively lower level of software engineering capability, such efforts can be expected to be limited in their impact. Shanghai has also attempted to boost software engineering awareness by setting up a software engineering network to exchange information. Especially when it comes to software engineering, industries such as those in Jinan have found that the local software engineering programs needed bolstering for their software project and other practical skills, and the local government and companies are trying to help the city's Shandong University with its software engineering programs by assisting in training. Such programs are also apparently going to be increasingly supported by Indian educational providers such as NIIT, which are opening more and more training sites across China.

Many companies appear to lack project managers and other managerial talent [24]. Various younger companies such as Tangram, which makes educational system software, and Intrinsic Technology, which makes mobile device software, noted that it was difficult to develop and grow because they lacked managers who could implement the company's vision. In general, the impression in the industry is that high-level systems analysts and project engineers are in short supply, and that software blue collar workers like coders are also scarce. As a result of this, the software talent structure is considered by some to be an unreasonable one, not a 'pyramid' but a 'spindle', with a middle part that is smaller (or greater unfulfilled needs) than both its ends. This lowers the competitiveness of the national software market, and also causes a number of undergraduate programmers to undertake simpler coding work. This in turn makes manpower costs higher than expected.

The monthly wage rates for professionals (i.e. developers with about two years experience) range from about $4,846–6,057 in China, versus about $4,913–9,212 in India [1]. However, the monthly wages also do not always include many other benefits that companies may provide, including housing and transportation. Some companies are even building campuses to house their employees and create a more convivial working atmosphere and corporate culture. Thus, wages actually vary substantially across regions and firms. With the level of software process skills as discussed, although some wages may be comparable to that in India's, it would appear to make parts of the Chinese industry less competitive than India's.

Many of the firms that we interviewed did not perceive a major shortage of most types of personnel, perhaps because they were product firms that were growing at a much slower pace. They seemed to believe that as long as they were able to keep their technical people, and to keep the core team happy, the labor turnover would be manageable. However, a few of the companies that we interviewed, such as Shanghai Grand Horizon, did note that the highest level technical-business people such as product managers were difficult to come by. Some other companies noted that having good sales staff with the connections to broker significant deals was critical.

5.3   Nature of the Domestic Market: Fragmented and Competitive

Our interviews, secondary analysis, and earlier discussion of the sectoral evidence provides several observations about the domestic market. The market is fragmented and competitive at the low end, making profit-making more difficult.

First, to reiterate the logic of Figure 6.1, the booming economy has created wealthier consumers and growing industries, and these in turn are increasing their demand for software, which will give software firms opportunities to grow. This effect benefits both domestic and multinational software firms.

Second, as noted earlier, many user enterprises are still barely capable of absorbing and using IT, requiring software firms to provide more services or customized software. Domestic firms may be better positioned to do this, and further, believe that they have a deeper understanding of their own markets than do the multinationals [18].

A third related issue was that markets were fragmented by provincial boundaries. For instance, the Jinan company SEPCO develops software for electric utilities— for both the back end (office automation) as well as the front end (running power plants). However, it faces a market with a large number of competitors, each one with an advantage in its own region.[29]

Finally, the combination of intense competition at both the high end (from multinationals) and low end (from the many local competitors) can put a 'squeeze' on many firms in the middle. At the low end, there are too many small and financially weak software firms. As one interviewee from SEPCO noted, many small firms compete with them on low cost and quality. On the other hand, at the high end, the market is also getting increasingly sophisticated, and foreign multinationals are increasing their presence, all of which adds up to competition at the high end. The open question is whether Chinese software firms can match this increasing sophistication with their products, or whether they will be able to graduate along with their market from being systems integrators or developers of less sophisticated products, to comprehensive packaged software solutions providers. If not, the multinationals will more easily dominate this emerging situation.

Other factors in the business environment also work against effective capability building and the growth of software firms. Piracy is also often mentioned as something that continues to hurt the software industry, and is now being officially recognized as a problem. Firms that we interviewed recognized that many software pirates are simply firms or individuals who cannot afford the software, and whom the state may be unwilling to penalize. Ideally, a form of price discrimination could be practiced, since software has almost zero marginal costs of reproduction, but we have not seen any firms devise strategies along these lines. As a result, many firms report very high piracy rates, with Microsoft being one of the hardest hit, with a reported piracy rate of 95 percent. It was also pointed out by TongRan that one incentive for firms not to pirate was when they found they needed TongRan's customer service. Hence, the need for services appears to mitigate piracy.

5.4 Strategies for Coping

In our interviews as well as in the broader observation of industry practices, all of the factors discussed above—organizational capability, human resources, market fragmentation, and competition—are sources of problems for software firms. At least three distinct strategies appeared to be adopted in order to address the need to survive and grow under these conditions.

The first strategy is that of specialization. Specialization is increasingly seen in the better product firms such as Kingdee, Kingstar, and Red Flag. Specialization is one way of deepening competencies and differentiating oneself from other firms that cannot do so. It is also useful in being able to develop brands. Specialized firms can presumably target the higher end of the value chain. Indeed, Kingdee is determinedly aiming at maturing ERP users, while Red Flag is aiming at newer markets (but dealing with sophisticated manufacturers). Specialization can help differentiate when there are hundreds of look-alike competitors. Of all the hundreds of companies developing ERPs, many may only be doing so for very localized markets, and for one client at a time. Their work will thus look more like contracted project work than a packaged product. It is possible that many of these firms that claim to be developing ERPs may in fact be developing MIS systems (or precursors to the ERPs of today), rather than full-fledged ERP systems. Without scale economies, it is unlikely that these firms will graduate to developing more packaged products. Thus, the ERP space is fairly easy to enter, but in reality, the bigger firms and the ones specializing in ERPs like But One and Kingdee appear to be doing better, and are probably more likely to survive than the others.

A second strategy is to produce a diverse range of products and services, although given the relatively small scale of these firms, diversification does not appear to be the best alternative. Many of the firms we interviewed were diversified across a few product lines or more, and systems integrators are diversified even further. Diversification could either be chosen in order to chase revenue in emerging sectors, or to survive, by moving away from the original product lines with limited prospects. Diversification in services could also help firms to fund their main activity with steady income. Finally, diversification could involve combining different types of products and services. That is, some firms may combine products with broader systems integration work. This also gives them the benefit of earning more revenue from hardware sales and services.

A third strategy is alliance building and consolidation. Alliances are quite common as firms try to exploit markets across provincial boundaries. Consolidations appear to be less evident in our interviews, but in the ERP realm, consolidation happens as domestic firms gear up to compete with larger, better funded foreign competitors. Kingdee's acquisition of another large firm—CASE—in 2001 was a case in point.

This raises a final issue: that of whether firms that are benefiting from the opportunity presented by the weaker users can upgrade themselves along with their users. This depends on stability in the firms' business as well as their ability to execute an upgradation strategy for their products. One example of this that was discussed earlier was Kingdee's improvements in its ERP product.

6 Conclusions

The Chinese software industry has developed quickly, with many new entrants over the last several years. It has benefited from the significant support of the government, which has spawned many of the software firms, and provides significant work for them. At the same time, the government's involvement can be traced back to its similar role in the development of the hardware industry. This industry is now a potential source of customers for the software industry. The government continues to be supportive and is willing to go to great lengths to support the still nascent software industry. The software industry is now effectively composed of larger systems integrators which are very diverse in both capability and scope, and smaller (and often financially weaker) product companies, which also face difficulty in increasing their size, or in keeping their focus. Many product firms still have to do systems integration work in order to earn or increase revenue.

Theoretically, the large growing domestic Chinese economy can provide opportunities to the domestic software industry in terms of a critical mass of work, and in terms of opportunities from other sectors. These are to some extent evident in our analysis. The Chinese market is indeed providing opportunities to many domestic firms to grasp a share of the market, as well as creating room for specialization in a variety of products and sectors. At the same time, however, the market has also opened the doors to foreign competition.

We have identified several major factors that shape the domestic industry's opportunities. First, there is the broad adoption of software across many sectors. A few sectors such as finance, telecoms, government, and consumer can be considered to be lead sectors in terms of size or growth rates. Second, the industry provides opportunities in that they require software which suits more local requirements, which can stimulate demand for select software firms. Third, some smaller commercial and manufacturing enterprises tend to have local business processes, which requires customization and more services at lower cost—something which multinationals are less willing to undertake. Fourth, there is the government's deep involvement.

As a result of the confluence of these factors, certain sectors and types of software activity tend to be emphasized. One is that of manufacturing and its needs for software, which comes about from the nature of Chinese products. A second is that of certain types of business software, which have unique domestic practices. A third is the need for large amounts of systems integration, partly because of the IT infrastructure building phase many customers are in, and partly due to the inexperience of customers. All these are areas of opportunity made possible by the lesser multinational dominance. Multinationals often first try to resell the same technology unmodified to Chinese conditions, which limits them to the upper end of select markets.

While each of these presents an opportunity, it also presents a challenge. Being 'too local', can also hurt domestic software companies if they only specialize in local practices (which customers may jettison as they mature), cannot upgrade themselves, or cannot gain economies of scale because they are working with disparate customers. This is the question facing the larger systems integrators, since if they rely on large custom systems installation contracts with heavy hardware components, they do not appear to have an easy basis for improving their technological capabilities. None of the systems integrators have made a clear transition to the status of major product players or made a name for themselves as services companies; slowing growth in some of them may be an indicator of this problem.

On the other hand, the medium-sized and growing product development firms do apparently have opportunities to grow in a number of sectors, but as they 'grow up' and have to compete with multinationals in the higher end product sectors, they may face resource limitations and require new strategies. Chinese firms have a greater problem in dealing with multinational competitors in that multinationals often have mature, tested technology and brand names. In select sectors like manufacturing or e-government, or certain products like security software, there may not be any large dominant multinationals, so these may present opportunities for local firms. The strong government handholding that is present in many technology areas may initially help these firms get off the ground and sustain themselves, but should also be viewed with caution in the long run, as it may lead to technology picking and could be used mainly to support the weakest firms.

Finally, the industry has to face a number of issues as it goes forward, not the least being the lack of process knowledge and good human resources at the experienced and inexperienced (but well-trained) end, and the fragmented market which does not lend itself to scale economies. The Chinese software industry is clearly an industry in transition with possibilities to succeed, but also with potential risks.

Appendix. Interview Sample

TABLE 6.A1. Firms that were Directly Interviewed and their Basic Characteristics[a]

Company	City	Origin	Employee	Capability maturity level (SEI)	Revenue (USD)	Founded
GrapeCity	Xian	Private (started in Japan)	70		1.21 Mn	1988
Calkai	Xian	XJTU	100			>10 yrs
But One	Xian	Split off from Calkai	360			1994
Sunny	Xian	Private, diversified from H/W	86		6.05 Mn[c]	1999
Suntek	Xian	Private				2000
ICE	Xian	Govt Investment Co, GM from XJTU	40		0.2 Mn	2000
Huawei	Shenzhen	Private				
TongRan (Neusoft)	Shenyang	N-E University	5,300	Lev. 5 (2002)	0.24 Bn, 9.02% growth	1991
Kingstar	Shanghai	Fudan University students	300	Lev. 2, ISO 9001		1995
Shanghai Fudan Grand Horizon	Shanghai	Fudan University	260	ISO 9000	11.7 Mn[b] 19.4 Mn[c]	1988
ASTI	Shanghai	Private	80			1990
Digital China	Beijing	Spin-off from Legend Group	400	Lev. 2	02/03 Turnover 1,605 million, 18.9% growth in 02–03	2000
CVIC	Jinan	Private	600	Lev. 3 (2003)	0.11 Bn[c]	1991
Cheelosoft	Jinan	Diversified from H/W	1,300	Lev. 2	0.18 Bn	2000

Name	City	Ownership/origin	Employees	Certification	Revenue/profit	Year
Shandong Luneng Jicheng (SLJ)	Jinan	University spin-off	176	ISO 9001	3.9 Mn	1999
SEPCO	Jinan	Government	488			2000
Human Technology	Beijing	Graduates from Tsinghua University	400			1996
Kingsoft	Beijing	Private	400–500			1988
Anyware	Beijing	Private	41			1997
Tsinghua TongFang DASCOM	Beijing	Tsinghua University spin-off				
Supermap	Beijing	Spin-off from government-funded research institute Chinese Academy of Sciences (CAS)	170	ISO 9001:2000	48.4 Mn[b]	1997
Beijing Listen	Beijing	Private	30 Tech			1996
Tongtech	Beijing	Private	200			1992
CASS	Beijing	CAS spin-off	500		7.3–8.5 Mn	1985
Red Flag Linux	Beijing	CAS spin-off	100	Lev. 1	0.36 Mn profit Desktop Linux	1999
Netsky	Beijing	Private	6 + 6			
Chongran (CS&S)	Beijing	Government	400 (1 site)			1980
Luan Xiang (Legend)	Beijing	CAS (originally), mainly H/W	12,000			1984
Yong Yu	Beijing					

[a]In addition to these firms, a venture capital firm and government officials from the following were interviewed: Ministry of Science and Technology, Torch Office; Chinese Academy of Sciences—Institute of Software; Beijing IT Promotion Center; Xian Software Park; Jinan Software Park.
[b]FY 2000.
[c]FY 2001.

Notes

1. Another estimate of the domestic share of products puts it at 40% [2].
2. Poor software process capabilities were cited by Huawei, a large Chinese telecom firm, as a reason for locating a major software development facility in Bangalore, India (interview with Huawei, 2001).
3. Attempting to gauge the Chinese software industry's current capabilities by adopting the measures favored by many international industry watchers can result in a negative view of the sector, while using Chinese statistics can lead to a misreading in the opposite direction. Because of this potential variance, we use both Chinese sources and international sources to arrive at a more balanced view of both the positive and negative features of the industry. In particular, we have tried to cross-correlate four different sources of consulting data: IDC, Gartner, CSIA, and CCID (where CSIA and CCID are governmental in background). We also based our analysis on a sample of thirty firms that we interviewed, comprised mainly of better performing small- and medium-sized companies. This provided a balanced account of the industry that encompassed both the positive and the negative (self evaluator) views.
4. Note that this is quite different from Gartner's figure of 150,000 software professionals in 2001 and 50,000 graduating a year [1].
5. Most of the data came from company websites (both in Chinese and English), with a more limited amount from our own interviews of firms or other secondary sources.
6. This data is based on the higher software industry numbers of the CSIA, so it is important to recognize that other sources will give lower numbers for the individual segments as well.
7. One of the difficulties in dealing with Chinese statistics is that different organizations use completely different ways of categorizing various types of products and services. In the CSIA category illustrated above, products consist of systems software, which includes operating systems and systems management software, while supporting software consists of middleware, database management software and software tools. The application software area is more straightforward, consisting of management software (such as financial, ERP, and so on), and consumer applications.
8. While this sample was not intended to be a representative sample of the total population of firms, for the most part, it was chosen to reflect the better known or growing software firms.
9. Information from CASS website (www.cass.ac.cn/En-company.htm).
10. Open source software is a type of software that is independent of any individual maker, so anyone can make it, contribute to it, and use it for free. However, more specific implementations of the software that rest on the base software and add more functionality or usability may be made privately and priced on the market, as with Red Flag's product. These will still derive the benefits of the 'open' (worldwide) developer community, and eventually have the opportunity to work interoperably with many platforms.
11. Based on website information.
12. First author's meetings with Ministry of Science and Technology Officials (formerly a more powerful State Commission on Science and Technology), 1998.
13. Interview with Ministry of Science and Technology Torch program official.
14. Cited in Saxenian [3].
15. The principal policies in this document concerned a reduction in the value added tax (VAT) for R&D and expanded production; preferred enterprises, enterprise income

tax elimination for two years and reduction by 50% for another three years; fast track approval for software companies desiring to use overseas stock markets for capitalization; exemption of software companies' equipment exports from tariffs and the VAT; and reductions in export hurdles for selected companies [12].

16. Some government programs that sought to develop talent for the local industry have apparently also failed. Most members of a group of a hundred top engineers trained in Beijing under a special software talent program left the country for the United States, while another group in Shanghai left mostly for Singapore and other regions. In recent years, however, the brain drain has reversed itself, with numerous entrepreneurs and trained IT professionals returning to China. One interviewee gave up a comfortable New York based position as an IT head with the United Nations to return home to help manage the Fudan Grand Horizon Company. It was, to paraphrase his words, a once-in-a-lifetime career opportunity.

17. At least one of the largest software firms—Top—is particularly well known for focusing on the real estate aspects of software parks around the country, partly as a means of developing infrastructure for specific regions, and it may now be suffering from this overinvestment.

18. Although GDP figures continue to be a source of scholarly dispute.

19. Based on an interview with Cheelosoft. Firms that we interviewed which specialized in the telecoms sector include But One, which focused on ERPs for the telecoms area, and Digital China and Cheelosoft, which attempted to specialize in systems integration for telecoms network and back office management.

20. Another way of saying this is that the Hopen software kernel or core code is smaller than Microsoft's, making it more efficient in terms of space, but less able to drive more devices with greater functionality.

21. Named after the Chinese goddess *NuWa*.

22. Local practices and requirements, especially at the low end, are very different from international practices and standards. This base is expected to expand the domestic (packaged) software market from $10 billion to $100 billion in 5–8 years [2]. The areas covered by this application area range from the simpler tasks of office automation (e.g. basic payroll and accounting) to more advanced activities such as enterprise resource planning, middleware and security software.

23. Defined by IDC to include industrial, business, and consumer applications.

24. The figure of 8.6 million is cited in Gartner [1]; the figure of 20 million is in CSIA [2].

25. Kingdee (which recently acquired CASE, another leading Chinese ERP firm) is an example of the new breed of Chinese firm which is doing well in the ERP market. Founded in 1993, Kingdee was originally a financial and accounting software company which moved into ERP. It has since grown to 1,500 employees and was the tenth largest ERP software company in 2001 [20,23].

26. Companies like Oracle are making aggressive moves, with Oracle entering into distribution agreements with local systems integrators and other distributors, as well as into partnerships with educational institutions and domestic software firms like Red Hat. Oracle had 1,100 distributors in China, and was taking steps to localize its products, with the opening of a product development facility in Shenzhen employing 100 engineers, and another one slated for Beijing [21].

27. One other concern is that the State Council's Document Number 18 seems to suggest that the government would be interested in promoting larger firms regardless of their ownership structure or capabilities.

28. *Far East Economic Review*, July 11, 2002, p. 38.
29. SEPCO is not related to the other Jinan company, SLJ, although they both have 'Luneng' in their Chinese names, and the same investor—the local Luneng power company.

References

1. Gartner (2002). Comparison: Indian and Chinese Software Services Markets. Gartner Research M-16-1762, May 2002.
2. CSIA (2000). Report on the Chinese Software Industry 2000, China Software Industry Association.
3. Saxenian, A. (2003). *Government and Guanxi: The Chinese Software Industry in Transition.* London Business School: Global Software from Emerging Markets, May 2003.
4. CSIA (2003). Report on the Chinese Software Industry 2002, China Software Industry Association.
5. Schware, R. (1992). Software industry entry strategies for developing countries: a 'walking on two legs' proposition. *World Development*, 20(2), 143–164.
6. NASSCOM (2003). Facts and Figures—Indian Software and Services Exports, www.nasscom.org/resourcecentre.asp?cat_id=408.
7. Lu, Q. (2000). *China's Leap into the Information Age.* Oxford: Oxford University Press.
8. Li, Zeng and Zhang (2003). Innovation systems in China, 1978 to 1998. In Grewal et al. (eds.), *China's Future in the Knowledge Economy.* Melbourne: Victoria University/Tsinghua University Press.
9. U.S. Embassy, Beijing (2002). An evaluation of China's science and technology system and its impact on the research community, October 2002, www.usembassy-china.org.cn/sandt/ST-Report.doc.
10. Lovelock, P., Petrazzini, B., and Clark, R. (1997). The golden projects: China's national networking initiative. *Information Infrastructure and Policy*, 5(4), 265–277.
11. CCID (2002). *Analysis of China's IT Application Market in Key Industries.*
12. SIIA-USITO (2002). SIIA-USITO Trade Mission to China Rethinking China's Software Market, June 24–July 2, 2002.
13. Wong, J. and Chan, S. (2003). *Why China's Economy can Sustain High Performance: An Analysis of its Sources of Growth.* London: The Royal Institute of International Affairs, Asia Programme Working Paper No. 6.
14. CCID (2002). *2001–2002 Annual Research Report on China's PC Market for Individual Consumers.*
15. CCID (2002). Growth of China's software market fell back in 2002. *News & Ideas*, http://202.108.101.203:87/detail?record=1&channelid=288&presearchword=ID=1312.
16. CCID (2002). *2001–2002 Annual Research Report on China's IT Application and Demand Market in Banking Industry.* Executive Summary.
17. CCID (2002). *2001–2002 Annual Research Report on China's IT Application Demand Market in Telecommunications Industry.* Executive Summary.

18. CCID (2001). *Research Report on the Software Industry's Development in China, 2001.*

19. CCID (2002). *2001–2002 Annual Research Report on China's IT Application Demand Market for SMEs.* Executive Summary.

20. Gartner (2001). *Financial Software Selection for the Chinese Market.* Gartner Research DF-14-5486, November 2001.

21. Gartner (2001). *Oracle's Expansion in China Faces Obstacles.* E-17-4283, July 2002.

22. IDC (2001). *ERP Market Trends in China.* Markets, IDC.

23. Gartner (2001). *Kingdee Seeks the Throne in China's ERP Realm.* Gartner Research, P-13-4714, May 2001.

24. Wilhelm, K. (2001). Tomorrow's IT powerhouse? *Far East Economic Review*, June 14, 2001, 36–39.

PART II

CROSS-CUTTING CHAPTERS

7

Organizational Capabilities and the Rise of the Software Industry in the Emerging Economies: Lessons from the History of some US Industries

ASHISH ARORA, ALFONSO GAMBARDELLA, AND
STEVEN KLEPPER

1   Introduction

Retrospectively one can provide reasons for the software industry prospering in the 3Is based on comparative advantage, deriving from abundant supplies of human capital. This explanation, however, is incomplete in many respects. Software is not the only human capital-intensive industry; many other service industries are intensive in human capital. Moreover, software encompasses a very wide variety of products and services, yet Israel, Ireland, and India are active only in a narrow subset.[1]

The comparative advantage explanation also runs into difficulty in explaining the persistence of the 3Is. After more than a decade of sustained high growth in software, the potential excess supply of software professionals in the 3Is has surely greatly diminished. The available evidence suggests that wages for software professionals in India, though they have remained below those in the United States and the United Kingdom, have risen more sharply than in those countries. For instance, Table 2.6 in Athreye's chapter (Chapter 2) indicates that in 1995 the wages of system designers in India were 20 percent of those in the United States, but by 1999 the ratio had increased to 24 percent. Similarly, the rates for quality assurance specialists increased from 28 to 33.5 percent. Even granting that demand for software professionals in the United States and other major markets remained high, surely the rising labor costs in India ought to have provided an opportunity for other countries to break into the software services market. Yet, Indian software revenues grew at an annual average rate of nearly 50 percent over this period and, contrary to the predictions of some pessimistic observers, the Indian industry did not lose ground to potential competitors from China, Singapore, Philippines, or Eastern Europe. Similarly, despite sustained increase in Irish software wages, the Irish industry has not as yet faced any serious competitive challenge from potential rivals such as Northern Ireland or Scotland.

Agglomeration economies involving knowledge spillovers across co-located firms are a common explanation for such persistent regional leadership. In this chapter, we offer a different, though not mutually exclusive, perspective by drawing upon recent work by Klepper on the experience of four other industries in the United States—automobiles, automobile tires, television receivers, and lasers. These are some of the first analyses of how the geographic structure of new industries evolves. Two of the industries, automobiles and tires, became extremely concentrated in two narrow regions in the United States, whereas geographic concentration declined over time in both TV receivers and lasers. The analysis of these industries shows that geographical concentration can emerge as a natural consequence of the clustering of early leaders in certain narrow regions, without any agglomeration economies. Klepper's findings also indicate an important role for related industries in producing the initial group of successful firms and for the persistence of the early leaders. Geographical concentration and persistence of leading firms are closely related. Industries grow and concentrate in the regions where successful firms enter early. Not only do the early successful firms often end up dominating their industries, they are also more likely to spawn other successful firms that locate nearby.

Producers in the United States were in the vanguard of all four of the industries reviewed, whereas the countries studied in the software industry were generally latecomers to the industry. This difference has important ramifications. Nonetheless, important lessons can be gleaned from the experiences of the four industries concerning how a region develops an initial presence in a new industry and the factors that condition how that presence evolves over time. In this chapter, we focus on the 3Is but we also draw upon the experience of Brazil and China where they illuminate our central themes.

2   Comparative Advantage and the Growth of the Software Industry in Emerging Economies

The limitations of comparative advantage in explaining the pattern of international specialization are not limited to software in the 3Is. Hausmann and Rodrik [1] provide some suggestive evidence about the limited explanatory power of comparative advantage. First, they point out that in developing countries, the bulk of exports consist of a narrow range of products.[2] Moreover, these are not usually part of a continuum of products falling in the same industry. For example, Bangladesh exports garments such as hats, but not bed sheets, and Pakistan exports bed sheets but not hats. As Hausmann and Rodrik note, this suggests that the specific product lines that will be export successes are typically uncertain and unpredictable.

Rhee and Belot [2] described Bangladesh's garment specialization as an example of a catalytic model of development, which they illustrated with eleven examples, Bangladesh's garment success being their flagship case. The catalyst to Bangladesh's garment industry was a joint venture between a local entrepreneur who had been exposed to international business as a senior official in the Bangladesh government and a leading Korean garment manufacturer whose growth was being stunted by international restrictions on imports from Korea. In Bangladesh, 130 workers that would fill 4 management positions, 97 production supervisory positions, and 29 production slots were selected for intensive on-the-job training with the Korean partner. The workers learned not only valuable production skills but the whole system of production, marketing, and management that had made the Korean partner so successful in international markets. The Korean partner also supplied intermediate inputs to the joint venture, helped develop administrative arrangements for basic export incentives, and provided international marketing of the joint venture's production. Within a few years, the joint venture cancelled its collaborative agreement with its Korean partner and was able to succeed on its own, expanding its work force to 1,500 within eight years.[3]

What is most striking about this experience is what happened subsequently. Of the initial 130 workers, 115 left to start their own, often competing, garment exporting firms. By 1985, there were more than 700 garment factories in Bangladesh exporting garments. Rhee and Belot recount the history of one successful firm that grew to have 900 employees, noting its specialization in shirts and its ability to respond to diverse European markets based on personal contacts developed by its dynamic marketing manager.

In Hausmann and Rodrik's theory a country needs to discover its strengths and comparative advantages via experimentation. Entrepreneurship consists of trying new activities or products and successful experiments. There are interesting parallels with the software industry in India. Athreye describes the many experiments that the pioneers undertook, trying to discover whether to target the domestic market and leverage capabilities there for exports, whether to produce products or services, and even among services whether to target high-end projects (such as ERP implementation) or more generic, lower-end services such as custom software development. The successful business model—generic software services provided through a mixture of onsite and offshore development—was rapidly imitated. Moreover, Athreye suggests that early multinationals, such as Texas Instruments, and firms set up by overseas Indians, such as Patni Computer Systems and Datamatics, may have played a catalytic role by demonstrating that India could be a good location for software development.

Though suggestive, the Hausmann–Rodrik theory is misleading insofar as it suggests that the potentially successful set of activities for a country are exogenously specified, awaiting discovery by a lucky entrepreneur, who is then rapidly imitated. Athreye's chapter (Chapter 2) on the Indian software industry shows that although the successful business model was rapidly imitated by a number of entrants, the leading firms have continued to grow rapidly and show signs of pulling away from the later entrants. The experience of the four industries studied by Klepper underscores even more forcefully the importance of firms acquiring the competencies required to be successful. Though there was significant entry in each of the industries, few of the entrants were eventually successful. In particular, emulating the leaders appears to have been extraordinarily difficult, particularly for entrants whose founders had not previously worked in one of the leading firms. Further, when production moved outside the regions where the industries had originated, it was not through firms in the lower-cost geographic areas but rather through the leading firms themselves branching out to the lower-cost areas.

So how are we to understand the success of the 3Is in software? It appears comparative advantage is simply a necessary but not sufficient condition for explaining export success. One way to think about this issue is that, in addition to comparative advantage, to be successful a country needs distinctive sources of competencies to breed successful firms in a new industry. This interplay between macro and micro, between comparative advantages at the country level and organizational capabilities at the firm-level, is the basic framework that we use to understand the growth of software in the 3Is.

3   The Rise and Evolution of New Industries in the United States

3.1   Industries Studied

We begin by reviewing evidence on the three US industries studied most extensively: television receivers, automobiles, and automobile tires. The three industries were originally studied to gain insights into how the market structure of new industries evolves. They followed a common evolution as reflected in Figure 7.1, which presents the annual number of entries, exits, and producers for the three products, as well as for lasers, from their inception through maturity.[4]

Each of the three industries initially experienced a sharp rise in the number of producers, the rise condensed into a much shorter period for televisions because the development of the industry was delayed by US participation in the Second World War. In each industry, the peak in the number of firms is followed by a prolonged period in which the number of firms falls sharply, eventually declining to less than 20 percent of the peak number.[5] All three of the industries also evolved to be oligopolies. Klepper [3] proposed and tested a theory to explain these patterns that features increasing returns from R&D imparting an advantage to earlier entrants and experienced entrants diversifying from related industries.

Subsequent work explored the heritage of entrants and how their heritage conditioned the evolution of the three industries [4–6]. The base location of all the entrants was identified. The pre-entry experience of the entrants was also traced. In televisions, entrants that diversified from radios were identified [7]. In automobiles, the heritage of all the entrants was traced and entrants were classified into one of four categories: diversifiers; firms founded by heads of firms in related industries; spin-offs, which were defined as firms with one or more founders that had previously worked for an automobile company; and other start-ups [4]. In tires, the heritage of the firms that entered the industry in Ohio, the leading state, was traced and firms were classified as either diversifiers, spin-offs, or other start-ups.

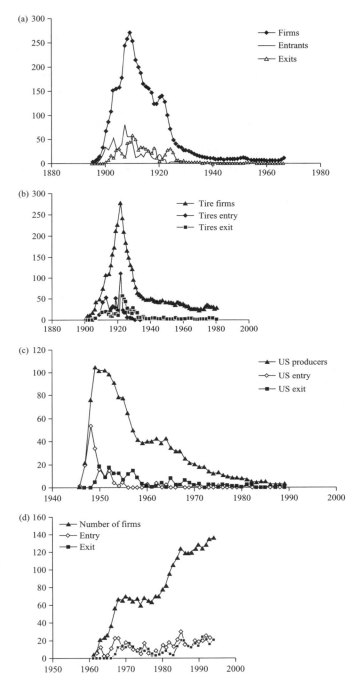

FIGURE 7.1. Entry, Exit, and Number (a) of Automobile Producers, 1895–1966; (b) of Tire Producers, 1901–80; (c) of Television Producers, 1946–89; (d) of Laser Producers, 1961–94

The geographic origin of each of the Ohio tire entrants was also traced according to the prior location of the diversifying entrants, the prior locations of the 'parents' of the spin-offs, and the prior locations of the founders of the start-ups [6]. The analysis of the evolution of each of the three industries features the role played by the heritage of the entrants, as reviewed below.

The evolution of the laser industry has also been analyzed by Klepper and Sleeper [8] and Klepper and Thompson [9]. It was originally studied because, as illustrated in Figure 7.1, it did not experience a shakeout over its first thirty-five years even though it is a high-tech industry. While to date the industry has not been analyzed as extensively as the other three, particularly regarding its geographic structure, it is reviewed because it adds an important perspective for the software industry.

3.2 TV Receiver Industry

The TV receiver industry is considered first because its evolution is the easiest to understand and it provides a useful backdrop for the other industries. A total of 177 firms entered the TV receiver industry in the United States from 1946 to 1989. Table 7.1 indicates they were heavily concentrated within 25 miles of three cities: New York, Chicago, and Los Angeles. Seventy-three percent located in one of these cities, with 44 percent entering in New York, 15 percent in Chicago, and 14 percent in Los Angeles. Figure 7.2 indicates how the base location of the firms that remained in the industry changed over time. Initially about 50 percent of the firms were based in New York and by the mid-1950s the percentage of firms based in Los Angeles peaked at around 20 percent. Subsequently, the share of producers based in both cities declined drastically. By 1970, no producers were based in Los Angeles and only about 10 percent were based in New York. In contrast, the percentage of producers based in Chicago remained steady at around 25 percent through about 1980. Subsequently it increased sharply, but this was when the number of firms based in the United States dwindled to three under intense international competition, and it was not long before there were no longer any television firms

TABLE 7.1. Location of Television and Radio Producers

	177 TV entrants (%)	58 TV entrants from radio industry (%)	119 TV other entrants (%)	266 radio firms (%)	Output of top 16 radio firms (%)
New York	44	26	53	33	11
Chicago	15	24	10	15	38
Los Angeles	14	5	18	7	0
Elsewhere	27	45	18	45	51

Source: Klepper [5].

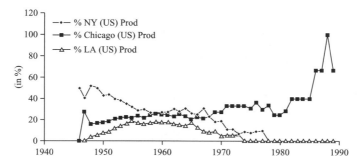

FIGURE 7.2. Percentage of Television Producers in New York, Chicago, and
Los Angeles, 1946–89

based in the United States. Thus, the history of the industry is one where firms
were heavily agglomerated into three regions but over time only one of the regions
maintained its share of producers, with the base location of the firms in the industry
increasingly dispersed geographically, primarily in the northeast and midwest.

The dominant force that shaped the geographic evolution of the base location of
the producers was the location of the firms in the radio industry. Of the 177 entrants
into the industry, 58, or approximately one-third, diversified from the radio industry. These firms dominated the TV receiver industry, particularly the firms that
were the leaders of the radio industry. Among the top fourteen manufacturers of
TV receivers over the history of the industry, thirteen were diversifiers from the
radio industry, and four of the top five TV receiver producers were among the
top five radio producers (the other radio producer in the top five was among the
top ten TV receiver producers). Consequently, it is not surprising that the entry of
TV receiver firms was concentrated where the radio producers were located, as
reflected in Table 7.1. Among the 266 radio producers at the start of the TV receiver
industry, 55 percent were located in New York, Chicago, and Los Angeles, which
mirrors the share of TV entrants that diversified from the radio industry that were
located in the three cities. Intriguingly, 82 percent of the entrants to the TV industry that did not diversify from the radio industry also entered in these same three
cities.

The location of the radio producers is also the key to understanding why only
Chicago maintained its share of producers. Table 7.1 lists the share of output of
the leading radio producers that was produced in each of the three cities. Only
one of the leading radio producers was based in New York, and it accounted
for 11 percent of the output of the leading radio producers, Los Angeles had no
leading radio producers, and Chicago had five leading radio producers accounting
for 38 percent of the output of the leading radio producers. Correspondingly,
Chicago had three of the top ten TV receiver firms, New York one, and Los
Angeles none, with the rest scattered throughout the northeast and midwest. The
leading TV producers were the longest survivors and consequently only Chicago

maintained its share of producers over time and the base location of the firms became increasingly dispersed over the northeast and midwest. In a statistical analysis of firm hazard rates, New York and Los Angeles firms had higher hazard rates than firms elsewhere, but once the backgrounds of the firms were controlled (whether they diversified from radios and if so whether they were a top radio producer, and also their time of entry) there were no significant differences in the hazard rates of firms by region [5].

Under intense international competition originating from Japan, US TV firms eventually moved much of their operations to low-wage countries, but this did not head off their ultimate demise. They were behind the technological frontier, particularly regarding the use of semiconductors, and lost their market to Japanese firms that were also experienced in radios and other consumer electronic products [10].

TV firms illustrate a few themes that will also show up in the other US industries and in our software cases. First, firms in related industries are important seeds for firms in a new industry and their location is an important influence on where entrants to the new industry will locate. Second, there is great heterogeneity in firms regarding their pre-entry experience that persistently affects their performance. In the television firms, experience in radios was so important that no new firm was successful in the industry, and the location of the leading radio firms determined the eventual locus of TV producers. Last, agglomeration economies were not a major factor shaping the base location of the TV producers. Two of the three regions in which the firms were concentrated declined over time, and regional differences in firm performance were primarily due to regional differences in their pre-entry experiences rather than to any regional effects per se.

3.3   Automobiles

The evolution of the automobile industry was different from that of the TV industry. Entrants were much more dispersed. A total of 725 firms entered the industry from its inception in 1895 through 1966, with all but 11 entering by 1925. Michigan had more entrants than any other state, but it accounted for only 18.6 percent of the entrants, followed by New York with 13.5 percent, Ohio with 12.3 percent, Illinois with 9.7 percent, and Indiana with 9.5 percent. Thus, the top three states accounted for 44.7 percent of the entrants versus 73 percent for the top three cities in the TV industry. The greater dispersion of the entrants in automobiles than TVs reflects that the industry that supplied the greatest number of diversifiers, carriages and wagons (C&W), was much more dispersed than radios, as were other supplying industries. The top five C&W states were the same as the top five automobile states, but the number one state, Ohio, accounted for less than 14 percent of the value of C&W production in 1899, followed by New York and Indiana with 11 percent each, Michigan with 10 percent, and Illinois with 7 percent. Similarly, other seeding industries were dispersed across the so-called manufacturing belt encompassing the leading automobile states plus a number

of others in New England, the northeast, and the midwest. Furthermore, diversifiers accounted for only 16.6 percent of all the automobile entrants, reflecting
the novel challenges faced by automobile firms. Automobiles soon required preci-
sion manufacturing to produce interchangeable parts, involved manufacturing on
an unprecedented scale, and were subject to much greater technological change
than C&W and other related industries.

Similar to TVs, automobile entrants that diversified from other industries,
particularly C&W, bicycles, and engines, performed better than the typical entrant,
as did new firms founded by individuals that headed firms in the same industries.
But what distinguished automobiles from TVs was that spin-offs—firms founded
by employees of incumbent automobile firms—also performed well, particularly
spin-offs from the leading automobile firms. Spin-offs accounted for 20 percent
of the entrants in the industry and they produced many of the leading makes of
automobiles, including eleven of the fifteen leading makes in the peak year of
1916. They were generally formed by high-level employees and tended to locate
near their parents. They were more likely to come out of better-performing firms,
with better-performing firms on an average spawning better-performing spin-offs.
One explanation for these patterns is that working in an incumbent firm was an
especially good venue to learn about tacit organizational best practices, and the
better the firm then the better the lessons learned. While there is no doubt that the
reasons for spin-offs varied, many of the spin-offs from the leading firms occurred
after disputes over strategy and/or technology in the parent firm, reflecting control
struggles that were common in the early years of the automobile industry. As such,
the better spin-offs from the better firms tended to expand the scope of products
and technology employed in the industry [11].

Spin-offs were the key force causing the automobile industry to become extraordinarily concentrated around one medium-sized city, Detroit, Michigan, that had
no compelling advantages for automobile production. Spin-offs took on special
significance for Detroit because the first great firm in the industry, Olds Motor
Works, was located there. Olds was in turn responsible for propelling the rise of
three other industry leaders that located in the area. Olds' scale was so large that it
subcontracted its engines and transmissions, which involved orders of unprecedented size, to two Detroit machine shops that were instrumental in the success of
the next two great entrants into the industry, Cadillac and Ford, both of which
entered in Detroit in 1902 and 1903, respectively. The next great firm to enter
the industry, Buick, was financed initially by another of Olds' subcontractees and
entered in Detroit in 1903.

These four firms basically unleashed a spin-off juggernaut that propelled
Detroit to become the automobile capital of the United States. They were the
most prolific parents in the industry, reflecting the greater rate of spin-offs among
the better firms, with forty-one spin-offs descending from them, nearly all of which
located in Detroit. Indeed, spin-offs accounted for 48 percent of the entrants in
Detroit versus only 15 percent of the entrants elsewhere. The spin-offs of the
four leading firms also performed distinctly well, reflecting the link between the

performance of spin-offs and their parents. The four firms accounted for eleven of the thirteen spin-offs that produced leading makes of automobiles after 1903, with each of the four firms spawning at least two of these spin-offs. The result was that by the mid-1910s nearly all the leading makes of automobiles were made by firms based in the Detroit area. Other than spin-offs, which performed distinctly well in Detroit, the rest of the entrants in Detroit performed comparably to those elsewhere. In a statistical analysis, the superior performance of the Detroit spin-offs was largely attributable to their superior heritage rather than being located in Detroit per se [4]. Similar to TV firms, the leading automobile firms remained based in Detroit, but over time they conducted more of their business outside of Detroit as they established branch assembly plants throughout the United States.

Some of the lessons that emerge from automobiles are similar to TVs. Like TVs, firms in related industries, such as Olds, were important seeds for the new industry. Also like TVs, there was enormous heterogeneity in entrants in terms of their pre-entry experience that persistently affected their performance. The key difference between automobiles and TVs was that spin-offs were competitive with, if not superior to, diversifiers. This reflected both the limited relevance of prior industries to automobiles and possibly the distinctive opportunities within firms, particularly the leading firms, for high-level employees to learn valuable tacit organizational knowledge that they could apply to their own firms. In sum, with better firms having higher spin-off rates and better-performing spin-offs, the spin-off process effectively led to a buildup of firms and activity around the leading firms in the industry. This was especially potent in automobiles because of the location of four of the most successful early firms in one narrow region, fueling a great agglomeration of activity there. Yet, it was not agglomeration economies from locating near other producers that were relevant here, but rather that the leading firms involuntarily spawned new firms that naturally located in the area where their originator firms were. Agglomeration seems to be more a consequence than a cause of successful capabilities. In this respect, there was no reason, other than the location of early successful firms, that made Detroit a particularly suitable location for the production of automobiles.

3.4 Tires

The evolution of the tire industry bears an uncanny resemblance to the automobile industry. The tire industry agglomerated around a small northeastern Ohio city, Akron, with no compelling advantages for tire production. Entry concentrated in the first thirty years of the industry, with 533 entrants dispersed over a number of states, with Ohio being the leading state, accounting for 24 percent of all entrants. The main seeding industry was rubber, but tires represented a considerable break from prior rubber products.[6] While the diversifiers, most of which came from the rubber industry, performed significantly better than the new firms, they represented only 15.6 percent of all the entrants. Moreover, Ohio was only the fifth leading state in terms of rubber production, accounting for only 3.5 percent of US rubber production in 1890 behind Massachusetts with 45.5 percent, New Jersey with 8.8 percent, Connecticut with 8.1 percent, and New York with 4.4 percent.

Unlike automobiles, Akron was an important center of tire production from the outset of the industry. Like Detroit in automobiles, though, it steadily grew in importance over time. By 1921, when the number of tire producers peaked, Ohio accounted for 59 percent of tire production in the United States, which increased further to 65 percent by 1929. Most of the production in Ohio was in and around Akron. Similar to automobiles, in the 1920s and the 1930s the leading tire producers began branching out by establishing manufacturing plants throughout the United States to save on wages and transportation costs [12]. Starting in the 1930s, this caused a much bigger exodus of the industry from Ohio than occurred from Michigan in the case of automobiles.

Similar to Olds, one Akron firm, BF Goodrich, was an important catalyst for the industry in Akron. At the start of the tire industry, it was a leading bicycle tire producer and successful producer of other rubber products and it produced the first pneumatic automobile tire in 1896. It was influential in four other tire firms locating and prospering in Akron—Diamond Rubber, Kelly-Springfield, Firestone, and Goodyear. Diamond was an 1894 rubber spin-off from Goodrich that became a very successful tire producer and merged with Goodrich in 1912. Goodrich produced Kelly-Springfield's initial carriage tire based on a patented design before Kelly-Springfield located in Akron in 1899 when it began producing pneumatic tires. Goodrich initially produced tires for Firestone after its entry in Akron in 1900 and then supplied Firestone with prepared rubber and fabric when it began producing its own tires in 1903. Last, Goodyear was founded in 1898 by the son of one of the original financiers of Goodrich that subsequently also operated a rubber firm.

Goodyear, Firestone, and Goodrich were three of the top four firms in the industry (the fourth, US Rubber, was originally located in Chicago and Hartford and then moved to Detroit), and Akron prospered as their market shares increased over time. Spin-offs also played an important role in the success of Akron. They accounted for 38 percent of the entrants in Ohio. The most prolific parents in Ohio were Goodyear, Goodrich, Firestone, and Diamond, followed by the next tier of leading firms, some of which had also descended from Goodyear, Goodrich, Diamond, and Firestone. The spin-offs of these firms outperformed the rest of the Ohio spin-offs, and a number of them made it to the ranks of leading tire producers.

3.5 Lasers

The evolution of the laser industry differs from the other three in that regional agglomeration is limited and the industry has not yet experienced a shakeout. The laser industry began in 1961, and through 1994 there were nearly 500 entrants, of which the pre-entry backgrounds of 465 could be traced. California attracted more entrants than any other state, with 15 percent of all entrants locating in Silicon Valley and another 13 percent in southern California around Los Angeles. Silicon Valley accounted for about 30 percent of the producers in the industry in the early

Ashish Arora et al.

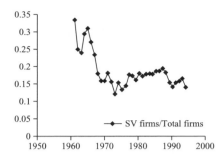

FIGURE 7.3. Fraction of Laser Firms in Silicon Valley, 1961–94

years, as reflected in Figure 7.3, and it was home to the industry's two leading
producers, Spectra Physics and Coherent. Furthermore, spin-offs were prominent
in the industry, accounting for 17 percent of the entrants, and the spin-offs performed distinctly well as a class, comparable to the best-performing diversifiers
with backgrounds in industrial electronics [13]. Thus, conditions were similar to
those in automobiles and tires, yet as Figure 7.3 indicates the percentage of firms
located in Silicon Valley declined over time and stabilized at around 15 percent,
and the industry did not experience a shakeout in its first thirty-five or so years
despite its research intensity.

So why did spin-offs not fuel the agglomeration of the industry in Silicon Valley?
A major factor appears to be the wide range of lasers produced in the industry and
the tendency of firms to specialize narrowly in a small class of lasers. Different
materials produce laser light of varying wavelengths, and the wavelength of the
light is key to the applications serviced by a laser. Much of the growth of the
industry was generated by new kinds of lasers that opened up new applications,
which helped fuel entry and the rise in the number of producers through 1994 [9].
Economies of scope across laser types were apparently limited judging from the
extent to which firms specialized in the types of lasers they produced. Dividing
lasers into nine broad categories, over their lifetime 55 percent of laser firms
produced only one type of laser, 20 percent two laser types, 23 percent three to six
laser types, and only 2 percent seven or more laser types, with an average of two
types of lasers per firm. Firms that produced a wide range of lasers generated more
spin-offs, as each type of laser was a separate source of spin-offs [8]. But spin-offs
tended to be much more specialized than their parents, which limited their effect
on the geographic structure of the industry.

In Silicon Valley, Spectra Physics and Coherent at one time each produced
eight different types of lasers, and they were the most prolific parents in the
industry with six and five spin-offs, respectively. The fifth most prolific parent
with three spin-offs, GTE/Sylvania, was also located in Silicon Valley, and it
produced four types of lasers. But the spin-offs of these three firms were far more
specialized than their parents. Spectra's spin-offs produced an average of 2.2 total

laser types over their lifetime, Coherent's 2.8, and GTE/Sylvania's 2.0. With their spin-offs so specialized it was inevitable that they would not spawn many second generation spin-offs—in total, they spawned only two. The fertility of all laser firms, including Spectra Physics and Coherent, fell at older ages, which was also true in automobiles. Consequently, over time spin-offs in Silicon Valley declined, and coupled with their limited scope they did not contribute to a major buildup of firms in Silicon Valley.

Lasers illustrate the potential importance of another random factor conditioning the role of spin-offs in the evolution of an industry, namely whether firms blossom into broad-based producers. In automobiles and tires, the spin-offs were generally broad-based, reflecting the narrower range of products produced in those industries than lasers. But in lasers spin-offs were destined to have less effect on regional concentrations of firms because only a small number were likely to become broad-based regardless of their parentage. In contrast to automobiles, TVs, and tires, early entry did not provide a competitive advantage and entry remained vigorous over time [13], which may also have limited the agglomeration of the industry, although this has yet to be investigated.

3.6 Summary

In all four US industries, the regions that were successful had a comparative advantage in terms of the supply of entrepreneurs and skilled labor in related industries. But in automobiles and tires in particular, the specializations developed by Michigan and Ohio defied prediction. In both instances, they were based on important catalysts, Olds Motor Works and BF Goodrich. These firms employed many of the workers who in turn left to form many of the successful firms in the industry, as was true of a few other notable local firms whose success was in part owed to the catalysts. Moreover, when the expertise of the catalysts and other early successful firms was not effectively transferred to new organizations, as was apparently the case in televisions, regional buildups of firms were limited. That it took the leaders of the industry to exploit the cost advantages of less agglomerated areas is testimony to the difficulty of firms imitating the tacit organizational knowledge underlying the success of the leaders without actually being part of their organizations.

The persistent effect of pre-entry experience on firm performance makes organizational competence of particular salience. Simply put, to be successful firms had to be able to draw upon organizational expertise and capabilities. For early entrants, this was typically located in successful firms in closely related industries, and successful early entrants themselves provided this, often involuntarily, to later entrants. Thus regional success was based upon the number and quality of firms in related industries and early entrants who catalyzed subsequent growth.

One can summarize the insights about catalyzing industrial development from the experience of these four industries as follows. First, in all four industries catalysts and the agglomerations they spawned were more likely in regions with related industries. Second, in automobiles and tires the catalysts spawned a number of the successful spin-offs around them. Third, judging from the automobile industry, spin-offs were not merely imitative of their parents but also contributed to technical advancement in their industries. This was perhaps even more pronounced in lasers [8]. Fourth, agglomeration benefits associated with firms locating close to each other appear to have been less important than is emphasized in much of the modern literature on agglomeration.

4 Implications for Understanding the Evolution of the Software Industry in Emerging Economies

4.1 Applicability to Software in Emerging Economies

The evidence presented so far was restricted to new manufacturing industries in the United States. To what extent would their experiences be applicable to industries like software in less developed countries? There are at least two important differences to be noted.

First, software is a sector with a range of different types of activities, as is evident from the discussion earlier in this volume of the differences across the countries studied. Indeed, software is a general purpose technology used in virtually every industry and business. Occupation data from the United States clearly show that two out of three software professionals in the United States do not work for IT firms but instead for firms in a variety of sectors, especially those that are intensive users of software, such as banking, finance and insurance, and telecommunications. One implication is that there are many different sources of competencies, including a large variety of user sectors. Another is that market leadership can only be defined relative to a particular submarket. Indeed, the software sector has a large number of submarkets, some of which are not dominated by well established incumbents and thus provide room for firms from emerging regions. In this respect, software is more like lasers than automobiles or tires.

The second, and perhaps more important, point is that latecomer regions face a distinctive set of opportunities and challenges. Unlike pioneers, followers do not start *tabula rasa*. Instead, as virtually all the chapters note, incumbents in the pioneer countries may already occupy the key market segments, forcing followers to focus on less competitive or underserved niches. Thus Irish product firms focus on banking and financial software and on telecommunication software. Israeli firms dominate security software where established US firms, such as IBM, though possessing the required technology, decided not to enter the market [14]. Until recently, even the leading Indian software firms did not directly bid on major software service contracts. On the other hand, followers often do not have to create and mould a market, and in many cases they do not need to create an entirely new set of input suppliers. For instance, whereas the electronics and biotechnology industries in the United States co-evolved with the venture capital sector, the Israeli and the Irish industries benefited from the well-understood model of how

venture financing worked, and in some cases could call upon US venture cap-
italists and financiers directly. Similarly, Indian software firms could tap into
the already existing business model of software outsourcing and provision of
temporary employees.

These differences notwithstanding, if comparative advantage alone does not
explain why only some emerging economies developed an internationally competitive software industry, can the lessons from the history of the four US industries
help in understanding the pattern of international specialization? The experience of
the four US industries highlights the role of organizational competencies. Simply
put, successful firms in these industries were those that were able to draw upon
organizational competencies of other successful firms in the industry or closely
related industries. Regions where early entrants were successful had an advantage.
Not only did successful firms persist for a long time, they were also more likely
to spawn other successful firms. Thus geographical concentration of industrial
activity could arise simply because entry by early industry leaders was geographically concentrated, and not because of agglomeration economies, which
are a commonly advanced reason for the geographical concentration of industries.
Accordingly, in this section we assess whether the software industries in the 3Is are
distinctive in their sources of organizational competencies, whether early leadership is persistent, and whether agglomeration economies appear to be important
for understanding their growth.

4.2 Sources of Firm Competencies

In the four US industries, the main sources of organizational competence were
firms in related industries and spin-offs of the successful early entrants. We shall
first consider these sources of organizational competence for our five countries,
particularly the 3Is. We then turn to two related sources of competence that have no
parallel in the four US industries: multinationals and expatriates. Last, we consider
a source for organizational competence that, although not prominent in the four
industries studied here, is sometimes prominent in the United States, namely the
public sector, including universities and the military.

In India, Brazil, and to some extent China as well, preexisting firms were a significant source of firm formation, and especially of successful firms. Table 2.2 in
Athreye's chapter (Chapter 2) list the origins of the top twenty Indian software
exporters. Six of the top twenty (and three of the top five) are the result of business
houses diversifying into software. Some, though not all, had experience in computer hardware.[7] One originated from a large multinational bank and another was
started by two employees of the same bank. Of the firms that were NASSCOM
members in 2001–02, firms diversifying into software were larger than average.
Though diversifiers account for 18 percent of the firms, they account for nearly
33 percent of the revenue and 30 percent of the employment.

Preexisting firms are the single most important source of leading Brazilian
software firms as well. A sample of fifty-five leading software Brazilian firms

discussed in Botelho et al.'s chapter (Chapter 5, Table 5.6), reveals that twenty-seven out of the fifty-five leading Brazilian software firms originated from existing firms.[8] Preexisting firms were also prominent entrants in the Chinese software industry. Table 7.2, which is adapted from Table 6.2 in Tschang and Xue's chapter (Chapter 6), shows that many of the leading Chinese software firms are diversifiers, often computer equipment manufacturers or systems integrators.

In contrast to India, Brazil, and China, the leading software firms in Israel and Ireland are product innovators targeting specific niches, and entrepreneurial start-ups are more prominent among them. Table 7.3 lists the leading Irish software firms (by revenue). Of the fourteen firms listed in the table, eleven are start-ups, with a couple formed to commercialize university technology. Interestingly, two of the leading Irish software firms originated in user organizations in the airlines and electrical power industries. Though Breznitz stresses the role of related industries, particularly computer hardware and electronics, as sources of competencies for Israeli software firms, the leading Israeli software firms also tend to be start-ups with distinctive proprietary technology.[9] Table 7.4, which provides information for a sample of fifteen leading Israeli software firms, shows that most of them are entrepreneurial start-ups.

The evidence thus far suggests that though preexisting firms gave rise to a substantial fraction of successful software firms, these preexisting firms belong to a diverse group of industries. This should not surprise us. As noted earlier, software is a widely used general purpose technology, with every large organization being a significant user of software-based systems for accounting, finance, human resources, and so on. Further, many users produce and develop a considerable amount of software, which is frequently industry or even firm specific. Consequently, firms in a large range of related industries, such as banks, insurance, and telecommunications, can spawn successful software firms. Since virtually all countries with per capita incomes greater than $1,000 are likely to have these industries, the presence of related industries does not distinguish the emerging economies studied here, with the possible exception of Brazil, which has very sophisticated banking and telecommunications firms. Thus, though we find evidence pointing to the importance of organizational competencies, related industries as a source of organizational competencies cannot explain why India alone developed a successful software export sector and Brazil and China have not.

The lesser importance of preexisting firms in Ireland and Israel compared to entrepreneurial start-ups reflects the greater importance of innovative technology relative to organizational competencies. The availability of venture capital, both homegrown and American, has also helped these innovators get access to experienced management and marketing expertise. Furthermore, many Israeli and Irish software firms with innovative products were acquired by leading European and American multinationals, complementing innovative technology with organizational competence.

Spin-offs from successful incumbent firms are another source of organizational competence, responsible to a substantial extent for the rise of Detroit and Akron

TABLE 7.2. Origins of the Leading Chinese Software Firms

Company	Business area and focus	Size	Origin	Year
Founder	Diversified IT products and services company	5000; >1000 S/W engineers	Academics: Beijing University	1986
Pu Tian	IT products and service provider for telecoms industry	>54,000 employees	State-owned	1980
Legend	Diversified IT products and services company	12,000	Academics: CAS	1984
Dong Fang (Neusoft)	Application software supplier and solution provider	>5,000 employees	Academics from local university	1991
CS&S	Product development, systems integration	2,020	State-owned	1990
Pansky	Solutions for: banking, airlines, airports	700	Start-up with foreign investors	1995
Tsinghua Tong Fang	Solutions for information industry and energy and environment	—	Academics: Tsinghua University	
Yan Tai Dong Fang	Integrates R&D, manufacturing and support for electric power	2,021 technicians	State-owned	1983
CVIC	Software development and systems integration: Banking, transport, retail	>600**	Founded in 1991	1991
Sichuan TOP Group	Application software and complete solutions for major industries	[Top S/W had 788 in 2001]	Academics: UESTC	1992
UFSoft co. Ltd.	ERP: Manufacturing, finance	>3,000 employees (600 in software development)	Start-up	1988
Kingdee	ERP: Manufacturing, finance, transport	>2,200	Start-up	1993
Beida Jade Bird Group	Embedded software products	180 (91 R&D staff) (Jade Bird Sci-Tech Universal only)	Academic: Beijing University spin-off	
Digital China	Systems integrator	3,800	Spun off from Legend	2001

** Based on interview by Tschang and Xue.
Source: Adapted from Tschang and Xue, Table 6.2.

TABLE 7.3. Origins of Some Leading Irish Software Firms

Company name	Year	Origin	Specialization	Empl. (2002)	Rev 2002 (mill.)	Notes
Iona	1991	Academic: Trinity College	Middleware—e-business	183	1,439.1	Founded by Chris Horn out of Distributed Computing Research Program at TCD
FINEOS	1993	Start-up	Banking and insurance	203	157.0	CEO is Michael Kelly who is ex DCU (Dublin City University) and ex Irish Life (Insurance Company)
Eontec	1994		Component based solutions for banks and financial services	154	104.1	Acquired by Siebel Systems in 2004
QUMAS	1994	Start-up	Enterprise compliance management solutions for lifescience and healthcare	63	86.7	Founder Paul Hands held senior management positions in technical companies
Precision Software	1984	Start-up	Shipping, logistics, transport solutions	73	78.0	
ESBI Computing	1989	Spin-out: State Elect. Board	IT solutions	65	48.3	Software arm of National Power Utility—Electricity Supply Board
Smartforce (Skillsoft)	1983	Start-up	Enterprise e-learning solutions	375	3.6	Founded by Pat McDonagh out of government e-learning initiative in 1980s. Merged with Skillsoft in June 2002

Company	Year	Origin	Product/Sector			Notes
Trintech	1987	Academic: Trinity College	Transaction management solutions for finance industry	149	n.a.	Founded by two brothers Cyril and John McGuire based on student project in engineering department at TCD
Baltimore Technologies	1976	Start-up	E-security products	92	n.a.	Founded by university lecturer, but hired Jim Mountjoy (previously worked for Dept of Post and Telegraphs) as its MD
Datalex	1985	Spin-out: Aer Lingus (Airline)	Technology solutions for airlines	78	n.a.	Spin-out from Aer Lingus—national state owned airline. Floated on Nasdaq in Oct. 2000
Kindle	1978	Start-up	Banking and insurance		n.a.	Got contract from Ansbacher Bank in Dublin to develop software application. Now owned by Misys
Aldiscon	1988	Start-up	Telecommunications		n.a.	Founder had a contract for laying cables for telecommunications system in Ireland in the 1980s
CardBASE	1993	Not available	Smart card solutions for secure e-commerce	56	16.3	
Riverdeep	1996	Spin-out: Smartforce	E-learning for schools		n.a.	Smartforce spin-out, founded by Pat McDonagh as well. Floated in March 2000

Source: Data supplied by Anita Sands, based upon NSD 2003 data, and company websites.

TABLE 7.4. Origins of Some Leading Israeli Software Firms

Company name	Year founded	Sales ($ mill.) 2002	Origin	Specialization
Amdocs Limited	1980s	1,613	Spin-off (Post and Telegraph)	Billing and Service Provisioning
Comverse	1984	736	Start-up	Telecommunications Equipment
Check Point	1993	427	Start-up (Univ)	Security
Mercury	1989	400	Start-up (overseas Israeli)	Development Tools, Operating Systems and Utilities
NDS Group PLC	??	368	BH	Messaging, Conferencing and Communications
Verinet	2002	120.6	Spin-off (Comverse)	Telecommunication
Tecnomatix Ltd.	1983	82		Supply Chain Management and Logistics
Retalix Ltd.	1982	77	Start-up	Retail, Point-Of-Sale and Inventory Management
Precise Software	1989	76	Start-up	Networking and Connectivity acquired by Veritas in 2003
Sapiens International	1982	65	n.a.	Information Technology Services
Magic Software	1984	60	Start-up (IDF)	Development Tools, Operating Systems and Utilities
Ulticom	2002	58.2	Spin-off (Comverse)	Telecommunications
TTI Team Telecom	1992	58	n.a.	Computer Networking and Connectivity
Verisity Ltd.	1996	53	Spin-off (DEC)	Engineering, Scientific and CAD/CAM
Aladdin Knowledge	1985	50	Start-up	Security; Network Security Devices

Source: Hoover.com and company websites, and data supplied by Dan Breznitz.

as the leading regions for automobile and tire production in the United States. Although we see evidence of spin-off activity, spin-offs do not appear to be as salient in the software industry in the emerging economies as they were in automobiles and tires. Of the top twenty Indian software exporters, Infosys is a spin-off from Patni Computer Systems and another, NIIT, is a spin-off from HCL. In more recent unpublished work, Athreye finds that out of 205 Indian software firms in 2003, fewer than 10 percent could be classified as spin-offs. Of the leading Irish firms in Table 7.3, one, Riverdeep, is a spin-off from Smartforce. Spin-offs are slightly more prominent in Israel. Three of the twelve leading firms for which the origin can be determined are spin-offs, including two from Comverse.

The relatively short history of the software industry in these emerging economies implies that spin-offs are likely to be less important. More importantly, the sources of competencies in a pioneer country, which in the United States were in automobiles and tires, would be expected to be different from those in follower countries. Simply put, spin-offs from successful incumbents play an important role because they act as channels for the transfer of organizational competence. However, follower countries can tap two distinct sources of competence not pertinent in the pioneer country: multinationals and expatriates. Expressed differently, when an industry first comes into existence, the only available sources of firm competencies are either firms in closely related industries or other successful firms in the industry itself. But to develop an industry in another region, one can look to successful firms in the industry (or, particularly in software, in related industries) in advanced regions, or to expatriates working in successful firms in advanced countries. We see ample evidence of the importance of both.

The importance of multinationals is evident in Ireland, where they were the main catalyst of the Irish software industry. As Sands shows in her chapter (Chapter 3), multinationals account for nearly half the software employment in Ireland, and even adjusting for accounting practices, a very substantial fraction of software revenues and exports. In addition, multinationals, both those developing software in Ireland and others, have catalyzed the indigenous software sector by acting as lead users and as a testing ground for potential firm founders and managers. For instance, Sun Microsystems was an early customer and investor in Iona and played an important role in Iona's success. Another leading Irish software firm, FINEOS, leveraged a software development contract from a Scottish bank to develop a successful banking product. The role of multinationals as training grounds for managers is particularly noteworthy. Of the thirty-eight Irish software firms surveyed by Sands, twenty-five (66 percent) had at least one founder who had worked for a multinational. Sixteen of these thirty-eight firms had a founder who worked for a multinational abroad and thirteen had a founder who worked for a multinational in Ireland.

Ireland also relied upon its diaspora of Irish software developers and managers working in the United States and United Kingdom. Sands's data show that twenty-nine of the thirty-eight companies had one or more founders who had worked abroad, and thirty-three out of fifty-eight of the founders had worked abroad.[10] The large Irish diaspora in the United States and United Kingdom is amply documented by Kapur and McHale (Chapter 9, this volume). They describe how an anemic economy and sustained investment in tertiary education created a serious imbalance in the labor market, leading to large-scale emigration in the 1980s, with 25 percent of male Irish graduates emigrating in 1990. The Irish born population in the United States by 1990 was nearly 170,000, a figure which dropped by 15,000 in the next decade as Irish graduates came home to fuel the software industry.

Multinationals and expatriates have also played an important role in the Indian software industry. Of the 657 NASSCOM member firms in 2000–01 reflected in Athreye's Table 2.3 (Chapter 2, this volume), 128 (19 percent) were multinationals. Of the top twenty Indian software exporters, three (Digital Soft, Perot Systems TSI, and Hughes Software) are multinationals, one is a joint venture involving a multinational (Mahindra–British Telecom) and another was spawned from Citibank (i-Flex). Expatriate Indians have been perhaps even more important than multinationals, though this may not be adequately reflected by the two firms founded by Indian expatriates (Patni Computer Systems and IGate) in the top twenty exporters.[11] As in Ireland, a number of top managers cut their teeth working overseas, particularly early in the history of the industry. One of the top twenty software firms, Mphasis-BFL, was founded by two top Citibank managers.[12] Of the 657 NASSCOM member firms in 2000–01, fifty-eight were founded by expatriate Indians overseas, almost all located in the United States.[13] Table 7.5 reports on more recent unpublished work by Athreye on 125 software start-ups in India involving 279 founders. She finds that fifty-six, or about 20 percent, of the founders had worked for a multinational.

TABLE 7.5. Entry Dates for 125 Indian Software Start-ups (Excluding Multinationals and Business Houses)

	Number	Percentage
Panel A: Year of establishment		
Pre-1984	9	7
1985–91	19	15
1992–99	76	61
2000 and after	21	17
Total	125	100
Panel B: Information on founder backgrounds		
Previous experience of marketing	156	56
Previous experience in IT	94	34
Previous experience in multinational	56	20
Total numbers of founders	279	

Source: Derived from survey data on 205 NASSCOM member companies, provided by Suma Athreye.

Although the Israeli software industry has also benefited from multinationals and expatriates, the evidence is more indirect. The Israeli born population in the United States as of 1990 was about 86,000, which is small compared to the contemporaneous Irish-born population at the time (170,000), let alone the Indian and Chinese born populations in the United States (450,000 and 530,000, respectively). But this figure underestimates the external expertise available to Israel because of the large Jewish diaspora in the United States and the strong cultural and economic ties between the United States and Israel. We lack systematic evidence on the precise contribution of expatriates to the Israeli software industry. Breznitz provides examples of two leading software firms founded by US based expatriates, Comverse, which also spun off two other leading software firms, and Mercury. We do know that few, if any, software firms were founded by Russian immigrants to Israel, even though these immigrants were better educated than their Israeli counterparts and accounted for 20 percent of the Jewish population in Israel. Breznitz cites an unpublished study which shows that none of the founders of the 151 publicly listed Israeli IT firms was an immigrant from the USSR. This intriguing result again points to the importance of organizational competence. It suggests that founding successful firms, even those that rely heavily upon technical innovation, requires more than mere technical expertise.

Breznitz also notes that multinationals have not been an important source of Israeli software firms. However, this is true only for technical expertise. Israeli firms have relied upon the United States for managerial and marketing expertise. To assess the background and competencies of the Israeli managers more systematically, we collected data on a sample of 200 top managers working as Chief Executive Officers (CEOs), Chief Technology Officers (CTOs), Chief Marketing Officers (CMOs), or Chief Financial Officers (CFOs) in thirty-six publicly listed Israeli software firms in 2000.[14] We found that about 25 percent of the top managers had US undergraduate degrees (the remainder had Israeli degrees). Moreover, 40 percent of these top managers had earlier worked for US firms, including Israeli subsidiaries of US multinationals. The competencies provided by the US firms were typically managerial and financial; 60 percent of CFOs and marketing managers had previously worked for US companies, whereas 69 percent of the CEOs and 72 percent of the CTOs had previously worked for other Israeli firms.

The available evidence, discussed in greater detail by Giarratana et al. (Chapter 8, this volume), also suggests that multinationals were not simply responding to market signals suggesting that the 3Is would be successful software exporters. Multinationals were drawn to Ireland by favorable tax policies and the prospect of easy access to the European market. Software multinationals found Ireland to be the ideal platform to distribute software, then to localize and finally develop software, and their entry clearly preceded and contributed to the growth of the software industry in Ireland. The role of multinationals in catalyzing the indigenous software industry in Israel and India is less clear cut. Although multinationals such as Hughes, IBM, Cognizant, and Digital are among the leading software developers in India, they entered the industry after the leading indigenous firms did. Athreye argues in her chapter, however, that Texas Instruments played a catalytic role in demonstrating the feasibility of developing software for the US market from India. In Israel, though multinationals have set up R&D operations, the contribution of these operations to the growth of the Israeli industry is unclear.

Multinationals are active in both Brazil and China. Botelho et al. (Chapter 5, this volume) note that IBM and Siemens have spawned a number of important Brazilian software firms. However, multinationals in both countries are primarily engaged in serving the respective domestic markets rather than international markets, perhaps because the domestic software markets in both countries are large and growing.[15] The firms they have spawned also appear similarly inclined towards the domestic market.

China and Brazil also have a substantial number of expatriates in the United States, although Brazilian graduates are of a more recent vintage, as shown in Table 7.6. However, neither Botelho et al. nor Tschang and Xue indicate that expatriates are a significant source of firm formation or competencies in Brazil or China. Differences in the expatriate population may partly explain why Indian expatriates are prominent in the Indian software industry, unlike in China or Brazil. Compared to the Chinese and Brazilian born populations in the United States, Indian expatriates are better educated, with a higher percentage having tertiary education. Other evidence provided by Kapur and McHale (Chapter 9, this volume) indicates that Indian expatriates in Silicon Valley are more likely to work in software firms and more likely to occupy managerial positions than Chinese expatriates.

The limited role of multinationals in spawning domestic firms and the apparent unimportance of expatriates suggests that the external sources of firm competence are markedly less important in Brazil and China than in the 3Is. We speculate that the key competence provided by multinationals and expatriates is primarily organizational competence, related to successful organizations in leading markets such as the United States, rather than technical competence. This is certainly true for Israel, and likely also for India and Ireland. Moreover, though software is technology intensive, organizational competencies such as those relating to

TABLE 7.6. Selected Foreign-born Populations in the United States Aged 25 and Above

	1990	2000	% Chng	% of 2000 population entering post 1990	Educational attainment (2000) %		
					Primary	Secondary	Tertiary
India	304	837	175	55	5	15	80
Brazil	54	154	186	49	9	36	55
China	405	847	109	66	20	26	54

Source: Kapur and McHale, 2003, from the US census.

marketing are more important than perhaps many realize.[16] Thus we conjecture that the inward orientation of the software industry in Brazil and China makes multinationals and expatriates less attractive sources of competence for domestic software firms.

Another distinctive source of firm competencies, largely absent from the four US industries studied for reasons that are self evident, is the public sector. Though Irish universities have spawned some successful software firms, Israel truly stands out in the contribution of the public sector to the success of its software industry. Breznitz details in his chapter (Chapter 4) how Israel has invested in R&D, looking to high-tech industries such as electronics, medical equipment, computer investments, and software to invigorate the economy. He emphasizes the role of the Office of the Chief Scientist, which provided key financing for R&D by firms, and a variety of government schemes to promote entrepreneurial start-ups by providing venture financing and other types of infrastructure. These measures appear to have directly helped Israeli software firms such as Comverse and Mercury, which benefited from a number of government R&D grants. They benefited Israeli software firms indirectly as well because other high tech Israeli firms were important lead users for Israeli software firms, especially early in the history of the Israeli software industry.[17]

Israeli investments in technology were impelled in large measure by its military needs. The leading role of the Israeli military in communication and software technology has meant that some of the leading firms drew upon military technology and also upon military networks. For instance, Breznitz points out that Magic Software Enterprise, one of the leading Israeli software firms, was founded by a team of former officers of the military's central computer unit (MAMRAM). Another leading firm, Fourth Dimension (later known as New Dimension), was formed to commercialize a software product for operation automation developed by the Israeli Air Force. Our data on the backgrounds of 200 Israeli managers in software companies confirm the role of the government and of the military in particular. The Israeli Defense Force (IDF) was the largest single former employer of these managers (12.5 percent), and approximately 20 percent of the Israeli software managers in the sample were formerly high-tech employees of the State.

In China, Brazil, and India, the public sector has also accounted for a large share of economic activity, particularly until the 1990s. In Brazil and China many of the leading software firms originated in the public sector. The dominance of the public sector in the Brazilian economy until the 1980s, particularly in informatics, made it a natural candidate for spawning software firms, and the five leading firms identified by Botelho et al. originated in the government. Similarly, given the leading role of the state in China's economy, it is only to be expected that state institutions would be an important source of software firms. Table 7.2, adapted from Table 6.2 in Tschang and Xue's chapter (Chapter 6), shows that other than two firms supplying business software, virtually all of the leading Chinese software firms originated in universities or public sector firms.

In contrast to Brazil and China, the public sector has not been prominent in the Indian software industry despite its leading role in the rest of the Indian economy. Athreye notes in her chapter (Chapter 2) that one of the earliest software service firms in India, CMC, was formed by the government to support IBM computers after IBM exited India in 1976. Although CMC was large and staffed by technically proficient engineers, its focus was on the domestic sector. The success of Indian software exports meant a steady attrition of its experienced managers and engineers to other Indian firms, and eventually the government sold CMC to TCS, the largest Indian software firm. Significantly, CMC does not appear to have spawned any of the leading Indian software firms.

The evidence suggests that whereas the public sector has seeded or directly spawned leading firms in Israel, Brazil, and China, only in Israel has this visibly contributed to an internationally competitive software industry. In general, the public sector and universities can be important sources of technical competence. They are less likely, however, to be important in providing organizational competencies that internationally competitive firms require. The extent to which different countries have successfully drawn upon the public sector as a source of firm competence depends obviously on the role of the public sector in the economy and less obviously on the type of competence required. Unlike Brazil, China, and India, organizational competence appears less critical for Israeli software firms because many are acquired by established firms. Further, it is easier for Israeli firms to leverage close cultural ties with the United States to acquire the organizational competencies they lack. Therefore, though the public sector accounts for a significant share of economic activity in all of the countries except Ireland, only in Israel is it a clear source of advantage for the software industry.

4.3 Summary

Are the 3Is distinguished by the sources of firm competencies they draw upon? As in the four US industries studied, related industries are an important source of organizational competencies for software firms as well. However, the range of related industries that can seed software firms is large and does not seem to be a distinguishing characteristic for the 3Is. Instead, it is the external sources of competencies that are noteworthy. We have seen evidence that multinationals and expatriates are more prominent in the software industry in the 3Is than Brazil or China. We lack systematic evidence on other countries with a potential comparative advantage in software, but it seems plausible that the 3Is are distinct in drawing upon expatriates and multinationals to the degree that they have.

In Ireland, the multinationals were clearly pivotal and once they catalyzed the indigenous software industry, expatriates fueled its growth. The early entry of multinationals clearly differentiates Ireland from comparable regions, such as Northern Ireland or Scotland.

In Israel, expatriates have been relatively more important than multinationals, although the great strengths that Israel enjoys in technology per se are probably the main reason for its successful software industry. That said, the importance of organizational competencies required to start successful technology focused firms should not be underestimated. Eastern European countries, particularly Russia, have a large stock of relatively underemployed scientists and engineers and significant strengths in mathematics and computer programming. Indeed, given the sustained increases in software salaries in India, Russian programmers are probably cheaper than Indian programmers. Recognizing this, firms such as Intel, Motorola, and Sun established software development operations in Russia. Yet, Russian software exports are small. In 1999–2000, the Russian software industry had revenues of around $500 million, with exports of only $100–200 million. The problem clearly is in organizational competencies. Leading Russian software development firms, such as Digital Design, employ 150–200 people, less than a hundredth of their Indian counterparts, and even well established systems integrators such as Lanit have only 1,500 employees. There are also few Russian software product firms. Quite simply, the Russian example shows that leveraging endowments of scientists and engineers to create companies that can develop new technologies or provide competitive software development services is not simple. Many factors may make Russia less hospitable to start-ups, but it is certainly plausible that the large public sector firms that dominated the Russian economy were not good sources of the competencies required by successful firms. The failure of Russian immigrants to Israel, many of whom had very strong backgrounds in computers and software, to found companies in Israel is perhaps telling in this respect.

Of course, given time, firm competencies can be developed and nurtured and early chance events can be important. The Indian software industry is a good example. The Indian economy suffered from a number of distortions at the start of the 1980s. Virtually all the large firms in the country were creatures of a protected and highly regulated market, more adept at navigating government regulations than their businesses. Most multinationals entered after the software industry was already on a growth path, and thus are unlikely to be the reason for India's emergence as a software power. Unlike Brazil or Israel, there were no strong lead user sectors in India. Nor was government support important, unlike China. True, there were a number of Indian expatriates, but this is also true for China, and likely also for Pakistan and Bangladesh. Chance events played an important role in the birth of the Indian software industry. As Athreye points out, early in the 1980s some Indian firms (especially TCS) began by sending people on temporary assignments to clients. These early exports were important because the people returned with knowledge about the needs of clients and also established credibility with the clients for their employers. It is also plausible that they established a good reputation for Indian programmers and for India as a place for software. Then, when IT demand began its explosive growth, Indian firms were well positioned relative to those in Russia, Pakistan, or Argentina to benefit from it. Of course, as already discussed, expatriates working in client firms were also sources of such knowledge, as were multinationals.

4.4   Persistence of Leadership and Accumulation of Capabilities

Klepper [18] develops a theory of increasing returns at the firm level that explains why, in automobiles, tires, and TVs, firms that entered early and were successful came to dominate the market. A similar persistence appears to characterize the software industry, although in differing degrees across the various countries.

Early entry appears to have been most advantageous for firms providing software services, such as software development in India. Table 2.2 in Athreye's chapter (Chapter 2) shows that all of the leading software exporters in India were founded before 1990, which is when the industry began its explosive growth period, and a substantial number were founded in the early 1980s, when total software exports were miniscule compared to $12 billion in 2003. Indeed, since 1990 only two firms have successfully entered the ranks of leading software producers in India, and both have been multinationals: Cognizant, previously a subsidiary of Dunn and Bradstreet, and IBM. The early leaders have continued to dominate the industry because they have developed distinctive capabilities. Specifically, they have become very good at managing large offshore software projects and in recruiting and managing the people to do the job. Athreye provides additional evidence. Table 2.11 in her chapter shows that larger firms have higher revenue per employee, and Table 2.12 provides examples of the ability of the leading Indian software firms to win large, multi-year contracts.

Since the Brazilian and Chinese software industries have even more recent origins, persistence in market leadership is less easy to discern. Even so, the top five Chinese software firms were founded before 1991 and the top three were founded in the 1980s. Of the fifty-five leading Brazilian software firms identified by Botelho et al. (Chapter 5, this volume), over 60 percent were founded before 1990 and eighteen were founded before 1980. The latter group includes industry leaders such as SERPRO, which employed close to 9,000 people and had revenues of $372 million in 2001.

Ireland and Israel have somewhat different patterns than the other three countries. Table 7.3 indicates that among the top five Irish software firms in 2002, four entered in the 1990s. Table 7.4 indicates that among the top five Israeli software firms, one entered in the 1990s and another in 2002. In part, the lesser advantage of early entry in Ireland and Israel relative to India, China, and Brazil is due to the high rate at which software firms in these countries, especially Israel, were acquired and thus ceased to be independent entities.[18] But it also reflects the distinctive nature of software firms in Ireland and Israel. Almost without exception, the leading Irish and Israeli firms entered with innovative products, focusing on specific market segments such as solutions for banking and finance, telecommunications, airlines, and e-learning (for Ireland), and data and network security products, software development tools, and solutions for telecommunication and e-commerce (Israel). This focus on product innovation, and the availability of many product niches, implies that the increasing returns that advantaged early entrants in automobiles, tires, and TVs are less salient in the Irish and Israeli software industries. This is similar to lasers, where the multiplicity of different user sectors appears to have provided significant opportunities for sustained entry. As in lasers, we see that successful firms like Iona in Ireland and Comverse in Israel are more likely to generate successful spin-offs. It is too early to tell whether these spin-offs will be more narrowly focused than their parents, as was the case in lasers. Lasers is also similar in that economies of scale and scope do not appear to be significant enough to preclude narrowly specialized firms from entering and surviving. Indeed, early entry was not a source of competitive advantage in lasers, suggesting that a similar pattern may obtain for Irish and Israeli software firms.

4.5   Modest Evidence of Agglomeration Economies

As noted in Section 3, the geographical concentration of the US industries studied by Klepper can largely be explained by the location of successful firms rather than agglomeration economies. The software industry in the emerging economies studied here also tends to be geographically concentrated. Bangalore, in particular, has been analogized to Silicon Valley in the United States, and by implication, the growth of the software industry in India is attributed in substantial measure to processes similar to those that drove the growth of Silicon Valley itself. Similar analogies have been made about Ireland (Silicon Glen) and Israel (Silicon Wadi).

Assessing the reasons for agglomeration in small countries like Ireland or Israel is difficult because companies will necessarily locate close to large economic centers and thus close to each other. Software firms locate mostly in the Dublin area in the case of Ireland and in the Tel Aviv and Jerusalem areas in the case of Israel, where most of the population and industry is located in any case. Table 7.7, which is based on a survey of Irish software firms in 2000, indicates that Irish firms appear to place less importance on benefits from locating near other software firms than on the availability of skills and transport and communication infrastructure.[19]

To test for the importance of agglomeration economies we have to turn to the larger countries. In Brazil and China, most of the software industry is located near centers of major economic activity. Tschang and Xue's chapter (Chapter 6) indicates that most of the Chinese software industry is concentrated in the largest cities, such as Beijing, Shanghai, Shenzhen, Jinan, and Xian. Many of these cities are in the prosperous eastern part of the country where much of the high-tech sector is located, the bulk of foreign investments are made, and many of the leading universities are located. Similarly, Brazilian software companies are mainly concentrated in the southeastern and southern areas of the country (59 and 22 percent of total companies in 2001), which are also the most industrialized and have better R&D infrastructure. Indeed, the State of São Paulo accounts for 40 percent of the total software market in Brazil, largely because the city of São Paulo is the major center for finance, telecommunications, and trade. Though not inconsistent with agglomeration economies, this clustering more likely reflects the need for

TABLE 7.7. Importance of Different Factors as Sources of Location Advantages in Ireland, Irish Software Firms

	Customers	Competitors	Partners	Business services	Physical infrastructure	Communication infrastructure	Skills	University
Average	2.68	1.68	2.32	2.96	3.54	3.74	4.54	2.93
Mode	1	1.00	2.00	3.00	4.00	4.00	5.00	3.00
Std deviation	1.33	0.77	1.16	1.14	0.92	1.21	0.69	1.12

Notes: Sample of 28 firms, interviewed over the phone.

Answers on a 5 point likert scale, 1 = unimportant, 5 = very important.

Source: Adapted from Arora, Gambardella, and Torrisi [19, table 12].

software producers to locate close to their customers, particularly for software firms supplying businesses, as is true of most of the leading Chinese and Brazilian software producers.

The evidence from India is the most extensive and the least favorable to agglomeration economies. Table 2.5 in Athreye's chapter (Chapter 2) reports the location and the entry dates of NASSCOM member companies in 2002. The table shows that there are at least five areas in India where software companies locate: Bangalore, Mumbai/Pune, Delhi, Hyderabad, and Chennai. None of them has a clear lead over the others in terms of number of firms located there. Indeed, the initial entrants were concentrated in Mumbai and Delhi, rather than Bangalore, which is commonly (and incorrectly) perceived to be the major software cluster today.[20] In terms of the leading firms, TCS and Patni are Mumbai based, Satyam is based in Hyderabad, HCL is Delhi based and Infosys and Wipro are Bangalore based, though Infosys was initially founded in Mumbai when it was spun off from Patni. Chennai, the other major city for software production, is home to Pentafour (which used to be among the top twenty software exporters) and Ramco, which is the leading producer of ERP systems in India. Both of these firms resulted from existing business groups diversifying into software.

It might be argued that the software industry is concentrated in southern India (which includes Bangalore, Hyderabad, and Chennai), well in excess of the share of GDP or population accounted for by these regions. As noted, these cities are home to some of the industry leaders. But the ability of the southern cities, particularly Bangalore, to attract software firms is itself due to a variety of factors that have little to do with agglomeration economies. The south and the west together accounted for nearly two-thirds of the accredited engineering capacity in India in the mid-1980s, noteworthy given that engineers were the key input for Indian software firms. Moreover, the available evidence suggests that this dominance in engineering education capacity predates the growth of software activity, partly because of education policies in some southern states (especially Karnataka, where Bangalore is located) that facilitated the earlier entry of private engineering colleges. Finally, Bangalore enjoyed a number of other advantages, including its favorable climate, its cosmopolitan tradition dating to British times, and the location of a number of advanced public sector research institutions in space, defense, and electronics.

In summary, the software industries in the emerging economies tend to concentrate near major centers of economic activity in those countries. Relative to the software industry, it appears that automobiles and tires are unusual because of the concentration of the early leaders in a narrow region, Detroit for automobiles and Akron for tires. By contrast, in India, Brazil, and China the early leaders were more dispersed and typically entered in centers of major economic activity. We do not dispute the possibility of agglomeration economies arising from thick labor markets or good infrastructure. However, the available evidence about agglomeration economies is inconclusive at best and instead provides some support for the role of early successful firms.

5 Conclusions

Though not conclusive, the evidence from the software industry in emerging economies, like that from automobiles, tires, TVs, and lasers in the United States, points to the importance of early industry leaders in the evolution of the industry. The automobile and tire industries concentrated regionally because entry by the early industry leaders was concentrated geographically. Not only did the early leaders persistently account for a large share of the output, they were also more likely to spawn other successful firms, typically in the same region. Where early leaders will come from is not entirely predictable, but as in TVs, they are more likely to come from successful firms in closely related industries.

Leaders in the software industries in the emerging economies also tend to be among the earlier entrants. However, software, with its diverse set of users, provides many niches and opportunities for product innovation, which has encouraged entrepreneurial start-ups in Ireland and Israel. Unlike TVs, automobiles, tires, and even lasers, many non-software vendors such as banks, insurance firms, and telecommunications firms develop software. These user organizations have been an important source of firm formation in the software industry in emerging economies. Furthermore, the 3Is in particular have drawn upon external competencies in the form of multinationals and expatriates, gaining access to vital organizational competencies that in the four US industries were available only through successful firms in the industry or in closely related industries.

Although it is dangerous to identify the success of an industry with those of its leaders, this chapter has argued that the firms that dominate an industry early in its history can greatly affect the future evolution of the industry. This holds an important lesson for developing countries and for economic policy makers in these countries.

Traditional economic doctrine has pointed to and even prescribed comparative advantage as the basis for the activities on which a country ought to focus. Hausmann and Rodrik [1] persuasively argue that within the broad range of alternatives offered by comparative advantage, the narrow set of activities in which a developing country will be successful is uncertain and difficult to predict. Discovering these activities requires economic experiments, or in a word, entrepreneurship. Since the private returns to entrepreneurship are significantly lower than the social returns, Hausmann and Rodrik [1] suggest that successful entrepreneurs be protected for a period before other firms are allowed to enter their industry. However, emulating leaders is not easy. The industry leaders are themselves not a stationary target. Instead, they deepen and improve their capabilities over time, making it difficult for followers to catch up with them unless the followers have some distinctive capabilities, such as markedly superior technology, or more likely, superior access to customers. More importantly, as the history of the four US industries illustrates, many later entrants do not merely imitate but actively try out new things.

Thus, although we agree with Hausmann and Rodrik on the importance of economic experiments, we do not think that countries ought to reward early leaders with temporary monopolies. Early leaders enjoy a variety of advantages. Instead, countries ought to encourage entry and entrepreneurship. Many countries and regions claim to have implemented such policies but few are truly committed to them. Frequently they try to provide 'strategic direction', blunting the edge of economic experimentation. Most policies end up trying to sustain existing firms, perhaps for political reasons, whereas the possibility of failure is an important part of entrepreneurship. Perhaps most importantly, government policies inherently tend to focus on technology and supply side variables, whereas successful firms are distinguished by organizational competencies, including marketing expertise. This is not to suggest that governments can successfully provide such competencies, for the evidence reviewed here suggests the opposite. Governments and universities can provide technical expertise but firms have to find organizational competencies elsewhere.

Science and technology parks and concessionary financing are common policy tools for attracting firms into 'high-tech' sectors. Insofar as these are a cost effective means of providing infrastructural services, science and technology parks make sense. However, such parks are frequently justified as facilitating knowledge spillovers across firms located close to each other. The evidence for such spillovers, in the four US industries studied as well as in the software industry in emerging economies, is limited at best. Instead, successful firms, particularly early in the history of the industry, appear to play a more important role in whether a region succeeds in an industry. Firms that enter early and succeed persistently account for a significant share of output and are also more likely to spawn other successful firms. Later entrants must differentiate themselves by opening other market niches or bringing markedly better technology.

Potential entrepreneurs and policy makers in developing countries eyeing India's success in software services (and since then, in other types of business services) must pay close attention to the last point. Even though the labor costs in India have risen steadily, the leading Indian firms in particular appear to be well entrenched. Potential challengers are unlikely to succeed if their only advantage is cheaper labor. Instead they must seek different market niches, as the Chinese firms appear to be doing by targeting the Japanese market, where Chinese firms naturally have a number of advantages.

Perhaps the most important lesson of all has to do with the importance of firms and firm competencies. Drawing upon the historical experience of four industries in the United States, this chapter takes the perspective that the growth of the software industry in emerging regions can only be understood as the interplay between comparative advantage deriving from the relative abundance of human capital and the specific institutions and sources of expertise that helped create software firms and shaped where these firms focused their attention. To paraphrase Karl Marx, firms do indeed make their own history, albeit in circumstances not of their choosing.

Notes

1. For instance, Indian firms focus on software services for software maintenance and custom software development, but do not design software products or semiconductor chips. The leading Irish firms tend to focus on banking and financial industry solutions, whereas Israeli firms dominate in security software, telecommunications software, and software development tools.
2. Hausmann and Rodrik [1] note that at the fine-grained 6-digit HS level, developing countries tend to export a small number of products, with their top twenty-five products accounting for between 60% and 80% of their total exports.
3. While the Bangladesh garment example is described in the most detail, Rhee and Belot provide ten other similar examples of a single catalyst involving a foreign and local partner that initiated a successful industry in a non-NIC developing country. In some of the examples, the prime local actor was the country's government. Not much detail is provided in a number of the examples about subsequent developments that took place after the success of the catalyst. However, in two of the cases involving Indonesia's plywood industry and Columbia's flower exports an extensive industry was catalyzed by the initial successful venture [2, p. 53].
4. The periods studied were dictated by data sources [3].
5. Only television receivers were affected in its formative era by international competition, which began in the later part of the 1960s after the industry had already experienced a sharp shakeout in the number of producers.
6. Bicycle tires did not readily scale to automobiles, tire manufacturing was much more complex than other rubber products, and tires were subject to much more technological change than other rubber products.
7. Among the top five, both Wipro and HCL also had prior experience with computer hardware (although Wipro originally started as a vegetable oil company) and TCS could draw upon the formidable managerial and technical resources of its parent, the Tata Group, which is involved in a variety of industries, including computer hardware, steel, and transport equipment.
8. The sample includes companies that were large or innovative and that obtained some form of risk capital financing. See Botelho et al.'s chapter (Chapter 5) and Botelho et al.'s [15] report for more details. They also show that in the 1990s these companies grew at a rate that was much higher than the industry average.
9. Breznitz claims that many software firms originated as hardware producers. He cites the example of Comverse, which started out producing telecommunication devices for voice and fax messaging before focusing on software.
10. As Sands notes, of those who worked abroad, 75% did so for a multinational corporation.
11. The list of top twenty software exporters excludes firms such as Syntel and Cognizant, which are US based firms headed by expatriate Indians.
12. Mphasis later merged with another leading Indian born software firm, BFL, whose corporate parent had run into legal difficulties.
13. In addition, a number of other firms have important international links. For instance, Taube [16, p. 11] notes that the founder of Satyam, a leading software firm, was educated in the United States, bringing back with him not '… modern technology but western business culture'.

14. These data were obtained from the *Hoover Database* (www.hoover.com). We thank Rafeal Lucea for collecting and analyzing these data for us. A manager could have more than one past employer. See also Lucea [17].

15. The Chinese software market is both large and growing rapidly since the Chinese economy has been growing at around 8% per year. Brazilian economic growth is not as stellar but Brazil appears to have invested very heavily in IT. In 2001, Brazil spent 8.3% of its GDP on ICT, far greater than the 3.9% spent in India and even the 5.7% spent in China.

16. For instance, Table 7.5 shows that of the 125 software firms surveyed by Athreye that did not originate from established firms (Indian or otherwise), 56% of the 279 founders had worked in marketing compared to 34% who had prior IT experience.

17. Breznitz provides a number of examples of leading Israeli software firms whose initial customers were the local Israeli computer industry. OptiSystems Solutions, established in 1982, focused on optimization of computer systems; Magic, established in 1983, developed a Rapid Application Development (RAD) tool for relational database applications; Attunity (formerly Nikov Haifa), established in 1988, developed RAD tools for reports programming; Sapiens, established in 1982, has been focused on rule-based systems for RAD; and Technomatix, established in 1983, developed a product to solve the problems of rapidly reprogramming factory robots. Breznitz also claims that these firms benefited from R&D grants from the Office of the Chief Scientist.

18. Only those Irish and Israeli software firms that also develop organizational competencies appear to survive as independent firms for any length of time. Amdocs, the largest Israeli software firm, is a case in point. Breznitz's chapter (Chapter 4) details how Amdocs added to its original product (automated directory systems) and currently provides a comprehensive solution to the billing and customer support needs of the leading telecom firms such as Nextel, which has outsourced its billing functions to Amdocs.

19. Arora, Gambardella, and Torrisi [19] report that their field analysis also shows that trade associations like the Irish Software Association, the Irish Internet Association, and the First Tuesday Club were not important in the development of formal or informal links with competitors and partners.

20. As Athreye points out, multinationals do favor Bangalore. However, one would imagine that multinational location decisions would be much less sensitive to agglomeration economies than to traditional factors such as the human and physical infrastructure.

References

1. Hausmann, R. and Rodrik, D. (2002). Economic Development as Self-discovery. National Bureau of Economic Research, Working Paper 8952.
2. Rhee, Y.W. and Belot, T. (1990). Export Catalysts in Low-Income Countries. World Bank, Washington DC, World Bank Discussion Papers.
3. Klepper, S. (2002). Firm survival and the evolution of oligopoly. *RAND Journal of Economics*, 33, 37–61.
4. Klepper, S. (2001). Firm Capabilities and Industry Evolution: The Case of the US Automobile Industry. Carnegie Mellon University, mimeo.

5. Klepper, S. (2003). The Geography of Organizational Knowledge. Carnegie Mellon University, mimeo.
6. Buenstorf, G. and Klepper, S. (2004). The Origin and Location of Entrants in the Evolution of the US Tire Industry. Carnegie Mellon University, mimeo.
7. Klepper, S. and Simons, K.L. (2000). Dominance by birthright: entry of prior radio producers and competitive ramifications in the US television receiver industry. *Strategic Management Journal*, 21, 997–1016.
8. Klepper, S. and Sleeper, S. (2000). Entry by Spin-offs. Carnegie Mellon University, mimeo.
9. Klepper, S. and Thompson, P. (2003). Submarkets and the Evolution of Market Structure. Carnegie Mellon University, mimeo.
10. La France, V. (1985). *The United States Television Receiver Industry*. Ph.D. dissertation, Pennsylvania State University.
11. Klepper, S. (2003). The Organizing and Financing of Innovative Companies in the Evolution of the U.S. Automobile Industry. Carnegie Mellon University, mimeo.
12. Jeszeck, C.A. (1982). *Plant Dispersion and Collective Bargaining in the Rubber Tire Industry*. Ph.D. dissertation, University of California, Berkeley.
13. Sleeper, S. (1998). *The Role of Firm Capabilities in the Evolution of the Laser Industry: The Making of a High-tech Market*. Ph.D. dissertation, Carnegie Mellon University.
14. Giarratana, M. (2004). The birth of a new industry: entry by start-ups and the drivers of firm growth. The case of encryption software. *Research Policy*, 33(5), 787–806.
15. Botelho, A.J., Stefanuto, G., Spinosa, M., and Veloso, F. (2002). *The Software Industry in Brazil: Strengthening the Knowledge Economy*. Campinas: Softex.
16. Tauebe, F.A. (2004). Proximities and Innovation: Evidence from the Indian IT Industry in Bangalore. Working paper, Department of Economic Development and International Economics, Goethe University, Frankfurt.
17. Lucea, R. (2001). Software in Israel: A Case of Globalization and Entrepreneurship. Unpublished manuscript, Software Industry Center, Heinz School, Carnegie Mellon University, Pittsburgh.
18. Klepper, S. (1996). Entry, exit, growth, and innovation over the product life cycle. *American Economic Review*, 86(3), 562–583.
19. Arora, A., Gambardella, A., and Torrisi, S. (2004). In the footsteps of Silicon Valley: Indian and Irish software in the international division of labor. In T. Bresnahan and A. Gambardella (eds.), *Building High Tech Clusters: Silicon Valley and Beyond*. Cambridge, UK: Cambridge University Press.

8

The Role of the Multinational Companies

MARCO GIARRATANA, ALESSANDRO PAGANO, AND
SALVATORE TORRISI

1 Introduction

This chapter analyzes the role of multinational corporations (MNCs) in the development of the software industry in India, Ireland, and Israel. These countries have experienced a high growth in the software industry especially during the 1990s. Software revenues reached $9.3 billion in Ireland and $8.3 billion in India in 2000. In Israel the software industry has reached a similar size (about $4.2 billion in 2001) [1–3]. Much of software growth in these countries is accounted for by exports, which represent about 75 percent of India's total sales and about 84 percent of Irish sales [1,2]. Similarly, exports represent about 73 percent of Israeli software sales [3,4], in fact, while in 1990, software exports from Israel amounted to $90 million, by 2000, overseas sales had soared incredibly to $2.6 billion and even if the staggering average annual growth of 25 percent could not be maintained in 2000, the forecast was that exports would surpass $3 billion by the end of the year. Domestic sales grew by 10 percent per annum and overall sales for the industry were expected to reach $4.2 billion in 2001.

These countries have benefited from historical linkages with the United States and the United Kingdom which have been reinforced by the communities of expatriates working for leading information and communication technologies (ICT) producers or large users such as financial institutions. Compared to other regions, these countries have been particularly successful in attracting foreign firms, which account for a significant share of national software activities, especially in India and Ireland. In the case of Israel and Ireland the local governments have introduced various incentives to attract MNCs. One reason for such policies is that MNCs

The authors thank all the participants at Workshops in Pittsburgh, Pisa, Urbino, and Catania, notably Ashish Arora, Alfonso Gambardella, and Steven Klepper for their comments on earlier drafts. Antonello Zanfei, Davide Castellani, Anita Sands, and Daniel Breznitz provided data and information in the research process. We also thank Elvio Ciccardini and Teymour Haider for their assistance in data collection. The financial support of the Italian Ministry of University Research (MIUR # 2003133821_005) is also acknowledged. The usual disclaimers apply.

are viewed as a channel through which technologies and business practices from abroad can be transferred to the economies of emerging countries.

The literature on MNCs and economic growth highlights three different channels through which the knowledge of MNCs spills over domestic firms:

(1) demonstration effects and imitation which may be favored by geographical proximity or contractual relationships with the MNCs [5–9];

(2) labor mobility which takes place when experienced workers leave the MNC to join a domestic firm or to found a new start-up [7,10–12];

(3) competition effects which may take place in the input and the final good markets. MNCs challenge domestic monopolies and spur domestic firms to increase their efficiency or to leave the market but they may also increase market power [13].

Another source of externality less explored in the literature on MNCs is represented by market access spillovers and reputation effects. The physical proximity to MNCs or the establishment of collaborative ties with MNCs may reduce the domestic firms' cost of market access, as pointed out by the literature on industrial clusters [14,15].

Most empirical works on MNCs and economic growth focus on productivity spillovers, entry of new domestic firms or firm survival.[1] This literature has not reached any clear-cut conclusions as to which are the benefits of MNCs, the conditions that promote the absorption of MNCs' spillovers, and the implications for public policies. Few studies provide direct measures of technology transfer, for example, through patent citations [23]. Even less is known about the channels of spillovers, such as labor mobility or alliances with domestic firms, with the exception of few works based on micro-level data and case-studies (e.g. [8–12]).

Our case studies look inside the 'black box' of MNC externalities by examining various types of linkages with domestic software firms. Specifically, we ask:

- What is the role played by MNCs in the development of the software industry in these countries? Did MNCs enter at the early stages of formation of the local software industry and place the building blocks of this industry or did they enter at later stages, when a domestic industry had been already established?

- What kind of activities do MNCs conduct locally? Do they conduct high-value-added activities like research and development (R&D) or low-value-added activities like assembling and customer support? What is the division of labor with local firms? Do their activities complement or substitute those of domestic firms?

- Which are the linkages established with domestic firms and what is their impact on domestic firms? Are MNCs a source of technology spillovers, new business models, skilled people, or spin-offs? Do they provide significant reputation effects for domestic firms? Do they represent a significant source of revenues and a bridge to foreign markets for domestic firms?

These issues are examined by drawing on different sources of data, including Dun and Bradstreet's (D&B) Who Owns Whom (WOW), corporate websites, and national industrial association datasets. An important source of information has been the collection of events concerning both domestic firms and MNCs reported by the InfotrackWeb database, which provides press information on several categories of corporate events, for example, new subsidiaries and strategic alliances. Finally, we conducted telephone interviews with managers of MNCs, founders of MNCs' spin-offs, managers of local firms involved in linkages with MNCs, and other industry experts (see the Appendix for details).

The chapter is organized as follows. Section 2 illustrates different patterns of entry strategies and compares software activities conducted by MNCs in the three countries in historical perspective. Section 3 analyzes different types of linkages between MNCs and indigenous software companies. Section 4 summarizes the main benefits of MNCs involvement in the local economies for domestic software firms while Section 5 concludes the study of the role of MNCs.

2   MNCs and the Evolution of the Software Industry

The main issue explored in this section is whether MNCs entered before or in parallel with the growth of a domestic software industry. We also examine the activities that they conducted in the sample countries and the division of labor with local firms. The analysis starts with addressing the entry of MNCs and the evolution of their local activities over time. The differences in historical background and market size across our three countries suggest that we first look at the role of MNCs in each country.

2.1   India

The domestic software industry in India developed in parallel with the entry of a few MNCs. Some MNCs which entered the first stages of development of this industry in the 1980s have influenced the business models of early domestic entrants (for a more extensive discussion of the Indian software industry see Chapter 2 on India in this book).

The first generation of MNCs that entered during the 1980s has not enjoyed significant government incentives. The Indian government introduced measures addressing specifically software exports and inward foreign investments only during the 1990s. The main factors that attracted MNCs to this country then have been the large pool of skilled (and English-speaking) labor force and, to a lesser extent, the domestic market. More recently, the proximity to other Far East markets have also contributed to attract some MNCs.

The relationship between MNCs and the Indian software industry is marked by two major events. First, the exit of IBM in 1977, which was induced by restrictive policies on international trade and foreign direct investment. Second, the establishment of a Texas Instruments (TI) R&D laboratory in Bangalore in 1985. The exit of IBM opened a window of opportunity to other MNCs like Honeywell, Digital Equipment, Burroughs, and Fujitsu; these firms filled the gap created by the departure of IBM by establishing alliances with domestic firms, as in the case of Burroughs with Tata Consulting Services (TCS), and Digital with Hinditron. Until the mid-1980s, domestic software firms were primarily involved in developing porting programs from IBM to other proprietary platforms, development and maintenance of custom applications for a variety of computer platforms. This represented an important learning ground for domestic firms. Over time several domestic firms adopted a business model based i) on the supply of software professionals who worked on the customer premises on a temporary basis (on-site servicing) and ii) on the adoption of 'time & materials' contracts [24,25].

The entry by TI in the mid-1980s marked another important change in the evolution of the domestic software industry since it pioneered the offshore model in India.[2] TI operations in Bangalore focused on high-end R&D activities, such as chip design and chip-related software. TI's digital signal processing (DSP) chip was developed by this R&D laboratory and then commercialized on a global scale. Moreover, TI brought in its satellite communication facilities which represented the frontier in communication technology. At that time private firms were not allowed to own and run their satellite communication facilities. TI then gave its 64 khp data link technology to the Indian Department of Telecommunications which in turn allowed domestic firms to use the excess capacity [25,26].

TI's business model, centered on the use of a powerful communication facility and high-end offshore R&D activities carried out on a global scale for the rest of the corporation, provided an important demonstration effect to domestic firms like TCS, Infosys, and Wipro. These firms have imitated this model and today most of their services are offered on an offshore basis [25,26].[3] The offshore model requires organizational capabilities such as process control, reporting and review procedures which are less necessary in the case of on-site services, where personnel has to adapt to customer organizational procedures already in place. TI India was willing to share organizational knowledge with Indian firms, which were not perceived as competitors.[4]

TI's successful experience in India gave also a demonstration effect to other foreign ICT firms which during the 1980s and, especially, the 1990s established offshore development centers in Bangalore and other Indian locations. This new wave of MNCs has also contributed to the progress of organizational and technological capabilities of domestic firms [26]. For example, in 1995, Motorola Development Center achieved Capabilities Maturity Model (CMM) Level 5 and this spurred both multinational and domestic firms to improve their software development process.[5]

Today in India domestic and multinational software firms employ over 500,000 people. Although the majority of exporters are Indian-owned firms, foreign affiliates in 1998–99 accounted for about 27 percent of India's software revenues ($10 billion) and 16 percent of software exports (*The Hindu*, September 18, 2002).[6] Many leading US and European ICT firms have established software facilities in India during the 1990s and 2000s and the bulk of foreign affiliates' exports is directed to their parent companies. In general, MNCs carry out two types of activities in India: (a) business process outsourcing (BPO) or IT-enabled services like sales and customer support services (e.g. GE Capital and Citibank); (b) R&D activities (e.g. TI and Motorola).

Most MNC R&D facilities support the parent company's R&D operations and have a limited autonomy from the corporate headquarters. Only a few local R&D facilities have a high level of autonomy. Besides TI, an interesting case is represented by Adobe's R&D center in Noida which developed a new version of Acrobat Reader for handheld devices, by carrying out autonomously all development stages, from the conception of the idea to final production. Its engineers have filed fifteen worldwide patent applications related to several Adobe products like Pagemaker and Photo Deluxe.[7]

Most MNCs do not compete directly with domestic firms. Several MNCs outsource low-level design, development, and testing to domestic suppliers and, on few occasions, establish joint R&D activities with domestic firms. The largest domestic firms such as Infosys and Wipro tend to compete directly with MNCs like IBM Global Services and Accenture in the market for global outsourcing services (*The Economist*, July 17, 2003).

2.2 Ireland

Unlike in India, several MNCs operating in the ICT industries have entered Ireland before a domestic industry started to grow. The main factors that have attracted MNCs in Ireland have been high fiscal incentives, a considerable pool of skilled people with low opportunity costs, and the proximity with the European Union (EU) market [27] (see also Chapter 3 on Ireland in this book).

Between the 1970s and the early 1980s a first wave of foreign computer and telecommunication equipment manufacturers, such as Digital, Amdhal, Ericsson, Apple, and Wang, started to establish their operations in Ireland. In this period software activities in Ireland were still very limited and MNCs outsourced low-value-added activities—for example, software manual printing, packaging, and language translation services—to local suppliers [28,29].

A second wave of MNCs entered during the 1980s. The most important MNCs were IBM, Lotus, Siemens-Nixdorf, Motorola, Lucent Technologies, Microsoft, Oracle, and EDS. These firms focused on personal computers manufacturing and software packages, and had limited linkages with local firms such as suppliers of manual printing, localization of legacy software packages, and distribution/logistics services.

The last wave of entry of foreign firms—such as Intel, Symantec, Novell, and Sun Microsystems occurred through the 1990s. These firms have a higher level of integration in the local economy as compared with earlier entrants and carry out a much larger variety of activities, including software development, on-line multilingual customer support services, localization, customization and porting of legacy software to new platforms, and centralized back office operations [28,30].

The domestic software industry developed during the 1990s, even though the earliest indigenous entries date back to the period between the 1960s and the 1970s. Most domestic firms focused on specific niche markets such as computer-based training (CBT) software (e.g. Financial Courseware and Courseware Interactive), telecommunication software (Baltimore Technologies, Euristix, a Baltimore spin-off, and Vistech), finance-assurance application software (Trintech and Allfinanze, formerly FM Systems), system software, and application development tools (Iona Technologies and Piercom).

Only few firms have grown rapidly and can claim an important share of the international markets (e.g. Iona, Trintech, and Kindle), while the majority of domestic firms have remained very small.

According to the National Software Directorate (NSD), over 900 software firms operated in Ireland by 2000, 770 of which were domestic firms. MNCs represent over 53 percent of total employment and almost 90 percent of Irish software exports. The average domestic firm employed about sixteen people by 1999 [31].

Like in India, MNCs and domestic firms do not compete in the same market. As mentioned before, domestic firms mostly focus on niche markets where MNCs have a limited stranglehold. The latter use Ireland as an export platform concentrating their local operations on low-value-added, low-skill manufacturing activities such as porting of legacy products on new platforms, disk duplication, localization (text translation, changing formats etc.), and assembling/packaging. For instance, Irish subsidiaries of Oracle and Novell outsource most of their work to Irish firms and specialize in project management, and administrative or sales back-office activities (including multilingual customer support).[8]

Indeed, some have argued that the initial attraction of low corporate tax has birthed an incentive system that rewards quick revenue sources and does not stimulate the location of R&D activities in Ireland [32]. Except for a few examples, such as Sun Microsystems and Motorola, the majority of R&D is probably undertaken in the home country [33].

The Irish software industry is then potentially vulnerable to sudden changes in investor sentiment. Typically, foreign direct investments in low-value-added activities are highly mobile.

2.3 Israel

The Israeli software industry originated independently from MNCs. The industry origins can be traced back to the sizable computer hardware sector, the military apparatus (the Israeli Defense Force) and the local universities as a source of competencies and scientific and technological infrastructure [34] (see also Chapter 4 on Israel in this book). MNCs' operations were limited until the 1990s. They accounted for about one percent of total employment in the 1980s [18]. Even if some MNCs like IBM, Motorola, and Intel entered Israel between the 1950s and the 1970s, their research activities often play the role of nodes integrated in the corporate global network rather than being embedded in the local economic environment [18].

Two major waves of MNCs entries can be highlighted. The first one is made of MNCs which started their R&D operations in Israel to poach into the local pool of highly skilled personnel with low turnover rates and the local scientific and technological research in computing and IT security [18,35]. Motorola and IBM were the first US firms to establish a R&D facility in Israel in the 1950s. Motorola's Israeli R&D activities focus on wireless product development (e.g. remote irrigation systems for agriculture). Motorola was followed by IBM, whose Haifa Research Lab, the largest IBM R&D laboratory outside the United States, works on medical imaging multimedia applications, very large-scale integration (VLSI) design and software R&D.

Intel is another important example of foreign firms who pioneered the establishment of R&D facilities in Israel. Intel set up a VLSI design center in Israel in 1974 [18]. Intel's research lab, located in Haifa's Matam technology park, is now the largest Intel R&D lab outside the United States. Intel, which has also located chip manufacturing facilities in Jerusalem and Kiryat Gat, employs in Israel over 5,000 people. Over time Intel's R&D operations in Israel have become responsible for critical components of Intel's technology such as the 8088 microprocessor and Pentium MMX technology [34].

A second wave of MNCs established their operations in Israel during the 1990s attracted by the local pool of talented people and promising domestic firms which have entered the market in the same period. A case in point is Microsoft, which established an R&D center in Haifa in 1991 (Windows and network applications).

The Israeli software industry is made of over 500 firms whose cumulative sales are about $4,100 million. Over 73 percent of total sales are accounted for by exports [4].[9] Domestic firms specialize in telecommunication software, data security and network management software, chip design, and other high-tech software products. Unlike the case of Ireland, domestic firms in Israel account for a large share of software exports: the top ten domestic firms represent over 50 percent of total exports (Israel Business Today, November 30, 1998: 23). The relatively low share of MNCs probably reflects the type of activities conducted locally. As mentioned before, most MNCs carry out R&D activities which do not result in significant outflows of services while some MNCs offer their services to local customers.

2.4   A Synthesis

The activities conducted by MNCs and the specialization of domestic firms show that these countries have different comparative advantages and therefore have attracted different types of FDIs. To give further support to our proposition, we studied the patents granted to domestic inventors in the three countries. The limits of patents as a measure of technological activities in the field of ICT, and particularly in the case of software, are known. However, the lack of alternative indicators such as R&D expenditures has spurred scholars to rely on patents. Moreover, USPTO data make international comparisons possible.

The patent data show interesting differences among our countries. Table 8.1 shows the patents granted by the USPTO to domestic and foreign (MNCs'

TABLE 8.1. Patents Granted to Domestic and Foreign Assignees (1976–2002)

Country	ICT patents (1)	Total patents	Total patents/ population (×1000)	RTA_1 (domestic assignees)[a]	RTA_2 (domestic and foreign assignees)[b]
India	257	1,681	0.002	0.214	0.561
Ireland	431	1,866	0.715	0.530	0.847
Israel	2,452	11,307	2.904	1.074	0.796
Taiwan	22,327	44,594	2.823	3.549	1.837
South Korea	22,297	27,405	1.114	3.164	2.985
California	107,924	285,352	13.715	2.108	1.387
World patents	768,270	2,818,378			

[a] The first 30 USPTO classes in which ICT (Information and Communication Technologies) MNCs were granted a patent plus all patents in USPTO class 700 (software) (including 704 e 702 classes).
[b] RTA, Revealed or Relative Technological Advantage, is the ratio between the country share in the world production of technology i and its share in the world production of all technologies. Values of RTA greater than 1 indicate a comparative advantage. RTA_1 is calculated with patents granted to domestic assignees only, while RTA_2 is calculated with all assignees (domestic and foreign).

Source: Elaborations on USPTO data.

subsidiaries) assignees between 1976 and 2002. All patents in this dataset have at least one inventor resident in our countries. Patent data of other leading ICT producing regions—Taiwan, South Korea, and California, are also reported in Table 8.1 for comparison. We must warn that the different product specialization profiles of these regions may affect our results. For instance, it is possible that the importance of hardware manufacturing in Taiwan explains in part the high number of patents compared with Israel, which specializes in software, an industry where patents have become important more recently. The different country size (population) obviously affects the levels but not the measures of relative technological advantage reported in Table 8.1.

Israel shows an absolute advantage in R&D activities measured by the total number of patents granted to domestic inventors in all technologies. The total number of patents granted to Israeli inventors is over three times the number of patents of Indian and Irish inventors altogether. Israeli innovative firms also show a comparative advantage in ICT innovative activities, as demonstrated by the relative or 'revealed technological advantage' (a measure of technological specialization) (RTA_1). When looking at the patents of both domestic firms and MNCs (RTA_2), the comparative advantage of Israel evaporates. This demonstrates that the comparative advantage of Israel in ICT is driven by domestic firms. The overall contribution of subsidiaries of foreign firms to the local production of this technology (29 percent of Israeli ICT patents) is limited compared to their contribution to all technologies (about 48 percent of Israeli patents). Both India and Ireland shows a comparative disadvantage in ICT patents, even when including the patents granted to foreign assignees (RTA_2).

Moreover, the average Israeli software firm appears to be much more productive in terms of patents than its Irish and Indian counterparts (see Table 8.2). This confirms that the Israeli IT industry is more innovation-oriented than its Irish and Indian counterparts. The technological productivity of Israeli firms, which has increased dramatically over time, is an important determinant of their specialization in high-tech market niches like Internet, data security, and network management software applications. Also compared to MNCs, Israeli domestic firms have made a big leap forward in innovation productivity. In turn, patent productivity of MNCs located in Israel is much greater than that of MNCs located in the other two countries. This is in line with the quality of the local scientific and technological infrastructure mentioned before.

By contrast, in India most MNCs have located sales and customer support activities, low-end software development activities (e.g. programming and testing), and BPO services. More recently, the location of R&D activities by foreign firms has gained momentum thanks to the demonstration effects generated by the R&D laboratories of early entrants such as TI. The level of technological activities by domestic firms has also increased recently. This progress is demonstrated by the rising average number of patents after 1990 reported in Table 8.2. Indian firms have improved their productivity (the average number of patents has doubled over time) in comparison with MNCs although they still lag behind the latter.

TABLE 8.2. Average Number of ICT Patents in Domestic and
MNC Firms

	Domestic firms		MNC firms	
	Before 1990	After 1990	Before 1990	After 1990
India	1.07	2.11	2.13	3.11
Ireland	1.24	1.33	1.68	1.99
Israel	6.64	17.18	11.81	12.21

Note: Average numbers obtained by dividing the number of patents by the
number of inventing firms (USPTO database only).

Source: Elaborations on USPTO data.

The performance of Irish domestic firms remained stable and therefore deteriorated in comparison with that of Indian and Israeli firms. The performance of Irish subsidiaries of MNCs is also below that of the other two countries. This is in line with the nature of activities carried out by MNCs in Ireland, such as packaging of software products, localization and logistics, customer sales and support for the European markets. Except for a few technologically productive domestic firms specialized in niche products like financial and telecommunication software applications, the majority of domestic firms have been granted few patents. Table 8.2 indicates that the average number of patents of domestic and MNCs have increased after 1990 but at a much lower rate than in India.

The overall direct contribution of MNCs to local R&D activities in the ICT field then is quite limited. In particular, MNCs are not important to determine the comparative advantage of our countries in the ICT sector.

3   Linkages with Domestic Firms

In order to assess more carefully the contribution of MNCs to the growth of the domestic software industry, this section examines various linkages with domestic firms. As mentioned before, our analysis aims to distinguish various channels through which the knowledge of MNCs spills over domestic firms. The literature suggests the following potential channels for spillovers: (a) MNCs' spin-off firms, that is, start-ups established by former highly skilled engineers or managers; (b) people mobility and patent citations; (c) alliances with domestic firms.

3.1   Spin-offs

Spin-offs are a typical channel through which established firms, including MNCs, can transmit their knowledge to domestic firms [36].[10] Earlier empirical studies on the software industry highlight the role of MNCs as incubators of spin-off firms. A survey of thirty-six Irish software firms conducted in the 1990s shows that two-thirds of entrepreneurs had worked for a multinational corporation (in the IT sectors or other sectors), at least at some stage of their career, before establishing

TABLE 8.3. Irish Software Firm Founders by
Previous Occupation (1981–2002)

Founder former employer	Number of founders
Irish software company	41
Multinational company	63
Worked abroad	51
Studied abroad	15
NA	22
Total	192

Source: Elaborations on data collected by Sands [38].

TABLE 8.4. Irish Software Firm Founders by Previous
Occupation and by Year of Firm Foundation (1981–2002)

Founder former occupation	Years	
	1981–95	1996–2002
Irish software company	0.123	0.179
Multinational company	0.271	0.380
Worked abroad	0.318	0.250
Studied abroad	0.039	0.080
NA	0.250	0.111
Number of firms	20	32

Note: The shares reported in this table are obtained by weighting the number of founders of the same firm; for example, if a company has two founders, one from a MNC and another one from an indigenous company, a 0.5 weight is calculated for each founder.

Source: Elaborations on data collected by Sands [38].

their own firm [37]. Another survey of twenty-eight Irish firms conducted in 2000 yields similar results—50 percent of their founders had worked for MNCs [27]. Sands's survey in this book produced yet further evidence of the importance of MNCs as a source of software spin-offs [38]. Table 8.3 shows the 192 founders of 52 Irish software firms classified according to their earlier occupations.

Moreover, Table 8.4 compares the shares of founders of two sub-samples, according to the period of foundation.

The significant number of founders of domestic firms who have worked for a MNC shows the importance of MNCs in the creation and development of the Irish software industry. The share of MNCs' spin-offs appears to increase over time while that of founders who had worked abroad decreases. This is probably the result of the growing density of the local network of professionals and firms (including MNCs) as a training ground for managers and entrepreneurs.

An important 'incubator' of new domestic firms has been Digital Equipment in Galway after the closing of its operations in 1993.[11] Our interviews with domestic firms confirm that after the shutdown about fifteen new firms were established by former Digital employees. One of these start-ups is AIMware, a firm established in 1995 and located at the Galway Business Park (software for process improvement).

Which type of knowledge MNCs transfer to their spin-offs? Our interviews suggest that technical expertise is less important than managerial skills and, to some degree, 'business sense'. Two examples illustrate this point. The first example is DLG Services (now Transware), a firm specialized in localization software development and testing. A typical example of MNCs' spin-offs in Ireland, DLG was set up in 1996 by a former Lotus employee. The founder and managing director of DLG has been able to transfer the experience accumulated at Lotus to his colleagues. Rather than technical skills, this experience helped the DLG's staff to learn organizational and management best practices from Lotus. These practices include project management (clear tasks definition, use of milestones, rigorous assessment criteria) and relational and marketing capabilities (ability to conduct a business negotiation, sales skills, and formal presentation skills). Finally, the experience with Lotus promoted the consolidation of collaborative links between the two firms and provides an important source of revenues for DLG.

The second example is Anam, a start-up established in 1999 by three former employees of Siemens Ireland (SSE) and Logica Ireland. This firm supplies a wireless Internet platform for mobile electronic commerce and its founders brought in technical expertise accumulated at the Irish Siemens Internet Security subsidiary, specialized in Internet and wireless products. This is a hundred employee subsidiary with a global mandate and a wide range of activities, from R&D to marketing. The founders of Anam also inherited expertise in the area of general management, international business management, and project and product management. Anam managers built upon this expertise to develop new capabilities in a complementary field, wireless software. Thanks to its specialization in complementary technologies, this start-up maintains strong collaborative ties with both Siemens and Logica.[12]

In India and Israel MNCs' spin-offs have played a more limited role, until very recently. The increasing importance of R&D activities conducted by MNCs in India has started to yield some high-tech spin-offs similar to the case of Anam in Ireland. Ittiam Systems is a case in point. Ittiam, active in R&D and embedded software development, was founded in 2001 by Srini Rajam, the former managing director of Texas Instruments India. Another six TI India engineers joined Srini Rajam bringing with them a high-level expertise in the area of DSP, a fast growing segment in the semiconductor business. Besides the technological expertise, the team inherited TI capabilities in general management and marketing. Moreover, working in a company like TI provided the founders of Ittiam with a global business perspective. One of the founders and the current Ittiam top management and CEO recognizes that the experience with TI helped the founding team to choose the market niche and to implement a business model centered on the sales of intellectual property rights, which is very different from the typical service-oriented approach adopted by many Indian software firms. Ittiam collaborates with TI and has been involved in the Third Party Development Network, a supply chain initiative recently launched by TI.

Finally, in Israel only recently MNCs have spawned a few software spin-offs. Founding teams often display a combination of business, military, and academic backgrounds. One relevant example is Riverhead Networks, a company established in 2000 and engaged in security software in the area of distributed denial-of-service mitigation. One of the founders gained experience in IBM Research Lab in Haifa, after serving in the military as a software engineer.

3.2 People Mobility and Patent Citations

Besides spin-offs, the mobility of skilled personnel is a relevant link with the local software industry in Ireland. Between the 1980s and the early 1990s several IT professionals emigrated because of the low job opportunities offered by the Irish labor market. The excess labor supply and low wages attracted several MNCs. Their local activities contributed toward reducing the outflows of professionals. From mid-1990s, the rapid growth of software activities, which was largely accounted for by MNCs, resulted in rapid growth of wages (about 20 percent a year), which attracted a large number of emigrants back to Ireland [39]. Thus MNCs in Ireland contributed to the maintenance of a local pool of software engineers and managers with expertise in system software, financial applications software, telecommunications software, and computer-based training software (or e-learning). MNCs in Ireland have also spurred the government to invest in IT skills [27]. Moreover, some senior managers have recently left MNCs to join domestic firms, bringing with them technical and managerial experience. Top manager mobility is also frequent in India and Israel even though it seems to be a more recent phenomenon compared with Ireland.

The analysis of patents granted by the US Patents and Trademarks Office (USPTO) to domestic inventors over the period 1976–2002 provides further insights over technical spillover from MNCs to local firms. A useful indicator is the number of domestic inventors who have been granted patents during their employment in MNCs and have then moved to a domestic firm. From the USPTO database we selected the inventors who are resident in Ireland, Israel, and India and looked at their firm affiliation (i.e. the patent assignee).

This indicator has some limitations. First, inventors who have worked abroad and have moved to a domestic firm are not classified as 'mobile' inventors. Second, inventors who have moved from MNCs to domestic firms but have not continued to patent are excluded from our analysis. Third, we are not distinguishing ICT from other technologies. The analysis of inventor mobility from patent data is in general difficult because of homonymy. However, in our study, the limited number of inventors made it possible to control for this source of error.

Table 8.5 shows that Ireland has a higher share of inventors with previous experience in MNCs compared to India and Israel. This corresponds to the longer history of MNCs and their spin-offs in Ireland. Conversely, the larger *number* of

TABLE 8.5. Domestic Inventors Formerly Employed by MNCs
(1976–2002)

Country	Inventors	As a share of total domestic inventors	Patents[a]
India	5	0.060	36
Ireland	14	0.100	30
Israel	38	0.022	83

[a] Total number of patents during inventors' life.

Source: Elaborations on USPTO data.

inventors moving from MNCs to domestic firms in Israel is consistent with the larger scale of R&D activities conducted by MNCs in this country.

Another proxy for technological spillovers is the number of patent citations. Table 8.6 shows citations reported in domestic patents (both inventors and assignees are resident in the sample countries).

The first two columns show the citations of world patents in all technologies while the remaining columns report citations of ICT patents granted to domestic assignees and to local subsidiaries of multinational firms (MNCs), respectively. These data lead to two considerations. First, the proportions of MNCs' and domestic firms' patents cited (columns IV and VI, respectively) are significantly higher than the average share of world patents cited by domestic patents, with the exception of India (column II).[13] For instance, the share of MNCs' ICT patents cited by Irish patents is over five times larger than the average share of world patents cited by Irish patents in all technologies. And the share of ICT domestic patents cited by other domestic patents is over thirty-one times larger than the average share of citations in all technologies.

Second, the share of MNCs' patents cited is always small in comparison to the proportion of cross-citations between domestic firms' patents.[14] MNCs' patents are more cited in Israel than in India and Ireland. But even in the case of Israel less than 2 percent of MNCs' patents are cited in domestic patents against 12 percent of patents granted to other domestic firms. The relatively high share of citations across domestic firms in Israel reflects the high density of the local network of scientists and engineers working for public research institutions and domestic firms mentioned before.

Patent citations show that MNCs' R&D activities, especially in India, are quite isolated from the local network of technological activities. An illustrative example is TI India. Its R&D laboratory in India has been granted seventy-five patents in the period examined but its patents have never been cited by Indian firms.

Even though these data may overlook the importance of informal knowledge trade among professionals, we cannot conclude that MNCs play a central role in the knowledge flows which take place in these industrial clusters.

The data on people mobility and inventors mobility discussed before suggest that MNCs are an important source of skills in Ireland and, more recently, in the

TABLE 8.6. Patents Citations in Domestic Patents, 1976–2002[a]

Country	Total world patents cited in domestic patents (all technologies) (I)	Share of world patents cited in domestic patents (II)	Domestic ICT patents cited (III)	Share of domestic ICT patents cited in domestic patents (IV)	MNCs ICT patents cited in domestic patents (V)	Share of MNCs ICT patents cited in domestic patents (VI)
India[b]	2,184	0.0008	2	0.050	0	0.00**
Ireland[b]	4,108	0.0015	6	0.046	3	0.01*
Israel[b]	10,483	0.0037	214	0.120	14	0.02**

[a] Domestic patents are granted to domestic inventors and domestic assignees. MNCs patents are granted to multinational subsidiaries located in the country.

[b] P-values (* $P \leq 0.02$ and ** $P \leq 0.01$, respectively) obtained from the chi-squared goodness-of-fit test under the null hypothesis that the shares of domestic patents and MNCs patents are not significantly different ($df = 1$).

Source: Elaborations on USPTO data.

other two countries. However, people mobility does not necessarily entail any spillover for domestic firms since the competition among firms to acquire talented employees may result in higher rents paid to employees which erode the extra-value (or competitive advantage) to the firm.

3.3 Inter-firm Alliances

Alliances with domestic firms represent another potential source of knowledge transfer and a measure of embeddedness in the local economy.[15] To this purpose, we collected data from D&B's WOW and other national data sources which are described in the Appendix. These data provide a representative sample of the population of domestic software firms and MNCs operating in our three countries in 2001.[16] However, our sample accounts for various generations of domestic firms and MNCs that have entered the market at different points of time, from the early formation of software activities in our countries until recent years.

Table 8.7 highlights marked differences across these countries. In Ireland MNCs account for about 34 percent of all sample firms against about 20 percent in India and only 10 percent in Israel.

Table 8.8 illustrates the entry time of domestic firms and MNCs in our sample. There are marked differences between MNCs and domestic firms across our countries which are consistent with the historical evolution of software activities illustrated before. In Ireland, many MNCs entered before the start-up of a domestic industry. While about 55 percent of MNCs currently located in this country has entered before 1990, only 41 percent of domestic firms entered in the same period.

By contrast, in India and Israel about 25 percent and 27 percent of MNCs, respectively, entered the market before 1990 against 39 percent and 43 percent of domestic firms. This picture shows that in these two countries a process of

TABLE 8.7. Sample Firms by Nationality of the Parent Company (2001)

India		Ireland		Israel	
Home country	Firms	Home country	Firms	Home country	Firms
India	412	Ireland	529	Israel	457
United States	82	United States	149	United States	53
Germany	6	England	50	Japan	3
France	6	Japan	16	England	2
Netherlands	3	Canada	14	Germany	1
Other	12	Other	46	Other	5
Total	521	Total	804	Total	521

Source: Elaborations on various sources (Who Owns Whom, NSD, NASSCOM, and corporate websites).

TABLE 8.8. Sample Firms by Year of Establishment

Year of establishment	Domestic firms	MNCs	Total	Domestic firms (%)	MNCs (%)
India					
Before 1980	35	10	45	0.08	0.09
1980 to 1990	125	17	142	0.30	0.16
1990 to 2001	252	82	334	0.61	0.75
Total	412	109	521	1.00	1.00
Ireland					
Before 1980	48	41	89	0.09	0.15
1980 to 1990	168	109	277	0.32	0.40
1990 to 2001	313	125	438	0.59	0.45
Total	529	275	804	1.00	1.00
Israel					
Before 1980	64	5	69	0.14	0.08
1980 to 1990	134	12	146	0.29	0.19
1990 to 2001	259	48	306	0.57	0.75
Total	457	64	521	1.00	1.00

Source: Elaborations on various sources (Who Owns Whom, NSD, NASSCOM, and corporate websites).

indigenous growth has occurred before or in parallel with the entry of MNCs. This is in line with the evolution of the software industry discussed earlier.

Overall about 43 percent of MNCs in our sample have entered these countries before 1990. This shows a long-term commitment to the local economy, which should be reflected in the linkages with domestic firms, especially in Ireland, where the entry process started earlier than in India and Israel.

In order to explore the patterns of linkages with domestic firms we collected information about events concerning the software industry in our countries during the period 1998–2002. We classified these events according to the following categories: establishment of new plants, units, and subsidiaries (new subsidiaries), organizational change (expansion of existing units or subsidiaries), mergers and acquisitions (M&As) of domestic firms, joint ventures, strategic alliances, and outsourcing agreements.[17]

The database includes 133 MNCs involved in 256 events (active firms). Table 8.9 indicates that in Ireland only thirty-three MNCs (12 percent of total MNCs in our sample) have been involved in events such as M&As of domestic firms, set up of new subsidiaries and alliances during 1998–2002. The number of alliances in particular is very small, especially in Ireland.

During this period, in Israel a larger share of MNCs (about 77 percent of our sample) have expanded their operations and have established linkages with local firms—primarily M&As of young, promising Israeli software firms.[18]

TABLE 8.9. MNCs Growth and Alliances with Domestic Firms (1998–2002)

Country	Active MNCs	JVs	Strategic alliances	Outsourcing agreements	M&As	New subs. & units	Organizational change	Total events
India	51	13	17	21	11	59	3	124
Ireland	33	0	0	1	19	27	10	57
Israel	49	4	8	1	39	20	3	75
Total	133	17	25	23	69	106	16	256

Source: InfotrackWeb database and corporates' websites.

This suggests that there is a greater activity by MNCs in Israel as compared to Ireland in recent years.

The case of India is different. As Table 8.9 shows, during 1998–2002 MNCs in India have expanded and restructured their operations to a larger extent than in the other two countries. They have also established several alliances with domestic firms, such as joint ventures, strategic alliances, and outsourcing agreements. As mentioned before, MNCs in India have entered later following the growth of the domestic industry. MNCs' activism in this case probably reflects the need to tap quickly the skills and resources available. Joint development centers and BPO facilities which MNCs have recently established in collaboration with Indian firms are a typical way to gain access to local resources.

Why have MNCs established only a few alliances with domestic firms especially in Ireland, where many foreign firms have entered before the growth of a domestic software industry? It is possible that some ties with domestic firms have been established before 1998 and are then not included in our database.[19] But there are also other more substantial reasons such as the type of activities carried out by MNCs in Ireland. As mentioned earlier, the majority of MNC subsidiaries specialize in manufacturing of packaged software. This activity commands a limited amount of local inputs. A local support industry has emerged over time but its activities (e.g. disk duplication, assembly and kitting, distribution and manual printing for MNCs) have little to do with software and IT services. A minority of firms, such as DLG and Banta Global Tunkey Systems, offer localization and testing services while the rest of the Irish software industry focuses on niche products which does not lead to much competitive or collaborative relationship with the local subsidiaries of MNCs. Moreover, interviews with domestic firms pointed out that the limited autonomy of local subsidiaries of MNCs inhibits the collaboration with domestic firms. Finally, unlike Indian firms, Irish firms have a limited presence in BPO services and so far the local subsidiaries of IT service providers like HP Services, IBM Global Services, and Fujitsu, which dominate the local market, have not involved local subcontractors in their activities [42].

So far we have compared the patterns of MNCs alliances across our countries but we cannot say whether the number of observed alliances is large compared to the expected number of alliances. For this comparison we analyzed all international

TABLE 8.10. Domestic Firms Alliances with MNCs and Other Foreign Firms
(1998–2002)[a]

Host country	Partner	Number of alliances (I)	Shares (II)	Number of potential foreign partners (III)	Shares (IV)	Relative shares (II)/(IV)[b]
India	MNCs	124	0.39	109	0.19	2.05
	All foreign firms	312		570		
Ireland	MNCs	57	0.28	275	0.48	0.58
	All foreign firms	206		570		
Israel	MNCs	75	0.45	64	0.11	4.09
	All foreign firms	166		570		

[a]Alliances include JV, M&As, strategic alliances, and outsourcing agreements.
[b]The Relative share is the share of alliances with MNCs in total alliances over shares of MNCs in total foreign ICT firms (MNCs and other foreign firms). Differences between shares (columns II and VI) are all significant at 0.01 significance level obtained from the chi-squared goodness-of-fit test ($df = 1$).
Source: Elaboration on InfotrackWeb database and corporates' websites; Business Week, The Global 1000, 2001.

alliances of domestic software firms in our dataset. These alliances were classified according to the type of partners. We distinguished between alliances with foreign firms which have a subsidiary in the country (*MNCs*) and alliances with foreign firms without subsidiaries in the country (*other foreign firms*).

Table 8.10 reports the share of alliances with MNCs over the total number of international linkages set up by domestic firms. We have then constructed a sample of the world's largest ICT firms listed in Business Week Global 1000, 2001 (Sectors 45, Information Technology, and 50, Telecommunications services), Who Owns Whom, and Infotrack databases[20] comprising of firms whose headquarters were in a country different from India, Ireland, or Israel. A subset of these firms are MNCs, that is, have foreign subsidiaries in at least one of our sample countries.

The last column of Table 8.10 gives the ratios between observed and expected frequencies of alliances with MNCs. Expected frequencies are obtained by calculating the shares of MNCs in our sample of the world's largest ICT firms. For instance, there are 109 foreign firms (19 percent of all potential foreign partners in our sample) which have at least a subsidiary in India. Under the hypothesis that colocation of partners does not affect the propensity to establish alliances, the share of alliances with MNCs in total international alliances should be similar to the MNCs' share in total potential foreign partners. In fact, the observed percentage of alliances with MNCs in total international alliances established by Indian firms is significantly larger than the expected share under the hypothesis that colocation is irrelevant to the establishment of alliances. Therefore, we cannot reject the alternative hypothesis that the propensity to establish international alliances of Indian firms is affected by the location of the foreign partner with a subsidiary. Also Israeli firms have established more alliances with MNCs than expected under the hypothesis of irrelevance of location; this result supports the hypothesis that colocation favors the establishment of inter-firm alliances.

On the contrary, in Ireland the share of alliances set up by domestic firms with MNCs is significantly smaller than the share of MNCs in total potential foreign partners. Overall, then, our data cannot reject the hypothesis that colocation does not play a significant role in the pattern of international alliances of domestic firms.

4   The Contribution of MNCs to Local Firms: Discussion

MNCs played a different role in the three countries analyzed. This is partially due to the different entry timings. The overall effect of MNCs on the domestic software industry is controversial. In line with earlier empirical evidence, our case studies confirm the difficulty to find unambiguous support for positive externalities.[21]

In Ireland most MNCs entered before the formation of an indigenous software industry and have generated a considerable number of spin-offs. They have also contributed to the training and mobility of human capital as showed by the relatively high share of inventors who have moved from MNCs to domestic firms. Our data cannot measure the effects of labor mobility on the performance of domestic firms. However, studies on MNCs in developing countries show that: (a) MNCs offer more training to their workers compared with domestic firms [12]; (b) founders' and managers' earlier experience in MNCs has positive effects on the performance of domestic firms [7,10].

Moreover, MNCs have shown that high-tech activities like software can be carried out in a country without an industrial tradition. Our interviews with domestic firms have pointed out that MNCs have given local firms confidence and international reputation. Although it is difficult to identify precisely the channels for reputation effects, collaborative ties with MNCs have been an important source of reputation for Irish partners. A case in point is Iona Technology. In 1993 Sun Microsystems bought 25 percent of Iona for $600,000 and two Sun's executives entered Iona's Board of Directors. Sun also became an important customer of Iona's integration technology and sold its stake for $60 million at the Iona's initial public offering (IPO) in 1997. According to Chris Horn, Iona's founder and CEO, the alliance with Sun had a huge importance not for the money but for Iona's credibility in the international market.[22]

Generally, however, MNCs have established only a limited number of alliances with software domestic firms when compared with other foreign firms without any subsidiary in Ireland.

Moreover, MNCs have not contributed substantially to patents in the field of ICT. Neither have they generated considerable technical spillovers as demonstrated by the limited share of MNCs' patents cited in domestic firms' patents. Therefore, the role of MNCs as a source of technical knowledge through patent citations and inter-firm alliances appears to be limited.

Finally, MNCs have represented an important source of demand for some firms in the early stages of their life. However, the bulk of MNCs suppliers in Ireland typically specialize in non-IT services such as translation, packaging, and logistics rather than software.

While MNCs in Ireland have clearly played an important role in terms of spin-offs, demonstration effects, and people mobility, their overall impact on the domestic software industry is debatable. Domestic firms have remained small and have a marginal position in this industry. By 2000 they accounted for only 10 percent of Irish software exports. Overall, about 62 percent of domestic firms' revenues are accounted for by exports. However, only one percent of all domestic firms account for about 30 percent of domestic exports.[23] This suggests that, except for a few firms like Iona, Massana, and Kindle Banking Systems, the majority of domestic firms have a limited presence in the foreign markets. Therefore, the question arises as to whether MNCs in Ireland have hampered the growth of a domestic software industry, by hiring the most skilled and experienced software professionals and attracting the demand away from domestic firms. It is possible that MNCs have produced some negative externalities in the labor market but this is not the case of the product market where most domestic firms do not directly compete with MNCs.

The case of Ireland corroborates the view that MNCs' spillovers do not occur automatically [11,43]. MNCs have contributed to the growth of a domestic industry by supplying skills and reputation. But, except for a few successful firms like Iona, the majority of domestic firms have not captured the externalities offered by MNCs. As discussed before, domestic firms have not improved their technological capabilities over time compared with their Indian and Israeli counterparts. Moreover, most firms have not developed robust marketing capabilities that are required to survive in international markets. The absence of a strong domestic industry, in turn, has limited the pressure on MNCs to improve the quality of their local facilities and extend the range of activities carried out, including R&D.

The entry patterns of MNCs in Israel are different. The majority of MNCs entered during the 1990s, after an indigenous software industry had already developed and a highly skilled labor force was available. Early MNCs have not been a source of spin-offs and people mobility; they have remained quite isolated from the rest of the domestic industry. This first wave of MNCs have set up primarily R&D laboratories while subsequent waves of MNCs have entered by establishing linkages (especially M&As) with promising local firms. These linkages provide domestic firms with managerial expertise and capital.

Only recently MNCs' spin-offs and people mobility generated by MNCs' subsidiaries have become more frequent in Israel. However, the low share of inventors who have left MNCs to join domestic firms shows that people mobility from MNCs is not a significant channel for spillovers in this case.

Moreover, even though MNCs account for a large share of Israeli patents in all sectors, they do not contribute significantly to Israel's comparative advantage in ICT. Finally, MNCs do not represent important customers for the average Israeli software firm. Most revenues of domestic firms arise from exports.

On some occasions, the acquisition of minority stakes in domestic firms by MNCs has increased the overall reputation of Israeli software firms and therefore has eased their access to foreign markets. But local subsidiaries of MNCs do not represent the main bridge to international markets for domestic firms. This is demonstrated by the fact that a large number of Israeli software firms have moved their headquarters to the United States to have a direct access to management, marketing, and financial resources, while maintaining their R&D activities in Israel.[24]

Finally, alliances with local subsidiaries of MNCs represent a high share of Israeli international alliances, given the small proportion of foreign ICT firms with a subsidiary in this country. However, we have limited evidence about the benefits of these linkages to domestic firms.

The overall benefits of MNCs for the Israeli software industry then appear quite limited. Like in Israel, the bulk of MNCs have entered India during the 1990s. MNCs have increased their activities over time but domestic firms overall still account for the largest share of Indian software exports. The Indian software industry then appears to be much more independent of MNCs as compared with its Irish counterpart.

The contribution of MNCs to the growth of the domestic industry in terms of people mobility and spin-offs is also quite limited. Only recently the number of software engineers who have left MNCs to join smaller domestic firms appears to be on the rise while in the past most domestic firms suffered from high attrition rates, which in part resulted from the competition of MNCs.

In the last few years several spin-offs have been spawned by MNCs. This is one implication of working experience and training activities which, according to recent accounts, are more intense in MNCs compared with domestic firms [12]. It is possible then that a new generation of Indian software firms is emerging by drawing on the expertise inherited from MNCs. An important benefit from MNCs in India is represented by demonstration effects of MNCs such as TI and Motorola.

More recently, several MNCs have engaged in cooperative linkages with smaller domestic firms for outsourcing low-value-added activities such as customized programming and testing. Some MNCs such as Nortel, Motorola, and Hewlett Packard have also established R&D outsourcing agreements with both small and large domestic firms like Wipro, TCS, and Infosys. These alliances have exposed domestic firms to the technology and business practices of large, global organizations. But these benefits are still limited because most of these alliances have been established very recently. For instance, Nortel Networks established non-equity joint ventures with four large domestic firms (Silicon Automation Systems, TCS, Infosys, and Wipro) in the period 1989–92 before setting up its own subsidiary in 2000. Most R&D conducted by Nortel in collaboration with its Indian partners focuses on development of products whose research activity has already been carried out elsewhere and on the adaptation of Nortel's existing products for the local market; research activity on new products is limited. Lately these collaborations have focused more on R&D and have yielded some co-patented inventions with one of the local partners [44]. Nortel has also transferred its latest telecommunication technology and international management practices to its partners [26]. Recently Nortel has announced the launch of a joint Wireless Centre of Excellence with Infosys.

5 Conclusions

Our analysis leads to three final conclusions. First, it shows that the evolution of software activities and the role of MNCs vary considerably across the three countries. The main differences concern the time of entry of MNCs relative to domestic firms and the type of activities conducted by MNCs, which appear to reflect different regional comparative advantages.

The different entry time across these countries is reflected in the different contribution of MNCs in terms of people mobility and spin-offs, which appears to be relatively more important in the case of Ireland. MNCs have also played a different role in terms of demonstration effects, which appear to be stronger in the case of India and Ireland compared to Israel.

These differences suggest that only in the case of Ireland MNCs have helped start the process of growth by providing the domestic industry with market access spillovers (demand, reputation, and linkages with foreign customers) and productivity spillovers in the form of people mobility and spin-offs. It is worth remembering that in the 1980s and early 1990s MNCs provided incentives to the skilled labor force to stay rather than migrate.

In Israel and India MNCs have provided important complementary resources, like finance, marketing, and managerial capabilities, to domestic firms but after a regional software cluster had already developed independently from the MNCs.

The second conclusion is that the overall impact of MNCs on the growth of the domestic software industry is controversial. Even in the case of Ireland, where MNCs contributed on various grounds to the emergence of a domestic industry, domestic firms on an average are still small and account for only a tiny share of Irish software exports. In Israel and India, the positive effects of MNCs on domestic firms, such as reputation, access to capital and managerial capabilities, have become apparent only in recent years and it is too early to forecast their impact on the future growth of the domestic industry. This suggests that analysts of MNCs' linkages and policy makers in emerging regions should pay attention to the timing of entry of MNCs in new industries and the host region's absorption capabilities. The examples of Israel and India show that an early entry of MNCs is not a necessary condition for the growth of a domestic industry while the experience of Ireland indicates that neither is it sufficient. This is not surprising because

MNCs' spillovers do not occur automatically. The relationship between MNCs and domestic firms' absorptive capacity is nonlinear and different outcomes are possible.

Finally, we found mixed evidence about the importance of localized spillovers generated by MNCs. The literature on MNCs' spillovers points out that geographical proximity favors the flow of technology, management practices, and business models into domestic firms. Our analysis shows that people mobility and spin-offs appear to be significant, especially in Ireland. On the other hand, we found very limited evidence of MNCs' technology externalities measured by patent citations. The proportion of patents granted to MNCs that are cited by domestic patents is significantly smaller than that of cross-domestic citations. Moreover, alliances between local firms and the subsidiaries of MNCs overall are not always significantly large compared with alliances with other foreign firms not located in the country.

Appendix: Data and Methodology

We have collected firm-level data from various sources, including publicly available material such as annual reports and corporate web sites. For Irish software firms and Indian firms we obtained information from their respective national industry associations and public agencies—that is, ISA and NSD for Ireland and NASSCOM for India. Publicly available information from the Association of Israeli software firms is more limited.

We integrated these data with information derived from Dun and Bradstreet's *Who Owns Whom Linkages* database (2001 edition) and from InfotrackWeb database (*Business and Company Resource Centre* and *Expanded Academic ASAP*). The former provides information about firms located in the sample countries by sector. The following data were extracted for each firm: primary and secondary SIC code (industry) of the firm, number of employees, year of establishment, name and country of the ultimate parent company.

For our purposes we selected all domestic firms operating in the software and IT services industry (SIC 737x). We also selected all foreign firms with local subsidiaries operating in ICT sectors (including computers, telecommunications equipment and services, microelectronics).

InfotrackWeb database reports articles in English from various press sources. We could gain access to detailed information about events and firms involved in each event only for the period between 1998 and 2002.

Our analysis draws some information on the role of MNCs from interviews conducted in a previous project where one of the authors was involved. We had access to the reports of 64 interviews with representative firms and sector experts conducted in Ireland in 2000 and 75 interviews with senior managers and software professionals of 40 Indian firms in Bangalore, Bombay, Hyderabad, and Delhi conducted in two separate visits in 1997–98 and in 1999 [24,27]. In addition,

TABLE 8.A1. List of Executives Interviewed by Telephone, 2003

Position	Company	Country
CTO	Vordel	Ireland
Editor-in-Chief	Irish Emigrant Publications (former Digital Equipment)	Ireland
Managing Director	Hewlett-Packard Software Operations	Ireland
Managing Director	SAP Service and Support Centre	Ireland
CEO	Anam	Ireland
Country Manager	Microsoft Ireland	Ireland
Chairman	Fineos	Ireland
Country Manager	Intel Capital	Israel
Vice-president	NASSCOM	India
CEO	Philips Software Centre	India
CEO	Aspire Communication	India
Director	Eastern Software Systems	India
CEO	Ittiam Systems	India
Chairman	Evalueserve	India

we conducted telephone interviews with company and business association managers during 2003 (Table 8.A1).

Notes

1. See, for instance, Lall [16]; Haddad and Harrison [17]; Felsenstein [18]; Barry and Bradley [19]; Aitken and Harrison [20]; Gorg and Strobl [21]; Haskel et al. [22].
2. Citibank Overseas Software Ltd. (COSL) has also pioneered the offshore business processing outsourcing (BPO) in India [25].
3. The relevance of TI's business model has been confirmed by NASSCOM VP, (telephone interview, September 2, 2003).
4. Telephone interviews with Ittiam Systems CEO, August 27, and October 14, 2003.
5. Telephone interview with NASSCOM VP, September 2, 2003.
6. According to more recent NASSCOM estimates, MNCs accounted for 22% of IT services exports and 45% of IT enabled services exports in 2001–02 (*source*: NASSCOM, August 25, 2003).
7. www.adobeindia.com.
8. See [24].
9. IASH's estimates for 2001. The IASH's website does not provide more recent data.
10. For our purposes it is not important to distinguish planned spin-offs, which are backed by the parent corporation, from other forms of spin-offs.
11. Some of Digital's units in Ireland survived the shutdown and have been inherited by Compaq and then by Hewlett-Packard.
12. Logica is still an important Anam customer. *Source*: telephone interview with Anam CEO (September 1, 2003).
13. This suggests that colocation affects the probability of citation. However, our data do not allow to test rigorously the importance of localized knowledge spillovers. Testing

this hypothesis would require a control sample of patents in the same class and time window of the citing patents which do not cite the same originating patent. The test of localized spillovers compares the probability of a geographical match conditional upon the existence of a citation link with the unconditional probability of a geographical match [23,40].

14. The observed shares of MNCs in patent citations are significantly smaller than expected shares. The latter are obtained from the shares of MNCs' patents in the country's patents.

15. The literature on MNCs often refers to linkages with domestic suppliers (see [22]). To our knowledge, however, the evidence about these linkages or other partnership with domestic firms as a measure of MNCs embeddedness is quite limited (e.g. [16,26,41]).

16. We do not know the number of firms that have exited the market before 2001. Despite this limitation, we believe that the problem of exit is not such to bias substantially our results which refer to linkages between domestic firms and foreign firms in recent years.

17. Joint ventures refer to the set up of a new firm while strategic alliances are non-equity alliances such as joint R&D and marketing agreements. Outsourcing agreements include dedicated development centers and other BPO activities managed by local firms in collaboration with MNCs. M&As includes also minority stakes in domestic firms.

18. Few MNCs, like Intel Capital Israel and Cisco, have invested in venture capital initiatives to support emerging start-ups. These events were also classified as M&As.

19. Moreover, purely commercial agreements with local distributors are not reported in our database, such as the contractual agreements between Microsoft Ireland and 130 Microsoft Certified Partners.

20. This sample was constructed on the assumption that only ICT firms represent potential partners for our software firms. Even if it is possible that software firms establish international alliances with non-ICT firms, most observed alliances were established with ICT firms.

21. See [45] for a survey.

22. *Source*: public speech, IST 2003 Event—The Opportunity Ahead, EC—Information Society Directorate—General, Centro Congressi della Fiera di Milano, Milan, October 3, 2003. More recently, another Irish firm, Vordel, has experienced similar benefits from its linkages with the Intel venture capital Fund (telephone interview with Vordel CTO, September 2, 2003).

23. Authors' estimates based on data collected through 64 interviews with a sample of domestic firms which includes the largest exporters in 2000.

24. By the end of 2002 there were about 250–300 Israeli technology start-ups in the New York area, most of which specialize in Internet and telecommunications (Crain's New York Business, November 13, 2000: 27).

References

1. NASSCOM (National Association of Software and Service Companies) (2002). *Indian IT Industry*. www.nasscom.org.
2. NSD (National Software Directorate) (2002). *Survey of the Software Industry*.

3. IASH (Israeli Association of Software Houses) (2002). *Software Industry*.
4. IASH (Israeli Association of Software Houses) (2004). *Software Industry*.
5. Rodriguez-Clare, A. (1996). Multinationals, linkages, and economic development. *American Economic Review*, 86, 852–873.
6. Markusen, J.R. and Venables, A.J. (1999). Foreign direct investment as a catalyst for industrial development. *European Economic Review*, 43, 335–356.
7. Gorg, H. and Strobl, E. (2002). *Spillovers from Foreign Firms Through Worker Mobility: An Empirical Investigation*. Discussion Paper 591. Bonn: IZA.
8. Young, S., Hood, N., and Peters, E. (1994). Multinational enterprises and regional economic development. *Regional Studies*, 28, 657–678.
9. Turok, I. (1993). Inward investment and local linkages: How deeply embedded is 'Silicon Glen'? *Regional Studies*, 27, 401–418.
10. Katz, J.M. (1987). *Technology Creation in Latin American Manufacturing Industries*. New York: St. Martin's Press.
11. Blomstrom, M. and Kokko, A. (2003). *Human Capital and Inward FDI*. Discussion Paper 3762. London: CEPR.
12. Daveri, F., Manasse, P., and Serra, D. (2002). *The Twin Effects of Globalization*. Centro Studi Luca D'Agliano Development Studies Working Papers, No. 171.
13. Caves, R.E. (1974). Multinational firms, competition and productivity in host-country markets. *Economica*, 41, 176–193.
14. Saxenian, A. (1994). *Regional Advantage. Culture and Competition in Silicon Valley and Route 128*. Cambridge: Harvard Business Press.
15. Porter, M.E. (1998). Clusters and the new economics of competition. *Harvard Business Review*, Nov.–Dec., 77–90.
16. Lall, S. (1978). Transnationals, domestic enterprises and industrial structure in host LDCs: a survey. *Oxford Economic Papers*, 30, 217–248.
17. Haddad, M. and Harrison, A. (1993). Are there positive spillovers from direct foreign investment? Evidence from panel data for Morocco. *Journal of Development Economics*, 42(1), 51–74.
18. Felsenstein, D. (1997). The making of a high technology node: foreign-owned companies in Israeli high technology. *Regional Studies*, 31, 367–380.
19. Barry, F. and Bradley, J. (1997). FDI and trade: the Irish host-country experience. *Economic Journal*, 107, 1798–1811.
20. Aitken, B.J. and Harrison, A.E. (1999). Domestic firms benefits from foreign direct investment? Evidence from Venezuela. *American Economic Review*, 89, 605–618.
21. Gorg, H. and Strobl, E. (2002). Multinational companies and indigenous development: an empirical analysis. *European Economic Review*, 46, 1305–1322.
22. Haskel, J.E., Pereira, S.C., and Slaughter, M.J. (2002). *Does Inward Foreign Direct Investment Boost the Productivity of Domestic Firms?* Cambridge, MA: NBER. Working Paper 8724.
23. Singh, J. (2002). *Knowledge Diffusion and the Role of Multinational Subsidiaries: Evidence using Patent Citation Data*. Boston, MA: Harvard Business School.
24. Arora, A., Arunachalam, V.S., Asundi, J., and Fernandez, R. (2001). The Indian software services industry. *Research Policy*, 30, 1267–1287.
25. Athreye, S.S. (2003). *Multinational Firms and the Evolution of the Indian Software Industry*. East West Working Paper Series: Economics Series, Honolulu, Hawaii, USA, January, www.eastwestcenter.org.

26. Patibandla, M. and Petersen, B. (2000). Role of transnational corporations in the evolution of a high-tech industry: the case of India's software industry. *World Development*, 30, 1561–1577.

27. Arora A., Gambardella, A., and Torrisi, S. (2004). In the footsteps of Silicon Valley? Indian and Irish software in the international division of labour. In T. Bresnahan and A. Gambardella (eds.), *Building High Tech Clusters: Silicon Valley and Beyond*. Cambridge: Cambridge University Press.

28. Tallon, P.P. and Kraemer, K.L. (1999). The impact of technology on Ireland's economic growth and development: lessons for developing countries. *Hawaii International Conference on System Sciences Proceedings*. Maui, Hawaii: IEEE.

29. O'Riain, S. (2000). The flexible developmental state: globalisation, information technology, and the 'Celtic Tiger'. *Politics & Society*, 28, 157–193.

30. Hanratty, P. (1997). *Ireland as a Software Location*. Dublin: Irish Development Agency.

31. NSD (2001). *Survey of the Software Industry*.

32. Grimes, S. (2003). Ireland emerging information economy: recent trends and future prospects. *Regional Studies*, 37, 3–14.

33. Coe, N. (1997). US transnationals and the Irish software industry: assessing the nature, quality and stability of a new wave of foreign direct investment. *European Urban and Regional Studies*, 4, 211–230.

34. Breznitz, D. (2003). *An Iron Cage or the Final Stage? Intensive Product R&D and the Evolution of the Israeli Software Industry?* Cambridge, MA: MIT. Working Paper.

35. De Fontenay, C. and Carmel, E. (2001). *Israel's Silicon Wadi: The Forces Behind Cluster Formation*. Stanford, CA: Stanford University. SIEPR Discussion Paper No. 00-40, Stanford Institute for Economic Policy Research.

36. Klepper, S. (2001). *The Evolution of the U.S. Automobile Industry and Detroit as its Capital*. Pittsburgh: Department of Social & Decision Strategies, Carnegie Mellon University. Mimeo.

37. O'Gorman, C., O'Malley, E., and Mooney, J. (1997). Clusters in Ireland. The Irish indigenous software industry: an application of Porter's cluster analysis. *Research Series*, 3, 41–62

38. Sands, A. (2003). *The Irish Software Industry*. Pittsburgh: Carnegie Mellon University. Mimeo.

39. FAS (Foras Aiseanna Saothair) (1998). *Manpower, Education & Training Study of the Irish Software Sector*. Dublin: FAS.

40. Jaffe, A., Trajtenberg, M., and Henderson, R. (1993). Geographic localization of knowledge spillovers as evidenced by patent citations. *Quarterly Journal of Economics*, 108, 577–598.

41. Castellani, D. and Zanfei, A. (2002). Multinational experience and linkages with local firms. Evidence from the electronics industry. *The Cambridge Journal of Economics*, 26, 1–25.

42. Wilson, S. (2003). Ireland: Is outsourcing the holy grail for IT services in 2003? *IT Europa*, 5, 8–11.

43. Strobl, H. and Greenaway, D. (2002). *Much Ado About Nothing? Do Domestic Firms Really Benefit from Foreign Investments?* London: Centre for Economic Policy Research, CEPR Discussion Papers Series No. 3485.

44. Basant, R., Chandra, P., and Mytelka, L. (2001). *Inter-Firm Linkages and Development of Capabilities in the Indian Telecom Software Sector*. Honolulu: Hawaii. East-West Center Working Papers.

45. Strolb, E. and Greenway, D. (2002). '*Much Ado About Nothing? Do Domestic Firms Really Benefit from Foreign Investment?*' CEPR Discussion Paper Series No. 3485, London Centre for Economic Policy.

9

Sojourns and Software: Internationally Mobile Human Capital and High-Tech Industry Development in India, Ireland, and Israel

DEVESH KAPUR AND JOHN McHALE

1 Introduction

Driven by a broadly based easing of rich-country immigration restrictions for skilled workers and booming high-tech economies, the decade of the 1990s saw a substantial increase in skilled emigration from emerging economies. To take an example, the Indian-born population in the United States aged 25 and over increased from 304,000 in 1990 to 836,000 by 2000—80 percent of whom have a tertiary education.[1] A key factor behind this increase has been the introduction and expansion of the H-1B temporary visa program for skilled workers.[2] The resulting outflow rekindled fears, prominent in the 1960s and 1970s, of a development-stunting 'brain drain'. The development costs of talent outflows are certainly hard to dispute when it comes to rich-country recruitment of African doctors, given already staggeringly high doctor-to-patient ratios and worsening disease environments. But the loss of talent in high-tech sectors such as software has produced a more ambivalent reaction, with commentators pointing to benefits as well as costs.[3] In this chapter, then, we explore the implications of skilled emigration on the development of the software sectors in three emerging economies—India, Ireland, and Israel.

What are the benefits of skilled emigration to a high-tech sector like software? We emphasize three classes of benefit. First, there are the benefits that result from the *prospect* of emigration, as young people are induced by the higher expected returns to skills to invest in more (and more internationally marketable) human capital.[4] Second, there are the economic benefits that stem from close links to the *diaspora*. The diaspora can be a direct source of advantage when its members have the desire and ability to trade with, invest in, and outsource to domestic businesses. It can also be an indirect source of advantage as its members act as 'reputational intermediaries'—matching trading partners, supporting contracting by leveraging its long-term relationships with people from their new and former homes, and, possibly most importantly, overcoming negative national stereotypes through demonstrations of their capabilities. Finally, there are the benefits that result when emigrants *return* with enhanced skills, connections, business ideas, and savings.

Before becoming overly excited about the potential benefits, we hasten to add that there are real costs to a country from having a sizable portion of its talent *absent* from the economy. The reduced supply pushes up domestic wages making it more difficult to compete on costs, leads to fiscal losses as net fiscal contributors leave, and undermines local knowledge spillovers. Possibly most damaging is the loss of specialized skills, talents, and energies that have few or no domestic substitutes, including the loss of crucial 'institution builders'. Recent work in economics has also stressed the importance of complementary skilled workers in providing the incentive to 'import' high-tech capital equipment and know-how (e.g. see [3,4]).

The loss of skilled workers may pose a particular challenge to an emerging economy that has managed to attain a surprising comparative advantage in a skill-intensive sector like software. A useful way to think about this advantage is in terms of a multi-sector Ricardian model (see [5]). Compared with other sectors in the economy, the software sector has relatively higher productivity (for reasons explored in other chapters in this volume). But skilled wages are low because of low average productivity. High productivity and low wages are an ideal basis for profitability. But the resulting international wage gap is also a threat as talent gets lured abroad by the prospect of higher living standards. As talent leaves—or even has the option of leaving—wages rise and productivity falls as specialized skills are lost.[5]

The tension between the costs and benefits of skilled emigration for an industry that relies heavily on outsourced business comes out clearly in a recent paper by Gene Grossman and Elhanan Helpman [6]. Their paper actually does not address emigration at all, but rather the extent and location of international outsourcing by rich-country firms. Firms outsourcing activities such as software development face the problems of finding qualified outsourcing partners and getting them to make relationship specific investments in customization without recourse to complete contracts. Emigration is clearly relevant to the extent of such outsourcing difficulties. On the negative side, it 'thins' skill markets, making it less worthwhile to search for partners in the skill-losing country. On the positive side, diasporic networks can improve 'technologies' for partner search and communication of customization requirements between the outsourcing firm and its suppliers, and also help overcome difficulties of contractual incompleteness by acting as 'reputational intermediaries'—ideas we explore in Section 3.

Notwithstanding the costs, we argue that international skill mobility has probably been on net an advantage for at least some of the countries in this project. For India, we think that the most important factor has been the role of the diaspora in overcoming reputational disadvantages in an industry where ex ante quality is very hard to discern. For Ireland, there is convincing evidence that returning Irish

professionals with enhanced human capital helped propel the booming high-tech
sector in the latter half of the 1990s and early 2000s. More directly, there is
evidence that a very high number of the founders of indigenous Irish software
companies had international experience. For Israel, the immigration of almost
1 million members of the human capital rich Jewish diaspora from the former
Soviet Union provided an unprecedented increase in the supply of skills to the
Israeli economy. Although it is hard to find an overt footprint of this inflow on
the Israeli software sector, it must have helped to maintain cost competitiveness
at a time of rapid economy-wide skill upgrading.[6]

We have organized the rest of the chapter in four sections. Section 2 describes
the evolution of the emigrant stocks in some key destination countries. Section 3
reviews the economics of the costs and benefits of emigration with a focus on the
welfare effects on home-country populations. Section 4 applies the economics from
Section 3 to better understand the effects on software industry development of the
migration episodes in Indian, Ireland and Israel noted in the previous paragraph.
Finally, in Section 5 we outline areas for future research.

2   Emigrant Stocks and Flows

The data on emigration stocks and flows are notoriously poor. In this section, we
nonetheless try to piece together a rough quantitative picture on the relevant stocks
and flows to get a sense of absent Indian, Irish, and Israeli human capital. We start
with crude estimates of broad Irish and Jewish ancestral diaspora and then try to
narrow our focus to measurements of overseas nationals that are more directly
relevant to the development of high-tech industries in the three countries.

2.1   The Broad Diaspora: Ancestry

Ireland's Department of Foreign Affairs has estimated that there are as many
as 70 million worldwide that claim Irish descent [7].[7] Although this diaspora is
in many ways the sad result of Ireland's politically and economically turbulent
history, the Irish government considers it a valuable resource: 'The existence of
this vast extended Irish family creates an immense reservoir of goodwill towards
Ireland and is one of our main assets as a nation' [7, p. 1].

Close to half of this broad diaspora reside in the United States. In the 2000
US census, some 30.5 million—10.9 percent of the population—claimed Irish
ancestry (though curiously this was down from 15.6 percent of the population—
38.8 million—in the 1990 census). From results released from the 1990 census
we know that the vast majority of those claiming Irish ancestry were *not* born in
Ireland, with some 98.8 percent having been born in the United States. Among the
270,000 foreign-born (not necessarily all Irish-born) claiming Irish ancestry, just
less than 50,000 had entered between 1980 and 1990. We return to the cohort of

Irish who were driven to emigrate by poor economic conditions in the 1980s in Section 4.

The Jewish diaspora is estimated to have been 8.4 million at the beginning of 2000, with a further 4.7 million Jews living in Israel [8]. Israel's Law of Return, the legal framework for acceptance and absorption of immigrants, defines a Jew as any person born to a Jewish mother or who has converted to Judaism. The law's provisions extend to all current Jews (as defined above) and to their non-Jewish spouses, children, and grandchildren, as well as to the spouses of these children and grandchildren [8].[8] As we discuss in Section 4, this broad diaspora has been a vast source of additional skill for the Israeli economy in the 1990s.

2.2 The Narrow Diaspora: Emigrants

We now turn to look more closely at characteristics of *emigrant* (or native born) Indian, Irish, and Israeli populations. We initially concentrate on US-resident emigrants because of their importance to each of the three countries and also because the US data is best. We then briefly discuss some other important destination countries.

Table 9.1 shows how the total numbers of these emigrant populations have evolved in the United States since 1960 for the three countries plus Brazil and China. The number of Indian-born emigrants has increased sharply since 1960, more than doubling in the 1990s alone to top 1 million. Ireland, which has been sending its people to the United States in large numbers since the 1840s Famine, has seen the number of Irish-born drop over the four-decade period as deaths outweighed new emigration, though the fall slowed during the 1980s and 1990s. The Israeli-born population has increased steadily between 1960 and 2000. Like the Indian-born population, both the Brazilian-born and Chinese-born populations also

TABLE 9.1. Indian-, Irish-, and Israeli-born Populations in the United States, 1960–2000

	1960	1970	1980	1990	2000
Number					
India	12.296	51.000	206.087	450.406	1,022.552
Ireland	338.722	251.375	197.817	169.827	156.474
Israel	17.724	35.858	66.961	86.048	109.719
Brazil	13.988	27.069	40.919	82.489	212.428
China	99.735	172.132	286.120	529.837	988.857
Percent of domestic population					
India	0.003	0.009	0.030	0.053	0.101
Ireland	13.378	8.521	5.816	4.841	4.121
Israel	0.828	1.235	1.792	1.907	1.878

Note: The 1960 and 1970 numbers for China include Taiwan.

Source: US Census (1960–2000); World Bank Development Indicators.

TABLE 9.2. Characteristics of the US-born and Selected Foreign-born
Populations in the United States

Year of entry (2001 March CPS)	Population shares (%)			
	US-born	Indian-born	Irish-born	Israeli-born
Before 1960	—	1	32	4
1960–69	—	3	19	1
1970–79	—	14	8	28
1980–89	—	24	23	35
1990–95	—	23	13	18
1996–2001	—	36	5	14
Age (average of 1999–2001 March CPS)				
<18	28	7	3	21
18–24	10	9	3	6
25–44	28	52	33	45
45–64	22	26	31	28
65+	12	6	31	0
Educational attainment (2001 March CPS) (Age ⩾25)				
Less than high school	13	6	9	6
High school	34	8	31	50
Some college	27	9	22	16
Bachelors degree	17	40	25	12
Masters/professional degree	7	33	11	14
Doctorate	1	4	1	4
Occupation (average of 1999–2001 March CPS) (Working population)				
Executive, administrative, and managerial	15	17	16	32
Professional specialty occupations	15	42	20	32
Engineers	1	7	—	—
Mathematical/computer specialists	1	16	—	—
Other	70	41	64	36

Source: US Census Bureau, Current Population Survey, March Supplement, various issues; and authors' calculations.

increased dramatically post-1990, though, as we discuss below, these populations are not as human capital rich as the Indian-born.

Who are these emigrants? Table 9.2 records some salient characteristics for the Indian-, Irish-, and Israeli-born populations based on Current Population Survey data for 2001. The first panel shows *when* emigrants residing in the United States in early 2001 came to the country. Consistent with the population evolutions in Table 9.1, a tiny minority (1 percent) of the Indian-born came before 1960, 59 percent have come since 1990, and 36 percent since 1996. The Irish-born population shows a very different pattern, with almost a third coming before 1960.

Interestingly, following an evident fall-off in US-bound emigration in the 1970s, there is evidence of a pick up in the 1980s and first half of the 1990s, before clearly falling as the 'Celtic Tiger' economy boomed in the later 1990s. Large-scale Israeli emigration to the United States is also a relatively recent phenomenon with an apparent peak during the 1980s.

The second panel shows the *age structure* of the US-born and the three emigrant populations using average shares from 1999 to 2001 March CPS's. Although there are clear differences in the population age structures, one common feature is the high concentration in prime working age years. Of the Irish-born, 52 percent are in the 25–44 age group, probably reflecting heavy graduate emigration in the second half of the 1980s and early 1990s. The age structure of the Indian-born population is somewhat surprising given the recentness of its emigrants, with an estimated 62 percent being 45 or older. The Israeli-born population is also concentrated in their prime earning years—45 percent between the age of 25 and 44—with a relatively high share under 18 (21 percent) and a negligible number above 65.

The third panel of Table 9.2 shows *educational attainment* for those 25 and above. All three emigrant groups have larger shares with a Bachelor's degree or better than the US-born population. What is truly striking here is the education level of the Indian-born population: 77 percent have a Bachelor's degree or higher, with 37 percent having a Master's, Professional, or Doctorate degree.

The final panel tells us something about the *work* these emigrant populations are doing. Clearly, the three groups are disproportionately represented in managerial and professional occupations. The pattern is most striking for the Indian- and Israeli-born populations, with 59 percent of working Indians and 64 percent of working Israelis involved in management or professional occupations. Forty-two percent of Indians are in professional occupations. Compared with the US-born population, the Indian-born are substantially overrepresented in the engineering professions (1 percent versus 7 percent) and as mathematicians/computer specialists (1 percent versus 16 percent).[9]

Table 9.3 uses recently released data from Census 2000 to compare the human capital intensities of the Indian-, Brazilian-, and Chinese-born populations. We limit our attention to the age group likely to have completed their educations, those 25 and above. Clearly, all three groups increased dramatically in size over the 1990s, with the largest percentage increase occurring for the Brazilian-born (186 percent). Of the populations residing in the United States in 2000, half or more had entered between 1990 and 2000, with Brazil again posting the largest share of recent emigrants (66 percent). In terms of education attainment, all the three populations in 2000 were relatively well educated. In each case, more than half of the population had at least some tertiary education (defined here as more than twelve years of education). For comparison purposes, only 14 percent of the Mexican-born population in the United States had tertiary education. However, in this regard the Indian-born had a substantially higher share (80 percent) than either the Brazilian-born (55 percent) or Chinese-born (54 percent).

TABLE 9.3. Selected Foreign-born Populations in the United States Aged 25 and Above

| | 1990 | 2000 | % change | % of 2000 pop. entering post-1990 | Education level (2000), % | | |
					Primary	Secondary	Tertiary
India	304.030	836.780	175	55	5	15	80
Brazil	53.904	154.250	186	49	9	36	55
China	404.579	846.780	109	66	20	26	54

Note: Primary is 0–8 years of schooling; secondary is 9–12 years of schooling; and tertiary is >12 years of schooling.

Source: Census 2000, US Census Bureau, and Adam (2003) based on special tabulations from Census 2000.

What explains the unusually high human capital intensity and emigration timing of the Indian-born population? An important part of the answer is the expansion of the H-1B program for highly skilled migrants through the 1990s as the tech boom gathered steam. The H-1B visa was introduced with an annual cap of 65,000 in the early 1990s. The cap first became binding in September of the 1997 fiscal year. The cap bound even earlier (May) of the following year, spurring industry lobbying efforts to pass legislation to expand the cap. Legislation passed in 1998 expanded the cap to 115,000 for 1999 and 2000, 107,500 for 2001, before returning to 65,000 in 2002. But as IT skill shortages continued to get worse, legislation was passed to relax the caps still further: 195,000 for 2001–03, before returning to 65,000 in 2004.

Table 9.4 shows a sample of results from an INS study of H-1B visa petitions approved during the first five months of Fiscal Year 2000 (October 1999 to February 2000). During this time 81,262 petitions were approved, of which 42.6 percent went to Indians. Of the total petitions 53.5 percent were granted for people in computer-related occupations. The sponsoring companies were a who's who of the IT world, and also included a number of Indian companies involved in hiring out personnel for on-site services ('body shopping') for its customer companies.

How did the tech slump affect petitions for H-1Bs? Not surprisingly, the number of approved petitions is down, and stories of hardship and returns home abound in the media. But the numbers are still well above mid-1990 levels before the original cap became binding. In the first nine months of fiscal year 2002 (October 1, 2001 to June 30, 2002), 60,500 people subject to the fiscal year limit were approved. But this is well down from the 130,700 people who were approved during the same period of fiscal year 2001.

So far we have concentrated on emigration to the United States, both because of its importance as an emigration destination and the quality of the available data. But of course there are other important destinations for emigrants from these countries as well. The United Kingdom, for example, is an important destination for emigrants from both Ireland and India.[10] Table 9.5 shows that the number of

TABLE 9.4. INS Approved H-1B Petitions, October 1999 to February 2000

Country of birth	Number	Percent	Occupation	Number	Percent	Company	Number
India	34,381	42.6	Computer related	42,563	53.5	Motorola	618
China	7,987	9.9	Architecture, Eng., and Survey	10,385	13.1	Oracle	455
Canada	3,143	3.9	Admin. specializations	6,619	8.3	Cisco	398
United Kingdom	2,598	3.2	Education	4,419	5.6	Mastech	389
Philippines	2,576	3.2	Medicine and Health	3,246	4.1	Intel	367
Taiwan	1,794	2.2	Managers and Officials	2,530	3.2	Microsoft	362
Korea	1,691	2.1	Social Science	1,963	2.5	Rapidigm	357
Japan	1,631	2.0	Life Science	1,843	2.3	Syntel	337
Pakistan	1,508	1.9	Miss Prof., Tech., and Mang.	1,659	2.1	Wipro	327
Russia	1,408	1.7	Math. and Phys. science	1,453	1.8	Tata Consult.	320
Germany	1,261	1.6	Art	1,066	1.3	PriceWaterhouse	272
France	1,204	1.5	Writing	548	0.7	People Com Consult.	261
Mexico	1,011	1.3	Law	428	0.5	Lucent	255
Brazil	861	1.1	Fashion models	344	0.4	Infosys	239
South Africa	838	1.0	Entertainment and Recreation	293	0.4	Nortel	234
Colombia	769	1.0	Museum, Lib., and Arch. science	146	0.2	Tekedge	219
Hong Kong	738	0.9	Religion and Theology	43	0.1	Data Conversion	195
Malaysia	722	0.9				Tata Infotech	185
Australia	644	0.8	Unknown occupations	1,714	2.2	Colligent USA	183
Indonesia	635	0.8				Sun Microsystems	182
Other countries	13,386	16.6	Total	81,262		Compuware	179
			Total (known occupation)	79,548			
Unknown country	476						
Total	81,262						
Total (known country)	80,786						

Source: US Immigration and Naturalization Service (2000), 'Leading Employers of Speciality Occupation Workers (H-1B): October 1999 to February 2000'.

TABLE 9.5. Irish and Indian Nationals in the United Kingdom

	1985	1990	1995	2000
Foreign nationals (thousands)				
Ireland	569	478	443	404
India	138	156	114	153
Foreign nationals in the laborforce (thousands)				
Ireland	269	268	216	206
India	—	—	60	74
Managerial and professional (percent)				
Ireland	—	—	22.4	28.6
Indian sub-continent	—	—	22.0	24.1
UK nationals	—	—	24.3	25.1
Other non-manual (percent)				
Ireland	—	—	31.5	35.0
Indian sub-continent	—	—	17.2	24.1
UK nationals	—	—	33.9	35.1

Source: Numbers of foreign nationals are from OECD (2001). Trends in International Migration.

Irish-born in the United Kingdom has fallen steadily since 1985 due to deaths in the generation who emigrated around mid-century, though it still numbers around 400,000. Their share in the labor force held steady in the late 1980s, however, as a new generation of economic migrants refreshed the working emigrant stock. Later their number fell by roughly 60,000 over the 1990s. The occupation shares for 1995 and 2000 show that the Irish have done relatively well in the United Kingdom, though the rapid increase in the share of the more skilled occupations between 1995 and 2000 suggests that the less skilled were more likely to return home.

Table 9.5 also shows that the Indian-born population in the United Kingdom now numbers around 150,000. Work permit data for 2000 shows that Indian nationals were the second largest recipient of permits (12,292) just after the United States (12,684) (see [9]). Of the total number of Indian nationals receiving work permits 2,616 were classed as 'engineers and technologists' and 5,973 were classed as 'computer analysts/programmers' [9]. No other country came close to India in number of work permits received for these highly skilled technical occupations.[11]

Technically skilled Indians were in high demand in other countries as well. In Canada, 5,738 Indians gained permanent residency under the points system for skilled workers in 2000.[12] In 1999/2000, Indians were the third leading recipient (after the United Kingdom and the United States) of employer sponsored temporary business visas for skilled professionals in Australia. And Indians were the largest beneficiaries of visas issued in the early stages of the German 'Green Card' program, receiving 1,403 of the 6,988 visas issued between October 2000 and April 2001.

3 Emigration and Industry Development: A Framework

How does the international mobility of a country's skilled workers affect its capacity to develop a domestic skill-intensive industry such as software? In this section, we briefly and selectively piece together what the economics literature has to say about the economic effects of emigration. Actually, much of the literature we draw from focuses on the effects of immigration rather than emigration. But since many of the effects are the same with the sign reversed there is much to be learned from this literature as well. In measuring the effects of emigration, our focus is always on the *welfare of domestic residents*—people referred to sympathetically in the literature as 'those left behind' or TLBs. Thus we ignore the (important) effects of emigration on the emigrants themselves unless their success or failure has some impact on home-country residents.

We aim for a broad coverage of the effects of home-country residents, which we discuss under four headings. The first deals with the impact of the *prospect* of emigration on the decision to accumulate human capital that may or may not be eventually taken abroad. The second deals with the direct effects of the *absence* of skilled workers on the domestic economy in terms of such factors as lost surplus, larger skill premiums, fiscal losses, diminished scale economies, and changed comparative advantage. The third considers how the *diaspora* can be an asset as a source and facilitator of international business. That is, we look at the ways that immigrants can have an impact on their home economies from afar. We finally turn to the part played by emigrants when they *return* to the home economy with augmented human capital, financial capital, foreign connections, and entitlements to foreign social insurance benefits.

3.1 Prospect

How does the prospect of emigration affect the incentive to invest in human capital? A number of recent papers have developed models in which the prospect of emigration increases the expected return to human capital investment (e.g. see [10–12]). This increase in the expected return can raise the overall level of human capital in the economy if the subsequent *actual* emigration is not too high. One example is where potential emigrants face a lottery for visas such as the diversity lottery run by the US State Department. The chance of winning, and thus of gaining access to a labor market with higher rewards to skill, induces more study and on-the-job learning. But many of those enticed by the prospect of a visa actually fail to win one, so that a portion of this increased human capital stays behind. The possibility of emigration may actually increase human capital if this portion is large enough.

Beine et al. [10,11] provide evidence that is consistent with an overall positive effect on human capital for a number of countries, though they readily admit their data has many limitations. Without forming an overall judgment on the empirical importance of this prospective channel, we note three factors that work to diminish its importance.

First, there will be income as well as substitution effects from an increased expected return to human capital. An Irish secondary (high) school student deciding on how hard to study to win a place at university might, for example, be enticed to slack off by the fall back of a relatively high paying job as a construction worker in London or a nanny in New York.

Second, an overall positive effect on human capital depends on the prospect of emigration inducing study but then many of these more skilled individuals deciding not to go or not qualifying to go. To the extent that the desirable destination countries screen immigration applicants with objective criteria (e.g. the Canadian or Australian point systems) or with jobs offers (e.g. UK work permits or US H-1Bs) the degree of uncertainty is diminished. In other words, those who *want to go* and make the necessary investments are likely to *qualify to go* (see [13]).

Lastly, there is evidence that the value of human capital acquired in one country—especially if it is a developing country—does not always travel well with an emigrant. Looking at the case of immigrants to Israel from the former Soviet Union, Friedberg [14] finds that education and experience acquired in the former Soviet Union is significantly less valued than human capital acquired in Israel. This suggests that would-be emigrants should wait to acquire their more advanced human capital abroad if possible. Interestingly, Friedberg [14] does find that education acquired in the adopted country raises the return to education acquired at home. This suggests that the prospect of emigration could still provide some incentive to acquire human capital provided that the individual is willing to pursue further education while abroad.[13] We return to the fascinating case of Israel-bound emigration from the former Soviet Union in the third of our applications in Section 4.[14]

Our discussion has focused on how the prospect of emigration affects the expected return to human capital. Having a (potential) emigration option might also affect an individual's willingness to take more risks with their human capital accumulation decisions. Suppose, for example, that the global software industry is growing strongly, but is at a nascent stage domestically. Investing in computer programming skills may be quite risky if options are limited in the domestic economy, which may fail to develop a substantial computer industry. Having the fall back option of emigration may make a young school leaver more willing to take a risk on an emerging industry. From the national perspective, such a propensity to take a more forward looking perspective in developing skills may help the country break out of traditional patterns of comparative advantage, and also to increase the national proclivity to 'explore' new industries for which the country's characteristics might turn out to make it particularly well suited.[15]

3.2   Absence

How are TLBs affected by the absence of a sizable portion of the native-born skilled labor force? Figure 9.1 shows the simple case of a closed economy producing

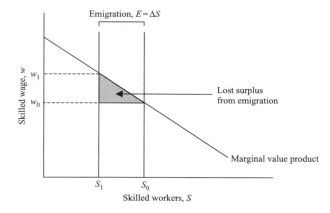

FIGURE 9.1. Lost Surplus from Emigration

a single good (GDP) with skilled workers and other factors under constant returns to scale technology, competitive markets, and no fiscal system. With diminishing returns to skilled workers, skilled emigration pushes up the domestic wage.[16] The size of the aggregate loss to TLBs is shown by the shaded area in the diagram.[17] A loss stems from a difference between an emigrant's marginal value product (their benefit to TLBs) and the wage they were paid (their cost to TLBs). Since in a competitive labor market skilled workers are paid their marginal product, the loss of a *single* skilled worker will have no effect on the aggregate surplus of TLBs. It is clear from the diagram that this is not true for the loss of multiple skilled workers. Moreover, it is easy to show that the total loss (approximately) rises with the square of the number of emigrants.[18] To understand better the source of this loss, note that in measuring this loss we are comparing the value lost from someone leaving with the wage they were paid before anyone left. The real source of the emigration loss is not that the *wage* is pushed up (though it will be in a competitive skill market) but that the *marginal value product* of remaining workers is pushed up as others leave (see Figure 9.1).[19] For example, the emigration of a few software engineers will drive the value of remaining software engineers above what they were all initially being paid. If then more software engineers leave, the loss in value to TLBs will be strictly greater than the amount of money they had been handing over to the engineers *before any of the engineers had left*.[20]

We now consider a number of complications to this simple model of emigration loss. The key to understanding the loss to TLBs is to compare the domestic marginal value product of an emigrant to the wage they were paid. Unlike in our simple model, the first three complications show how the loss of even a single skilled worker can harm TLBs. The last complication considers how things change when the labor-losing economy is open to international trade.

(i) *Fiscal effects*: Our simple analysis assumed away the existence of a fiscal system. In reality emigrants pay taxes and receive benefits from the government.

Under a progressive fiscal system it is likely that skilled workers—and especially young high-tech workers—are net contributors to the fiscal system. Desai et al. [1] estimate the fiscal loss to Indian TLBs from skilled Indian emigration to the United States. Their method is to infer what fiscal contributions emigrant Indians would be making had they stayed in India by combining estimates of what their Indian incomes would be and summary measures of the progressive tax and expenditure system. Using their preferred income inference method and a conservatively high estimate of expenditure saving, they find a tax loss equal to 0.58 percent of GDP and a net fiscal loss equal to 0.24 percent of GDP. The largest component of the tax loss is the loss of central government income tax revenues (0.44 percent of GDP), which represents a substantial fraction of central direct tax revenues.

(ii) *Scale effects*: The assumptions of constant returns to scale and strictly diminishing returns to skilled workers may lead us to miss important channels through which emigration harms domestic industry. The scale of the skilled labor may affect an emerging software industry in a number of ways. As examples, the 'thickness' of skill markets could affect the willingness of foreign firms to search the economy for investment locations or outsourcing partners [6], or there may be uncompensated knowledge spill-overs between skilled workers.

(iii) *Non-competitive wage setting and heterogeneous skills*: In our simple model, we assume that skilled workers are paid their marginal product so that the emigration of a single worker will not (assuming no fiscal effects) harm the welfare of TLBs. Another situation where this is unlikely is when particular worker skills are uniquely matched to a particular firm. This skill specificity is important for knowledge intensive industries such as software, where competitive advantage can attract and retain 'core competents' (not to be confused with core competence). In this case, it is more appropriate to assume that the wage is determined by bilateral bargaining, with the surplus between the worker's value to the firm and their next best wage offer being split according to their relative bargaining power. Assuming the firm has at least some bargaining power, the wage will be set below the workers marginal value product. Thus the loss of this worker to emigration will result in a loss to TLBs.[21] The likelihood that it is uniquely talented workers that are lost to emigration also suggests that we cannot look simply at the number of emigrants, or even the number of emigrants in broadly defined skill categories. The loss of even a few 'institution builders', for example, might have large development effects. Studies of the graduates of the elite Indian Institutes of Technology provide a good illustration of this concern. The acceptance rate in these institutions is between 1 and 2 percent of an applicant pool that is already highly selective. Analyses of the graduating classes of IIT Mumbai in the 1970s have revealed that 31 percent settled abroad, of which 7 percent were engineers. Moreover, 43 percent of the top quartile of graduates had emigrated compared with 27 percent in the rest of the class [22].

(iv) *Open economy effects*: Our models have so far assumed economies closed to international trade. India, Ireland, and Israel are, of course, very much open to world trade in information technology products and services. How do our results about the effects of immigration on industry development change when we move from a closed to an open economy setting? The most widely used open economy framework for studying the effects of changes in factor endowments is the Heckscher–Ohlin model. For a small open economy facing given terms of trade, internationally equalized factor prices, and using the same technologies as its trading partners, the emigration of skilled workers will cause a reallocation of resources away from skill-intensive sectors. But in contrast to our simple closed diminishing returns to skill model there is no change in the skilled wage or any other factor price. Since software is a skill-intensive sector, this model predicts that emigration shrinks the software sector, but does not harm the welfare of TLBs as factor incomes are unchanged. The mechanism at work is that described by the well-known Rybczynski Theorem: output is reallocated away from the skill-intensive sector until the demand for skill is reduced to match the shrunken supply.[22]

Few governments around the world would be sanguine about the shrinkage of high-tech sectors even if convinced that current factor prices are not affected. There are several reasons for this and not just the 'prestige' of high technology. Policy makers want to promote sunrise industries because of future growth prospects. There are good reasons to believe that high-tech sectors such as software— especially at the more innovative end of the industry spectrum—generate ample opportunities for learning by doing and knowledge spillovers (for arguments along these lines see Lucas [24]). Software and IT are 'general purpose technologies' with large spillover effects in other economic sectors. Capabilities built up in software can be leveraged in other high-technology fields such as bio-informatics, pharmaceuticals, and media and entertainment (on the role of General Purposes Technologies in economic development see Helpman [25]). An open economy setting moves attention away from current income losses to TLBs, to shifts in the allocation of remaining resources to industries with lower growth potential.[23]

3.3 Diaspora

It is increasingly recognized that a country's overseas nationals, and even those who claim distant ancestral heritage, can be a valuable economic asset (e.g. see [27,28]).[24] In this section, we briefly explore the broad mechanisms through which such a connected diaspora can be a boon to a country's emerging high-tech industries in doing international business.[25]

3.3.1 Willingness to Interact/Transact. The act of emigration rarely leads to the breaking of all connections, not least emotional connections, with a person's original home—emigrants may be gone, but they are rarely completely forgotten. Whereas the emigrants who were forced to leave Ireland through economic adversity in the decades following the Irish Famine in the late 1840s were able to retain few links with the country of origin, modern transport, media, and communications allow for much richer interactions. From a narrowly economic point of view these interactions can be a source of information on new technologies and trading opportunities. Emigrants may also have a preference for goods produced in their home countries, especially when they have developed a taste for home-country specific products. The dedicated, country-of-origin arranged import isles of supermarkets in larger American cities are one visible sign of the importance of such trade.

Such attachments to home-country products are probably not of great importance for the high-tech sector. Of more importance is the knowledge that emigrants have of trading and investment opportunities back home, possibly combined with a desire to put business and advice the way of emerging home-country businesses where feasible. This willingness to trade and invest goes beyond preference and information; it also reflects *ability to pay*. Skilled emigrants from poorer countries often earn substantially more in their adopted countries than they earned prior to leaving—which can grow into substantial purchasing/investing power as the emigrants sacrifice consumption to accumulate financial wealth. To the extent that this wealth leads to business with home-country firms, the origin country gets to share in the emigrant's gains from leaving or 'emigrant's surplus'.

The transnational economic role of diasporas is the subject of a good deal of informal speculation but less formal analysis.[26] Have the large Irish and Jewish diasporas in the United States, many of whom are in positions to influence the location decisions of multinational direct investors, tilted decisions at the margin to favor their ancestral homes? It is suggestive that 43 percent of the 1,500 companies that have chosen to establish bases in Ireland are from the United States [30]; and Ireland's industrial development agency calculates that Ireland wins close to a quarter of US manufacturing investment in Europe while accounting for roughly 1 percent of the population [31].[27]

3.3.2   Reputational Intermediaries. International business is greatly complicated by poor information on distant trading partners and the difficulties of contracting across national boundaries. To examine how a connected diaspora might facilitate such business, we take the example of a US software firm looking to outsource a once-off software development project, with all the attendant difficulties modeled in the Grossman and Helpman paper referenced in the introduction [6]. The US firm lacks information on the capabilities of the software firms in various locations, and is worried about being 'held up' by any overseas party due to difficulties in writing and enforcing contracts with opportunistic trading partners. We note three distinct ways in which members of the diaspora can serve as what we loosely call 'reputational intermediaries'.[28]

(i) *Search*: If the member of the diaspora has an ongoing relationship with the US firms (possibly an employment relationship) they may be able to 'put their reputation on the line' by vouching for a particular overseas firm. The incentive to risk reputation in this way could be monetary. For example, an employer pays a premium for foreign country nationals that are well informed about the home-country business scene. But it could also reflect a desire to help home-country businesses.[29] Rauch and Watson [35] develop a model in which an employee can build up knowledge about suppliers through the normal conduct of their business over time. The employee then faces the choice of going out on his own as a network intermediary (i.e. becoming an entrepreneur) or staying in employment. A network intermediary sells the service of matching buyers with suppliers. Members of the diaspora might be well placed to act as such intermediaries if they have richer knowledge of home-country firms or ways of finding this information out. Reputational intermediaries are likely to matter more where knowledge is tacit. Information is distant invariant, knowledge is more contextual. Unlike many manufacturing sectors where ex ante knowledge of quality is more easily discernible through third party certification (like ISO, ASTM etc. . . .) this is much less the case with services where quality can only be discerned after use.

(ii) *Contract fulfillment*: Moving beyond the search process, reputational intermediaries can ensure that each side lives up to its side of the deal.[30] Once the deal has been signed, the supplying firm may be willing to act opportunistically with its outsourcing partner, but may be unwilling to risk its reputation with the member of the diaspora vouching for their trustworthiness. The power of the vouching party can be greatly enhanced if they can 'blacklist' an offending home-country businessman within the diasporic network. On the other side of the deal, the outsourcing firm may also value its reputation for fair dealing with the intermediary and the diasporic network they belong to. In essence, the intermediary is leveraging its long-term relationship with each party to overcome the often severe difficulties with one-shot contracts across weak legal systems.

A diaspora's influence is a function both of its own characteristics as well as of the country of origin. There are five features of a diaspora's reputational role that are important to note. First, there is a threshold of the country of origin's economic openness, below which diaspora's have little effect. The three countries examined in this chapter (as well as China) were all closed economies for many years during which period their diasporas played little role. It is only after the countries began to open up that the effects of diasporas became more important. Second, the diaspora can play a reputational role only when it itself has a reputation. A good proxy for this is the size and education of the diaspora. Thus despite their sizes, the diasporas from Central America and the Caribbean appear to have had little effect (low education) as do those from countries like Germany and Chile, whose higher educational levels cannot compensate for the handicap of smaller size. Third, even the existence of the first two factors while necessary is not sufficient to ensure that a diaspora's reputational potential is actually realized. The reasons for leaving are critical. If the diaspora was forced out for political reasons, then it is likely to leverage its reputational role to block, not promote, investments in the country of origin. Jews of German origin, Cuban Americans, East European immigrants in North America prior to 1990, successful Israeli Arab immigrants or Indian Gujarati

Muslim immigrants are all examples of this phenomenon. Fourth, the role of reputation might be even greater in the current context when most countries have liberalized and a MNC potentially has several equally viable investment locations to choose from. Then diasporas within firms can act as champions for their country of origin in internal management battles. Note that the need to protect their *internal* reputation within the firm ensures that they will only do so if their country of origin is indeed a viable candidate to begin with. Finally, as a few MNCs locate investments in these countries, it is the reputation of the MNCs themselves that will signal to other MNCs on the locational viability of that country. Thus the reputational role of diasporas may have its greatest leverage in acting as a 'tipping point' with far reaching consequences.[31]

(iii) *Altered profiles*: At a more general level, members of the diaspora can also act as reputational intermediaries to the extent that their business behavior affect the 'profile' or 'brand' of their countrymen. Firms looking for outsourcing partners under uncertainty will rationally engage in statistical discrimination, whereby they form an expectation of the quality of any given potential trading partner based on observed characteristics *and* their priors about the distribution of characteristics in the population that this firm belongs to. These prior beliefs can be altered through contacts with members of the diaspora. For example, if a firm dealing in the United States with Indian engineers from the elite IITs, show them to be excellently trained, this experience can lead to upward revision of priors about the quality of Indian engineers in India from these institutions, and possibly other institutions as well. This mechanism will be especially important if the industry and firms in question do *not* share the negative attributes of other more prominent industries in their country—a fact that may be poorly appreciated by the outsourcer.

3.4   Return

Lastly, we turn to the impact of returned emigrants. Our interest is how the fact that some part of the population having spent time abroad affects the welfare of that population, including the welfare of the returned emigrants themselves. This is consistent with our intention to examine how emigration—prospective, present, and past—affects the existing population at a particular point in time. Time spent in work or study abroad can augment human capital as emigrants acquire knowledge of frontier technologies and market opportunities, management know-how, languages, business contacts, and so on. In addition to direct individual productivity enhancing effects, emigrants may have saved part of their 'emigration surplus', accumulating financial capital they can bring back with them for investment at home. If they have been away for long enough they may also have acquired entitlements to foreign social insurance benefits. For example, ten years of contributions to the US Social Security system creates entitlement to retirement income benefits. The return on contributions can actually be quite high for returned emigrants given that the average monthly earnings used in the benefit formula is an average of the worker's highest earning thirty-five years, and the benefit formula is a progressive function of thus calculated average earnings.[32] However, the available evidence suggests that the probability of migrants returning declines with time—hence very few of those who stay for a decade return in the first place. In contrast, most of those who do return do so well within ten years—in which case the loss from uncollected social security benefits is substantial.

Of course, the benefits from past emigration must be weighed against the negative impacts on the economy during the time they were gone. One factor increasing the probability of an overall positive balance is that temporary emigrants engage in a form of inter-temporal substitution—leaving when times are bad (and the domestic value of their skills is low) and returning when the domestic demand for their skills is higher. This seems a reasonable description of the well-educated Irish graduates who left a slumping Irish economy in the 1980s, many of whom returned to propel the 'Celtic Tiger' economy of the 1990s. We return to this example of 'brain circulation' as the second of our applications in the next section.

4 Applications

4.1 Transnational Connections: India's Silicon Valley Diaspora

In Section 2, we outlined the large increase in the number of highly skilled Indians residing in the United States. The Indian-born population in the United States increased by more than half a million over the course of the 1990s alone, and an analysis of the March 2000 CPS reveals that 78 percent of these recent arrivals had a Bachelors degree or higher—with exactly half of these in the 'or higher' category.

In a widely discussed study Saxenian [37] drew attention to the impact these absent Indians (and Chinese) were having on economic success of high-tech industries in Silicon Valley. One fascinating finding was that Indians were running 9 percent of Silicon Valley start-ups from the period 1995–98—almost 70 percent of which were in the software sector.[33]

These findings have, however, raised obvious questions about the effect that such absent talent and entrepreneurship is having on the domestic Indian economy. But the study also hints at the connections that these 'absent' Indians retained and cultivated with people and businesses back home. Saxenian [38] followed up on the possibility of these connections with an extensive survey of Indian (and Chinese) members of professional associations in Silicon Valley.

Before reviewing Saxenian's findings, we first recap the ways our framework suggests that a human capital rich diaspora could be an international business asset. We saw that the combination of preference, knowledge, and ability to pay may make members of the diaspora willing customers, investors, and purveyors of information. Their knowledge of the needs and capabilities of both US- and India-based firms make them potentially useful intermediaries in the search and matching process. Their ongoing relationships with both United States and Indian firms (and with other members of the diaspora) make them well situated to use their reputations to support complex transactions when legal contracting is difficult. And their success as technologists, managers, and entrepreneurs in Silicon Valley can change the perceptions of the Indian technology businesses in general.

In Section 3, we grouped the last three of these functions together under the heading of 'reputational intermediaries'. It is well known that reputational concerns have been an obstacle to Indian software firms. Banerjee and Duflo [39] provide evidence that reputation affects the form of contracts that firms outsourcing customized software enter into with Indian software firms. Indicators of weaker reputations are correlated with opting for fixed-price contracts over riskier (for the buyer) time and materials contracts. Kapur [40] points out various ways that Indian firms have tried to lessen reputational constraints, including joint ventures with US firms, acquiring or setting up US firms, getting independent quality certifications, getting listed on US stock exchanges, and working on-site for the buyer.

Table 9.6 records some basic demographic information about the respondents to Saxenian's survey. The Indian respondents are generally younger, more educated, and more concentrated in executive/managerial occupations than the overall Indian-born population in the United States (see Table 9.2 for a comparison). Of the total Indian respondents 38 percent classed themselves as being in the software industry, which compares with 26 percent of Chinese-born and 19 percent Taiwanese-born respondents. Of the total Indian respondents 98 percent had a Bachelor's degree or higher, and 77 percent had a Master's or a PhD. Interestingly, 68 percent of Indian respondents said that they earned their highest degree in the United States, but this is still lower than the 81 percent of Chinese and 92 percent of Taiwanese who received their highest degree from US institutions.

In Table 9.7 we reproduce a sample of Saxenian's findings on the degree of connectedness of these admittedly elite Indian professionals to those in India. Seventy-seven percent of the Indian-born had one or more friends who returned to India to start a company. At least once a year 52 percent travel to India on business. Twenty-seven percent report regular exchanges of information on jobs/business opportunities with those back home, while 33 percent report regular exchanges of information on technology. In terms of the potential role of Silicon Valley Indians as reputational intermediaries, 46 percent have been a contact for domestic Indian businesses. On the investment side, 23 percent have invested their own money into Indian start-ups—10 percent more than once. And, finally, when asked about the possibility of bringing their much augmented human capital home, 45 percent report returning as somewhat or quite likely.

Saxenian's results, while suggestive of strong connections between the Silicon Valley resident Indians and those in India, should however, be interpreted with care. There are strong problems of self-selection into such associations and in the choice to respond to the survey.[34] There is also reason to believe that diasporas will exaggerate their contribution to the country of origin. These figures contradict what is known about the activities of Indian diaspora from other sources.

TABLE 9.6. Demographic Characteristics of Professional Associations
in Silicon Valley

	Country of birth		
	India	China	Taiwan
Age (% shares)			
18–35	60	58	37
36–50	34	34	51
50+	6	8	12
Educational attainment (% shares)			
Less than Bachelor's/no answer	2	1	0
Bachelor's degree	21	13	15
Master's degree	68	58	69
PhD	9	28	16
Highest degree earned in United States (%)	63	81	92
Current job (% shares)			
Executive (corporate officer)	41	10	24
Manager	26	13	31
Technical professional (non-manag.)	28	68	35
Other professional (non-manag.)	3	9	9
Clerical/administrative/other	0	0	1
Industry (% shares)			
Semiconductor	9	18	20
Computer/communications	20	26	24
Software	38	26	19
Professional services	13	7	9
Internet content/services	9	7	6
Other	11	16	22

Source: Saxenian, Annalee (2002). *Local and Global Networks of Immigrant Professionals in Silicon Valley*. Public Policy Institute of California.

One problem is that the investment data is silent on the magnitude of investments. Foreign direct investment from the Indian diaspora is less than 5 percent of its Chinese counterparts—even though the propensity to invest is comparable for the two diasporas in Saxenian's survey. Similarly, the finding that 45 percent would consider returning is belied by reality. While aggregate data on return migration is unavailable, segment specific data such as NSF longitudinal data on PhD students suggests a number closer to 10 percent.

These survey results indicate that the Silicon Valley based Indian diaspora have transnational links with the Indian IT sector. At least for this group, skilled emigration is not simply a one-way 'brain drain'. Although the results are revealing, we are still left with the question of whether the loss of such evident productive/entrepreneurial potential form the Indian economy is counterbalanced by the diaspora's role in breaking down barriers to international business for

TABLE 9.7. Leveraging the Diaspora: Indicators of Emigrant Connectedness in Silicon Valley

	Country of birth		
	India	China	Taiwan
How many of your friends have returned to their country of birth to start a company? (% shares)			
10 or more	4	6	17
1–9	73	68	70
None	23	26	13
How often have you traveled to your country of birth for business purposes, on average, in the past three years?			
Never	48	56	36
Once a year	39	31	38
2–4 times a year	9	8	20
5+ times a year	4	5	6
Percentage of respondents reporting regular exchanges of information with friends, classmates, or business associates in their country of birth			
Jobs or business opportunities in the United States	27	23	16
Jobs or business opportunities in home country	17	12	8
Technology	33	20	19
Have you ever helped businesses in your country of birth by serving as an advisor or arranging a contract? (% shares)			
Advisor	34	24	15
Contract	46	42	34
Percentage of respondents who have invested their own money in start-ups or venture funds in their country of birth (% shares)			
More than once	10	4	12
Only once	13	6	5
Would you consider returning to live in your country of birth in the future? (% shares)			
Somewhat likely	20	29	18
Quite likely	25	14	7

Source: Saxenian, Annalee (2002). *Local and Global Networks of Immigrant Professionals in Silicon Valley*. Public Policy Institute of California.

Indians who remain. One suggestive piece of evidence from the survey itself is that 73 percent of Indians responding to the question 'Which factors would figure most importantly in your decision to start a business in your country of birth?' listed the 'availability of skilled workers'.[35] This answer is interesting in the context of the trade-off we discussed earlier between emigration thinning domestic labor markets (and thus reducing the incentive to search for business opportunities) and the role of the diaspora in helping to facilitate and fund such opportunities.

4.2 Fueling the Tiger: Irish Grads Come Home

Showing few hints of the 'Tiger' economy that would emerge in the 1990s, Irish economic performance through much of the 1980s was anemic. Between 1982 and 1989 employment actually fell by 5 percent, and the unemployment hovered in the mid-teens [41]. Throughout this period tertiary education enrollments continued to expand strongly, growing by 64 percent over the course of the decade [42]. This growth followed rapid growth in the 1950s (56 percent), 1960s (129 percent), and 1970s (92 percent). It is not surprising that with such a dire labor market, and Ireland's tradition of emigration in hard economic times, a number of new graduates choose to emigrate.

Figure 9.2 shows the course of Irish graduate emigration from 1982 to 1997 based on surveys done by Ireland's Higher Education Authority of the first destinations of jobs/places of study in the year following graduation (see [43]). Male graduate emigration rose from around 6 percent in 1982 to around 25 percent by the end of the decade. Female graduate emigration shows a similar trend with a peak of around 20 percent. Clearly the Irish economy was losing a substantial fraction of the human capital it was producing.

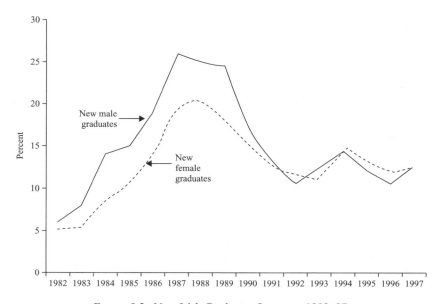

FIGURE 9.2. New Irish Graduates Overseas, 1982–97

Source: Adapted from Lydon [43]. Original data from Higher Education Authority, First Destinations Survey.

TABLE 9.8. Residents of the Irish State on Census 2002 Night Who Lived
Outside of Ireland for One Year or More

Year of taking up residence in Ireland	Total	Country of previous residence			
		UK	Other EU	US	Other
Before 1951	7,520	5,980	191	604	745
1951–60	16,048	12,973	369	1,153	1,553
1961–70	50,615	39,492	1,330	4,573	5,220
1971–80	86,967	66,752	3,375	5,825	10,745
1981–90	89,258	56,263	6,844	9,899	15,892
1991–95	98,379	62,171	8,952	10,489	16,767
1996–2002	252,383	121,226	27,991	24,431	78,735
Not stated	43,544	9,961	2,700	1,708	29,175
Total	644,444	375,178	51,752	58,682	158,832

Source: Central Statistics Office (2003) Census 2002, Principal demographic results.

Economic performance in the 1990s has been quite different. In terms of
the labor market, employment almost doubled—47 percent—between 1989 and
1999 [41]. From Figure 9.2 we can see that graduate emigration fell sharply as
slump gave way to boom, with the turnaround being especially large for male
graduates. Moreover, as the boom gathered pace graduates who had left during
the 1980s began to return home.

Figure 9.3 shows the history of migration since Irish independence in the
1920s. The 1950s was a particularly bleak decade for the Ireland Republic's
capacity to provide livelihoods for its young people, many of whom left for the
United Kingdom with limited education. Better economic conditions in the 1960s
and 1970s stemmed the outflows (leading to a significant net inflow during the
1970s), but macroeconomic mismanagement, industrial restructuring away from
indigenous labor intensive manufacturing, and poor global economic conditions
combined to produce net emigration again in the 1980s. There are arguments in
Irish policy and academic circles about what changed in the late 1980s, and a good
deal of ex post rationalization, though there is little disagreement that Ireland began
a 'growth miracle' that gathered pace through the 1990s.[36]

Table 9.8 records the number of people aged one year and over (usually resident
in Ireland and present on census night in 2002) that spent at least one year outside
the country. This measure captures both immigrants and returning Irish. In total,
644,444 were so classified, or 16.5 percent of the total population. It is striking
that 42 percent reported taking up residence in Ireland between 1996 and 2002.[37]
Assuming that relatively few US citizens took up residence in Ireland over this
period, it is reasonable to suppose that most of the 24,431 individuals who reported
their previous residence as being in the United States are returning Irish.

Figure 9.4 shows the number of *returning Irish* between 1995 and 2001. The
number of returnees peaked at over 26,000 in 1999, before falling to just over

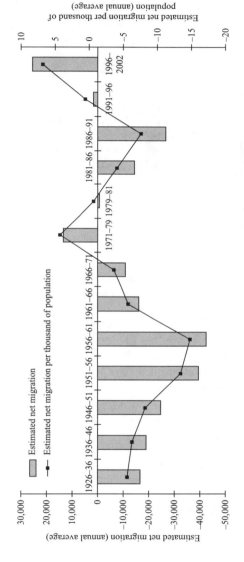

FIGURE 9.3. Estimated Annual Net Migration to Ireland

Source: Central Statistics Office (2002), Census 2002, Preliminary Report, Dublin: Stationary Office.

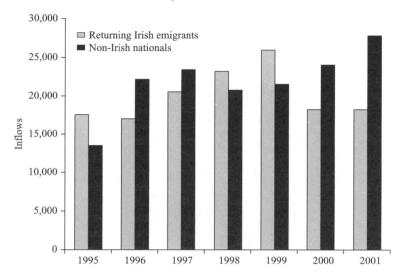

FIGURE 9.4. Migration Flows to Ireland: Returning Irish Emigrants and Non-Irish Nationals, 1995–2001

Source: Central Statistics Office (2001), Population and Migration Estimates.

18,000 in 2000 and 2001 as the emigrant stock diminished, Irish house prices rose, and commuting times in the major cities lengthened. Barrett and O'Connell [44] report labor force survey data from the mid-1990s that confirm that the returning Irish were relatively highly educated. Fifty-eight percent of returning Irish emigrants—that is, those born but not resident in Ireland in the preceding twelve months—had a third-level degree. This compares with 29 percent for non-returnees in the labor force. For the 30–39 age group, 50 percent of returnees had a third-level education compared with 26 percent in the non-returnee population. Thus returning emigrants provided a significant boost to human capital resources at a time that skill shortages were becoming more apparent.

How does their time spent abroad affect the productivity of these returnees? Barrett and O'Connell [44] have estimated an earnings equation to examine how emigration affected the 1992 cohort of graduates. Using earnings data from 1998, they found that returnees earned 5 percent premium over those who never left. The premium differed sharply between men and women, with male returnees earning a 10 percent premium and female returnees earning no premium at all. For emigrants who were deemed to have left for labor market reasons the premium was even higher—8 percent overall and 15 percent for men. Again, the premium for women was essentially zero (with a point estimate of −1 percent).

Of particular interest to the present study, Barrett and O'Connell also separately examine the premium for different industries. The computer sector had the highest overall premium at 16 percent. In contrast to the all-industry results, women actually had a higher premium in computers (21 percent) than men (11 percent).[38]

There is also evidence that returning skilled emigrants have significantly limited the rise in skill premiums at a time of strongly rising demand for skill [45]. Since the increase in surplus of existing factors of production in Ireland from returning emigrants depends, in part, on their effect on domestic wages, this is consistent overall beneficial effect from returnees. Barrett et al. [45] show that with net immigration of 16,000 per year between 1996 and 1999, and assuming that all of this net immigration is skilled, the supply of skilled labor increases by 3.2 percent and skilled wages decrease by 4.7 percent. A standard social surplus calculation based on these estimates yields a total gain to the preexisting population of less that one-tenth of one percent of the skilled wage bill.[39] This calculation, however, ignores any fiscal benefits from bringing in individuals likely to make positive net fiscal contributions, any benefits from increased scale or spillovers from the expanded skilled labor supply, the benefits of providing unique skills to the Irish economy, or the investment induced by larger (and cheaper) supplies of skills.[40]

While evidence on how returning migrants have affected the development of the Irish software sector is limited, Sands [46] reports survey evidence on the background of Irish software entrepreneurs that suggests a significant role for international experience. Sixty-six percent of company founders have worked abroad and 55 percent have worked for multinational companies.[41] Seventeen percent of Irish entrepreneurs have studied abroad. Moreover, the entrepreneurs who worked for a multinational are almost twice as likely to have worked for that company abroad as they are in Ireland. Sands speculates that this reflects the fact that the lower end activities conducted by these companies in Ireland are less conducive to spurring 'indigenous innovators'.

Summing up then, it appears that the Irish economy in general, and the software sector in particular, were fueled over the latter half of the 1990s by returning Irish with augmented skills. With current evidence it is hard to determine exactly how much the software industry has benefited from the resulting improvement in skill availability and cost. One sign that the software industry had much to gain by attracting skilled workers home is that it was an active recruiter of the Irish abroad. An example of this recruitment effort was the setting up of *Opportunity Ireland* in 1998 by Enterprise Ireland (the agency responsible for indigenous industry development). The purpose of this new service was to highlight opportunities for expatriates in the software and electronics industries. That Opportunity Ireland has been disbanded is a sign that the pendulum may be swinging once again.

4.3 Almost One Million Soviets Come to Israel: What Boost to Israeli Software?

Between 1990 and 2000, 847,600 members of the Jewish diaspora of the former Soviet Union immigrated to Israel—a number equal to 21 percent of the 1990

Jewish population of Israel [47]. These new immigrants were on an average more educated than resident Israelis [15], and contained a disproportionate number of scientists and engineers. Of the 534,000 immigrants aged 15 and above who had worked abroad, 30 percent classed their occupation as scientific or academic,[42] with a further 32 percent classed as 'professional, technical and related workers' [47].

One would expect that such a huge inflow of skilled workers was a boon to Israel's emerging high-tech sector including its software sector. However, finding a large immigration footprint turns out to be harder than, at least we, expected.

The first surprise is that this skilled-biased inflow has not lowered the skilled wage premium [15,48]. Gandal et al. [49] explore two open economy mechanisms that could explain this puzzling absence of a wage effect. The first explanation is that the timing of the inflow coincided with a global burst of skill-biased technical change (SBTC) that increased the demand for skilled workers across sectors.[43] This technical change explanation is consistent with a gain from skilled immigration as the increased supply of skill moves the economy down along the (now higher) skill demand curve. Put in another way, the immigration prevents the rise in skilled wage costs that would have occurred due to surging skill demands.

The second explanation applies the Rybczynski Theorem to predict a sectoral reallocation of resources toward industries intensive in the use of the newly abundant factor of production.[44] The resulting expansion of skill-intensive sectors increases the demand for skill sufficiently to offset the increased supply, which could explain the lack of wage change.[45] Gandal et al. [49] note their 'mild surprise' that the latter mechanism—sectoral output changes—did not play a role in absorbing immigrant inflows.[46]

One limitation of the Gandal et al. analysis is that it is applied at a broad level of industry classification. Thus it is possible that it misses a skill availability-driven increase in certain high-tech sectors. A recent study by the Israeli statistics agency, however, casts some doubt on this explanation as well [50]. The study reports that high-tech employment in Israel increased from 6.6 percent of total employment in 1995 to 8.0 percent in 1999. Of this high-tech employment in 1999, 49 percent was in manufacturing, 14 percent in communications, and 37 percent in computers/related services and R&D. Interestingly, the computer services sector underwent the largest percentage expansion of the three sectors over this period, increasing its total employment by 83 percent from 34,700 to 63,400, so the increase in skill availability may well have fueled the expansion of this sector.[47] Given the skill requirements of these industries and the skill intensity of the immigrants, we might expect that immigrants would be over-represented in these sectors. But this is not the case. In 1999, post-1990 immigrants represented 18.5 percent of total employment, just less than the share of post-1990 immigrants in high-tech employment. Immigrants are overrepresented in high-tech manufacturing, with a share of 25.3 percent of the employment in that sector. But for computers and related services and R&D—which includes software—the share is actually slightly below the share of immigrants in total employment at 17.3 percent. In a survey of Israeli software firms that went public on foreign stock exchanges, Breznitz [32] finds no immigrants from the former Soviet Union among the founders.[48]

What can we conclude? Given the massive expansion of the skilled Israeli labor force due to Jewish immigration from the former Soviet Union, it is hard to believe that it did not aid the rapid expansion of the software sector. Yet the studies reviewed here hardly point to a significant effect. The expansion of the skilled labor force does not appear to have led to a disproportionate increase in skill-intensive sectors, at least at a broad level of industry classification. When we look more narrowly at the computer services sector we do see evidence of rapid growth, though we do not see disproportionate participation by the post-1990 immigrant group. We cannot rule out the possibility, however, that the inflow is having its effect more indirectly by easing the overall tightness of the skilled labor market at a time of economy-wide skill upgrading, thereby freeing new Israeli graduates for the software sector.[49]

Our discussion of the Israeli case has focused on inflows of skilled workers. One concern on the outflow side stems from the substantial number of acquisitions of Israeli start-ups by foreign (typically US) firms. Such acquisitions raise the possibility that Israel-based human capital will be moved to the acquirer's home base. Based on an examination of the successful Israeli data security industry, Teubal and Avnimelech [51] emphasize a different concern: that the opportunity to leverage R&D capability into broader capabilities, be it manufacturing or international marketing, will be lost when the Israeli operation is integrated into a larger entity. In the case of the server security firm MEMCO, for example, the firm's international marketing operations were dismantled after being acquired by Platinum (which was subsequently acquired by Computer Associates). So, rather than a direct loss of human capital from the country, Israel loses the opportunity to develop human capital that is complementary to its existing R&D capability.

A second concern relates to Israeli students who leave to study in the United States and do not return. National Science Foundation numbers do not suggest this is a severe problem [52].[50] Looking at just PhDs, an NSF survey found 81 Israeli nationals received PhDs from US Universities in 1990. Of these, 51 percent planned to stay on in the United States, with 31 percent having 'firm' plans to stay. By 1999, the number of Israelis receiving PhDs from US universities had dropped to 61, though the percentage planning to stay had risen (57 percent with plans to stay of whom 41 percent had firm plans to stay).

5 Concluding Comments

Although the details of the software industry development stories differ a great deal between the three countries, the broad outlines are similar. All three countries produce impressive levels of high-end human capital; country-specific inefficiencies had meant that the human capital was poorly utilized and thus relatively cheap; and the software sector, for reasons that other chapters in this volume examine, has proved relatively effective in taking advantage of this cost advantage. This is the opportunity side of the story. Yet the same international wage gap that created the opening for software also creates a strong incentive to emigrate, possibly undermining the competitive advantage. But although skilled emigration is usually seen in such threatening 'brain drain' terms, its effects are multifaceted and poorly understood. In addition to the harm done by the absence of domestically produced human capital, we must also consider such factors as the commerce facilitating effects of diasporas and the possibility of skill-enhanced emigrant return. Overall, the evidence is strongly suggestive that the benefits of skilled migration have outweighed the costs for the three countries. The Indian experience in Silicon Valley, for example, shows how the diaspora can be a valuable national asset in facilitating international commerce, especially where the business is transactionally complex and reputation concerns are paramount. Although a full cost–benefit analysis is beyond our scope, our judgment is that highly skilled Indian emigration has played a key part in the development of an internationally competitive Indian software sector. The Irish experience shows how one decade's lost human capital can, under the right conditions, become a skill reservoir that can be tapped to ease resource constraints and sustain economic expansion as domestic labor markets tighten. The experience also suggests a positive productivity effect of time spent abroad that is especially pronounced for the computer sector. And although it is difficult to find a substantial entrepreneurial footprint of Russian emigrants in the Israeli software industry, such a massive influx of skilled workers almost certainly has helped to relieve wage cost pressures in this rapidly expanding sector, in part by easing supply constraints in competing sectors.

The foregoing sections have reviewed available measures of international human capital flows for the three countries, provided a (hopefully) comprehensive list of the channels through which such flows could help or hinder the development of their software industries, and applied parts of the framework to look at some specific episodes that we think have been especially important for the countries in this project. In closing we note some questions relating to each of the three countries we think provide opportunities for fruitful research.

The Saxenian [38] study has painted an optimistic picture of the role played by the Indian diaspora in facilitating international business for home-country firms. Our assessment is that the Indian diaspora is less tightly linked than suggested by her survey respondents. More work is needed to confirm and extend our understanding of the diaspora's role. In this vein, we are currently using data on the location of patenting inventors and the location of patent citations to investigate the extent of knowledge flows into inventors' former homes (e.g. see [53]). We are also beginning a project that uses comprehensive lists of ethnic surnames to track knowledge flows between co-ethnics. Too little is also known about the negative effects from the absence in the Indian economy of some of the country's most talented individuals. Together with a colleague (see [1]), we have taken a modest step to measure part of this loss by describing the characteristics of the US-resident Indian-born population and estimating the net fiscal impact of their absence. An open question is what emigration has done to the cost and availability of technology and management skills in India. We have found evidence of significant increases in the return to higher education in a preliminary comparison of earnings regression results from the 1993/94 and (recently released 1998/99) rounds of Indian National Sample Survey. In future work we hope to untangle the effects of changing demands and supplies to identify the impact of high-skilled emigration on the domestic cost of human capital. In addition, we believe it is critical to test the strong assumption that with high levels of skilled emigration there will be no bottlenecks in the supply of new human capital in critical sectors. One of us has been finding in recent field work that even India's most elite institutions—the Indian Institutes of Technology and Indian Institutes of Management—face increasing constraints in finding and hiring new faculty.

Turning to Ireland, we need to know more about the backgrounds of Irish software workers from detailed survey evidence to gauge the impact of returning emigrants on the development of Irish software firms (see, however, the work of Sands, Chapter 3 this volume). How many software professionals are returned emigrants? And how has their international experience increased the value of these returnees through further education, frontier firm exposure, business contacts, etc.? What is the importance of the multinational sector as supplier of talent to indigenous firms? On the issue of the multinationals more generally, it would be interesting to go beyond anecdotal evidence about the role of the Irish, Indian, and Israeli diasporas in tilting foreign direct investment in their country's favor to some harder evidence. One possibility is to adopt a difference-in-difference approach, comparing, say, the difference in gap between US investment per employed worker in Ireland and Scotland and the gap between Japanese investment per employed worker in these two countries. Of course, a significant difference-in-difference could be due to factors other than a larger Irish diaspora. But a significant finding would be highly suggestive nonetheless.

Finally the work of Gandal et al. [49] has provided some intriguing evidence of how mass skilled immigration affected the Israeli labor market and industry structure. Their industry analysis, however, was conducted at too aggregated an industry level to get a good feel for how the software sector was affected in particular. A more disaggregated analysis would give a better idea of how this immigration affected Israeli comparative advantage in software.[51] Other issues we think are worth exploring in greater depth are the extent of 'hollowing out' of skills due to foreign takeovers of emerging Israeli software firms and Israeli company listings on US stock markets, the effect of the prospect of a foreign takeover or stock exchange listing on the incentive to pursue a high-tech start-up in the first place, and the long-run human capital impact of Israeli students getting advanced education abroad.

Notes

1. We estimate from the 2001 March CPS that 38% of Indians aged between 25 and 64 have a graduate degree. This compares with 9% in both the US-born and other foreign-born populations. In the 18–64 age group, 37% of the Indian-born have incomes more than 200% of the US-born median income ($23,925 in 2001); only 20% of the US-born and 13% of the other foreign-born have incomes above this level (see [1]).

2. The most widely discussed case of skill-focused immigration reform was the expansion of the H-1B professional worker temporary visa program in the United States. But skill-focused immigration policy change was a much wider phenomenon in the late 1990s and early 2000s (e.g. see [2]). Germany introduced a 20,000 a year 'Green Card' program for IT professionals (now ended), and its parliament passed legislation introducing permanent residency for high-earning skilled workers (now under court challenge). The United Kingdom announced at the end of 2001 that it is implementing a points-based Highly Skilled Migrant Programme on a pilot basis, and has dramatically increased the number of work permits it issues to skilled workers since the mid-1990s. Canada recently revamped its points system to make it more focused on education and adaptability to the Canadian skill market, and put in place a pilot program for fast-tracking temporary visas for IT workers. Australia introduced a major new class of employer sponsored temporary visa in 1996, in addition to increasing the share of its permanent migration visas that are granted on the basis of skills. Although the current high-tech slump and post September 11 fears have stemmed this reform momentum, continued skill-biased technical change, educational system deficiencies (particularly in science and computing), and aging populations make it a fair bet that the competition for skill will reassert itself before long.

3. For example, NASSCOM, the leading lobbying group for the Indian software industry, actually supported increasing the annual cap on H-1B visas in the late 1990s, and in the late 1980s senior Irish ministers were actually advising ambitious young Irish graduates to go abroad to get valuable experience.

4. Potential entrepreneurs may also be induced to take greater risks with start-up companies by the prospect of being able to move their companies abroad with foreign takeovers or stock market flotations.

5. It is sometimes said that these countries have an 'excess supply' of human capital. However, care must be taken in using this term as it draws attention to just one side of the skill market. Successful economies can absorb large increases in human capital through such changes as complementary capital accumulation, induced skill-biased technology adoption (and even technology invention), and increases in the share of skill-intensive industry. One indicator of 'excess supply' is a large negative differential between domestic and foreign wages. But given the forces pushing towards factor price equalization in an open economy, a sustained wage gap is more likely to be due to country-specific factors that affect the utilization of skills than their overabundance.

6. The prevalence of Israeli company flotations on US stock markets also suggests that the prospect of company (as opposed to individual) mobility has also been a spur to software industry development.

7. The department also estimates that there are roughly three million Irish citizens living outside Ireland. Of these three million, around two-thirds live in United Kingdom

and one-sixth live in the United States. It is estimated that 1.2 million of the total number of overseas citizens were born in Ireland. The entitlement to Irish citizenship is relatively generous compared with other countries. People born in Ireland, their children born abroad, and in some cases their grandchildren and great grandchildren, are entitled to Irish citizenship [7].

8. It is estimated that 43% of the world's Jewish population lives in the United States, compared with 37% in Israel. Not surprisingly, the number of US residents claiming Israeli ancestry is much smaller. Although results are not yet available for the 2000 US census, 1990 census results show that just under 70,000 claimed Israeli ancestries. Of these, just over 39,046 were 'foreign born', 21,980 of whom had entered between 1980 and 1990. Of the broader population claiming Israeli ancestry, 44.6% of those over 16 and employed were in managerial or professional occupations and 42.3% of those 25 and over had a Bachelor's degree or better. In comparison, 28.5% of those in the same age group claming Irish ancestors were in managerial or professional occupations, and 21.2% had a Bachelor's degree or better. The numbers in the native-born populations were 26.4% and 20.3%, respectively.

9. Sample sizes for the Irish and Israeli born in the CPS are too small to reliably estimate shares at this level of disaggregation.

10. Indeed, the Irish-born and Indian-born populations are respectively the first and second largest foreign-born populations in the United Kingdom.

11. The United States sent 1,767 'engineers and technologists' and 1,004 'computer analysts/programmers'. The United States sent many more 'managers and admin-istrators', however; 5,247 compared with 1,203 in this category from India.

12. 6,649 Indians came as the dependents of skilled workers in 2000. Across all categories of permanent immigration to Canada—skilled, business, and family—26,064 Indians immigrated to Canada (11.5% of total permanent immigration in that year). Indians account for a relatively small share of temporary workers in Canada. In 2000 the stock of Indian temporary workers was 1,358 (1.7% of the total). India is also not among the top senders of students to Canada.

13. Weiss [15] reports significant occupational upgrading by Soviet Union immigrants to Israel over time.

14. We have focused on how the prospect of emigration affects the willingness to invest in human capital. Given the importance of foreign takeovers and foreign stock exchange listings to Israeli software companies in particular, it is worth noting that the prospect of foreign investor interest can spur high-tech entrepreneurial activity as well. Thus, even if foreign ownership eventually curbs the domestic contribution of the firm (including the possibility of moving staff abroad), the prospect of a big payoff may be an important spur to high-risk entrepreneurship in the first place.

15. See Hausmann and Rodrik [16] for a model that emphasizes the social value of discovering the costs of domestic activities when such activities can be easily imitated.

16. The wage rise will be larger the less substitutable other factors are for skill. We assume that domestic skilled labor is supplied perfectly inelastically.

17. Skilled emigration has distributional implications in addition to this loss of aggreg-ate surplus. Remaining skilled workers clearly gain as their wage goes up. If we make the plausible assumption that skilled workers had above average incomes *before* the emigration, then the emigration will make the distribution of income more unequal.

18. The size the loss can be approximated by using the formula for the area of a triangle. Expressing this loss as a share of total income yields the formula,

$$\frac{\text{Loss}}{\text{GDP}} = \frac{1}{2} \times \varepsilon \times s \times \left(\frac{\text{Skilled Emigration}}{\text{Skilled Laborforce}}\right)^2,$$

where ε is the elasticity of the skilled wage with respect to the skilled labor supply and s is the skilled worker share of GDP.

19. There is a large empirical literature that attempts to measure the effect of immigration on local wages (see [17,18] for surveys). There are three main types of studies: area studies that compare wages across labor markets receiving different numbers of immigrants; natural experiments that look for immigration changes that are independent of developments in local labor markets; and calibration studies that estimate how relative factor supplies affect relative wages for different skill groups and then calculate how immigration with a given skill mix affects relative wages. Advocates of the latter method argue that the first two types of study fail to account for native outflows in response to immigrant inflows. The first two types of studies tend to find small wage effects (see [19,20]). The third type of study tends to find larger wage effects (see [21]).

20. The key to identifying such losses is that we consider the skilled emigration in total with the initial wage as our reference point rather than taking each emigrant one-by-one taking previous emigration as given.

21. Monopsonistic wage setting—where wages are set by a single buyer in the relevant skill market—provides another example of noncompetitive wage setting in which the skilled wage will be below the marginal value product. Employers with monopsony powers in the labor market will weigh increases in the quantity of skilled workers offered to them when they increase the wage with the cost of raising the wage for everyone. (We assume that the monopsonist employer must pay the same wage to everyone.) The optimal employment equates the marginal cost of hiring more workers with the marginal value product. At this optimal employment the wage is again less than the marginal value product. Such a monopsony skill market could develop where a large firm, say a Microsoft or an Intel, is a dominant presence in the area.

22. Trefler [23] examines the effects of migration in a variety of trade models. Though he focuses on immigration in an attempt to dismiss the myth of an 'immigration surplus', his results can be turned around to examine the effects of emigration in an economy open to trade. Trefler's results show that an emigration surplus loss is present in a specific factors trade model, whether skilled workers are the mobile factor or one of the specific factors. He also shows how the Heckscher–Ohlin results change when technologies differ across countries. It turns out that it matters whether the technological (or productivity) differences are inherent to workers (so that any technological backwardness travels with them) or to countries (so that an emigrating worker can leave their backwardness behind). When technology differences are inherent to workers, he shows that the standard Heckscher–Ohlin results are not affected as factor price equalization occurs for productivity adjusted factor prices. This is not true when technology differences are specific to countries as emigration leads to favorable movements in the terms of trade and an increase in the welfare of TLBs.

23. In a provocative recent paper, Davis and Weinstein [26] have examined the impact of balanced flows of factors to an economy (they focus on the United States) with a superior CRS technology. To the extent that the resulting increased size of the economy leads to a worsening of its terms of trade, the balanced inflow of productive factors leads to lower welfare (see also [23]). They argue that the United States has been made *worse off* due to its openness to foreign capital and workers. On the sending side, a balanced outflow of factors will lead to an improvement in welfare provided it is large enough for its terms of trade to change. A welfare loss to the sending country could reemerge if the factor outflows are unbalanced (say all skilled workers) or if there are economies of scale.

24. Rauch [27] provides a comprehensive recent survey.

25. In passing we note that although conventional transportation costs may be lower for 'weightless' output such as software, its often nonstandard nature makes it subject to substantial nontransport related transaction costs, increasing the potential importance of a trade-facilitating diaspora.

26. A recent paper that looks at the determinants of US foreign direct investment in Ireland is Gunnigle and McGuire [29]. The main source of information is interviews with high-ranking executives from ten major US multinationals. The chapter addresses more objective determinants of the decision to invest such as the corporate tax regime and labor cost and quality. Intriguingly, Table 3 in the chapter does list one vice president for strategy of an electronics firm as listing 'culture and identity' as one of the key factors behind the decision to locate in Ireland.

27. Among other examples of diaspora influence, Breznitz [32] describes how a member of the American Jewish diaspora, venture capitalist Fred Adler, was instrumental in arranging an important early IPO for the technology firm Elscient in the early 1970s.

28. As far as we know the term 'reputational intermediary' was first introduced in Kapur [33].

29. An interesting *Fortune* magazine article profiling the Indian Silicon Valley businessman and technologist Kanwal Rekhi describes a reputational intermediary of the form we have in mind in action [34]. Rekhi is the former CTO for Novell and a founding member of the Silicon Valley professional organization The Indus Entrepreneurs, or TiE. Commenting on one Indian-American businessman who had come to him looking for a reference to investors, Rekhi is quoted as responding, 'I wouldn't send you to anyone until I figure out your plan. I have to feel good about someone when I refer them. Or else people call me up and say "Why did you send me that one?"' Rekhi's value as a reputational intermediary comes out clearly in the article from the number of Indian entrepreneurs that come to him seeking his help. The aforementioned quote also shows how seriously he takes the value of reputation.

30. See Dixit [36] for a game theoretic model of such intermediary-based contract enforcement.

31. The fact that the share of India's IT exports—North America 62%, Europe 24%, Japan 4%—is roughly the average of these regions share of India's skill migration and the region's share of global IT industry—is suggestive that incorporating the size and skills of diasporas in gravity models of global IT trade may be worthwhile.

32. Many returned emigrants will have worked far less than thirty-five years meaning that there are many zeros in the numerator of the average wage calculation.

33. The 70% figure is based on all Indian-run start-ups from the period 1980 and 1998.
34. The overall response rate was 21%.
35. Of the Indian-born who had actually set up business relationships in India, 85% listed the availability of skilled workers as a key contributing factor to their decision. 73% listed the low cost of labor.
36. The most plausible explanation is that Ireland was on a long-term fast growth path for some time, underpinned by its initial relative backwardness and thus opportunity of catch-up growth, increased investments in education starting in the 1950s, and its openness to trade and foreign investment. The 1980s debacle was the result of poor macroeconomic conditions—partly brought on by earlier fiscal profligacy— and the working through of a process of creative destruction of older labor intensive manufacturing industries in the context of rigid and excessive real wages in low productivity firms.
37. 36% of total were between the ages of 25 and 39 on census night.
38. Barrett and O'Connell [44] considered different explanations for why returnees have higher earnings than those who stay. In addition to the human capital accumulation story, they also considered the possibility of emigration as a signal of quality (positive or negative) and the possibility that it is the more able (with ability unobserved by econometrician) that choose to emigrate. Although they are cautious in their conclusions, they view their results as more supportive of the human capital based explanation than the signaling or self selection explanations.
39. Applying the standard social surplus calculation (ignoring fiscal effects and externalities) yields a small surplus gain equal to 0.07% of the skilled wage bill. We can calculate the surplus gain as a share of the initial skilled wage bill as $1/2 \times \varepsilon \times (N/S)^2$, where ε is the elasticity of the skilled wage with respect to the skilled labor supply, N is the net immigration of skilled workers, and S is the initial supply of skilled workers (see [17]). The elasticity of the wage with respect to the supply of skilled labor is given by the ratio of the percentage change in the wage divided by the percentage increase in skilled labor, approximately 1.5.
40. On the other hand, it also ignores negative spillovers from rising road congestion and increased pollution. It also ignores any distributional effects that stem from rising housing and land prices.
41. 74% of Irish software companies have a founder who worked abroad. Not surprisingly, company founders are also highly educated: 83% have a Bachelor's degree, 31% a Master's degree, and 9% a PhD [46].
42. 60% of these scientific and academic workers are classed as engineers or architects [45].
43. That is, there is a broad shift in production methods towards using relatively more skilled workers, though the extent of the relative shift can differ across industries.
44. In other words, rather than within-industry changes in the use of skilled workers, industries that use skilled workers intensively expand at the expense of other industries. This leads to an overall increase in the demand for skill.
45. Weiss [15] offers the additional explanation that an increase in skill-complementing capital accumulation led to the offsetting increase in the demand for skill. He also considers the possibility that immigrant inflows did not initially compete strongly with domestic skill due to the poor transferability of Soviet skills and qualifications. He finds evidence of increasing substitutability between the skills of veteran Israelis and immigrants over time.

46. One puzzling aspect of the Gandal et al. results stems from the fact that skill-biased technical change has raised the skilled wage premium in the United States. If factor price equalization was truly operating and Israeli firms had access to the new technologies, then skilled wages should rise in Israel as well—no matter what was happening to skill supplies. The mechanism to bring about the increase in Israeli wages given the common skill-biased technical change and Israel-specific increase in skill supplies should have been a reallocation of resources to skill-intensive industries.
47. The share of computers and related services and R&D sector employment in total employment remained small: the share was 1.7% in 1995 and rising to 2.8% in 1999.
48. Breznitz [32] highlights an indirect effect of the immigration wave: it acted as an inducement to various government initiatives in venture capital, incubation, and cooperative R&D designed to support the high-tech sector.
49. In 1999, 55% of workers in the computer and related services and R&D sector were aged between 18 and 34. The share of such young workers was 45% in the high-tech industry overall, and 43% in the total economy (authors' calculations from table 3 of Central Bureau of Statistics 2002 [50]).
50. Statistics are unpublished tabulations from the Survey of Earned Doctorates, Division of Science Resources Statistics.
51. Breznitz [32] also discusses the role of the Israeli diaspora in helping to penetrate foreign markets, transfer technological knowledge, and facilitate multinational investment in Israel.

References

1. Desai, Mihir, Kapur, Devesh, and McHale, John (2001). The Fiscal Impact of the Brain Drain, Indian Emigration to the US. Paper prepared for the Third Annual NBER-NCAER conference, Neemrana, India.
2. McLaughlin, Gail and Salt, John (2002). *Migration Policies Towards Highly Skilled Foreign Workers*. Report to the United Kingdom Home Office, available at: www.homeoffice.gov.uk/rds/pdfs2/migrationpolicies.pdf, last accessed in March 2002.
3. Caselli, Francesco and Wilson, Daniel (2003). *Importing Technology*. NBER Working Paper No. w9928.
4. Acemoglu, Daron and Zilibotti, Fabrizio (2001). Productivity differences. *The Quarterly Journal of Economics*, CXVI(2), 563–606.
5. Dornbusch, R., Fischer, S., and Samuelson, P. (1977). Comparative advantage, trade, and payments in a Ricardian Model with a continuum of goods. *The American Economic Review*, 67(5), 823–839, December.
6. Grossman, Gene and Helpman, Elhanan (2002). *Outsourcing in a Global Economy*. National Bureau of Economic Research Working Paper 8728, available at: www.nber.org/papers/w8728.
7. Government of Ireland (1996). *Challenges and Opportunities Abroad*. White Paper on Foreign Policy, available at: www.irlgov.ie/iveagh/information/publications/ whitepaper/default/htm, last accessed in September 2003.
8. DellaPergola, Sergio (2000). World Jewish population, 2000, from *American Jewish Year Book*, Vol. 100. New York: The American Jewish Committee.

9. Dobson, Janet, Koser, Khalid, McLaughlin, Gail, and Salt, John (2001). *International Migration and the United Kingdom: Recent Patterns and Trends.* Research, Development and Statistics Directorate, Occasional Paper No. 75.

10. Beine, Michael, Docquier, Frederic, and Rapoport, Hillel (2001). Brain drain and economic growth: theory and evidence. *Journal of Development Economics*, 64, 275–289.

11. Beine, Michael, Docquier, Frederic, and Rapoport, Hillel (2002). *Brain Drain and LDCs' Growth: Winners and Losers.* Center for Research on Economic Development and Policy Reform, Working Paper No. 129.

12. Stark, Oded and Wang, Yong (2001). *Inducing Human Capital Formation: Migration as a Substitute for Subsidies.* Institute for Advanced Studies, Vienna, Economic Series No. 100.

13. Commander, Simon, Kangasniemi, Mari, and Winters, L. Alan (2002). The Brain Drain: Curse or Boon? A Survey of the Literature. Paper prepared for the CEPR/NBER/SNS International Seminar on International Trade, Stockholm.

14. Friedberg, Rachel (2000). You can't take it with you? Immigrant assimilation and the portability of human capital. *Journal of Labor Economics*, 18(2), 221–251.

15. Weiss, Yoram (2000). *High Skill Immigration: Some Lessons from Israel.* Mimeo, Tel Aviv University.

16. Hausmann, Ricardo and Rodrik, Dani (2002). *Economic Development as Self Discovery.* NBER Working Paper No. 28952.

17. Borjas, George (1994). The economics of immigration. *Journal of Economic Literature*, 32(4), 1667–1717.

18. Friedberg, Rachel and Hunt, Jennifer (1995). The impact of immigrants on host country wages, employment, and growth. *Journal of Economic Perspectives*, 9(2), 23–44.

19. Altonji, Joseph and Card, David (1991). The effects of immigration on the labor market outcomes of less skilled natives. In John Abowd and Richard Freeman (eds.), *Immigration, Trade, and the Labor Market.* Chicago: University of Chicago Press.

20. Card, David (1990). The impact of the Mariel boatlift on the Miami labor market. *Independent Labor Relations Review*, 43(2), 245–257.

21. Borjas, George, Freeman, Richard, and Katz, Lawrence (1996). Searching for the effect of immigration in the labor market. *The American Economic Review*, Papers and Proceedings, pp. 246–251.

22. Sukhatme, S.P. (1994). *The Real Brain Drain.* Bombay: Orient Longman.

23. Trefler, Daniel (1997). Immigrants and Natives in General Equilibrium Trade Models. National Bureau of Economic Research Working Paper 6209, available at: www.nber.org/papers/w6209.

24. Lucas, Robert E. (1993). Making a miracle. *Econometrica*, 61(2), 251–272.

25. Helpman, E. (ed.) (1998). *General Purpose Technologies and Economic Growth.* Cambridge, MA: MIT Press.

26. Davis, Donald and Weinstein, David (2002). *Technological Superiority and the Losses from Migration.* National Bureau of Economic Research Working Paper 8971, available at: www.nber.org/papers/w8971.

27. Rauch, James (2001). Business and social networks in international trade. *Journal of Economic Literature*, 39, 1177–1203.

28. Saxenian, Annalee (2002). *Local and Global Networks of Immigrant Professionals in Silicon Valley.* San Francisco, CA: Public Policy Institute of California.

29. Gunnigle, Patrick and McGuire, David (2001). Why Ireland? A qualitative review of the factors influencing the location of US multinationals in Ireland with particular reference to labour issues. *The Economic and Social Review*, 32(1), 43–67.

30. PricewaterhouseCoopers (2001). *Doing Business in Ireland*. Dublin: Pricewaterhouse-Coopers.

31. IDA Ireland (2002). Achieve European competitive advantage in software. Available at: www.idaireland.com/industry/software_industry.asp, last accessed in September 2003.

32. Breznitz, Danny (2002). *The Development of the Software Industry in Israel*. Mimeo, MIT.

33. Kapur, Devesh (2001). Diasporas and technology transfer. *Journal of Human Development*, 2(2), 256–286.

34. Warner, Melanie (2000). The Indians of Silicon Valley. *Fortune*, 141(10).

35. Rauch, James and Watson, Joel (2002). *Entrepreneurship in International Trade*. National Bureau of Economic Research Working Paper 8708, available at: www.nber.org/papers/w8708.

36. Dixit, Avinash (2001). *On Modes of Economic Governance*. Mimeo, Princeton University.

37. Saxenian, Annalee (1999). *Silicon Valley's New Immigrant Entrepreneurs*. San Francisco, CA: Public Policy Institute of California.

38. Saxenian, Annalee (2002). *Local and Global Networks of Immigrant Professionals in Silicon Valley*. San Francisco, CA: Public Policy Institute of California.

39. Banerjee, Abhijit and Duflo, Esther (2000). Reputation effects and the limits of contracting: a study of the Indian software industry. *The Quarterly Journal of Economics*, August, 989–1017.

40. Kapur, Devesh (2002). The Causes and Consequences of India's IT Boom. *India Review*, 1(2), 91–110.

41. OECD (2000). *Economic Outlook*, No. 67, June. Paris: OECD.

42. Clancy, Patrick (2001). *College Entry in Focus: A Fourth National Survey of Access to Higher Education*. Dublin: Higher Education Authority.

43. Lydon, Reamonn (1999). Aspects of the labour market for new graduates in Ireland: 1982–1997. *The Economic and Social Review*, 30, 227–248.

44. Barrett, Alan and O'Connell, Philip (2001). Is there a premium for returning Irish migrants. *The Economic and Social Review*, 32(1), 1–21.

45. Barrett, Alan, Fitzgerald, John, and Nolan, Brian (2000). Earnings Inequality, Returns to Education and Immigration to Ireland. CEPR Discussion Paper No. 2493.

46. Sands, Anita (2002). The Irish Software Industry. Mimeo, Carnegie Mellon University.

47. Central Bureau of Statistics (2001). *Statistical Abstract of Israel 2001*.

48. Friedberg, Rachel (2001). The impact of mass migration on the Israeli labor market. *The Quarterly Journal of Economics*, CXVI(4), 1373–1408.

49. Gandal, Neil, Hanson, Gordon, and Slaughter, Matthew (2000). Technology, Trade, and Adjustment to Immigration in Israel. National Bureau of Economic Research Working Paper 7926, available at: www.nber.org/papers/w7926.

50. Central Bureau of Statistics (2002). *Development of High-Tech Industry in Israel, 1995 to 1999: Labour Force and Wages*. Working Paper Series, No. 1, available at: www.cbs.gov.il/publications/hitech/pages_hitech_eng.htm, last accessed in September 2003.

51. Teubal, Morris and Avnimelech, Gil (2001). *Which Peripheral Countries Benefit from Globalization: Lessons from an Analysis of Company Growth, Acquisitions and Access to Complementary Assets in Israel's Data Security Sector.* Mimeo.
52. NSF Conference (2002). www.eng.iastate.edu/nsf2002/, last accessed July 2004.
53. Agrawal, Ajay, Cockburn, Iain, and McHale, John (2003). *Gone But Not Forgotten: Labor Flows, Knowledge Spillovers, and Enduring Social Capital.* Mimeo, Queen's University and Boston University.

10

Bridging the Gap: Conclusions

ASHISH ARORA AND ALFONSO GAMBARDELLA

1 Introduction

We began this book by asking how some developing countries had come to be so visibly associated with a high-tech industry such as software, and what could be learned from their experience. Our journey has covered the three emerging software exporters, the so-called '3Is'—India, Israel, and Ireland. It has also covered Brazil and China, two large developing countries with a substantial software sector, albeit driven by domestic demand rather than exports. To complete the picture, the book explored three important crosscutting topics: The role of multinationals, the international movement of people, and the sources of firm formation and entrepreneurship.

This chapter attempts a synthesis. It summarizes what is common and what is not in the experiences of the individual countries studied here; it develops an interpretive framework for understanding the growth of the software industry in these countries; and finally, it attempts to distill the lessons that others can learn. In other words, first come the facts, then how to interpret the facts, and then what it all may mean for other regions with software ambitions of their own.

We begin, however, by sketching the main elements of the interpretive framework. There is a key difference between the export-led-growth model of the 3Is and the model represented by China and Brazil, which, if successful, might be dubbed development-led exports. To be sure, there are important differences within the countries in each of the two groups. Indian software firms provide software services, while Israeli firms, as we have seen, are mostly focused on developing technology intensive products. But these differences should not obscure the important similarities: each of the 3Is had an abundant supply of English-speaking, technically skilled workforce and a substantial diaspora in its major export markets. Moreover, all these conditions were in place when worldwide IT demand began to grow in the early 1990s. There are other countries that have abundant supplies of trained human capital, which have manifestly failed to benefit from the boom in international demand, either because they lacked the links to the major markets or because they failed to form and grow firms that could penetrate these markets. English, or the lack thereof, is also a frequent concomitant factor. But even this is not the whole story. After all, if Ireland and Israel could make it in software, why not Scotland or Singapore? If India can make it, why not Pakistan or the Philippines? Furthermore, the 3Is have sustained their initial advantage, even as the principal foundation of that advantage, access to a cheap and skilled workforce, has eroded over time. The very success of these countries resulted in increased demand and tighter labor markets. Yet, no major competitors have emerged to capitalize on this opportunity.

In other words, any interpretive framework must go beyond delineating the initial determinants of comparative advantage. Increasing returns, resulting from agglomeration economies, is the usual suspect in such cases. However, the country chapters point to another likely cause: the development of firm capabilities. Comparative advantage and good timing may explain how the software industry in 3Is got started. But the software industry is sustained in the 3Is, and especially in India, because of the capabilities that the leading firms have accumulated.

All of this is not to imply that Brazil and China are failures. Given China's size and its economic performance, and in particular, its spectacular success in manufacturing, it would be foolish to bet against its success, and there are many promising signs from Brazil as well. These two countries represent an interesting alternative path to possible software success, albeit one whose contours are still under construction and whose ultimate fate is as yet unknown. Hence, the broad question we speculate on in the end is how software helps understand development. Are the successful stories that we have uncovered special or are there lessons other developing countries can learn as well? An even more ambitious question is to ask whether these stories have uncovered potential new paths for development. Is software-led growth a viable alternative to the classical development processes in which development of manufacturing precedes the development of high-tech sector? Or will the software short-cut to development end up as another instance of globalization that enriches the middle class but leaves the poor behind?

2   Empirical Regularities

2.1   Size, Growth, and Export Performance of the Industry in the 3Is, Brazil, and China

Table 10.1 provides a summary picture of the software industry in our five countries in relation to the three leading software producers: the United States, Germany, and Japan.[1] Table 10.1 shows that the software industries in our five countries are of comparable size. In 2002, the Irish industry reached $13.9 billion in total sales, of which $12.3 billion was due to multinationals and $1.5 billion due to indigenous companies. The 2002 sales of the Indian and Chinese industries are $12.5 and $13.3 billion, respectively, while the 2001 figures for Brazil and Israel are $7.7 and $4.1 billion, respectively.

Table 10.1 also reports wide differences in the employment base across these countries. The Indian association of the software firms, NASSCOM, estimated the employment of software professionals in India to be over 650,000 in March 2003.

TABLE 10.1. The Software Industry in Brazil, China, and the 3Is, and by Comparison in the US, Japan, and Germany

Countries	Sales ($ billion)	Employment ('000)	Sales/ employment (000)	Software sales/GDP (%)	Software development index
Brazil[a]	7.7	160[b]	45.5[b]	1.5	0.22
China	13.3	190[b]	37.6[b]	1.1	0.23
India	12.5	230	54.3	2.5	0.96
Ireland (MNC)	12.3	15.3	803.9	10.1	0.34
Ireland (domestic)	1.6	12.6	127.0	1.3	0.04
Israel[a]	4.1	15	273.3	3.7	0.17
United States	200	1,024	195.3	2.0	0.05
Japan[b]	85	534	159.2	2.0	0.08
Germany[a]	39.8	300	132.7	2.2	0.09

Notes: Table based on 2002 or latest available figures. The Software development index is the ratio between Software sales over GDP (in %) and the GDP per capita of the country (in '000 US$) (see also Botelho et al., in this book).
[a] 2001.
[b] 2000.

Of these, the software industry employed 230,000.[2] The 2000 figures for China and Brazil are respectively 160,000 and 190,000. The total employment in 2002 in the Irish software industry was about 28,000 (15,300 and 12,600, respectively for multinational firms and indigenous firms), while the 2001 employment figure for the Israeli industry was about 15,000.

This produces notable differences in sales per employee. Revenue per employee in the Israeli software industry has increased significantly over the 1990s, reaching over $255,000 in 2000 and over $270,000 in 2001. The corresponding figure for the Irish multinationals is higher (about $800,000) although this is almost certainly an accounting artifact. Data from the Irish National Software Directorate (NSD) indicates that the revenue per employee of the indigenous software firms in Ireland have also increased in the 1990s, from slightly over $50,000 in 1991 to the $127,000 as shown in Table 10.1.[3] Finally, Table 10.1 indicates that the revenue per employee figures for India, Brazil, and China are about one-fourth of those of Ireland and Israel.

It is seen from Table 10.1 that the ratio of total software sales to GDP in our five countries is higher than 1.0 percent, a figure typical for countries such as the United Kingdom, Italy, and France. For China, Brazil, and Ireland (indigenous) the share is slightly below the 2–2.2 percent figure for the United States, Germany, and Japan. For India and Israel, it is higher than the latter three countries. Moreover, in all our five emerging economies, software ranks particularly high when compared with their overall level of development. Following Botelho et al. (Chapter 5, this volume), we divided the ratio of software sales to GDP by the GDP per capita of the country, which yields a plausible index of the size of the software industry relative

TABLE 10.2. Brazil, China, and the 3Is: Software Industry Growth, GDP Growth, and Software Export Shares

Countries	Average growth of software sales in the 1990s (%)	Average GDP growth in the 1990s (%)	Software exports as % of sales (2002 or latest available year)
Brazil	20	2.5	1–2
China	>35	9.8	11
India	40	3.4	80
Ireland	20	7.0	85
Israel	20	7.4	70

Source: Average GDP growth computed from the Penn World Table Version 6.1. Heston, A., Summers, R., and Aten, B. Centre for International Comparisons at the University of Pennsylvania, Oct. 2002.

to its country's level of development. With the sole exception of the indigenous industry in Ireland, in all our countries the index is far higher than that of the United States, Germany, and Japan.

But the most impressive figures about the software industry in our emerging economies are their growth rates. Table 10.2 provides an estimate of the average growth rate of software sales in our five countries in the 1990s derived from the individual country chapters. Table 10.2 also reports the growth rate of GDP during the decade. The Indian software industry grew more than 35 percent a year between 1993 and 2002, which is orders of magnitude higher than the growth of GDP. The growth of software dwarfs the growth of GDP in all other countries as well. Israeli software sales jumped from $0.54 billion in 1991 to $4.1 billion in 2001, growing at about 20 percent per year. The Irish indigenous software industry recorded a similar growth rate, with revenues growing from $0.19 billion to $1.4 billion between 1991 and 2003. Precise data on the growth of the Chinese software industry for the whole decade are not available. However, Table 6.4 in Tschang and Xue (Chapter 6, this volume) reports that the whole industry grew at an average of 35 percent per year during 1999–2002. Presumably the growth was even higher in the years immediately earlier, as the industry started from scratch around the mid-1990s. Finally, Figure 5.1 in the Botelho et al. (Chapter 5, this volume) shows that the Brazilian software industry grew at an average of 13 percent per year in 1991–2001.

Table 10.2 also shows that there is a clear distinction between the 3Is on the one hand and Brazil and China on the other in terms of export orientation. The 3Is have high-export shares: 70 percent for Israel in 2001, almost 80 percent for India in 2002, and 85 percent for the indigenous Irish industry in the same year.[4] By contrast, exports accounted for only about 1.2 percent of total Brazilian software sales and about 5 percent of the total Chinese sales in 2001.

Even among the 3Is there are differences. Figure 10.1 portrays the trends in the export share of the Indian, Israeli, and indigenous Irish software industry since

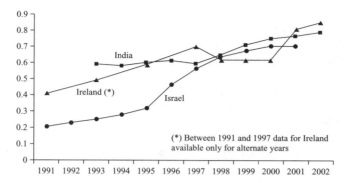

FIGURE 10.1. India, Ireland, and Israel: SW Export Shares 1991–2002
Source: Country chapters and other sources.

the early 1990s. It shows that although their export shares are converging in the late 1990s, the starting points differ greatly. In the Indian software industry, exports constituted a large share of sales from the early 1990s. In 1993, the first year for which Athreye reports export and total sales data, the share was 59 percent, while in 1991 it was 41 percent for the indigenous Irish industry and 20 percent for the Israeli industry.

Thus, not only have exports been the main driver of the Indian software industry, but they have also provided the initial impetus. The indigenous Irish industry shows a less pronounced initial dependence on exports, although Sands argues that multinationals were an early source of demand for the indigenous software firms. At the outset Israel relied less on the export market compared to India and Ireland. Breznitz argues that the rapid expansion of R&D (including military research) and sophisticated lead users in computer hardware and telecommunication created local demand for software.

2.2 Domestic Market

The focus on the domestic market underpins many characteristics that are common to the software industries of Brazil and China. The first is the relatively small size of even the leading firms compared to their Indian counterparts. The three largest Indian software firms have sales in excess of $1 billion and employ more than 25,000 persons each, the leading Brazilian and Chinese firms are less than one-fifth in size. Another striking characteristic is the broad range of activities and firm types. In the 3Is, software firms are easy to characterize. In India, they are software services firms; in Ireland, they are product firms, and in Israel, they are technology firms. China has them all, from systems integrators to custom software developers to firms developing operating systems for hand-held computers. Similarly, though the leading Brazilian firms have naturally focused on banking and telecommunications, Brazilian firms develop Enterprise Resource Planning (ERP) systems and a number of them provide software services and systems integration services. A related characteristic is that the leading firms in Brazil and China are often heavily diversified. Once again, this is only to be expected because firms attempt to maximize the returns from what they perceive to be their major asset, namely preferential access to domestic buyers.

Israel and Brazil, and possibly also China, are similar in relying upon sophisticated domestic users as lead users. However, Israel is a much smaller market than Brazil or China and exports have been and are crucial for the growth of software. Moreover, the Israeli software industry has benefited from the strong economic and cultural ties with the United States, especially to get access to financing, and organizational and marketing expertise. On the whole, the other similarities among the 3Is outweigh the greater role of the domestic market in the development of the Israeli software industry. These similarities include the excess supply of human capital and the strong links with the principal export markets, facilitated by cultural ties and emigration.

2.3   Human Capital and the Supply of Skills

One regularity among the 3Is is an 'excess' supply of human capital in the 1980s, and specifically, an excess supply of engineering and technology graduates. Needless to say, the 3Is are not always the countries with the largest proportion of science and engineering graduates. Rather, the excess supply was relative to the demand from manufacturing and related services. Simply put, the 3Is have produced more engineers than their hitherto lackluster industrial sector could absorb, especially between 1970 and 1990.[5] In the more advanced countries, and most likely in the rapidly growing Asian countries such as South Korea, Taiwan, and Singapore, science and engineering graduates faced a high opportunity cost of working in the software sector. Plentiful job opportunities in industry, in well-established firms, meant that there would be fewer entrepreneurs setting up software firms, and nascent software firms would find it difficult to attract talented engineers.

Our excess supply story is confirmed by a simple quantitative analysis of the determinants of the stock of scientists and engineers in the early 1980s. We regressed the log of the stock of scientists and engineers in 1980 (or in the earliest available year thereafter) on the log of population and GDP, and a dummy variable for the countries for which we had the stock of scientists and engineers in years later than 1980.[6] We found that the residuals for Brazil, China, Israel, and India are all positive, suggesting that these countries had more scientists and engineers in the years just before the start of their software industry than explained by their population size and GDP level. Thus, it appears that for these four countries an excess supply of human capital existed prior to the growth of the software industry. Exploring why these countries were abundant in technically skilled workers in time to catch the IT wave is not a goal of this book, but their being in such a position was crucial.[7]

TABLE 10.3. Stocks of Scientists and Engineers in
Selected Countries, 1981 and 1990, in '000s

	S&E		Increase (%)
	1981	1990	
Brazil	2,951	4,667	58
China[a]	26,457	34,420	30
India	7,094	n.a.	—
Ireland	155	200	29
Israel	290	371	28

Notes: n.a = not available.
[a] 1982.

Only for Ireland is the residual slightly negative. Compared to the other four countries much of the increase in human capital in Ireland took place in the 1990s.[8] Our regression results imply that by 1990, just around the time when the indigenous software sectors began to grow, Ireland also had a substantial surplus. The surplus represents both the increase in human capital and also the anemic economic growth during the 1980s. Even so, substantial immigration prior to 1970 had left Ireland with a large diaspora in its main markets, which would grow in the 1980s before many of the migrants returned home to fuel the growth of the Irish software industry. Thus, the Irish investments in human capital in part followed, or at least coevolved with, the growth of new industries like software.

The education sector in each of the countries appears to have responded quickly to the needs of the growing software industries in the 1990s. Table 10.3 shows that the stock of scientists and engineers in Israel, Ireland, and China grew by about 30 percent between 1981 and 1990, and in Brazil, it was more than twice that, growing by nearly 60 percent. We lack comparable figures for India. However, the available data on engineering graduates and IT graduates in the 1990s show similar growth patterns in India as well. NASSCOM figures indicate that in India the number of IT admissions in universities increased from slightly over 50,000 in 1992 to a predicted 158,000 in 2004. NASSCOM also estimates that the number of IT professionals graduating each year increased from 42,800 in 1997 to 71,000 in 2000 and about 99,000 in 2004. By comparison, the number of IT graduates in the United States increased from 37,000 in 1998 to 52,900 in 2000. Other countries show a similar pattern. Tschang and Xue report that in China the number of IT graduates increased from 29,000 to 89,000 in 1999–2002. Botelho et al. note that the 18,000 graduates in IT in Brazil in 2000 amounts to a greater per capita number than China and India. For Ireland, the share of Irish population between the ages 25 and 64 with a college degree was 14 percent in 2001, up from 11 percent in 1999 [1,2]. For those between 25 and 34 this was 20 percent in 2001 versus 16 percent in 1999. These figures compare favorably with the top four European countries.[9]

The increase in human capital required to power the software industry was accomplished through a mix of private and public efforts, with the mix varying across countries. In Israel and China, the bulk of the efforts were probably in the public sector. In Ireland, though education is largely in the public sector, the latter appears to have been very responsive to the economic environment. Sands describes how the Irish system for channeling the high-school students to academia helped direct them towards the new disciplines for which there was rising demand, and how polytechnics modified their curricula to serve the needs of major local industries.

In India, a substantial fraction of additional engineering capacity created during the 1990s was in the private sector. Data from the All India Council on Technical Education show that sanctioned capacity for undergraduate engineering disciplines combined was about 340,000 in 2002–03, and about 240,000 for IT-related engineering disciplines. Well over 85 percent of the IT capacity, and a somewhat smaller share of the overall engineering education capacity, is in private colleges that do not receive public grants. Moreover, this ignores the non-accredited but valuable private training institutes such as NIIT and Aptech, which for a time enjoyed considerable commercial success. Needless to say, such a rapid expansion of engineering training capacity has raised valid concerns about the quality of the education and a variety of other social costs. Nonetheless, this supply response does speak of a flexibility that is rare in more advanced countries.

2.4 The Diaspora

The diaspora reflects the excess supply but also affects this supply of skills, albeit in different ways for different countries. Both China and India have experienced a substantial net outflow of skilled workers.[10] Brazilian emigration of skilled workers is smaller in absolute volume but as a percentage of the stock of skilled population, the figures are comparable with India and China.[11] A recent set of estimates provided by Carrington and Detragiache [3] indicate that the stock of high-skilled (more than thirteen years of schooling) immigrants in the United States from China, India, and Brazil were about 400,000, 300,000, and 60,000, respectively. Moreover, the fraction of such immigrants coming to the United States as compared to other OECD destinations was slightly higher for China at 51 percent compared to about 44 percent for the other two countries. This is also reflected in Table 9.1 in Kapur and McHale, which shows that the Indian-born population in the United States over 25 years of age increased from less than 350,000 in 1990 to more than 830,000 in 2000, while the Chinese born population increased from about 400,000 to just under 850,000. Moreover, 78 percent of the newly arrived Indians in the 1990s have Bachelor's degrees or better, frequently in IT-related areas. This is confirmed by independent estimates of the US IT workforce which indicates that more than 15 percent of this workforce is from Asia, of which slightly less than one-third are from India [4].

Even though only a small proportion of the Indian and Chinese immigrants return, Kapur and McHale argue that there have been notable benefits from the diaspora to the Indian software industry. These benefits have taken the form of opportunities for linkages, ties, market access, and other collaborations between India and the United States. As Arora et al. argue in their chapter (Chapter 7, this volume), a particularly important benefit has been the number of software firms, particularly successful software firms, started by Indian expatriates. Of the 657 NASSCOM member firms in 2000–01 reported in Athreye's Table 2.3 (Chapter 2, this volume), 128 (19 percent) were multinationals and 58 (9 percent) were founded by expatriate Indians overseas, almost all located in the United States.[12] Of the top twenty Indian software exporters, three (Digital Soft, Perot Systems TSI, and Hughes Software) are multinationals, one is a joint venture involving a multinational (Mahindra–British Telecom) and another was spawned from Citibank (i-Flex). The importance of expatriate Indians is suggested by the presence of two firms founded by Indian expatriates (Patni Computer Systems and IGate) in the top twenty exporters.[13] Unpublished work by Athreye on 125 software start-ups in India involving 279 founders shows that fifty-six, or about 20 percent, of the founders had worked for a multinational firm.

The role of Irish expatriates as source of firm formation is also noteworthy. Sands's survey of fifty-eight Irish software entrepreneurs indicate that 57 percent of the founders of the Irish software firms in her sample have worked abroad, 55 percent have worked for multinational companies, and 76 percent of the companies had one founder who worked abroad, largely consistent with earlier findings that roughly a third of all entrepreneurs had worked for a multinational firm directly before starting their company [6]. The large Jewish diaspora in the United States has been catalytic to the growth of the Israeli software industry, as discussed in greater detail in Chapter 7.

The diaspora can provide links, act as 'reputational intermediaries', and upon returning, can bring back valuable skills and expertise. On the other hand, the outflow of skilled engineers, scientists, and doctors represents a net loss of talent and of the considerable investment in training the emigrants. The broad question about the net effects of the international mobility of skilled people on the home country is a complex one and well beyond the scope of this book. However, Kapur and McHale conclude that the benefits from the diaspora outweigh the costs for the 3Is for the development of the software industry. In other words, setting aside the question whether the brain drain represented by the diaspora was a good thing or not for their country as a whole, the software industries of India, Ireland, and Israel certainly benefited from having a diaspora. Given the domestic market orientation of software industry in China and Brazil, the tradeoff has likely been less favorable.

2.5 The ICT Multinationals

Multinational firms have been a sizable presence in the software industries of our countries. At the risk of some exaggeration, one can say that ICT multinationals came to Israel to do R&D, to India for inexpensive skilled workers, and to Ireland to leverage tax incentives and access the European market.[14] Over time the set of activities expanded. Giarratana et al. (Chapter 8, this volume) provide evidence of these different patterns. They first show that in Ireland the entry of ICT (computers, telecom equipment and services, electronics) and software multinational firms precedes the rise of the domestic software industry. By contrast, in Israel and India, industry growth and multinational entry both happen during the 1990s.

Analysis of business linkages (such as mergers and acquisitions, joint-ventures, and alliances) between the domestic software companies in the three countries and the foreign firms provides further evidence of the different role of multinationals in the 3Is and changes over time. Giarratana et al. find that the earliest of these linkages are detected in Ireland. However, currently these links are the strongest in Israel. Overall their analysis confirms Sands's observation that in Ireland, multinationals have played an important role in nurturing the growth of firms in the domestic industry. However, it is in Israel that one observes a more active set of relationships between the ICT multinationals and the domestic software companies. By contrast, the Indian software industry does not seem to have developed tight linkages with the India based ICT multinationals. Giarratana et al. do not provide comparable evidence for Brazil and China but the available evidence suggests that multinationals are contributing to the domestic software competencies in China and Brazil as well. For example, the chapter by Botelho et al. underscores the role of Siemens and Ericsson, which have provided significant background opportunities for the growth of the Brazilian software industry.

2.6 Firm Formation and Sources of Competencies

One conclusion of the analysis conducted in this book is that firm formation and organizational competencies have been an important determinant of the observed growth of the software industry in our region. The chapter by Arora, Gambardella, and Klepper illustrates this point. It starts from Klepper's pioneering work on the origin and the evolution of the TV, automobile, tire, and laser industries in the United States, which showed that successful new firms and industries come from two sources: related industries and spin-offs especially from successful entrants. Thus, for example, successful TV producers in the United States originated from the radio makers diversifying into the new field. Three leading automobile firms in the Detroit area—Buick, Cadillac, and Ford—originated from the first successful firm in the industry, Olds Motor Works. In turn, these four companies were prolific sources of other automobile firms. The tire industry also exemplifies the importance of spin-offs. Goodrich in particular nurtured four important new firms, Diamond Rubber, Kelly-Springfield, Firestone, and Goodyear.

Compared to the four US industries studied by Klepper, software is more pervasive in the economy, especially because software activities are performed by many user firms. In addition to firms in obviously related industries such as computer hardware and telecommunications, lead users such as banks have been important sources of software firms in the five countries studied in this book. For instance, banking and telecommunications were important sources of competencies in Brazil, and the hardware and other related sectors have been responsible for a good deal of the origin of software production in China. In Israel too the large domestic electronics sector fed the growth of software in various ways. Many of the leading Indian software firms originated from business groups diversifying into software. Thus it is probably safe to say that related industries have not figured as prominently in software firms in the emerging economies as they have in the four US industries studied by Klepper. Although firms originating from existing software firms feature among the leaders in virtually all countries for which we have data, spin-offs are not a prominent source of firm formation in the software industry in emerging economies.

The pervasive use of software implies that the potential origins of software competencies are far more widespread than in automobile, tires, TVs, or lasers. As a result, any country with a minimal level of industrial activity host a set of industries that could incubate software competencies and give rise to a potentially successful software industry. Thus we cannot look to related industries to account for Pakistan, which also has a large number of English-speaking engineers but did not grow a software industry, or why Israel developed a strong capability in software innovation but not the former Soviet Union, which also had strong capabilities in mathematics and programming.

The software sectors in our countries emerged when software was already maturing as a sector elsewhere. Follower countries and regions can exploit external sources of competencies not available to the pioneering regions. Arora et al. highlight two factors: the multinationals and the diaspora, whose contribution to the software industries in our countries, and especially in the 3Is, has been discussed extensively already. They also highlight a third source of competence that emerged in some of our countries, and that was not present at the birth of the US industries studied by Klepper: the public sector. There is evidence that universities have spawned a number of the leading Irish software firms as well as many of the top Chinese software firms. But the most significant example of public sector competencies nurturing the growth of the software industry is Israel's military sector. The influence of the military provides a natural explanation for the observed specialization of the Israeli software industry in areas like security software.

While the public sector can be an important source of competencies, it may lead to patterns of specializations that are not as valuable in the international arena as they are at the domestic level. The Chinese software industry may suffer from this problem. As Saxenian [7] also noted, Chinese government policies, especially procurement policies, encourage the formation of competencies in areas such as operating systems where there are well-established international alternatives. The peculiarities of the Chinese language and the large size of the domestic market are plausible justifications for this strategy. But there may be a substantial opportunity cost of not specializing in other subsectors of the software industry in which China enjoys a clear advantage (e.g. providing software services to Japan and Korea) over competitor.

In sum, the point made by Arora et al. is that firm formation and the creation of firm competencies have been crucial for the growth of the software industries in our countries. While one may think that the point is pleonastic ('competencies have to come from somewhere'), it is worth contrasting it with some alternative perspectives. In particular, while emphasizing organizational competencies, our cases do not provide much evidence in support of agglomeration economies, other than classical 'thick labor market' economies or 'lower average cost' for infrastructure. Simply put, in all countries, the software industry tends to locate in areas with significant economic activity. Among other things, this has intriguing policy implications. It suggests that attempts to develop new industries by concentrating activities in a given area (e.g. Science Parks) may not yield the desired outcome. Specific sources of firm competencies are a necessary condition, and these are not replaceable by mere geographical proximity.

2.7   The Ubiquitous Role of Government

Perhaps the most contentious issue of all is what the governments did and did not do. The role of the government in promoting the software industry has ranged from *laissez faire* (India) to active sector specific interventions (China), with Ireland, Israel, and Brazil lying somewhere along this continuum.

Arora et al. [8] approvingly characterize government policy towards software in India as one of benign neglect. Athreye's chapter (Chapter 2) shows that for the most part, software flew 'under the radar', in large measure because the domestic market was small and because as a service, it was naturally exempt from many of the laws and regulations that have stifled the growth of Indian manufacturing. Neither were the large investments in the 1960s and 1970s in science and engineering directed at software. Instead, the objective was to supply the manufacturing sector, whose slower-than-hoped-for growth resulted in the excess supply of engineers we referred to earlier. In more recent years, of course, the software industry and its industry association have come to exercise substantial political influence. But that has been the consequence of its success, not its cause.

Some have argued that the Indian software industry arose from specific government investments in IT and software capability. For instance, Parthasarathi and Joseph [9] point to policies such as easier imports of computers for software exports, looser restrictions on foreign direct investment aimed at exports, and the provision of communication bandwidth. However, government support for other sectors such as electronics and hardware was much stronger but much less effective. Software benefited not as much from the science and technology policies of the Indian state as from the relatively liberal economic policies put in place after 1984.

China is at the other extreme with targeted industry specific policies, as for instance in the tenth Five Year Plan. Perhaps even more important are the unwritten policies. The Chinese government helps the formation of the companies either directly or through institutions like the Chinese Academy of Science; it employs procurement as a means to support them even when this means sustaining national alternatives to well-defined international products. All of this is overlaid on a personal network of ties between the industry and the government bureaucracy—the *guanxi* as Saxenian calls it—that are very important for commercial success. That said, given the large role of government enterprises in the Chinese economy, it is natural to expect the domestic market oriented Chinese software industry to depend upon government sector demand. Further, just as defense sector demand has driven a great deal of IT (and software) development in the United States, it is reasonable to expect that the Chinese concerns about national security would lead to substantial support for software sectors such as operating systems, embedded software, and network security products.

The biggest government impact of the Brazilian government on the software industry has been through procurement and incentives for R&D. Apart from projects like electronic voting, procurement contracts have helped the growth of the domestic firms, and have attracted some foreign software companies as well. In recent years, Brazilian software firms have originated mainly from other companies rather than government or universities.

Two Irish policies, neither one targeted at software, stand above the others: the substantial investments in science and technology education since the 1980s, and the favorable company tax rates.[15] The favorable tax rate attracted multinational firms, which account for much of the industry's revenues today and have benefited the indigenous sector as well in a number of ways. The education policy greatly enhanced the supply of human capital, an important attractor for multinationals. Sands points out specific education policies such as the institutional arrangement for channeling incoming students into academic disciplines that potential employers valued more highly, which have supported the expansion of the IT and software industries.

Breznitz's chapter (Chapter 4) deals with government's impact at two levels. The first were the policies that built Israel's comparative advantage in R&D, such as R&D subsidies, incubators for start-ups, and publicly funded venture capital funds. The chapter describes the extent and variety of these policies although their impact is unclear; at the very least it is not evident how vital these affirmative state policies were for the success of the Israeli software industry. However, perhaps more importantly, the government was also the technology supplier, the first buyer, and many other things besides, for the software industry. For instance, the MAMRAN, the central computer unit of the Israeli defense forces, was very helpful in creating a community of technically skilled people, similar to the sorts of networks that one finds in the Silicon Valley [20]. Thus government played a catalytic role early in the life of the Israeli software industry, although at least some of it was unwittingly so.

3   An Interpretive Framework: The Interplay of Comparative Advantage and Firm Capabilities

3.1   The Key Elements: Comparative Advantage, Opportunity, and Firm Competencies

There are now extensive studies of the growth of new firms and industries, especially in the context of regional clusters and regional processes of growth. Many explanations have been advanced. The evidence presented in this book indicates that the growth of an internationally competitive software industry in emerging economies is best seen as the outcome of a dialectic between comparative advantage at the macro level and firm capabilities at the micro level.

The great increase in demand for information technology, including software and software services, in the OECD countries opened a window of opportunity. The 3Is were well positioned for this opportunity. In a human capital intensive industry like software the key input is skilled people. The 3Is had abundant supply of engineers (relative to the needs of their slowly growing sectors), strong links to their major external markets, stable macroeconomic environments, and government policies that facilitated entrepreneurship and firm entry. They also had sources of firm competencies. And they were lucky enough to have this in place when the big boom in global IT demand started.

The diaspora provided the all important links to the US market for the Indian software industry. A couple of multinationals like Citibank and Texas Instruments helped illuminate the way forward, and the domestic software firms seized the opportunity to grow their internal capabilities and reputations. In Ireland, the multinationals were the key, first using Ireland as an export platform and then opening the door for the indigenous Irish firms, by example and by providing experienced and confident managers who would run these indigenous firms. As in Ireland, the leading Israeli firms were intent on competing in the world market on the basis of innovative technology. In both countries, these innovations were the result of public investments in higher education and research.

3.2   Discovering and Exploiting Comparative Advantage: Entrepreneurship and Firm Competencies

Demand growth, though important, is not critical. The recent downturn in international IT demand provides an informal test. The most recent evidence shows that in the United States, aggregate IT-related employment fell between 2001 and 2003 by over 200,000 or about 9 percent from its high in 2001. By contrast, software employment in India has continued to grow, with growth rates in employment averaging an impressive 25–30 percent. Virtually all the leading firms have continued to grow at or above industry rates, with the brunt of the impact of demand slowdowns felt by second tier and smaller firms. The growth in revenues and employment of the market leaders in Indian firms has come in part through lower profits but it has also come through large multi-year IT outsourcing contracts, evidence of the firm capabilities gradually acquired.

Similarly, it would be incorrect to conclude by saying that the 3Is are simply exploiting their comparative advantage in human capital intensive activities and their good luck in having English-speaking engineers and links with their major export markets. As noted at the beginning of this chapter, many countries have a comparative advantage in human capital intensive activities but few have emerged as serious players in the world software industry. Comparative advantage is simply too coarse to explain this.

In a thought provoking article Hausmann and Rodrik [11] point out in an uncertain world, figuring out where and how to exploit a certain type of resource abundance is not straightforward. For instance, Bangladesh's abundant supplies of cheap labor give it a comparative advantage in labor-intensive products as opposed to high-tech machinery. But labor-intensive manufactures range from a range of textiles to diamond polishing. Even in textiles, it turns out that Bangladesh's exports to the United States are narrowly concentrated in men's cotton shirts and trousers and knitted hats. By contrast, Pakistan, with a similar resource endowment, exports bedsheets to the United States but few hats. Both countries can be said to have a comparative advantage in textiles, but at a more disaggregated level, the countries focus on a very narrow range of products with very little overlap. This is not an isolated example. Hausmann and Rodrik show that of the top twenty-five export items from each country, there are only six items in common. They find the same pattern for other pairs of comparable countries, such as Honduras and the Dominican Republic, and Taiwan and South Korea. They conclude that in most developing economies, 'industrial success entails concentration in a relatively narrow range of activities'. Moreover, what precise product lines and activities will eventually prove to be a success is very difficult to predict. As they put it, 'learning what one is good at producing', which may be key to the process of economic growth in follower countries, is not yet well understood. In their model, economic experiments or entrepreneurship is the way such learning takes place.

The implications for our story are several. First, the initial conditions that positioned these countries for developing a software industry are necessary but not sufficient. One also needs to understand better the process by which firms and entrepreneurs in these countries learned what would work. The evidence presented in this book suggests that entrepreneurs who had prior experience working in established firms in the software industry or in related industries are more likely to be successful at discovering what works. Second, although not featured prominently in Hausmann and Rodrik's analysis, firms have to build the in-house competencies and capabilities to implement what has been discovered to work. These capabilities are also a key to understanding how why certain countries and certain regions can retain international leadership even as the initial advantages fade.[16]

Breznitz's account makes clear that while it was evident that Israel's comparative advantage lay in R&D intensive sectors, it was not at all clear in the beginning that software would emerge as a prominent instantiation. Indeed, the Office of

Chief Scientist did not even include software in the technologies to which R&D subsidies would be provided until 1985. Multinationals demonstrated the viability of developing software in Ireland, but it was left to some indigenous firms to demonstrate that Irish universities could provide world class technology and that Irish managers could convert this into commercial success. The leading firms in Israel and Ireland have had to feel their way along as they attempted to imitate the Silicon Valley model, albeit with only limited venture capital support initially. Many Irish firms (and a few Israeli firms as well) tried to fund product development from consulting and service revenues but only a few have succeeded. In Israel, the success of other technology-based sectors helped. So did generous State support for R&D and commercialization, made more efficient by lessons learned earlier with other Israeli high-tech sectors. By the late 1990s, venture capital appears to have become plentiful in both countries, leading to firms more focused on commercialization of innovative technology.

Athreye's chapter (Chapter 2) shows how Indian firms experimented during the early 1990s, producing products or trying to go after large systems integration contracts in India and similar markets, before settling on a model which targeted the US market with simple software development services, frequently as subcontractors to leading systems integrators. Initially, the business model was simply as a supplier of temporary software developers working at the client's site in the United States. As Athreye goes on to show, from such humble beginnings, Indian firms have grown in capability and reputation. This growth has required systematic investments, for instance in implementing high-quality software development processes, and careful project planning and risk management capability.

But the process also involved a number of mistakes and missteps. Even successful software services firms unsuccessfully attempted to develop products for the US market. Fortunately, these mistakes did not prove to be very serious, in part because of the very rapid growth in demand. Moreover, departing from its customary habits, the Indian government did not do much to push firms toward one or the other model. For instance, in the mid-1990s most observers viewed onsite work as little more than an attempt to arbitrage wage differences and by definition unsustainable in the long term, and contrasted it unfavorably with onshore software development. Yet the government did not penalize or discourage onsite work. This was fortunate for onsite work has been valuable in helping Indian firms learn about their clients and win their trust.

China and Brazil present a different picture. The software sector, especially in China, is composed of a wide variety of firms, suggesting that the process of searching for comparative advantage is still under way. In Brazil, the learning is farther along, with telecommunication and banking software being the plausible domains where Brazilian software firms may acquire significant expertise.[17] A very important question about the Brazilian strategy is that even if Brazilian software firms could reach or exceed the technical frontier, they would still have to contend with established incumbents and their marketing and organizational capability. Klepper's study of the four US industries teaches us that technical superiority will rarely prevail in such a contest. In other words, even if Brazilian software firms reach their technical goals using a domestic market strategy, that is not enough, and paradoxically, may actually make things worse.

As Arora et al. [13] point out, the successful software firms in the 3Is have specialized in areas that are complementary to—as opposed to competing with—the specializations of the world leaders. The specialization of the Indian industry in lower end software development meant that at least initially, Indian firms could partner with or subcontract from US software service firms and systems integrators. Only over time have Indian firms been able to compete with them for certain types of large projects.

The specialization of the Israeli and Irish software firms has been in product niches where they did not compete head to head with well established incumbents. The complementarity in the case of Israeli firms has been manifest in other ways as well. Many rising Israeli firms in the software industry have been acquired by leading American and European firms. This has raised some concerns in as much as it represents the loss of potentially very valuable capabilities. However, this is also the purest manifestation of Israel's comparative advantage in R&D. The parallels with the Cambridge region in England are intriguing. Arguably R&D is also that region's comparative advantage. However, though there are many high-tech start-ups, few of these have grown into Sun or Intel or Genentech. Indeed, when the technology start-ups in the Cambridge region have tried to commercialize their technology and grow into full fledged firms, they have usually failed (e.g. [14]).[18]

In other words, one wonders whether the Israeli firms would do quite as well in selling software products on a large scale, particularly if they have to compete with well established American or European IT firms. Instead, getting acquired may be the most efficient form of cashing in on their technical and innovative advantage.[19]  In short, when faced with established leaders in world markets, attempts to become world leaders—or at least to become like them—are unlikely to succeed. Indian software succeeded in part because they entered the US market in the lower end software development rather than attempting to enter higher up the value chain, in systems integration or consulting. This is a lesson for the industry in Brazil and China. As they try to reach into the international market, it will be hard to compete if they present themselves as competing producers of relatively high end products. The question can be particularly important for China, which appears to be nurturing national and regional champions.

This is not to condemn followers to remain as such in perpetuity. Indeed, the 3Is are examples to the contrary. Instead the lesson is simple, even obvious; 'moving up' will be more successful if it is a market driven process, where one begins by leveraging the existing comparative advantage and complementarities and learns the best way to move to more paying activities. Conversely, trying to enter and compete with established market leaders in the advanced countries at the 'high end' is less likely to succeed. A related lesson is that while often 'high-tech' and high-value-added activities are also the most profitable ones in developed economies, the same may not always hold for poorer countries. Indeed, in recent times, many

Indian software firms have moved down rather than up, branching into business process outsourcing, involving even lower tech activities such as customer support services and call centers. In so doing, these firms are trying to exploit their two major assets—strengths in organizing and managing human capital activities *and* the relationships with clients for whom they have done software development work in the past. The broader point is that organizational innovation can be a very powerful source of productivity increase even in high-tech industries, and new business models and new sources of supply can also provide the motivating force for economic growth that technical change is often assumed to provide.

4   Exportable Lessons

4.1   What is New and What is Not

Before we turn to distilling lessons for other countries and assessing whether others can replicate what Ireland or Israel or India have achieved, it is worth noting that much of the story has a familiar ring to it, or at least, there are many familiar features. Export-led growth is not a new phenomenon and neither is development-led export a new strategy. Moreover, though governments in many of the Asian tigers which had followed an export-led growth strategy intervened to promote exports and got 'the prices wrong', not all did. If Japan and South Korea are the poster children of the successful *dirigiste* state, Hong Kong and Taiwan, equally successful in their own ways, are not.

Perhaps what stands out in our story is the role of human capital and human capital flows, and the role of those flows in opening these countries to the outside world. Openness and the importance of human capital are not new, but surely they have been insufficiently appreciated. Also not new, but insufficiently appreciated till now has been the importance of firm capabilities, and hence, of the sources of firm formation. As we noted earlier, the software industry in the 3Is, as well as in Brazil and in China, is far more the story of successful firms than of successful regions. None of the country chapters have highlighted geographically localized spillovers or special regional infrastructure.

To be sure, the growth of firm competencies is related to the mobility of people across different firms or institutions. Thus, for example, the multinationals in Ireland were a fertile source of managers for Irish software start-ups. However, as Sands shows, nearly as many founders of domestic software companies in Ireland had worked for multinationals abroad as did for multinationals in Ireland. It is possible that the presence of the multinationals in Ireland implied other links, such as those between Irish affiliates and their foreign headquarters, that facilitated the mobility of employees from abroad as well.

What is important is access to certain types of competencies rather than proximity to other firms. Put differently this is not a story of spillovers of knowledge across firms located close to one another. The process has been more structured. Software firms have frequently drawn upon competencies developed in other software firms and firms in other industries. In the main this has been through the movement of people. Mobility across firms could well have resulted in knowledge spillovers. But these are not spillovers in the sense of knowledge exchanged in a pub or through personal and informal acquaintances. In other words, this is not a Marshallian story of the secrets of industry being in the air. Rather, it is a story of the mobility of people. And though geographical proximity helps mobility, what appears crucial in this case is not geographical proximity, but cultural connections, often mediated by the diaspora.

4.2   Software: A Model for Other Emerging Economies?

Potential emulators are likely to find it difficult to replicate two central features of the successful growth of the software industry in the 3Is: the excess supply of skills and the international connections. Most developing economies are short of skills, with an excess supply of unskilled labor. There are a number of developing countries with substantial numbers of underemployed college graduates. However, few are English-speaking countries with a diaspora or other means of linking to their potential export markets. Therefore, it is unlikely that others can replicate a success of similar proportions, even more so because they would be playing catch-up.

Nonetheless, there are a few regions in the world where software has thrived, even though not at the rates that we have observed for our 3Is. Two of the most successful examples are Finland and Korea. Finland is not an emerging economy. However, it is an interesting case because it is becoming an important software exporter. The Finnish software industry received the boost in the second half of the 1990s with the growth of its packaged software market. In 2001, the total turnover of software packaged products was estimated to be almost €800 million, employing about 10,000 people, and employment in packaged software is expected to double in 2002–04. Software product companies have also grown from 450 in 1999 to 700 in 2000 and over 1,000 in 2001. In 2001, product software exports totaled €340 million, many from companies founded for the export market. The software service market in Finland is about as large, also employing another 10–11,000 people, in more than 2,000 firms.

The Finnish case fits our framework. The country has an educated workforce. OECD [1] reports that in 2001 the share of the population aged between 25 and 64 with an academic degree was 15 percent, higher than Germany (13 percent), France (12 percent), and Italy (10 percent), and slightly below Sweden (17 percent) and the United Kingdom (18 percent). Compared to Sweden, which has a more developed and diversified industrial base, Finland's economy has depended upon primary products to a much greater extent. Thus, Finnish graduates have a lower opportunity cost of working in the new software industry.[20] Finland did not have the same international connections as the 3Is though English is widely spoken in

Finland. The export strategy of the packaged software industry has been gradual, tapping the nearby markets first. The bulk of Finnish software products are exported to Sweden, Germany, the Baltic countries, and the United States. This is an export strategy that Brazil and China may wish to follow.

Another country that appears similar to Brazil and China is South Korea. The Korean software industry is much larger than the Finnish one. In 2000, its estimated total sales were $6.1 billion, and its 1996–2000 average growth rate was 30.6 percent per year. About 17 percent of the industry sales consist of packaged products while the rest is services. Exports, however, are negligible (around 1 percent of total industry sales). Korea has a large technical workforce. In 2001, 17 percent of the Korean population of age 25–64 had an academic degree, and this share rose to 25 percent for the population of age 25–34 [1], more than Sweden (20 percent) and the United Kingdom (21 percent). On the demand side, the electronics, computer hardware, and manufacturing industries in Korea are natural sources of software demand. Moreover, the computer hardware and electronics industries provide the foundation for expertise and competencies that feed the software sector.

The other emerging regions are in Eastern Europe, such as Hungary and the Czech Republic. Both countries have high share of college graduates in the 25–64 age group; 14 percent for Hungary and 11 percent for the Czech Republic, similar to Germany (13 percent) or Italy (10 percent) [1]. Today software development has become a major driver of the ICT industry in the Czech Republic and it is becoming increasingly important in Hungary. The main sectors are e-business applications, ERP-based solutions, and networking software. Both have received significant investments by ICT and electronics foreign firms. The growth of software activities in these countries has followed the rise in domestic demand. The missing factor here is clearly that the international connections of the two countries are not as prominent as in the 3Is, which may also imply absence of sources of firm competencies.

4.3   The 'Exportable' Lessons

The exportable lessons should be plain by now. First and foremost, our case studies have underscored the importance of openness. Export markets can facilitate scales of operation and opportunities for learning that would otherwise not be possible. However, as we have emphasized, this is more than simply a prescription for free trade. Openness includes openness to multinationals. In Ireland, for instance, multinationals have been important as sources of demand and competencies, and in India, they appear to have helped in legitimizing India as a source of software. In both countries, multinationals also account for a substantial fraction of software exports. Doubtless, relying upon export markets also makes one more vulnerable to the vagaries of the business cycle and policies in those markets, policies over which one can have little control. Openness has other costs as well, as domestic firms may be squeezed out of learning opportunities (as in

Brazil) and experienced managers and engineers may be lured away to jobs in the developed countries, as in India or Israel. Such mobility of people, which is an important component of openness, can, however, be turned into an advantage because ethnic links often underpin important trade links (e.g. [16]), and in a human capital intensive industry such as software, such links are vital. If conditions are right, some of the emigrants may also return, as was the case in Ireland, bringing with them valuable skills and experience, both technical and managerial.

A second exportable lesson is that the 'upgrading' to overcome the inevitable erosion of initial competitive advantage can take many forms. In particular, it does not have to take the form of rapidly moving up the value chain. For instance, many observers of the Indian software industry have noted that with the growth of the industry the advantage of low wages would decline. Many even characterized the growth of the Indian software industry as unsustainable unless firms began to invest in R&D to undertake sophisticated product development. The prescription that emerged was that Indian firms would have to move rapidly from merely performing programming to 'higher value' activities such as design and product development [17–19].[21] Such recommendations are often part of a broader mindset wherein progress in technology intensive industries must necessarily take the form of moving up the technology ladder, to parallel (if not imitate) the activities undertaken in the rich countries. Indeed, policy makers in developing countries often point with pride to the technological accomplishments achieved in their countries, treating them as indicators of success. Considerable pride is staked on the formation of national champions and the ability to undertake high-tech projects and produce technically sophisticated products, regardless of their commercial feasibility.

The lessons from the Indian experience are the opposite. To be sure, in recent years the leading Indian firms have managed to take on a larger range of activities. But, for the most part, developing new products or undertaking high-level design has not been the principal means of offsetting the wage advantage. Rather, Indian firms upgraded their ability to take on and manage larger projects. Instead of product design and development, they focused on taking on lower end functions such as maintenance and support. Although not as lucrative, such activities involve a steady and predictable stream of revenues since maintenance contracts are typically three to five years in duration. Moreover, this focus leveraged the capabilities Indian firms had developed, which was to manage projects with large teams of skilled people. These capabilities are further evidenced by their more recent move into business process outsourcing, such as customer support. These activities are even less technology intensive and require lower skilled workers. They do, however, build on the capabilities these firms have developed on the one hand as well as the credibility that they enjoy with their overseas customers.[22]

This also speaks to the validity of the development-led export model of Brazil and China. Growth based on domestic demand can give rise to development processes that then help the firms to move down their learning curve, even though the drawback of any strategy that relies too strongly on the domestic market is that there can be too narrow a focus on the idiosyncratic needs of local users, as the Brazilian case suggested. The Chinese strategy, which is essentially one of import substitution, is even less promising in terms of the export markets in the West. It may, however, prove of some value in terms of the East Asian export markets of Japan and Korea.

The implications for government policy are more diffuse. Israel and Ireland are instances where enlightened government policy did help the software industry. Even here, the evidence for the efficacy of targeted sector specific policies is limited at best. Israel's software industry benefited from general support for R&D and human capital development, and from the earlier growth of the computer hardware and electronics industries. The benefits of government venture capital funding and incubators are difficult to assess, and in particular, whether the benefits outweigh the costs. Ireland's welcome for foreign direct investment was aimed at boosting employment rather than promoting software. Software did benefit directly because these multinationals were initial sources of demand and competencies, and legitimized Ireland as a place to develop software. The Indian case shows that a weak and inefficient bureaucratic structure works best when it attempts not to do too much. It also shows the virtues of decentralization. There is no doubt that competition among Indian states to develop software has kept political excesses in check and has focused government policy on addressing issues such as physical infrastructure instead of attempting to channel the industry into 'high-tech' and 'high-value-added' directions, or attempting to regulate entry and entrepreneurship. This is an instance also of the political economy of success—the success of the software industry has provided celebrity status for Indian software entrepreneurs and political clout to the industry, which the industry has used to push for sensible tax and capital market policies [13].

Given the service export orientation of the industry, procurement policies in India have been of much less importance than in Brazil or China. The Chinese case is an extreme one. There the government openly encourages the creation of products and even basic technologies such as operating systems. Given the importance of standards and network externalities, this is likely to confine the use of these products to the Chinese domestic market. But the curse of the domestic market can take forms that are less direct but no less important. The Brazilian case shows how the large domestic market has prompted many firms to focus on providing a wide range of services to local clients. This may hamper the development of firm capabilities that will be valued in export markets and that can sustain long term growth.

Finally, our case studies highlight the importance of entrepreneurship: in each of the countries, firms have sprung up to exploit the opportunities opened up by the growth of demand for software. The findings in this book also provide a message of hope in this regard. For India and Ireland, and to a lesser extent for Israel, the entrepreneurship in high-tech industries had hitherto been the exception, not the norm. These countries had mostly lacked a culture of risk taking that one takes for granted in the United States. Financial institutions and capital markets were not set up to promote entrepreneurship, and there were few role models to follow. In India, commercial success had hitherto required preferential access to government permits and capital markets to exploit the protected Indian market. In Ireland, few believed that Irish scientists and engineers could develop and commercialize world-scale technology until the Ionas and the Baltimores proved them wrong.

Quite simply, the elasticity of entrepreneurship has proven to be high. For policy makers in developing countries, this should be welcome news. What is required is not special programs to encourage entrepreneurship, but a clear opportunity and an economic environment that minimizes legal barriers to entry and exit. For software, this welcome news must be tempered. Not only is the sustained boom of the 1990s unlikely to repeat itself in the near future, even if such a boom arose, entrants would have to contend with established incumbents from the 3Is.

5   A New Model for Economic Development?

In the traditional neoclassical model, capital and labor are symmetric. Countries relatively abundant with labor can just as easily specialize in labor-intensive sectors and adopt labor-intensive technologies as countries with abundant capital can specialize in capital intensive sectors. However, as we all know, labor and capital have been anything but symmetrical. Poor countries have had to follow in the footsteps of richer countries, moving from agriculture to manufacturing, moving from labor-intensive to capital intensive sectors. Might software, with its dependence on human capital but relatively low intensity in physical capital, offer a new way for labor abundant countries? Can developing countries leverage their abundant labor endowments to target human capital intensive service sectors for exports and growth, without having to invest the large amounts of capital that manufacturing requires?

It is true that software, particularly software services, do allow a country to participate in the high-tech sector with only a limited physical infrastructure. However, even a successful software industry is likely to account for a small share of GDP and employment. For instance, even in the United States, total IT employment amounted to a little over 3 million out of a total workforce of 127 million, or a little less than 2.5 percent. The software industries in the countries we have studied account for less than 2 percent of the respective GDP, and an even smaller fraction of the total labor force, so that the direct impact on economic growth is likely to be small.[23] Hence we turn to examine the indirect effects.

One possible set of indirect effects work through the links to other sectors. Some authors have argued that software is to the knowledge-based economy what capital goods were to manufacturing—an input source whose importance for productivity and innovation was far greater than was reflected in revenues or share of GDP. Software does supply basic inputs to virtually every industrial sector. Better software would therefore increase productivity across the board. Economic growth would result from the externalities produced by software on the large array of application sectors that employ it as an input.

Though superficially attractive, this argument has a problem. In our 3Is most of the software is exported. Hence, domestic software production benefits firms and industries in other countries. The logic may be applicable to Brazil and China wherein most of the software is produced for the internal market. But could not the application sectors in Brazil and China use software developed in other countries? After all, software is widely traded internationally and user firms need not rely on a domestic software industry. There may be some advantages to have a domestic software sector which could tailor software to local requirements at lower costs. However, this must be weighed against the possible lower efficiency in developing software domestically. The net effect of all these factors is that having a domestic software industry provides at best a modest contribution to the overall growth of the economy even when considering the potential effects on the large set of domestic user firms and industries.

Moreover, software is labor intensive but it does require skilled and trained labor. Indeed, in software, there is very little use of workers with modest education and training, unlike most other skilled labor-intensive sectors, and in marked contrast to large-scale manufacturing operations. Most developing regions have abundant labor, but abundant skilled labor is less frequently found. By contrast, developing economies are characterized by large reservoirs of unskilled labor typically employed in lower end manufacturing or agriculture. The rise of software could therefore mostly benefit the small segment of the population of the highly skilled and educated, and leave the rest virtually untouched. Indeed, the growth of the software industry draws away skilled engineers from other sectors. This may not only increase inequality, but may also reduce rather than increase total output.

Perhaps the more important contributions are indirect. The software industry can act as an exemplar to the rest of the economy, particularly for other sectors that rely upon skilled workers, of a business model that features flatter organizations, individual incentives, competition, and export orientation. Most of the successful software firms in the 3Is, in modeling themselves after their Silicon Valley counterparts, have also stressed shareholder value, and responsible and transparent corporate governance and accounting. Though American corporate governance is under attack, and with good justification, it is likely to be superior to the practices of the traditional firms in many developing economies, which frequently resemble family fiefdoms more than the shareholder-owned corporations. It is likely that the software will be an immediate role model only for services such as accounting, but over time may apply more broadly as well.

Success at an export-oriented industry also has spillovers for other industries in terms of enhanced reputation. China's initial success in producing and exporting light manufactures of all kinds has earned it the reputation of being a desirable location for all manufacturing. Conversely, years ago, Japanese automakers had to fight the reputation for shoddy quality that its early exports of light manufactures had earned it. Today, India enjoys a reputation for quality service, largely due to the software industry. It is no accident that it is the favored destination for other service exports, ranging from call centers, customer care, and medical transcription to high-end R&D services.

But perhaps most important of all, the success of an export-oriented software industry can demonstrate to potential entrepreneurs what is possible with talent, luck, and hard work. If they can convince enough people that success is not reserved for those with good connections or *guanxi* or for those born to wealth, they would succeed in unlocking the drive and creativity that is the mainspring of economic growth under capitalism. In Ireland, the success of the software industry provided others with the confidence that Irish high-tech firms can compete with any in the world. In India, software was virtually the first instance where wealth was created honestly and legally, and more importantly, visibly so. Before this, wealth came either from breaking laws or at least bending them to one's convenience, using existing political and economic power. Partly as a result, commercial success had invited envy, cynicism, and even outright hostility, and only rarely, admiration. While envy and hostility are not gone by any means, there is much more of admiration, and more importantly, a desire for imitation.

Of course, entrepreneurs can only succeed if other conditions also obtain. Some of these, such as international links and supply of skills, are not easy to create. The task, however, is not impossible and for any underdog region it is probably easier today than at any other time in the past.

Notes

1. Table 10.1 is adapted from Table 5.1 in Botelho et al.'s chapter. Here, we focus on our five countries plus the United States, Germany, and Japan, and we update their table by using some more recent figures from the other country chapters.
2. This excludes what NASSCOM calls IT-enabled services, such as call centers and help desk operations, which employ 160,000. Another 260,000 software professionals are estimated to work in what NASSCOM calls user organizations.
3. See www.nsd.ie/htm/ssii/stat.htm (last visited in July 2004).
4. As Sands's chapter makes clear, the software multinationals in Ireland have consistently accounted for 90% or more of the total Irish software exports over the past decade.
5. In the Israeli case, the economic crisis in the early 1980s and with the growing military alliance with the United States after the 1973 war led to a significant downsizing in the defense industry, the most notable instance of it being the decision to stop the development of the latest fighter-jet ('The Lavi'). The result was that thousands of highly trained and experienced engineers became available. Breznitz also notes that generous redundancy packages became seed capital for many of these would be entrepreneurs.
6. Data on the stock of scientists and engineers was obtained from the International Data Base (IDB) compiled by the US Bureau of the Census. Data on population and GDP is from the World Bank Development Database (WBDD). Our sample consists of sixty-seven countries with complete data. More details on the analyses are available on request.

7. One can safely rule out the possibility that this abundant supply of engineers was the result of a carefully thought out attempt to be in a position to leverage the growth in IT demand.

8. Sands notes in her chapter that Ireland used the European Structural Funds (which aim at supporting investments in less advanced regions of the Union) mainly for enhancing its human capital in the 1990s. More generally, the acceleration of their education policy took place during the past decade rather than largely before it.

9. Between 1999 and 2001, the share of population between 25 and 64 with a college degree in the United Kingdom moved from 17% to 18%, Germany remained stable at 13%, Italy moved from 9% to 11%, and France from 11% to 12%. For the population between 25 and 34 years, the United Kingdom moved from 19% to 21%, Germany from 13% to 14%, France from 15% to 18%, and Italy from 10% to 12%.

10. There are suggestions that return rates have increased substantially after 2001, particularly for those on H1-B visas.

11. Unfortunately, the small absolute size of the stock of Brazilian immigrants in the United States has meant that little is known about their role in the growth of the Brazilian software industry.

12. In addition, a number of other firms also have important international links. For instance, Taube [5, p. 11] notes that the founder of Satyam, a leading software firm, was educated in the United States, bringing back with him, not '... modern technology but western business culture'.

13. The list of top twenty software exporters excludes firms such as Syntel and Cognizant, which are US-based firms headed by expatriate Indians.

14. In time, they also established software development and R&D facilities in Ireland. Of course, India is too large a market to ignore for software products and so firms like Oracle and Microsoft also came to sell in India.

15. There are several references to the high public investments in science and technology education in Ireland, and on the corporate tax rates. See for instance O'Riain [10].

16. Thus, Germany and Switzerland have retained a pre-eminent position in organic chemicals and pharmaceuticals, whereas the United States remains the leader in petrochemical technologies. The dominance of the German chemical industry owes much to the fortunate establishment of the big three, BASF, Bayer, and Hoechst, which doubtless benefited from the German strengths in organic chemistry in the late nineteenth century. However, many other countries have since developed good organic chemists without seriously challenging Germany. Similarly, the US petrochemical industry leveraged the large market and abundant oil and gas reserves in the United States. Oil is now an internationally traded commodity and has been for at least fifty years, and the United States is a prominent net exporter. Yet, the United States continues to be the leader in petrochemical technologies. See also Arora et al. [12].

17. In both cases, imports and multinationals are encountered primarily in the domestic market. Although domestic incumbents are leveraging their advantage in terms of language and knowledge of the users, it is not at all clear that this type of competition will be very effective in uncovering their comparative advantage. Insofar as overseas products and competitors wipe out incumbent domestic firms, it will reveal where comparative advantage does *not* exist. However, such extreme outcomes are rare. In Brazil, the opening up of the domestic market to imports resulted in domestic firms ceding ground and moving down-market. For instance, Botelho et al. note that in ERP,

the incumbent Brazilian firms have conceded the large enterprise segment to SAP and Oracle and are competing for the small enterprise market.

18. Another example cited in Arora et al. [15] is that of Cambridge Display Technologies, an innovative firm developing polymers to replace LED displays. After nearly going bankrupt trying to commercialize its technology, it has settled on a different business model. It has withdrawn from manufacturing and focuses solely on technology, licensing its technology to partner companies such as Dow Chemicals and Sony.

19. Of course, some Israeli software firms have remained independent and prospered. Many of them were indeed the pioneers in their submarkets, as for instance is the case with Checkpoint and Amdocs. Breznitz describes the growth of Amdocs, which developed from a single directory product into a provider of billing and customer support solutions and services for the telecommunication industry. However, Amdocs is in many ways now an American rather than an Israeli firm. Checkpoint is similarly in many ways an American firm with Israeli ties.

20. Finland is also the home country of Linus Torvalds, the founder of Linux, the first open source software operating system, which is indicative of the bent towards software production in this country.

21. Frequently, this recommendation was accompanied by a complementary recommendation for firms to focus on the domestic market, which would provide the initial demand for more sophisticated products and services. Arora et al. [8] conclude that the competencies developed in the domestic Indian market were not helpful for exports. Athreye's study i-Flex, a Citibank subsidiary earlier known as CITIL, indicates that the Indian market could provide a fruitful learning base for products (in this case, a backend banking product) that could be successfully exported [14]. The study also makes clear, however, that this strategy depends on a number of concomitants for its success. In this case, Citibank's own internal use of the product (albeit in India and other developing country markets) provided important legitimization. Further, i-Flex's strategy was to initially focus on other developing country markets, particularly in the British Commonwealth, avoiding head to head competition with incumbent producers in developed countries, most of which were not large established firms. Only after succeeding in other export markets did i-Flex enter the developed country markets.

22. Conversely, most of the early forays of Indian software firms into product development did not pay off. We do observe other Indian software firms, mostly later entrants that do not have the same possibilities in software services, investing in developing products for targeted niche markets as a means of differentiating themselves. Some of these are likely to succeed. However, even if they fail, this is unlikely to shake the foundations upon which the Indian software industry has grown.

23. Software accounts for a higher share of Irish GDP but that is likely an accounting artifact.

References

1. OECD (2002). *Education at a Glance*. Paris: OECD.
2. OECD (2001). *Education at a Glance*. Paris: OECD.
3. Carrington, W. and Detragiache, E. (1998). *How Big is the Brain Drain*. IMF: Washington, DC. IMF working paper no. 98.

4. IT Workforce Update (2003). The outlook in 2003 for information technology workers in the USA. Commission on Professionals in Science and Technology, available from www.cpst.org/ITWF_Report.cfm (last viewed, May 3, 2004).

5. Tauebe, F.A. (2004). *Proximities and Innovation: Evidence from the Indian IT Industry in Bangalore.* Department of Economic Development and International Economics, Goethe University, Frankfurt. Working paper.

6. O'Gorman, C., O'Malley, E., and Mooney, J. (1997). *Clusters in Ireland. The Irish Indigenous Software Industry: An Application of Porter's Cluster Analysis.* NESC, National Economic and Social Council, Research Series, Research Paper No. 3, November.

7. Saxenian, A. (2003). Government and guanxi: The Chinese software industry in transition. Paper presented at the Conference *Global Software from Emerging Markets: An Engine for Growth?* London Business School, May 12.

8. Arora, A., Arunachalam, A., Asundi, J., and Fernandes, R. (2001). The Indian software services industry: structure and prospects. *Research Policy*, 30(8), 1267–1288.

9. Parthasarathi, A. and Joseph, K.J. (2001). Limits to innovation set by strong export orientation: the case of India's information and communication technologies sector. Conference paper, *Future of Innovation Studies*, Eindhoven University of Technology.

10. O'Riain, S. (2000). The flexible developmental state: globalisation, information technology, and the Celtic Tiger. *Politics & Society*, 28(2), 157–193.

11. Hausmann, J. and Rodrik, D. (2002). *Economic Development as Self-Discovery.* NBER Working Paper 8952, Cambridge, MA.

12. Arora, A., Landau, R., and Rosenberg, N. (eds.) (1998). *Chemicals and Long-Term Economic Growth.* New York: John Wiley and Sons.

13. Arora, A., Gambardella, A., and Torrisi, S. (2004). In the footsteps of Silicon Valley: Indian and Irish software in the international division of labor. In T. Bresnahan and A. Gambardella (eds.), *Building High Tech Clusters: Silicon Valley and Beyond.* Cambridge, UK: Cambridge University Press.

14. Athreye, S. (2004). Agglomeration and growth: a study of the Cambridge high-tech cluster. In T. Bresnahan and A. Gambardella (eds.), *Building High Tech Clusters: Silicon Valley and Beyond.* Cambridge, UK: Cambridge University Press.

15. Arora, A., Fosfuri, A., and Gambardella, A. (2001). *Markets for Technology: The Economics of Innovation and Corporate Strategy.* Cambridge, MA: MIT Press.

16. Rauch, J. (2001). Business and social networks in international trade. *Journal of Economic Literature*, 39, 1177–1203.

17. Heeks, R. (1996). *India's Software Industry: State Policy, Liberalization and Industrial Development.* Sage Publications, Thousand Oaks, California.

18. DaCosta, A. (1998). Technology leapfrogging: software industry in India. Presented at the 2nd International Conference on Technology Policy and Innovation, Calouste Gulbenkian Foundation, Lisbon, August 3–5.

19. NASSCOM (2002 and various volumes). *Indian IT software and services directory*, accessible at www.nasscom.org/artdisplay.asp?Art_id=1608.

20. Breznitz, D. (2005). Collaborative public space in a national innovation system: a case study of the Israeli military's impact on the software industry. *Industry and Innovation*, 12(1), forthcoming.

INDEX

Note: Most references are to the software industries in India, Ireland, and Israel.